Lecture Notes in Computer Scie

Commenced Publication in 1973
Founding and Former Series Editors:
Gerhard Goos, Juris Hartmanis, and Jan van Leeuwen

Editorial Board

Bruce Christianson   James A. Malcolm
Vashek Matyáš   Michael Roe (Eds.)

Security Protocols XVII

17th International Workshop
Cambridge, UK, April 1-3, 2009
Revised Selected Papers

 Springer

Volume Editors

Bruce Christianson
James A. Malcolm
Michael Roe
University of Hertfordshire
Computer Science Department
Hatfield AL10 9AB, UK
E-mail: {b.christianson; j.a.malcolm}@herts.ac.uk
E-mail: mroe@cornstalk.org.uk

Vashek Matyáš
Masaryk University
Faculty of Informatics
Botanicka 68a
602 00 Brno, Czech Republic
E-mail: matyas@fi.muni.cz

ISSN 0302-9743   e-ISSN 1611-3349
ISBN 978-3-642-36212-5   e-ISBN 978-3-642-36213-2
DOI 10.1007/978-3-642-36213-2
Springer Heidelberg Dordrecht London New York

Library of Congress Control Number: 2012955819

CR Subject Classification (1998): K.6.5, E.3, C.2, D.4.6, H.4, H.3

LNCS Sublibrary: SL 4 – Security and Cryptology

Typesetting: Camera-ready by author, data conversion by Scientific Publishing Services, Chennai, India

Printed on acid-free paper

Springer is part of Springer Science+Business Media (www.springer.com)

Preface

Welcome to the proceedings of the 17th International Security Protocols Workshop. Our theme this year is "Brief Encounters."

Traditionally, protocols are built on the assumptions that message payloads are expensive and that state is evil. Perhaps it is time to revisit these assumptions. Often the real requirement is to authenticate the state, rather than the identity, of the client. Techniques for doing this, such as hard cookies, are already being inserted as performance optimizations into protocols that still model the old assumptions. Can we take the next step? We are used to having dynamic address assignment, could we have dynamic identity assignment as well?

The presentations are deliberately structured in such a way as to encourage audience participation, and you are now a part of the audience. Please join in: you know how to contact us.

As usual, our thanks to Sidney Sussex College Cambridge for the use of their facilities. Particular thanks to Lori Klimaszewska of the University of Cambridge Computing Service for making the initial transcription of the audio tapes, and to Frank Stajano and Bruno Crispo for acting as members of the Programme Committee.

September 2012

Bruce Christianson
James Malcolm
Vaclav Matyas
Michael Roe

Previous Proceedings in This Series

The proceedings of previous International Workshops on Security Protocols have also been published by Springer as *Lecture Notes in Computer Science*, and are occasionally referred to in the text:

16th Workshop (2008), LNCS 6615, ISBN 978-3-642-22136-1
15th Workshop (2007), LNCS 5964, ISBN 978-3-642-17772-9
14th Workshop (2006), LNCS 5087, ISBN 978-3-642-04903-3
13th Workshop (2005), LNCS 4631, ISBN 3-540-77155-7
12th Workshop (2004), LNCS 3957, ISBN 3-540-40925-4
11th Workshop (2003), LNCS 3364, ISBN 3-540-28389-7
10th Workshop (2002), LNCS 2845, ISBN 3-540-20830-5
9th Workshop (2001), LNCS 2467, ISBN 3-540-44263-4
8th Workshop (2000), LNCS 2133, ISBN 3-540-42566-7
7th Workshop (1999), LNCS 1796, ISBN 3-540-67381-4
6th Workshop (1998), LNCS 1550, ISBN 3-540-65663-4
5th Workshop (1997), LNCS 1361, ISBN 3-540-64040-1
4th Workshop (1996), LNCS 1189, ISBN 3-540-63494-5

Table of Contents

Introduction: Brief Encounters (Transcript of Discussion)   1
  Bruce Christianson

Evolutionary Design of Attack Strategies.   3
  Jiří Kůr, Václav Matyáš, and Petr Švenda

Evolutionary Design of Attack Strategies (Transcript of Discussion)   18
  Petr Švenda

Below the Salt: The Dangers of Unfulfilled Physical Media
Assumptions   24
  Matt Blaze and Patrick McDaniel

Is the Honeymoon over? (Transcript of Discussion)   28
  Matt Blaze

Below the Salt (Transcript of Discussion)   34
  Matt Blaze

Attacking Each Other   41
  Wihem Arsac, Giampaolo Bella, Xavier Chantry, and
  Luca Compagna

Attacking Each Other (Transcript of Discussion)   48
  Xavier Chantry

Bringing Zero-Knowledge Proofs of Knowledge to Practice   51
  Endre Bangerter, Stefania Barzan, Stephan Krenn,
  Ahmad-Reza Sadeghi, Thomas Schneider, and
  Joe-Kai Tsay

Bringing Zero-Knowledge Proofs of Knowledge to Practice
(Transcript of Discussion)   63
  Stephan Krenn

Towards a Verified Reference Implementation of a Trusted Platform
Module   69
  Aybek Mukhamedov, Andrew D. Gordon, and Mark Ryan

Towards a Verified Reference Implementation of a Trusted Platform
Module (Transcript of Discussion).   82
  Aybek Mukhamedov

The Least Privacy-Damaging Centralised Traffic Data Retention
Architecture (Extended Abstract)   87
    George Danezis

The Least Privacy-Damaging Centralised Traffic Data Retention
Architecture (Transcript of Discussion)   93
    George Danezis

Pretty Good Democracy   111
    Peter Y.A. Ryan and Vanessa Teague

Pretty Good Democracy (Transcript of Discussion)   131
    Peter Y.A. Ryan

Design and Verification of Anonymous Trust Protocols...............   143
    Michael Backes and Matteo Maffei

Design and Verification of Anonymous Trust Protocols
(Transcript of Discussion)   149
    Michael Backes

Brief Encounters with a Random Key Graph   157
    Virgil D. Gligor, Adrian Perrig, and Jun Zhao

Brief Encounters with a Random Key Graph
(Transcript of Discussion)   162
    Virgil D. Gligor

Trust*: Using Local Guarantees to Extend the Reach of Trust   171
    Stephen Clarke, Bruce Christianson, and Hannan Xiao

Trust*: Using Local Guarantees to Extend the Reach of Trust
(Transcript of Discussion)   179
    Bruce Christianson

Alice and Bob in Love: Cryptographic Communication Using Shared
Experiences   189
    Joseph Bonneau

Alice and Bob in Love (Transcript of Discussion)....................   199
    Joseph Bonneau

Why I'm Not an Entropist   213
    Paul Syverson

Why I'm Not an Entropist (Transcript of Discussion)   231
    Paul Syverson

Deriving Ephemeral Authentication Using Channel Axioms   240
    Dusko Pavlovic and Catherine Meadows

Deriving Ephemeral Authentication Using Channel Axioms
(Transcript of Discussion) 262
   Catherine Meadows

A Novel Stateless Authentication Protocol 269
   Chris J. Mitchell

A Novel Stateless Authentication Protocol (Transcript of Discussion) ... 275
   Chris J. Mitchell

The Trust Economy of Brief Encounters 282
   Ross Anderson

The Trust Economy of Brief Encounters (Transcript of Discussion) 285
   Ross Anderson

Qualitative Analysis for Trust Management: Towards a Model of
Photograph Sharing Indiscretion 298
   Simon N. Foley and Vivien M. Rooney

Qualitative Analysis for Trust Management
(Transcript of Discussion) 308
   Simon N. Foley

Establishing Distributed Hidden Friendship Relations................. 321
   Sören Preibusch and Alastair R. Beresford

Establishing Distributed Hidden Friendship Relations
(Transcript of Discussion) 335
   Sören Preibusch

Not That Kind of Friend: Misleading Divergences between Online
Social Networks and Real-World Social Protocols 343
   Jonathan Anderson and Frank Stajano

Not That Kind of Friend (Transcript of Discussion) 350
   Jonathan Anderson

The Final Word 365

Author Index 367

Introduction: Brief Encounters
(Transcript of Discussion)

Bruce Christianson

University of Hertfordshire

Welcome to the 17th Security Protocols Workshop; the theme this year is "Brief Encounters".

Traditional authentication protocols were designed to be re-run every time you had an interaction with the system. That's because, as Roger Needham was fond of saying[1], the original protocols were designed on the assumptions that message payloads were expensive, and state was evil. By this he meant that the cost of maintaining any significant amount of state, for the duration of time between presentations by the client to the system, was prohibitive for systems with any significant amount of throughput. And the option of bundling the state up and moving it across the network to the client in the way that we do with stateless file-servers was out, because the high costs of message payloads wouldn't allow you to transfer significant amounts of state in that way.

Since then we've gotten lots of new protocols, but they're all built on the same set of assumptions. Meanwhile we have a situation where message payloads are practically free, state is still evil, but now it's evil for the opposite reason, that it's really difficult to get rid of. Maintaining the presence and consistency of state is trivial both technically and technologically, but once you've had a particular state it's very, very hard to get rid of it, and you never know who you're going to be forced to hand it over to.

For several years now we've had the capability of designing the underlying protocol in a different way: we could see the requirement as being authenticating not the identity of the client but the state of the client, or rather certain attributes of the client state (which might include the attribute of you being the one that I spoke to this morning), and doing that in a way that doesn't allow us to obtain any more information than we absolutely need to do the next step of the protocol. Although we're seeing a certain insertion of these techniques into protocols that are being deployed, for example, the hard cookies that are starting to be fashionable, these are mainly being put in as performance optimisations to protocols that are still designed on the original old-fashioned assumptions. And as Roger was also fond of saying, performance optimisation is when you take something that works and replace it by something that's faster, and almost works.

So we've got all the pieces, but the bad attitude from some of those underlying protocols has gradually permeated into the things that are built on top of them, and perhaps it would be a good idea to revisit some of those assumptions. We've

---

[1] For example, in LNCS 1796, p 1.

B. Christianson et al. (Eds.): Security Protocols 2009, LNCS 7028, pp. 1–2, 2013.

gotten used to having dynamic IP address assignment, perhaps we want to have dynamic identity assignment as well.

There's a good mixture here of people who have been before and people who haven't, so I'll just go over the rules of engagement. This is a workshop, not a conference: it's intended to be interactive, so if a thought occurs to you, or you have something that you think would be of general interest, don't wait for the speaker to finish, just interrupt them. That "if" was supposed to be an "if and only if" though; just bear that in mind. Similarly, if you're presenting and you've got something that you really, really want people to take away at the end of the presentation, try and get to it within the first three minutes, because that might be as far as you ever get along the talk that you've prepared. It's OK, because you can rewrite your position paper to say whatever you want after the workshop, and also, although we're recording this, and we do publish transcripts, they are very heavily edited.

So don't worry about saying something stupid and making a fool of yourself, we can edit all that out afterwards. It's better to take the risk in this sort of environment.

Please don't feel constrained to give the talk that you planned to give when you stood up, even if it wasn't your turn to give a talk. The other rule is that all breakages have to be paid for, if you break somebody's protocol during their talk it's polite to help them try and fix it during the coffee break.

Evolutionary Design of Attack Strategies

Jiří Kůr, Václav Matyáš, and Petr Švenda

Masaryk University, Brno, Czech Republic
{xkur,matyas,svenda}@fi.muni.cz

Abstract. We propose and investigate a new concept for automatic search for attack strategies and demonstrate its use in the area of wireless sensor networks. We exploit mechanisms inspired by the biological evolution, known as Evolutionary Algorithms and we use a combination of simulation (or real system execution) with a candidate attacks generator. Each candidate is evaluated, its success is measured and used as a guiding input for the next generation of candidates. Evolutionary Algorithms perform well in case they evaluate a large number of candidate attack strategies, and thus we have focused on applications where quality can be assessed fast (in order of seconds and optimally less).

1 Introduction

The fundamental asymmetry between the attacker's and defender's position is that an attacker needs to find only one successful attack option where the defender should take care of all possibilities. This asymmetry is similar to the relation between a guided search without processing the entire search space and an exhaustive space search. We based our work on the assumption that guided search for new attacks is possible – at least at the same level as searching for defenses against attackers. While this in principle is search for attack strategies, this approach has clear benefits for defenders as well – discovery and study of new attacks should help the defender to build a better protection.

The advantage of automatic search provides us with the possibility to reliably examine all configurations within a constrained search space as formal verification does (see [Mea03] for an exhaustive review). If we use some form of guided search instead of brute force search we can search through even larger spaces (yet without examining all configurations).

So far, automated constructions of attacks were proposed mainly for construction of testbeds for Intrusion Detection Systems (IDSs) or optimization of parameters for known attacks. Automated construction of attack graphs was proposed in [SHJ+02], using symbolic model checking algorithms and with an example application in the area of network security, where a potential violation of the safety property is constructed from four atomic attacks. And all possible attack vectors are constructed.

In [MGL+06], a virtual network is used to capture all network traffic with traces of known attacks from vulnerability databases. These traffic logs can be

B. Christianson et al. (Eds.): Security Protocols 2009, LNCS 7028, pp. 3–17, 2013.

later used to test a particular IDS. In principle, recombination of several attacks can be run in parallel to produce more obscured network traffic and more successful attacks (against a particular IDS) can be found.

Automatic generation and analysis of attacks against IDS systems is proposed in [RJM04]. Formal transition rules are specified to transform the attack footprint from one known to a particular IDS to one that bypasses the detection. Soundness property of rules ensures that only valid attacks are derived; therefore method allow easy evaluation whether the attack was detected or not. Several significant bugs were found in the well known Snort IDS using this method.

A formal derivation method capable of generating polymorphic blending attacks that use encryption to hide the attack code is proposed in [FL06]. IDSs are modeled as finite state automata and problem of finding suitable encryption key that would not trigger IDS detection in an incoming packet is shown to be NP-complete. A hill climbing heuristic method is used to search through a potentially large space of possible encryption keys for near optimal solution.

Simulation with discrete event system specification (DEVS) is used to automatically generate attacks by recombination from several groups of shell commands in [LLL+04]. All possible combinations of the commands valid within given constraints are generated via DEVS and attacks are obtained as a paths between initial and compromised state.

Inspiration for the proposed concept of automatic generation of attack strategies comes from our previous work on secrecy amplification protocols [vSM09]. We used Evolutionary Algorithms[1] to automatically generate candidate protocols and our own network simulator then provides a metric of success in terms of secured links. The approach was verified on two compromise patterns that arise from the key infection approach [ACP04,CS05] and probabilistic key pre-distribution [EG02,CPS03,LN03,SM07a]. For these patterns, all published protocols we were aware of were rediscovered and a new protocol that outperforms them was found. The approach was particularly successful when the relative positions of nodes were included into protocol steps, leading to a secrecy amplification protocol with only linear instead of exponential increase of necessary messages making it practical also for dense and battery limited networks. See [SM07b] for details on automatic protocols design, examples of discovered protocols, their performance comparison and used settings of Evolutionary Algorithms.

It was an earlier work on the evolutionary design of secrecy amplification protocols with a suspiciously high fraction of secured links (typically 100%) that lead us to a deeper inspection of the protocol with such a high performance.

---

[1] *Evolutionary Algorithms.* are stochastic search algorithms inspired by Darwin's theory of evolution. Instead of working with one solution at a time, these algorithms operate with the *population* of *candidate solutions* (candidate attack strategy in our case). Every new population is formed by genetically inspired operators such as *crossover* (part of strategy instructions are taken from one parent, rest from another one) and *mutation* (change of instruction type or one of its parameter(s)) and through a selection pressure via fitness value, which guides the evolution towards better areas of the search space.

Here we discovered either our program mistake or incomplete specification of the evaluation function that was exploited by the evolution. Repetition of this behaviour then lead us farther to the idea of using Evolutionary Algorithms to search not only for defenses (like the secrecy amplification protocol), but also as a tool for discovering new attacks (mistakes in code or incomplete specification).

The rest of the paper is organized as follows: The next section discusses relevant issues of proposed schemes for automatic generation of attack strategies in a combination with a simulator or real execution environment. The following section focuses on generation of candidate attacks using Evolutionary Algorithms. Then the next section demonstrates the usage of this concept in the area of the Wireless Sensor Networks – automatic generation of eavesdropping pattern, selective node capture and attacks against routing. This is followed by conclusions summarizing results achieved.

2   Automatic Design of Attacks

We propose to use an automatic attack strategy generator together with simulated or real execution environment to generate and test large amount of candidate attacks. Additionally, we propose to use Evolutionary Algorithms instead of brute-force or random search over the space of the possible attacks.

We have developed a general concept for automatic design of attacks. It consists of the following sequence of actions:

1. Execution of the X-th round of candidate attack strategy generator → attack strategy in a metalanguage.
2. Translation from the metalanguage into a domain language.
3. Strategy execution (either by a simulation or in a real system).
4. Evaluation of the fitness function (obtaining attack success value).
5. Proceed to the (X+1)-th round.

Details are as follows: Prior to actual generation we have to inspect the system and define basic methods how an attacker may influence the system (create/modify/discard messages, capture nodes, predict bits, etc.) and what constitutes a successful attack. Subsequently we decompose each basic method into a set of elementary rules and identify its parameters (e.g., modification of x-th byte in the message, delay a message certain time x, capture a particular node, ...). These elementary rules serve as basic building blocks of new attack strategies. Having these blocks, we can start generating the strategies.

1. The candidate strategies are generated from elementary rules using specified mechanisms like:
   - *Educated guess* – field expert selects combinations of elementary rules that might work.
   - *Exhaustive search* – all possible combinations of elementary rules are subsequently examined and evaluated. This becomes very inefficient for large search spaces.

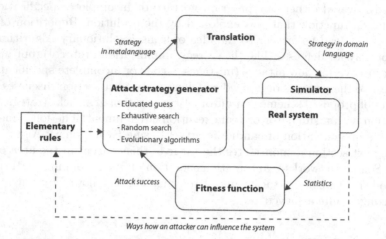

Fig. 1. Automatic attack generation process with success evaluation. A new attack strategy is generated in a metalanguage from elementary rules created for a specific environment. Based on the used evaluation context, strategy is transcribed from the metalanguage into actions in the target environment. Statistics about attack are obtained and evaluated using a fitness function to provide guidance for the next generation of attacks.

- *Random search* – combination of elementary rules is selected at random. No information about the quality of the previous selection is used during the following one.
- *Guided search* – actual combination of the rules is improved according to some rating function able to compare between quality of previous and newly generated candidate strategy. We will use the Evolutionary Algorithms for this task.

2. Candidate strategy is translated from the metalanguage used for generating into the domain language, which can be interpreted by the simulator or real system.
3. Candidate strategy is executed inside simulated or real environment.
4. Impact of the attack is measured by a fitness function.
5. The whole process is repeated until a sufficiently good strategy is found or the search is stopped.

We propose to use Evolutionary Algorithms as the mechanism for generating candidate strategies. In contrast to the conventional design, the evolutionary method is based on the generate&test approach that modifies properties of the target design in order to obtain the required behavior. The most promising outcome of this approach is that an artificial evolution can produce intrinsic designs that lie outside the scope of conventional methods.

The tricky part and key to a successful usage of evolution is specification of a proper fitness function. The fitness function must fulfill the following conditions:

Capture the Progress towards the Optimum – the fitness value of candidate solutions within relevant properties must capture the relationship between actual quality of a candidate solution and the intended goal we would like to achieve.

Sufficient Granularity – if the fitness function outputs only two values like "0% keys compromised" and "100% keys compromised", there is no potential for evolution to gradually increase the quality of the solution. Either the solution for 100% compromised keys is directly found by a chance or the solution is no closer to optimum than any other 0% solution.

E.g., if we want to identify 100 nodes (carrying overlapping sets of keys) to compromise in order to capture most keys, replacing one node by another within this set will probably change the amount of captured keys (progress towards the optimum) only a little.

Fast to Compute – evaluation of a single candidate solution must be fast enough to evaluate 10^2 to 10^6 or more candidates in reasonable time. The exact time constraint depends heavily on the solved problem, but evaluation of one candidate should typically be completed in the order of seconds or less. The faster the evaluation is, the higher is the fraction of examined search space and the better is the chance to find a satisfactory solution.

3   Evolution of Attack Strategies

The described concept does not need to generate complete attack strategies starting from very basic rules. In the simplest case, new attack strategies are generated only as a recombination of already existing generic elementary attacks (e.g, replay a message, change the IP address in a packet header, capture a node). Evolutionary Algorithms are searching only for a sequence of such elementary attacks that together lead successful attack. If we give more freedom to evolution by increasing the granularity of rules, which means we decompose the generic attacks into more elementary rules (e.g., modification of X-th bit of message regardless of the structure of message), we get more possibilities. Results range from improvements of existing attacks by optimization of their parameters up to finding completely novel attacks. Note that the transition between recombination-only and novel attacks is not discrete as it depends on the granularity of the elementary attacks we are using, and the level of freedom we allow is often relative to the solved problem.

3.1   Re-combination of the Existing Attacks

Generic attacks are written as a sequence of elementary rules and evolution creates combinations only at a generic attack level, not on the rule level. Pre-specified generic attacks also serve as a significant evolution speed-up as it is not necessary for evolution to develop known attacks from scratch. Example generic attacks can be replay, reflection or interleave message attacks, forged IP addresses in a packet header, forged ARP packets, captured packets in a promiscuous mode or claim fake identity. Generic attacks alone may or may not be a successful attack strategy alone. E.g., if the target of an attacker is DoS for a selected computer, then a forged ARP packet alone is often sufficient. In the case of data traffic exposure, it must be combined with a subsequent packet capture of the redirected traffic.

3.2   Improvement (Optimization) of Known Attack Strategy

In this case, a particular attacker's strategy is known in advance (e.g., capture and extract keys from some nodes and use them to compromise communication), we are only optimizing parameters of the strategy (e.g., which particular nodes should be captured). This is the most common usage of Evolutionary Algorithms in other domains – as a tool for parameter optimization.

3.3   Finding Novel Attack Strategies

Looking at the granularity of elementary rules, we can extend the re-combination approach to find novel attack mechanisms. If we do not restrict ourselves only to known attacks and their parameters, but introduce more general rules describing what else might an attacker be able to observe and manipulate inside the system, Evolutionary Algorithms might be able to evolve a completely novel attack. However, as the additional rules also increase the search space, the evolution progress will often be slower than in previous cases and with an uncertain outcome. But the ability of evolution to come up with unique solutions that can be beyond human capabilities as was demonstrated in the area of hardware circuits [Tho98] and may lead to novel attack strategies difficult to be conceived by a human expert.

3.4   Promising Areas

Not all areas have the same potential for automatic search within the described concept. Systems with straightforward and accurate fitness functions (like the fraction of compromised messages) are generally more suitable. Evolutionary Algorithms typically work well within systems with complex relations depending on multiple input variables, where the fitness landscape[2] is not discrete but contains local minimums and maximums with gradual transition. In case of attack strategies, it is important to have a gradual decrease in security after an attack instead of only "0% or 100% compromised". In discrete cases, evolution is just as effective as random search (might be still useful under some circumstances). Particularly suitable are the environments with already existing partial compromise due to security/resources tradeoff that can be unbalanced by a better attack strategy.

We expect that recombination and optimization of known attacks will provide the most useful results. But different "way of thinking" of evolution may lead

---

[2] Virtual hyper-plane of fitness values for all possible points inside search space.

to unexpected and surprising discoveries of novel attacks. Here, the success rate will be highly dependent on the proper choice of the elementary rules used to build up the attack strategy.

4 Applications

Our inspiration for this work came from research on security of Wireless Sensor Networks (WSNs), and therefore we applied the described concept to search for attacks mainly in this domain. But the concept is not limited only to WSNs.

4.1 Optimal Eavesdropping Pattern

Lightweight key distribution presented in [ACP04] requires no pre-distributed keys as link keys are exchanged directly in plaintext between neighbours "in situ" with secrecy amplification protocol executed afterwards. Weakened attacker with limited ability to eavesdrop in the network is assumed, where attacker's eavesdropping nodes are on an equivalent technical level (radio sensitivity) to legitimate nodes of the network owner, but present only in a fraction amount (results for 1-5% ratio for which a reasonably secure network can be set were originally presented [ACP04], and then improved up to 20% in [CS05]). The attacker's success is influenced by the placement of eavesdropping nodes. Original results presented in [ACP04,CS05] were based on an assumption that eavesdropping and legitimate nodes are both deployed in a random fashion. However, placing nodes in a specific pattern may consistently provide better results than for the random case. We can increase the number of secured links when evolving the pattern for legitimate nodes or increase the number of eavesdropped links when evolving the pattern for eavesdropping nodes.

We performed automatic search of an attacker that can precisely deploy its nodes (e.g., manually) using our new concept. Our network simulator was used, and candidate attack strategies were used to encode the eavesdropping deployment pattern. Square deployment field was assumed for simplicity, divided into k^2 equivalent cells, where k is the number of cells per axis. The same deployment pattern was used for every cell. A single genome is used for encoding positions (x and y axis) of nodes within one cell.

The fitness function is based on our simulation result as a fraction of compromised link keys after executing a plaintext key exchange and fixed amplification protocol (we used the PULL protocol as best performing yet simple amplification protocol with a low message overhead). When evolving the pattern for eavesdropping nodes, a higher fraction of compromised links implies a better fitness for a given genome.

Two possible scenarios were examined. In the first scenario, actual deployment of legitimate nodes is random and not known to the attacker in advance. One of the well performing patterns for this scenario with group of four nodes is on figure 2. The comparison of the evolved pattern with a naïve grid-like distribution shows only a slightly better result for the evolved pattern and basically minimize the distance of eavesdropping nodes from any point at the deployment plane.

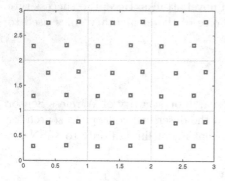 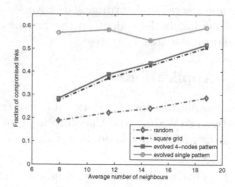

Fig. 2. Deployment pattern for eavesdropping nodes found by an evolution. Nine neighbouring cells are displayed to show the pattern tying.

Fig. 3. Comparison between eavesdropping nodes placement, grid-like pattern and evolved patterns with and without information about position of legitimate nodes. Eavesdropping to legitimate nodes ratio = 20%.

In the second scenario, the attacker knows the distribution of legitimate nodes in advance and can place eavesdropping nodes according to this knowledge. Such scenario fits situations when secrecy amplification is used in later phases of network lifetime when attacker might be aware of nodes positions. A simple experiment with a single pattern for the whole (fixed) deployment of white nodes shows that significantly better results can be obtained (with respect to unknown deployment). A highly successful pattern of eavesdropping nodes is evolved not only to cover by eavesdropping an area as large as possible, but also to joint effort of eavesdropping nodes to cancel an effect of secrecy amplification based on local positions of legitimate nodes. Such attack would be very successful in case when legitimate nodes do not start key exchange and amplification right after their deployment, leaving attacker some time to obtain information about the network topology and to distribute its limited number of eavesdropping nodes accordingly.

4.2 Selective Node Capture

Pre-distribution of the keys is not an easy task in the context of WSNs due to limited memory, large set of potential neighbours, susceptibility to node capture and battery-expensive communication. Novel pre-distribution schemes were proposed, including probabilistic pre-distribution [EG02] and later variations [CPS04,CPS03,DDHV03,LN03,SM07a] where a random subset of the initial key pool is assigned to each node (without replacement). Two randomly selected nodes can find at least one shared key with a surprisingly high probability, but an attacker can also recover the original key pool by capturing only a fraction of the deployed nodes. Yet the typical attacker strategy is not to capture as many keys as possible, but to compromise enough data traffic with least possible effort. In contrast to the limited eavesdropping model for the previous attack, the assumption here is that an attacker is able to monitor all transmissions and capture few selected nodes as well. Different schemes have different node capture resilience and results presented in original papers typically assume the random capture of nodes. An optimization algorithm designed only to maximize the number of captured keys (when identifications of keys carried by every node are known to the attacker, like in the case of seed-based pre-distribution [PMM03]) might not be an optimal strategy as it is not taking the network topology into an account.

We used our concept to generate a selective node capture strategy that is significantly more successful at the whole network level (selective node capture is an easy task if we want to compromise only selected link(s)). For simplicity, we used the original probabilistic pre-distribution by Eschenauer and Gligor [EG02] (will be denoted as EG or 1-EG) or EG that requires at least 3 shared keys to establish the link key (denoted as 3-EG). The ring size with 200 keys and initial pool size with 96359 keys and 19393 keys for later variation [CPS04] are used to maintain probability of connection equal to 33%, same as most common settings used for evaluations in relevant papers [EG02,CPS04,DDHV03]. The same method can be used for more complicated schemes and we expect comparable results.

We compare four different results from 1) random node capture, 2) capture based on a deterministic algorithm maximizing number of extracted keys with high occurrence inside network, 3) capture based on a deterministic algorithm maximizing number of keys most commonly used to form link inside network and 4) nodes selected to capture by our newly proposed concept. For simulation purposes, network with 1200 nodes was used, with the attacker compromising a fraction of them (from 30 to 150 nodes). The average density of the network was 9 neighbours within one's node transmission range[3]. Note that in order to find an optimal node capture using brute force just for 30 nodes requires $\binom{1200}{30} \cong 6.2 * 10^{59}$ enumerations.

Deterministic algorithms for case 2) and 3) is constructed as follows: During each iteration, frequency of occurrence as a) number of nodes carrying a particular key in its keyring (maximization of captured key set) or b) number of links secured with a particular key (maximization of compromised links) is computed for each key from the original key pool. More common keys have one of the higher values of occurrence. If a key is already compromised then its value is set to zero. Significance value for each node is computed as a sum of values of occurrence for keys carried by this node. For a given iteration of an algorithm, the node with a highest significance value is selected for capture. No node can be selected twice[4] as its value decreases to zero in the next iteration due to the zero value of occurrence assigned to keys compromised from its keyring.

The results for the random case are an average from ten random selections of nodes. To allow for a fair comparison with automatic design, the result for

---

[3] Such number of neighbours yields to 3 directly connectable neighbours when predistribution settings 33% probability of sharing key is used.

[4] Until all keys are captured.

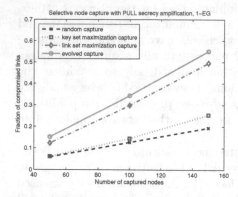
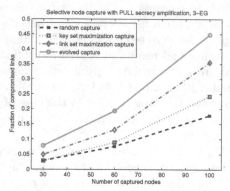

Fig. 4. Attacker's success for different selective node capture techniques for EG pre-distribution with initial pool size 96359 keys and ring size 200 keys with PULL secrecy amplification protocol

Fig. 5. Attacker's success for different selective node capture techniques for EG pre-distribution with at least 3 keys required for link establishment with initial pool size 19393 keys and ring size 200 keys with PULL secrecy amplification protocol

random capture should be taken as the best value obtained from a random selection of subsets of nodes for the same time as was given to the evolution. We performed such evaluation and the results were only about 10% better than the average from ten selections only and still lower than the method which maximizes captured keys. Therefore we did not plot these results into figures for clarity reasons.

Figure 4 shows results for basic version of EG scheme with different amounts of captured nodes (50, 100, 150) and PULL secrecy amplification protocol [CS05] executed at the top of the established links after the key discovery phase. A significant improvement with the use of evolution can be seen over random capture and slightly better results than link capture maximization algorithm as well. Maximization of captured key set is not an efficient strategy as it does not take into the account actual distribution of nodes. Figure 5 shows results for the same settings, but with the 3-EG instead of 1-EG. Here we present results for compromise of 30, 60 and 100 nodes as 3-EG scheme generally provides a better node capture resilience than 1-EG for a smaller number of compromised nodes (see [CPS04] for detailed comparison) both having approximately same resilience for 100 nodes (for random capture). Improvement of evolution over deterministic link maximization algorithm is more significant here (ranging from 30 to 60%) as the relation between captured keys and compromised links is more complex here – if all keys used to establish a link key are not compromised together, this link remains secure.

4.3   Attacks against Routing

Search for the optimal eavesdropping pattern and selective node capture attack demonstrated the ability of our concept to optimize parameters of known attacks. However, the concept can be used to successfully search for completely novel attacks as well. We employed the Evolutionary Algorithms to search for attacks on routing algorithms for WSNs. The elementary rules were designed to maximize attacker's possibilities. Evolved strategy could involve elementary instructions like `drop_message`, `store_message`, `save_message_attribute_x` or `set_message_attribute_x`. We assumed that the attacker would have captured and control a small number of nodes randomly distributed along the network.

We have focused on two insecure routing protocols, Implicit Geographic Forwarding (IGF) [BHSS03] and Minimum Cost Forwarding (MCF) [YCLZ01]. The aim was to verify whether the evolution is capable of finding the known attacks on these protocols.

MCF. Minimum Cost Forwarding indirectly constructs a minimum spanning tree rooted at the base station. The routing is based on *cost fields* (cost of the optimal path from a node to the base station) established by periodic broadcast of beacons. The process starts at the base station, which broadcasts its cost field 0. Nodes in the range of the broadcast set their cost field to the sum of their own cost and the broadcasted cost field. Then they broadcast their cost field. After some time, all nodes have their cost field equal to the cost of the optimal path to the base station. Messages then float along these paths to the base station.

Two trivial MCF specific attack strategies were generated. First attack strategy involved impersonation of the base station. Attacker was sending the beacon packets with cost field equal to 0. In case the impersonation was not allowed, the attacker kept broadcasting as low cost field as possible. We consider this result as trivial, because one of the instructions was `send_beacon` with parameter `cost_field`. However the attacker understood the need of broadcasting the low cost field to attract traffic. To enable the search for different attacks, we banned forging the beacon packets by removing the instruction `send_beacon` from the set of elementary rules.

Without the ability to forge the beacons, evolution generated the replay attack. In order to decrease his own cost field, attacker copied the beacon obtained from his neighbor and rebroadcasted it without proper modification of the cost field.

IGF. Implicit Geographic Forwarding is a stateless hybrid routing/MAC protocol. The next hop is determined at the transmission time, during the MAC-layer handshake. The IGF is built on the RTS/CTS MAC protocol. The routing procedure starts when a source node broadcasts Open Request To Send (Open RTS). Nodes, which are supposed to forward the message, set their Clear To Send (CTS) response timers. The more a node is suitable for forwarding the message, the shorter time it sets. When the response timer expires, the node sends CTS. Then the source node sends it the data. Nodes hearing CTS cancel their timers.

Evolutionary Algorithms generated several known attacks on IGF: rushing attack, selective forwarding, black hole attack and jamming.

By the rushing attack, attacker's node aims to attract the traffic flowing through the neighboring nodes. The point is that the node does not respect

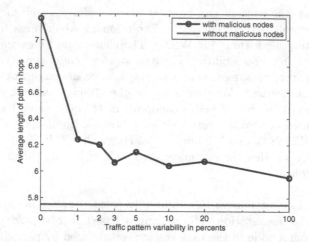

Fig. 6. Attacker's success in extending the length of the message path. The success is strongly dependent on the traffic pattern variability and is maximal in case of static traffic pattern. The results for situation with malicious nodes is average over 30 separate network deployments.

the CTS timer and immediately answers the Open RTS. Thus the source node chooses it as the next hop regardless of the real suitability.

Selective forwarding is a variant of the DoS attack. Malicious node forwards only chosen messages and drops the rest. The ultimate variant of this attack, in which the malicious node drops all the messages, is called the black hole attack. Evolutionary Algorithms has found out several techniques for dropping messages. The trivial one is using `drop_message` instruction from the set of elementary rules. Other techniques are more complicated. For example, the attacker does not forward the message and just stores it into a memory slot. Subsequently he overwrites the memory slot with another message. This approach is complicated and unnecessary indeed, but it demonstrates the capabilities of Evolutionary Algorithms to come up with several different ways to achieve the same goal.

Since IGF is integrated in the RTS/CTS handshake, the set of elementary rules contains instructions such as `send_open_RTS` or `send_CTS`, which enable the attacker to control access to the medium. Generated attacks thus exploited these instructions to cause frequent collisions on the medium, which totaly crippled the neighborhood of the attacker's node. Another variant of the attack exploited the node's limited buffer size for storing incoming messages. Attacker repeatedly sending data and blocking the medium was able to fill up these buffers. Congested nodes were then forced to drop subsequent incoming messages.

The primary goal of our search for attacks against routing was to demonstrate the ability to find novel attack strategies. However, Evolutionary Algorithms have shown their potential for optimization again. In order to extend the average length of the routing path (this goal was set and evaluated by the fitness function), attacker dropped the messages that traveled short distances.

To improve this attack strategy, we have used fixed network topology and the static traffic pattern during evolution. The attacker was thus able to learn which messages to drop to extend the average path. This can be seen as the optimization of the drop pattern. Figure 6 shows how the traffic pattern variability influences the attacker's success. Even small traffic variability significantly decreases the attacker's influence on the system as his strategy is optimized on the specific traffic pattern. Note that the extension of the average length of the routing path is caused by a massive drop rate of the messages. Thus we cannot consider this as a successful attack on extending the routing paths, because in fact the paths remain the same. These results have confirmed the predominating opinion that evolution algorithms are primarily suitable for optimization problems for this particular situation.

5 Conclusions

We have proposed a novel concept for automatic generation of attack strategies based on combination of Evolutionary Algorithms and a network simulator. The main advantage of the approach is possibility to test and find well working attacks in close to real or even real usage.

Usability of the proposed concept was verified on several attack vectors for wireless sensor networks, but is not limited only to this area. Firstly, well performing pattern for the deployment of eavesdropping nodes was developed as an attack against Key Infection plaintext key distribution [ACP04] achieving roughly twice as many compromised links compared to the random deployment. Secondly, several variations of attacks based on selective node capture were examined. Approximately 50-70% increase in the number of compromised links was obtained with respect to the random node capture (for the whole network) or 25-30% decrease in the number of nodes to capture, lowering the cost of attack. These two groups of attacks are examples of automatic optimization of known attacks.

The third examined group of attacks demonstrates the ability of our concept to search for novel attack strategies. Two insecure routing algorithms (Minimal cost forwarding, Implicit geographic routing) were targets of our attacks. The Evolutionary Algorithms were able to find all known trivial attacks. Furthermore, they confirmed their usability for optimization of known attacks by finding a several patterns for dropping messages.

References

ACP04.   Anderson, R., Chan, H., Perrig, A.: Key infection: Smart trust for smart dust. In: Proceedings of the 12th IEEE International Conference on Network Protocols, ICNP 2004, pp. 206–215. IEEE Computer Society, Washington, DC (2004)

BHSS03. Blum, B., He, T., Son, S., Stankovic, J.: IGF: A state-free robust communication protocol for wireless sensor networks. Technical Report, CS-2003-11. Department of Computer Science, University of Virginia, USA (2003)

CPS03.   Chan, H., Perrig, A., Song, D.: Random key predistribution schemes for sensor networks. In: Proceedings of the 2003 IEEE Symposium on Security and Privacy, SP 2003, pp. 197–214. IEEE Computer Society, Washington, DC (2003)

CPS04.   Chan, H., Perrig, A., Song, D.: Key distribution techniques for sensor networks, pp. 277–303 (2004)

CS05.   Cvrcek, D., Svenda, P.: Smart dust security - key infection revisited. In: Security and Trust Management 2005, Italy. ENTCS, pp. 10–23 (2005)

DDHV03.   Du, W., Deng, J., Han, Y.S., Varshney, P.K.: A pairwise key pre-distribution for wireless sensor networks. In: Proceedings of the 10th ACM Conference on Computer and Communications Security, CCS 2003, Washington, DC, USA, pp. 42–51 (2003)

EG02.   Eschenauer, L., Gligor, V.D.: A key-management scheme for distributed sensor networks. In: Proceedings of the 9th ACM Conference on Computer and Communications Security, CCS 2002, Washington, DC, USA, pp. 41–47 (2002)

FL06.   Fogla, P., Lee, W.: Evading network anomaly detection systems: formal reasoning and practical techniques. In: CCS 2006: Proceedings of the 13th ACM Conference on Computer and Communications Security, pp. 59–68. ACM, New York (2006)

LLL+04.   Lee, J.-K., Lee, M.-W., Lee, J.-S., Chi, S.-D., Ohn, S.-Y.: Automated Cyber-attack Scenario Generation Using the Symbolic Simulation. In: Kim, T.G. (ed.) AIS 2004. LNCS (LNAI), vol. 3397, pp. 380–389. Springer, Heidelberg (2005)

LN03.   Liu, D., Ning, P.: Establishing pairwise keys in distributed sensor networks. In: CCS 2003: Proceedings of the 10th ACM Conference on Computer and Communications Security, pp. 52–61. ACM Press, New York (2003)

Mea03.   Meadows, C.: Formal methods for cryptographic protocol analysis: emerging issues and trends. IEEE Journal on Selected Areas in Communications 21(1), 44–54 (2003)

MGL+06.   Massicotte, F., Gagnon, F., Labiche, Y., Briand, L., Couture, M.: Automatic evaluation of intrusion detection systems. In: ACSAC 2006: Proceedings of the 22nd Annual Computer Security Applications Conference, pp. 361–370. IEEE Computer Society, Washington, DC (2006)

PMM03.   Di Pietro, R., Mancini, L.V., Mei, A.: Random key-assignment for secure wireless sensor networks. In: 1st ACM Workshop Security of Ad Hoc and Sensor Networks, Fairfax, Virginia, pp. 62–71 (2003)

RJM04.   Rubin, S., Jha, S., Miller, B.P.: Automatic generation and analysis of nids attacks. In: ACSAC 2004: Proceedings of the 20th Annual Computer Security Applications Conference, pp. 28–38. IEEE Computer Society, Washington, DC (2004)

SHJ+02.   Sheyner, O., Haines, J., Jha, S., Lippmann, R., Wing, J.M.: Automated generation and analysis of attack graphs. In: SP 2002: Proceedings of the 2002 IEEE Symposium on Security and Privacy, p. 273. IEEE Computer Society, Washington, DC (2002)

SM07a.   Svenda, P., Matyas, V.: Authenticated key exchange with group support for wireless sensor networks. In: WSNS 2007: Proceedings of the 3rd Wireless and Sensor Network Security Workshop, pp. 21–26. IEEE Computer Society Press, Los Alamitos (2007)

SM07b.   Svenda, P., Matyas, V.: Key distribution and secrecy amplification in wireless sensor networks. Technical Report, FIMU-RS-2007-05, Brno, ČR, Masaryk University (2007)

Tho98.   Thompson, A.: Hardware Evolution: Automatic design of electronic circuits in reconfigurable hardware by artificial evolution. Distinguished dissertation series. Springer (1998)

vSM09.   Švenda, P., Sekanina, L., Matyáš, V.: Evolutionary design of secrecy amplification protocols. In: ACM WiSec 2009, Zurich, Switzerland (2009)

YCLZ01.   Ye, F., Chen, A., Liu, S., Zhang, L.: A scalable solution to minimum cost forwarding in large sensor networks. In: Proceedings of Tenth International Conference on Computer Communications and Networks, pp. 304–309 (2001)

Evolutionary Design of Attack Strategies
(Transcript of Discussion)

Petr Švenda

Masaryk University

The motivation for this presentation came from our work on trying evolutionary approaches on building protocols for security. We eventually came to an understanding that evolutionary approaches help us in finding problems that we would not be aware of, and that generated the idea of trying evolutionary approaches not to generate new protocols, but to generate attacks.

The basic motivation is that there is a fundamental symmetry between the attacker and the defender, in the sense that an attacker needs to only find one attack path to successfully compromise the system, where a defender must be able to secure all of them to have a secure system. So by this analogy, the brute force search over the space of all possible attack paths is more suitable for a defender, whereas some kind of informed search where not all possibilities in the search space are examined is more suitable for an attacker.

This is based on our previous experience with generation of secrecy amplification protocols, and in this talk I will examine two basic types of generated attacks. The first one is the attack where we are just optimising already known attack strategies, and we are just tuning the parameters of this attack. And the second one is search for novel attacks, built from some small elementary rules, and will we use our generation based on evolutionary algorithms. These algorithms are used in situations where brute force search is either not possible or it's not affordable, the search space is too large. There is some kind of algorithmic function to evaluate the fitness of the candidate, in our case, the metric that gives us how well an attacker is performing, and it's a kind of clever search for a function maximum, and this function should have some properties. The first one is that it should capture the progress towards the optimum from bad solution, in our case bad attacks, to good attacks. Then sufficient granularity, which means that there should be a gradual way how to come from the very bad attacks to well-performing attacks. And not least, it should be fast to compute because we are searching over quite a large search space.

We are not working with only one candidate solution at a time, but with a multiplicity of them, it's called the generation, and the next generation of the candidate solution is generated from the previous one, but not from all of them, but from the better performing. So there is the basic concept. At first we have some real system, we observe this system, look for the ways how an attacker can influence such a real system, by influence I mean not just direct things, but things like, what information is available to an attacker, what actions an attacker can do in the system.

B. Christianson et al. (Eds.): Security Protocols 2009, LNCS 7028, pp. 18–23, 2013.

This leads us to elementary rules that are then used to generate candidate attacks. We can generate candidate X in several ways. If we are a human attacker then we are making some educated guess, selecting some elementary rules, combine them together to get a candidate attack strategy, and then try if it works. We can also try exhaustive search, we can use a random search, or we can use evolutionary algorithms that hopefully work better than random search, not all the time but sometimes. So then we have a candidate strategy. We translate this candidate strategy into the representation that is suitable for testing, if you are using a simulator, we transfer this to simulator language, or in a real system. Then we run this attack strategy, obtain some statistics about the results of the attack, feed it into the fitness function, and this fitness function will give us the attack success of these candidates' strategy. We are repeating this again, and again, and again, until we either find a successful attack that is well performing for us, or we quit because we have no more time.

I will give you an overview of two examples of attacks we were examining. The first one is focussing on the optimisation of already known attacks, it is taken from the area of wireless sensor networks where it's a hard task to pre-distribute keys. One new idea that is proposed is a probabilistic pre-distribution, where the nodes have overlapping key sets. What the attacker can do is to capture the nodes from such a network, extract all secrets or keys carried by these nodes, then use this information to compromise links, have a lot of extracted keys, cause degradation, and so on; these are the goals of the attacker. And the attacker has some information about the actual deployment, for example, at least three keys at minimum are necessary to establish the link between two nodes. And a secrecy amplification protocol is over the top of this basic pre-distribution. And we compare this to several deterministic algorithms. So here is a graph that gives you the fraction of compromised links based on the number of captured nodes, and the blue line shows the result when you are capturing the nodes randomly; capture random nodes, extract the keys, see which links will be compromised by that. That's random capture.

Then there is the red line, that's a deterministic algorithm that tries to maximise the set of the keys that are extracted. Then if the attacker is even more clever and uses a kind of algorithm that tries to maximise the fraction of links that are compromised, he will get the pink line, and if you use our proposed architecture to generate an automatic attack, then you will the green one. The problem here is that you are not able to examine all possibilities because the number of nodes in the network is too large to examine all possible sets of captured nodes, so you need to do some local optimisation.

So that was the example of an optimisation attack, and now maybe a more interesting attack, where we are trying to come up with completely new attacks. Again it's from the area of wireless sensor networks. We assume that there is a network, and there are some misbehaving attacker nodes in it; we search for attacks against standard routing, I will examine two of them. The attacker's goals are to increase, for example, the number of non-delivered messages or to increase the number of hops that the messages are going, because this will increase the network delay and most importantly, consume energy inside the network. To increase the number of messages that are routed over the malicious nodes and so on, we are using very simple actions like, we can store the value, we can load the value from the memory register, we can send the message that is constructed in the memory, we have time counters to allow some timing actions. Then we have triggers that are based on some specific action like node hears some specific messages in the air, then some chunk of code is executed. We were using a multiple network deployment to avoid optimisation of attacker strategy on particular network topology, and the very first thing that came to us was that it's usually hard to analyse the resulting strategy. It works well, it increased the number of message hops, for example, but to get an idea why, we need to really analyse this protocol. It turns out that there is a complex behaviour, a complex interleaving between these actions, so we came up with a technique of pruning where we were able to automatically discard the actions that were not relevant to the attacker's strategy, but even after that we still not able to fully interpret all the details of the attacks we found.

At first we were trying to attack the Minimum Cost Forwarding algorithm, in short this algorithm routes the messages over the minimum spanning tree that is built by beacon messages from the base station to the end node, and this spanning tree is not built only by number of hops, but also by the remaining energy in the network and so on. The initial attacks were found when we were searching for how an attacker can influence the network so that more than average messages will be routed over the attacker node. The first thing that the attacker came up with was the forging of beacons. At first he was impersonating a base station, which is a very simple attack. Then when we banned this type of impersonation from further search he broadcast as low a value in the cost field as possible. When we banned this one, he came up with replaying of the message that contained the beacon, and so on, so we had a quite simple attack in principle, but such an attack is very powerful in terms of this goal, and it prevents evolution towards more complex, more difficult attacks, so we reached some local maximum in fitness space.

So we were banning these transactions, but it turns out that the same goal, for example, impersonating a base station, can more or less be achieved by different techniques. It turns out that it's really hard to ban even such simple attacks to force evolution to search for the more difficult ones. But on the other side this might improve signature based intrusion detection systems. There is already research in this area, but they are not using evolutionary algorithms, they were using more simple techniques.

The second type of routing protocol is Implicit Geographic Forwarding, where the next node that is selected for the next message hop is based on its geographic position, remaining energy, and some random element. Attacks that the evolution was able to come up with: at first it was a rushing attack, where the attacker was manipulating the waiting time period to get the advantage to be always, or most of the time, the next hop in the network. Then selective collisions, where the attacker was trying to jam the transmission that prevents him from getting the advantage of maximising the number of hops, maximising the number of undelivered messages. Also an interesting attack was that he was overloading the message buffers of neighbour nodes, and then indirectly causing a message drop by these neighbour nodes. And once again it was finding such attacks then optimisation: once one such quite powerful attack was found, then it was just optimising this attack.

The selected protocols, I must say, are known to be insecure; we selected them so as to be able to compare with already known attacks, there are several simple attacks like impersonation of base station, and the problem sometimes is that Evolutionary Algorithms are only running to specific topologies, so we try to prevent that by multiple deployments, multiple different topologies at the same time.

So, the final conclusion. In the situation where we have environments that are pretty complex, or are variable, then automatic approaches are welcomed here because they can be tuned to a specific environment, and once in place, if we change one environment variable it's easy to run the evolution again and get a well-performing result again. The general observation was that most complex relations in the environment bettered the results with respect to algorithmic solution. The not so surprising thing was that the Evolutionary Algorithm works well for optimisation of already known attacks, optimisation is the area where Evolutionary Algorithms are usually used. The next important thing was that the selection of the basic rules is very important. If we make a lot of simple rules, this will increase the search space a lot, on the other hand this will increase the description of the attack so there is some kind of trade-off, and usually human intervention is necessary here. There is the potential to search for any attacks, but the progress of the search must be controlled because these very simple yet powerful attacks appear, and we need to ban them to get more complex attacks. And on the other side we are using simulators, it's hard to provide an exhaustive list of implicit assumptions that we have in our mind about the environment, and implement all these implicit assumptions in the simulator. And another problem is that with some attacks it's hard to have an appropriate fitness function that satisfies these three requirements of speed, sufficient granularity, and progress towards optimum.

Ben Laurie: You have not described the Evolutionary Algorithm.

Reply: No, but I can explain. You encode your candidate solution in a bit stream, the interpretation of this bit stream is up to you, so if you are using a simulator, we have in this bit stream instruction of the actions that the attacker is performing. Then evaluate this attack, get the fitness function, for example, in the case of the number of compromised links, more is better. Then if we have initial population of ten candidate solutions we sort them according to this fitness function, select, let's say, the better half, generate a new population from them, and it's not a direct copy, there is mutation included so some instructions are changed, and also crossover is possible, that two well-performing solutions are combined together to hopefully have a new candidate solution that is working better.

Ben Laurie: Have you tried simulating so that sometimes you accept bad solutions, so fitness can go up, but also down?

Reply: In the case of Evolutionary Algorithms you are working with multiple candidate solutions at the same time, so at the same time you are in a different part in the search space, so this, and the crossing-over operation, allows you to escape from the local maximum, and hopefully go to the global one.

Chris Mitchell: I wonder what applications you might have in mind for this? I can see that it might be rather useful for sophisticated malicious software to adapt its behaviour in these ways, but do you have any nice applications instead of nasty ones?

Reply: The changing of the behaviour of the variables to bypass the intrusion detection system was an area that was already researched. My view is that if you have a well-performing attack, then you, as the defender, can use this knowledge to fix the problem. So just generate attacks, fix them, and you will have at least a few attacks less.

Chris Mitchell: So what you're saying is, yes, this is designed for the bad guys, and the fix is, you don't have an automatic fix, just do your job better?

Reply: Yes, exactly, I think the usage is for both.

Cathy Meadows: Usually what people do now, particularly in sensor network security, is run a lot of simulations on your different scenarios, and this looks like a good way to make your selection of scenarios a lot more intelligent. It looks like something that could be very useful for evaluating various types of complex protocols that right now don't really have a good method of evaluation. Have you thought of that much?

Reply: Our initial work was on secrecy amplification protocols, where we were automatically generating secrecy amplification protocols that worked well in particular settings of the network, particular topology, particular restrictions. And then we turned to this area and we examined so far these two protocols, but we plan to extend this to other protocols. We initially selected insecure protocols, but now we would like to go for a secure one and try to find holes exactly like what you said.

Cathy Meadows: It looks like you could try to use the kind of protocol that works well just about every time, but . . .

Reply: Yes, you need a pretty fast simulator for that. We write our own simulator because we need to evaluate the attack strategy in order of seconds maximum because usually you have hundreds of thousands that you need to evaluate. There is limitation if the topology is too complex, or the protocol itself is too complex, this might be a problem.

Nasser Abouzakhar: You mentioned that Evolutionary Algorithms are capable of signature based intrusion detection. Does that apply to your work?

Reply: I think yes as well. The situation in that research was that they were taking the known attack that was detected by the intrusion detection system or an automatic detection system, and then they have a set of rules that transforms this attack to the basically same attack, but looking a different way. So it depends on what normally detection systems are actually looking for, but there is this possibility, and you can easily test whether the modified version of the attack is still detected by the automatic system, so you can use it for this.

Nasser Abouzakhar: Or if the detection systems are actually using the same variables that we are trying to play with, so what would happen to them?

Reply: These automatic systems are not perfect, so there is the chance that the Evolutionary Algorithm (but also other ways how to search over the whole search space), can come up with the situation that is not covered by automatic detection, so there is no straight answer, but there is the possibility.

Stefano Ortolani: If I know that if establishing this attack, the fitness function would show a behaviour in the network, in the system, so this could be like a signature attack if somebody has actually sensors all around the network.

Reply: I think the situation is slightly different, you as an attacker have the current protocols that are used in the real network, current settings in the real network, and then you define your fitness function as maximum of compromised links, and run your simulation. Then when you apply your attack, a defender will probably notice that something is going wrong and try to fix that.

Stefano Ortolani: I'm not saying where the defender is evaluating fitness functions, my point was that if the defender was able to get this information . . .

Reply: So before deployment of the network he will just run his own search for attacks, for some obvious fitness function, and then fix them.

Stefano Ortolani: But finding something that would make this easier for the attacker, is that in a way predictable?

Reply: I think it's predictable that an attacker will like to maximise the number of compromised links, for example.

Stefano Ortolani: But for example, can you detect test messages?

Reply: I think you will know that because these basic actions are interpreted from the real system, and that's something that also the defender can interpret, basically observing the communication traffic, maybe inserting some bogus messages, and maybe some side-channel information, so this situation is the same for the attacker and the defender as well.

Jonathan Anderson: I wonder if this mightn't be applied to social engineering, where you have some model of an organisation and you're trying to maximise the quantity of information you can get out of someone. Maybe you're trying to reply to the model of how the representation actually works.

Reply: There I can see two directions. The first one is optimisation of already known attack strategy, and then the second one is the new one. Probably the easier way is optimisation of already known strategy, so you somehow do social engineering in the network. If there are parameters of this method, you can let the Evolutionary Algorithm search for well-performing parameters. But on the other hand you need to compute a fitness function, so you need to be able to quickly verify if the social engineering by this particular candidate solution is working well, because you need to be able to come up with a fast easy to compute function, but if you need to wait days for the result for one candidate strategy, then it's probably not suitable.

Below the Salt
The Dangers of Unfulfilled Physical Media Assumptions

Matt Blaze[1] and Patrick McDaniel[2]

[1] Computer Science Department, University of Pennsylvania
mab@crypto.com
[2] Systems and Internet Infrastructure Security Laboratory,
Department of Computer Science and Engineering, Pennsylvania State University
mcdaniel@cse.psu.edu

1 Introduction

The physical access media communication traverses is increasing in diversity. Users now access data and services from wired computers, wireless laptops, PDAs, cell phones, and any number of embedded devices. All of these devices now share the same network — the Internet. Of course the Internet itself consists of many media including traditional long haul, ISP, home, and telecommunication networks. Uncertainty introduced by the media diversity has historically led to insecurity simply because the threat models upon which a protocol or security technique may depend, make false or unfulfilled assumptions about the attacker. This has direct consequences on security protocol requirements.

Consider for a moment a simple but ubiquitous case: the move to personal wireless networks. Only a few years ago it was the norm to access the Internet via modem and later cable modem physically connected to a personal computer. The security needed at the physical location was limited to host-level protections, e.g., virus scanners, access controls, etc. When commodity wireless networks were introduced, unknowing users did not anticipate any increased threats. However, the nature of the media completely changed the security profile of the home. Things got even worse when the poor security was added, e.g., WEP [1, 2]. Adversaries could sit up to several hundred meters outside a home while accessing its network and traffic. Thus, users who once freely accessed web, email, and other content could not longer trust the media in their home. This led to massive war-driving[1]. To this day, anyone with a wireless card (and absent ethics) can obtain access to the Internet in any moderately populated location within minutes.

The failure here is not one of security; it was a problem of a moving target. Because the user assumed that the communication was physically secured between the wall socket and his computer, she need not provide any security. As the access moved from the cable to radio frequencies, all of those assumptions

---

[1] War-driving is the act of scanning a geographic area for "open" networks. This has become a kind of sport where websites like http://www.wardriving.com/ list open networks.

B. Christianson et al. (Eds.): Security Protocols 2009, LNCS 7028, pp. 24–27, 2013.
© Springer-Verlag Berlin Heidelberg 2013

were no longer valid. In this paper, we argue that a consequence of this reality is that protocol designers should assume the adversary has total control of the media in all circumstances. The media that any protocol will be used on in all possible futures is unknowable. Therefore, one must assume the worst case or accept your fate.

Vulnerabilities introduced by new media can be substantially more subtle in other media, networks, and applications. We argue this case at length in the following sections by exploring the use of telecommunications networks as universal vehicles for data and services. We begin in the next section by exploring the transition of these networks to open systems.

2   Telecommunications Networks

The ongoing transition from closed, proprietary telecommunications networks to open services, open-source mobile phone systems, and diverse applications and content has radically changed traffic patterns and end-point behavior. The provider community views this change with both excitement and unease — while the new revenue streams and business models afforded by open networks will re-invigorate the industry, it is un-clear how the infrastructure will respond to the malicious behavior that is sure to follow.

Even more so than in IP, the misbehavior of a client (mobile phone or tethered lap-top) can negatively affect the health of a telecommunications network. In prior work we studied the effects of open interfaces and abusable protocols in telecommunications networks [3, 4, 5, 6, 7]. We found that the subtle manipulation of traffic violates the underlying "voice-only" design of these systems [3]. A consequence of these violations is vulnerability; we have shown that very low rate attacks can incapacitate voice, text messaging, and data services in large areas (such as Manhattan, see below). Such vulnerabilities not only exist in legacy networks, but also in next generation wireless data networks. These realities strongly suggest that such vulnerabilities are going to become more damaging and prevalent as networks expose open interfaces. Moreover, the move to open mobile phone platforms will increase adversaries' ability to compromise and control large numbers of end-points in the network — thus increasing the networks' and users' vulnerability to abuse. As a consequence, telecommunications networks are likely to increasingly find themselves in an Internet-style morass of unstable services, compromised endpoints, and widespread malicious behavior. Telecommunications networks are fundamentally unprepared for such environments.

3   Attacks on the Telecommunications Network

A central observation we draw from our past experience is that security of the network is not a consequence of one entity enforcing security policy, but it is the collaborative behavior of providers, phone manufacturers, mobile phone operating system and application developers, and ultimately, end users. This leads to diverse requirements and sometimes complex interactions between the phones, the media, and applications.

Instant messaging is tool for providing synchronous communication between endpoints on the Internet. In an effort to boost highly profitable text messaging revenues, cellular providers introduced network interfaces through standard IM clients, browsers, etc. They provided generalized gateways open to the public that would translate these missives into SMS messages (text messages) that were delivered to the phones. Tension between the applications assumed access to high-speed packet switched networks (IP) and the relatively constrained cellular network led to substantial new vulnerability [5].

To illustrate, a cellular network must perform multiple tasks before delivering a text-message. The network first conducts a series of lookups to determine the location of the destination device. The device must then be awoken from an energy-saving sleep state and authenticated. A connection can then be established and the incoming text message delivered. Critical to this process is the Standalone Dedicated Control Channel (SDCCH), which is responsible for the authentication and content delivery phases of text messaging. With a bandwidth of 762bps [8], this constrained channel is shared by the setup phases of both text messaging and voice calls. Consequently, by keeping the SDCCH saturated with text messages, incoming legitimate voice and text messages cannot be delivered by the network. Understanding this, an adversary attempting to exploit this system can use web-scraping and feedback from provider websites to create hit-lists of targeted devices. By sending traffic to these targeted devices at a rate of approximately 580Kbps, the adversary would be able to deny service to all of Manhattan.

Conversely, note that a protocol can also have a negative effect on the underlying media. In prior work [3], we showed one such circumstance that introduces a vulnerability. To simplify, GPRS/EDGE (cellular data access protocols) use allocated voice channels to transfer data. Each such channel is reserved when the first packet of data is sent from a phone, and held until a period of no use is reached. Because the channels are finite and the bandwidth is fixed, this can lead to severe under-utilization of the network. Moreover, attackers who control groups of cell phones can seize entire cells simply by sending infrequent ping packets. Here the upper layer protocol can abuse the access media because of protocols that assume packet switching but are accessed by circuit switching (channels).

4   Conclusions

Returning to the home network example in the introduction, posit an alternate reality in which the host operating system developer and ISP made no assumptions about the access within the user's home. The two would create a secure tunnel between the host and the ISP access point, e.g., via IPsec [9]. In this case, the adversary would be severely restricted in the kinds of attacks that could be mounted (see below). In addition to providing for the integrity and confidentiality of communication content, the adversary could not access to the Internet through the invaded network — the ISP would simply filter out all traffic not emerging from the secured tunnel as a matter of policy.

Note further that there are attacks that are specific to the media. Jamming and traffic analysis would still be possible, but other more direct attacks. We observe that addressing these attacks within the protocol, rather than within the access layer is problematic for two reasons. First, any protocol that attempts to address the threats of every possible media type is a practical impossibility. Second, even if such a protocol were possible, the overheads of its execution would enormous and possibly prohibitive.

Of course, the challenge here is to figure out which threats are specific to (and best solved by) the access media, and those that are fundamental to the target protocol. In the case of the home wireless network, the access protocol requires the communication from the paying customer's computer to be confidential and integrity-checked. The use of IPsec is sufficient in this case. The potential for jamming and traffic analysis is an artifact of the media, and thus are best dealt with at that layer. When implemented with the access layer, techniques like frequency hopping and nulling could effectively mitigate these attacks.

References

[1] Stubblefield, A., Ioannidis, J., Rubin, A.: Using the Fluhrer, Mantin, and Shamir Attack to Break WEP. In: Proceedings of the Networking and Distributed Systems Security (NDSS) Symposium (2002)

[2] Bittau, A., Handley, M., Lackey, J.: The Final Nail in WEP's Coffin. In: Proceedings of the IEEE Symposium on Security and Privacy, S&P, Oakland, CA, USA (May 2006)

[3] Traynor, P., McDaniel, P., Porta, T.L.: On Attack Causality in Internet-Connected Cellular Networks. In: Proceedings of the 16th USENIX Security Symposium, Boston, MA (August 2007)

[4] Traynor, P., Enck, W., McDaniel, P., Porta, T.L.: Mitigating attacks on open functionality in SMS-capable cellular networks. In: Proceedings of the Twelfth Annual International Conference on Mobile Computing and Networking, MobiCom, Los Angeles, CA, pp. 182–193 (September 2006)

[5] Enck, W., Traynor, P., McDaniel, P., Porta, T.L.: Exploiting Open Functionality in SMS-Capable Cellular Networks. In: Proceedings of the 12th ACM Conference on Computer and Communications Security, CCS, Alexandria, VA, pp. 393–404 (November 2005)

[6] Traynor, P., Enck, W., McDaniel, P., Porta, T.L.: Mitigating Attacks on Open Functionality in SMS-Capable Cellular Networks. IEEE/ACM Transactions on Networking, TON 17(1), 40–53 (2009)

[7] Traynor, P., Enck, W., McDaniel, P., Porta, T.L.: Exploiting Open Functionality in SMS-Capable Cellular Networks. Journal of Computer Security 16(6), 713–742 (2008)

[8] 3rd Generation Partnership Project: Technical realization of the Short Message Service (SMS). Technical Report 3GPP TS 03.40 v7.5.0

[9] Kent, S., Atkinson, R.: Security Architecture for the Internet Protocol. Internet Engineering Task Force, RFC 2401 (November 1998)

Is the Honeymoon over?
(Transcript of Discussion)

Matt Blaze

University of Pennsylvania

I apologise, but after hearing the theme I realised I have yet again stumbled close to what the theme of the workshop is, which I've never done. But I'm going to break the rules anyway by giving two talks instead of one. Some timely things have happened to my talk from last year, so I'm going to start with a brief follow-up from last year, and if there's time I'll give the talk that I originally planned.

Last year[1] we observed that a property of security protocols and secure systems in general has been that attackers seem to take a while to catch up with new technology, that is, even when you deploy hideously horrible technology, there's a certain amount of time in which you can get away with it, even if what you're protecting is very valuable, even if attackers are heavily motivated, there is some learning curve in which attackers have to learn about the existence of your system, figure out how to react, and develop an attack, during which even very poor defences seem to be sufficient. An example of such a honeymoon period has been the early days of the Internet; everything was much less secure than it is now but yet it was attacked less often that it is now.

The example that I've been particularly looking at has been electronic voting, particularly as it has been inflicted on the United States. The systems are demonstrably horrifically insecure, everyone who has looked at them, I mean, if you look at the reports by independent academics, they run out of paper in writing up the list of all of the vulnerabilities. I recall in one of the reports we wrote we ended up omitting the line: "the best thing we can say about these systems is there's a minimum of toxic materials in the terminals so they won't do too much damage when they end up in the landfill," because it turned out not to be true because they had lead acid batteries in them, so we had to take that out. So these systems are just demonstrably awful, and yet in spite of that there's been this perplexing question, why is it that there has not been any substantiated instance of these weaknesses being exploited in practice in the United States. The US has a long history of many, many different kinds of fraud with its elections, it is an extremely high-stakes very hostile environment, and it seems that these electronic voting systems, one would think, give a tremendous gift to those who would like to steal elections, and yet it has appeared that either the attackers are doing such a perfect job that they never get caught, or they just haven't started trying, which seems like the more likely scenario.

So I made that statement last year at the Protocols Workshop, and I'm pleased to report that I was completely wrong. Two weeks ago in Clay County, Kentucky,

---

[1] See LNCS 6615, pp 241–255.

B. Christianson et al. (Eds.): Security Protocols 2009, LNCS 7028, pp. 28–33, 2013.
© Springer-Verlag Berlin Heidelberg 2013

eight election officials were arrested and indicted for a conspiracy to steal votes starting in 2002, which is when the Statute of Limitations would have allowed them, so they may have been at it for longer than that. This was apparently just a complete top to bottom case of corruption, according to the indictment, assuming they're guilty. Essentially it was bi-partisan: if you wanted to get elected to any office you basically had to pay this cabal of officials for them to allow you to get elected. They did hold elections, they went through the process of voting, but they managed to adapt to every new voting technology that was put in place.

Among the things that they were accused of, and which got my attention, was they were accused of changing the votes on their new touch screen voting machines after the votes had been cast, and that got my attention because the particular model of machine they were using was one of the voting systems that we looked at in our review for the state of Ohio. I immediately wondered which of the large catalogue of vulnerabilities were they exploiting? And it turned out they weren't exploiting any of the ones that we had found. Instead what they exploited was a user interface weakness: a human factors usability and instructions for voting weakness. Essentially, the version of the user interface that they managed to get the machines to use encouraged voters to omit the last step of committing their vote, and they would simply go and "correct" the vote to the correct candidate after the voter left, if the voter hadn't already voted for the correct candidate, because the voter hadn't actually committed the vote if they behaved in the way that the instructions told them to behave.

Now the interesting thing about this is that there were no buffer overflows, there was no cryptanalysis involved, there was no altering of records involved, there were no viral propagation of attacks, and while all those things are quite easily possible, they exploited a much lower tech of vulnerability, simply in the instructions for voting that voters would follow. So essentially there's a big red mechanical vote button on the top of the screen that flashes red when it's ready to accept your vote, and according to the instructions, when you're done, wait for the red light to start flashing, and then press that button at the top of the screen above the touch screen itself.

So here are the official instructions from the company, this is a flash demo that they provide of how the machines work in general, the printed instructions basically reflect this behaviour. You put this little activator cartridge in, the poll worker generally does that, you touch the screen, you vote for your candidates, there's a 1, there's a 2, and then next page, we're going to vote for taxes because I'm a liberal (tax and spend), review ballot, and then press the vote button, thank you for voting. So I press this button at the top of the screen and then I'm done.

But in fact it's possible to configure the machines so that they don't work that way at all, and there is a flash demo of that, but no printed instructions associated with it. Again you put the ballot activator in, it flashes this little thing, we're going to vote there, vote for our two candidates there, and then, something goes wrong — alright we're going to do it again, well let's vote against taxes, whoops, it doesn't let us do that, so we'll review our ballot and press the vote button, and it says ballot complete, you've made choices in all contests, but in fact, in order to actually finish you have to press this extra confirm button on the bottom of the screen, and then if you do that it correctly casts it. So lots of voters were just abandoning it before that step because the printed instructions essentially told them that they were done as soon as they pressed the button at the top of the screen.

So you might say, what do we have to contribute here? This is pretty simple stuff, and we might take some comfort in the fact that this is a low tech kind of an attack, it didn't exploit any of the technical weaknesses. But on the other hand, low tech was quite sufficient for their purposes, they didn't need to resort to any of the more electronic and computerised attack vectors for this machine because they had one that met their needs that didn't require that. In particular it was also quite subtle, and I'll say it's subtle because it makes me feel better to think it's subtle because we didn't notice it, I mean, we reviewed this voting system, and we just never thought... Now we weren't charged with looking at the user interface, but we were trying to figure out how to attack the system, and we didn't find this particular one.

Cathy Meadows: Did you look at the user interface at all, I mean, for attacks?

Reply: We had ten weeks to look at seven hundred thousand lines of source code and all of this unfamiliar hardware, so we took the point of view of, we can't possibly do an exhaustive analysis, we're going to simply try to put ourselves in the position of an attacker and try to attack it, and you know, when we've succeeded finding one way, we said, alright now we have to write this down.

Bruce Christianson: But did you put yourself in the position of a clever attacker?

Reply: We were trying to be in a position of a technologically sophisticated attacker, I wouldn't say clever attacker, because they out-clevered us, right.

Sandy Clark: But we did find some problems with the user interface.

Reply: We did find some, right, but not this particular one.

Chris Mitchell: Do you think they found it just by watching the behaviour of people?

Reply: Well no, because in fact these guys were pretty good; this is where it gets interesting from the question of, what can we learn about the honeymoon. They discovered the weakness very, very quickly, they took delivery of these machines at the end of 2003, and were stealing votes in the very first election that they were used, so they examined these machines enough to find a weakness that they could exploit, and were able to get an attack up and running that let them go for about four years without getting caught, and the only way they were caught was, well we don't quite know yet, but it appears there was somebody who squealed.

Frank Stajano: The other attacks that you mentioned you were looking at, are things that once you find the attack it works every time. Here it works if the voter is sufficiently careless, that he doesn't notice that there's a button that says, confirm. So you need enough people to be careless for this attack to work.

Reply: That's right, and in particular you need someone on the ground in each polling place to take advantage of it, so this attack doesn't scale as well as some of the more technological attacks, but it scales well enough for these people.

Frank Stajano: But do they have a backup in a case where there weren't enough people?

Reply: Well as a practical matter this was simply the way they enforced their attack; the real attack was, you have to pay us a certain amount of money or don't bother running, so the only candidates who would run for office in this county were ones who already understood that it would be very hard to win if they weren't paying off.

Cathy Meadows: So did the candidates know how this rule was enforced, about the flaw, and about the attack, did they know there was some mysterious way?

Reply: Well they had other things that they had been doing before this, so this is part of a large catalogue of tools available to the conspirators. Among the things that they would do, they would also get absentee ballots and help people fill them out, and other things along those lines.

Joseph Bonneau: It seems like this attack requires the poll worker to go to the machine every time after somebody has made an incomplete vote. Does the poll worker normally have to go and do some clearing of the machine after a completed vote?

Reply: Yes, they have to re-enable the machine for the next voter using a cartridge. So no suspicious behaviour was involved. One could do this opportunistically but it turns out from reading the indictment they had a little class for poll workers explaining exactly what they're expected to do: wait for this screen to appear, and when it does you can go correct their vote. So it turns out not to have been opportunistic but rather systematic, but it could have been done opportunistically as well.

Paul Syverson: You were concerned about the talk being on the theme from last year but I think this fits very nicely with the theme of *this* workshop.

Reply: Yes, I apologise for that.

Paul Syverson: And many of the other attacks that you found required some work to clean up the state that stays behind, but ignoring the minds of the poll workers, this is a nice attack because there's no state left behind.

Reply: That's right, there's essentially no forensic evidence beyond the fact that it requires a conspiracy, and conspiracies, you know, are messy in practice, which is why ultimately they were caught. But it also raises the question, how many other people have figured this out.

Peter Ryan: Talking of conspiracy, it also feels like the system was somehow kind of primed to facilitate this kind of attack, is there any suspicion of that?

Reply: I should point out I'm not representing the state of Ohio or California for whom I've done voting machine analyses in the past, but I would have to say that that there is no evidence that any of the vendors are capable of being systematic enough to have thought of this first.

Bruce Christianson: So if they accepted an equal bribe from everybody taking part, why didn't they run a fair election?

Reply: Well it's unclear. Apparently if you google Clay County, Kentucky, it has a long history of election day shenanigans that pre-dates this sort of thing, so pay for play appears to be a built-in part of the local culture.

Joseph Bonneau: So to get this functionality to work where it didn't complete without an extra confirmation, they had to change the firmware or something in the machine?

Reply: No, it's a configuration option in the ballot definition.

Joseph Bonneau: So it seems like nobody ever ran an election with that option set because very quickly you'd have the poll workers go in and see that the thing is left incomplete.

Reply: Right, so part of the problem is that the user interface for the version that they exploited was clearly not very good, but on the other hand, it was superficially alright, I mean, it didn't say anything directly misleading, but the problem is that it conflicted with the instructions that the vendor supplied for posting in the polling places, so voters were kind of primed to expect a behaviour different from the one that they actually saw, and that kind of exacerbated the problem.

Joseph Bonneau: I'm wondering why this didn't get caught when, if any other county that was honest used the same voting machine with the same setting, they would have a ton of poll workers saying, what am I supposed to do with I see an incomplete ballot?

Bruce Christianson: But they don't have the correct instructions posted on the walls.

Joseph Bonneau: So this is the only county that ever had that configuration?

Reply: Well I don't know if it's the only one that ever had, certainly it's the only one where people have been arrested for exploiting this, but I will say also that these systems are kind of clunky and difficult, so the fact that something doesn't quite match the instructions, you know, this would not be the only example where it's confusing and hard to use.

Joseph Bonneau: That's why I'm surprised that the flaw didn't come up just from the fact that it's hard to use, even if the election people are being honest.

Reply: Right, but when you report back that something is hard to use about these systems you're told, oh yes, you're right, they're hard to use.

Sandy Clark: One of the things they learn to expect is that there's a certain percentage of under votes, so a machine is not going to count the correct number of votes anyway, and they expect it.

Joseph Bonneau: Right, so if the poll worker is honest and he goes in and sees an incomplete ballot he just cancels the whole thing?

Reply: So the point here is not so much that one needs to look at the user interface, I think we all kind of understand that one needs to think about the user interface as part of a system like this and as part of what one needs to do the security analysis on. I think the instructive take-away for us is simply just how good the attackers were at figuring out how to find something to exploit, that the threat environment is a higher temperature one than we had estimated it to be, and in fact from very early on these systems were being exploited, at least in this one county, and perhaps in other places. So that will teach me to make an assertion about something never having happened, because it turns out that at the time I made it, it had been happening, so there you go.

Below the Salt

(Transcript of Discussion)

Matt Blaze

University of Pennsylvania

The talk that I came here to give is about some work that we're just getting started with, joint work with Sandy Clark (who is here) and Patrick McDaniel (who is out with pneumonia, so I'm standing in his stead). This is based on the observation that one of the ways in which we get into trouble is by designing protocols based on incorrect assumptions about the security of components at a lower level than the one that we're reasoning about; we tend to make assumptions that change out from under us. And in particular I'm going to focus on various kinds of wireless networks. Wireless networks have of course increased in importance, partly during the time since many of the underlying protocols used for them had been designed, and in fact wireless networks are also where many of the most spectacular protocol failures that we point at to show why protocol design is important and interesting. If you want to know what happens when you don't ask a smart protocol designer to help you, we can look to examples in wireless networks. I think we can expect this to be a rich source of cautionary tales for some time to come.

So it's worth asking the question, why is this particular area so rich for bad protocol designs that turn out to be exploitable in practice. Now to look at the engineering of wireless networks, you know, we tend to have very heavily engineered protocols, that is there is a strong desire to squeeze out the maximum bandwidth, and the minimum hardware possible to operate the network, so there is strong pressure for a large degree of optimisation. There's a particular desire to accommodate, particularly in public networks, very minimal hardware, that is telephone handsets should be able to be made cheaply and mass produced. Because these networks require large economies of scale, a property of designing a protocol for something that works only in a large network is that there will be years between the design and the deployment, so the initial assumptions are cast in stone, and so we are deploying something designed for assumptions that were valid often years earlier, and the protocols tend to last forever, particularly when they're successful, they get used for more and more different kinds of things, and the more they're used the harder they are to change. For example, at least in the United States, analogue mobile telephone service is still available, because there are some people who still have the old analogue handsets, and even though it would be much cheaper to simply buy a new handset for everybody who has one of the old analogue ones, it's logistically very difficult to do that in practice.

So this is the kind of environment in which these protocols are designed, and from a security point of view, we can think about that from the attacker's point of view, heavy engineered protocols means they're trying to design for the minimum amount of security that can be gotten away with. Being able to

B. Christianson et al. (Eds.): Security Protocols 2009, LNCS 7028, pp. 34–40, 2013.

accommodate minimal hardware, particularly means that there is a tendency to tolerate weaker cryptographic algorithms than we might prefer. The years between design and deployment means that the security assumptions of various things have often changed. And the fact that the protocol lasts forever means that when we find something wrong there's really very little we can do about it.

So let's look at some recent spectacular failures. Analogue cellular networks in the United States were vulnerable to easy spoofing of the electronic serial number of the phone which enabled people to steal service from the carriers back when phone service was expensive enough that that was worth doing. This continued even after phone service was cheap, and people would spend far more to clone telephones than the service they were stealing was worth, and it turned out that the motivation for most of the attackers was to get anonymity. So it was generally criminals trying to do other things, drug dealers who didn't want phones linked to their own service to make them harder to investigate.

George Danezis: Your previous slide kind of suggested that there are fundamental design difficulties in getting security right in this context, but at least three of the examples you showed there actually there was surveillance as an issue.

Reply: The regulatory environment certainly is a constraint, but interestingly the regulatory environment in many of these cases provided a convenient excuse for a weaker or more compromised design that they wanted to do for other reasons as well. If we look, for example, at WEP (which is not a mobile telephone protocol, but rather a local networking wireless protocol), there was weak crypto built in, but that was only the beginning of the problem, there were all sorts of other protocol failures that didn't depend on the cryptanalysis as well.

There have been denial of service attacks caused by incorrect bandwidth assumptions, for example, the SMS denial of service attacks that Patrick and his students looked at, partly were a consequence of the signalling channel being overloaded with actual content traffic, and then gateways provided to the Internet which would allow somebody to selectively flood some of these inherently low bandwidth channels. So some of these attacks are not against the security protocol, but rather are against the network as a whole. So some forthcoming spectacular failures that we can anticipate with smart handsets and convergence, for example, are bugs in the security model of something like Android being able to breach the barrier between the RF side and the application side means that you can have attacks against the network itself caused by applications running on the network, we're almost certainly going to see things like that.

Ross Anderson: But handsets have had such attacks for almost ten years

Reply: That's right, it's certainly true that they've been out there, this may be going back to the honeymoon question, but also convergence itself contributes to the threat, because once your handset and your laptop become less distinguishable, the ways in which your laptop becomes attacked will also become the ways in which your handset becomes attacked, but it's talking to a different kind of network altogether.

We have asymmetric security assumptions, for example, it is easy to do man-in-the-middle attacks against most wireless protocols, GSM and so forth, because the authentication model is heavily asymmetric, and intended to authenticate the handset to the network rather than the network to the handset. But people like to be able to roam, so you can simply put up something that claims to be a base station, and people will happily pair with it. That was not a high threat when a base station was an expensive thing, software radio[1] changes that significantly.

So what we've seen is a combination of good old-fashioned incompetent protocol design mistakes, but also the effects of Moore's law against something designed right on the edge of security, the effect of new applications that a protocol wasn't designed for but that it gets used for, the effect of changing security properties of underlying media, particularly things like radio where we assume that it is difficult to implement a pirate version of the over-the-air protocol, as new technology comes out that stops being true. And what happens to exacerbate this is that these changes tend to be largely invisible, somewhat incremental, and very subtle. Things continue to work until they don't.

So this talk is intended to ask questions rather than give answers, so I just want to point out the focus of our research programme, and to kind of encourage you. Our security religion has been to say, shame on you you stupid designers, you should have listened to us in the first place: always design your protocol to make ridiculously generous assumptions about the attacker and protect against anything and everything that you can think of. In fact this is extremely good advice which one should always continue to give and to follow, but designers of these protocols were not ignorant of that advice, they simply found it unrealistic for their needs. Designers want to engineer for a realistic threat, as they perceive it, but our community is not helpful at all in designing against a realistic threat because we don't understand the threats, we don't know how to design protocols that aren't perfect, we think that if we can find an attack it's fatal and we move on, and as someone has said in a slightly different context[2], we've invented a religion and turned ourselves into fundamentalists. And so one question is, can we do better without having to convert the designers to this fundamentalist state, and I think this is a very, very rich area for us to be looking at.

Ross Anderson: Economists and psychologists have thought a bit about why various professions are as they are, why do we get fundamentalists in religion? It can be understood perfectly well in the terms of microeconomics and game theory. Being a fundamentalist in religion has many advantages, if you say, for example, if you don't pay enough celestial income tax then there will be an eclipse of the moon and your crops will fail, this prediction is bound to come true because nobody ever pays enough celestial income tax for the priest, and eclipses of the moon are always eventually going to happen. And similarly there is an attraction for someone working for a chartered accountancy firm to think up an infeasibly long list of tick boxes for firms to tick saying, if you don't tick

---

[1] Like http://www.gnuradio.org
[2] See LNCS 2133, pp 1–4.

all these boxes then eventually you will be hacked, the firm is hacked, the boxes are unticked, and the accountant says, I told you so, and ups his fee for next year. So the incentives make themselves.

Reply: Yes, but what I don't figure out is, if this is true why aren't we all rich. [laughter]

Ross Anderson: Because we are optimised to become famous rather than to become rich. People who work for DeLoittes are optimised to become rich rather than to become famous.

Reply: Ah, made a bad career choice.

Cathy Meadows: I find this very interesting because this is a problem I've been thinking about too, and there is a talk I've been giving on what we should be doing about designing protocols, not to be secure, but to be securable. The idea is that we don't know what sort of environment they're going to wind up working in, so we want to leave enough room in there so that when changes are necessary they can be made, and I think at some point there's going to have to be some sort of regulation in there, it's not something that can come completely from the inside, because it doesn't meet short-term needs, it meets some longer term needs. But if we can come up with intelligent ways of doing this we could reduce the immediate negative impact this would have on the short term as well. It's an interesting problem.

Reply: One of the very frustrating things I found as someone who's consulted with the implementers and designers of systems that aren't intended for security but that need security is, it's very hard to have an answer to the very reasonable question, well how likely is it someone would do this. We have no good answer to that question in general. Ten years ago, how likely was it that something like GNU radio would exist, and completely violate the assumption that a wireless base station running sophisticated digital protocols is hard to build. That was a reasonable assumption ten years ago, and it's a completely unreasonable one today, but how could we have anticipated it?

Chris Mitchell: This is really interesting, and there's a connection between your two talks, well many connections, you've given them both, but this notion that one has to design to deal with the problems as they are kind of effects your first talk in that it wasn't these sophisticated problems they found, it was a funny bit of user interface design, and it seems to me there's a parallel here with EMV Chip and Pin. Right now in the UK we're using the cheapest smartcards that we can, which are not RSA capable. Now the banks I believe are considering switching to the more sophisticated version. Had I been asked five years ago should they do this, I would have certainly said yes, but now I'm not so sure, because this isn't where the big fraud is happening. OK, you can clone these cheap cards, and you can't clone so easily these expensive cards, but my point is that there are plenty of other places where fraud can happen, such as on the Internet, such as using mag-striped cards in domains where you don't need to use chip cards, and so on and so on. There is very little benefit as far as I can see, from deploying the more expensive technology. I guess this also relates to Ross' point that it's an economics issue, but we as security experts always want the fanciest solution because it eliminates some threats, but that may not be the right answer, and I think that's what you're saying.

Reply: Yes, and what we don't have a good way of doing is giving an answer of, alright, I understand you don't want the gold-plated security, but here's the minimum you're actually going to need to deal with the threats you're realistically going to have, it might not be the immediate threat that exists today, but the realistic one, We don't have a good way of degrading a little bit.

Sören Preibusch: I think just arguing economics doesn't get the point here, because as you said, people were seemingly attacking networks for having free air time minutes, but this was not be the real motive. Saying that it's not worth it because my payback for attacking is not worth the cost of the attack, may eclipse some attacks, and cause us to say that these are unrealistic. It's the same for hackers, if they attack for fame and not for money, then it's like terrorists, it's very hard to actually cope with that.

Paul Syverson: So two observations; one is, I remember when I gave a talk about onion routing at Financial Crypto in 1997, and a whole bunch of people immediately stood up to say Chaum mixes are so much more secure, like why on earth would you do this? And I'm like, well for realistic threats for intended applications it's a better solution, and similarly people that design security for RFID stuff aren't going to pursue things that require more expensive chips than people want to deploy. But there are people that are frightened to design things for a realistic threat given what they know is there.

Another thing I kept thinking about was the old adage in the military, that you always fight the last war, you're always designing for the thing that was there. In some sense this in inevitable because you can't design against the threats you can't even imagine, but as Cathy was saying, it's good to try to design so that when the unimaginable happens you have some hope of recovery.

Reply: Well at least the slightly imaginable, right; we can't deal with the unimaginable, but the slightly imaginable.

So what can the research community do? Onion routing which led to Tor, is obviously extremely important, but would you be able to publish your original onion routing paper today (had it not already been published in 1997)? Probably it would be a lot harder to get published today, because our community has become more fundamentalist over time; the answer you would get from a reviewer would be, well there's already a better protocol than this.

Paul Syverson: The first Tor paper[3] *was* rejected. I think it's much harder to publish a design paper, even a pretty good one; you can always throw a dart at it somewhere. But if you have an attack, well it's an attack, right, so that's inherent.

---

[3] Paul F. Syverson, David M. Goldschlag, Michael G. Reed, "Anonymous Connections and Onion Routing," IEEE Symposium on Security and Privacy, 1997.

Reply: Right, so our community is becoming less helpful to the real designers in that sense.

George Danezis: OK, I'll dissent from that actually, and I will use exactly the example of Tor on why it is a really good idea to have a very generic and very strong threat model because why do we have strong threat models: in order to really take out very broad categories of threats, so that we can effectively put a big "don't care", on a lot of things. Traditionally cryptography has put a "don't care" on the security of networking communications. We don't care if the observer can see the messages, change them, do whatever basically. Now Tor is a good example where we relaxed that, and suddenly we opened the floodgates for the most weird attacks we had never seen before, like looking at the temperature of the host, and then doing traffic analysis[4]. We never had to consider any of this before because we said, well, we won't make any assumptions about this thing and we'll still have a secure system, whereas now we relax the assumptions, effectively we realise we have to do a lot of engineering to make it secure.

Paul Syverson: DEC's secure VAX kernel was targetted at A1, but was discovered to have a bus-contention channel of well over a thousand bps. There was much subsequent analysis and work to mitigate this channel, although a system with the recommended fuzzy-time countermeasures was never built[5].

George Danezis: Yes but it's the same pattern.

Paul Syverson: Yes, so that's not a new thing.

Bruce Christianson: But it is a common response to finding an attack is to leave the protocol as it is and go away and fix the threat model.

Joseph Bonneau: So you seem to be saying that the fundamental problem is that people don't get the threat model right, and that's because they can't project 10 years into the future. There's thousands of individually unlikely events, like GNU radio coming out. I wonder if there are parallels to other areas where people try and model risks. We also seem to fail on finance. We do well for a while, and then we realise there are all these huge unlikely risks we were ignoring, so I wonder if we could learn more from other areas where people have managed extreme uncertainty.

Reply: That's a very good point, but I wonder what communities we can look to, I'd be hesitant to look at finance these days. [laughter]

Paul Syverson: Their experts said they warned about this failure, right.

Reply: There's probably a talk at an accounting conference, giving the same slides, but we've been saying these systems have to be audible against all sorts

---

[4] "Hot or not: revealing hidden services by their clock skew", by Steven J Murdoch in CCS '06: Proceedings of the 13th ACM conference on Computer and communications security.

[5] *cf* "On Analyzing the Bus-Contention Channel Under Fuzzy Time", by James W. Gray, III in the IEEE Computer Security Foundations Workshop VI (1993).

of improbable economic collapses, and you know, well told you so. We get to say, I told you so, a lot in our community.

Paul Syverson: Or maybe there's some kind of a balance that needs to be struck whereby you can have a very generic threat model where anything could happen, or you tell the designers you have to have a really short shelf life for this product, which they don't mind because then they make more hardware, but that that way we can stay rather current with our assumptions.

Reply: The problem is that the short shelf life just doesn't work in practice; we often find that something is useful for something a little bit different from what was anticipated, and once it becomes successful the protocol can't change.

Paul Syverson: They want it short on the consumer end, right; they can just tweak their manufacturing process by epsilon, and your stuff doesn't work, but it doesn't have to cost them anything more.

Virgil Gligor: Well part of the problem with figuring out what attacks are important, and why we don't get it right usually, is because we don't anticipate technologies. Some years ago at this workshop the point was made that new technologies tend to introduce new vulnerabilities, and once in a while the accumulation of vulnerabilities is such that we have to introduce a new threat model. So the idea here is that if we don't project what technologies are down the road, we cannot do the security analysis. So essentially security will always lag technology. It will be so forever, so we have to live with it.

Reply: Well that's a pessimistic note to end on, I like that.

Attacking Each Other

Wihem Arsac[1], Giampaolo Bella[2], Xavier Chantry[1], and Luca Compagna[1]

[1] SAP Research Labs, 805 Avenue du Dr Maurice Donat, 06250 Mougins, France
{wihem.arsac,xavier.chantry,luca.compagna}@sap.com
[2] Dipartimento di Matematica e Informatica,
Università di Catania, Viale A.Doria 6, 95125 Catania, Italy
giamp@dmi.unict.it

Abstract. The theme of this year's workshop emphasises the widespread use of security protocols in the current epoch. The Web 2.0 for example demands secure transactions for "brief encounters", that is between principals that share a shortlived goal such as an e-bay purchase.

In this setting, the untouchable Dolev-Yao threat model is inappropriate. It seems more suitable to assume that principals do not share private knowledge and that each of them pursue personal interests without colluding with anyone else. They may attack each other.

This position paper attempts at exceeding Dolev-Yao. It analyses the best-known protocol scenario (which pertains to the Needham-Schroeder-Lowe protocol) under the new threat model, and discusses some novel findings. It shows that current validation methods based on machine-assisted finite-state enumeration scale up to our extended analysis.

1 Introduction

The standard threat model for symbolic protocol analysis is the Dolev-Yao model (DY in brief), which sees a powerful attacker control the whole network traffic. The usual justification is that a protocol secure under DY certainly is secure under a less powerful, perhaps more realistic attacker. By contrast, a large group of researchers consider DY insufficient because a DY attacker cannot do cryptanalysis, and their probabilistic reasoning initiated with a foundational paper [1]. This sparked off a research thread that has somewhat evolved in parallel with the DY research line, although some efforts exist in the attempt to conjugate them [2–4].

This position paper is not concerned with probabilistic protocol analysis. Its main argument is that security protocols may hide important subtleties that cannot be discovered under the traditional DY.

These subtleties can be discovered by symbolic protocol analysis under a new threat model that adheres to the present real world more strictly than DY does. Also, it is not so clear how the current "brief encounters" would support the principals' collusion and knowledge sharing forming the stable DY attacker.

The new model we define here is the *General Attacker* (GA in brief): each protocol participant has the same offensive capabilities as a DY attacker but

B. Christianson et al. (Eds.): Security Protocols 2009, LNCS 7028, pp. 41–47, 2013.
© Springer-Verlag Berlin Heidelberg 2013

does not collude or share private knowledge (such as private credentials) with anyone else. GA appears to reflect to the absence of continuing relationships between principals in the Web 2.0. Anyone can be an attacker by exploiting his own private knowledge enriched with the entire network traffic, and then principals may even attack each other. Therefore, any principal who somehow learns a piece of information not meant for him can exploit this.

Innovative concepts are best illustrated in contexts that the readers know well. We have thus decided to adopt as our running example the most known protocol scenario of all: Lowe's attack on the public-key Needham-Schroeder protocol (NSPK). In particular, we consider (§2) the protocol continued with the final money transfer, where the exchanged nonces are used as a session key (NSPK++).

Our example scenario is analysed in the GA threat model from each principal's viewpoint (§3). A systematic analysis of the permutations of the three principals involved in the scenario features Lowe's attack and an attack mounted by the previous victim, recently published as an *indirect retaliation attack* of Lowe's [5]. It also unveils an unknown attack and a corresponding *direct retaliation attack*.

The paper continues by outlining our extensions to an existing set-rewriting formalisation of the classical DY model to capture the GA model, and how to use an established model checking tool such as SATMC to tackle the new validation problems that arise (§4). The presentation ends by elaborating its general thesis that today's protocol participants may attack each other (§5).

2   Example Scenario

The public-key Needham-Schroeder protocol (NSPK in brief) is intended to provide mutual authentication between two parties communicating on a network. The protocol version studied here, which we address as NSPK++, is its original design terminated with the completion steps for reciprocal, authenticated money transfers (Figure 1).

$$1. \quad A \to B : \{Na, A\}_{Kb}$$
$$2. \quad B \to A : \{Na, Nb\}_{Ka}$$
$$3. \quad A \to B : \{Nb\}_{Kb}$$
$$4a. \quad A \to B : \{\text{"Transfer X1€ from A's account to Y1's"}\}_{\langle Na, Nb \rangle}$$
$$4b. \quad B \to A : \{\text{"Transfer X2€ from B's account to Y2's"}\}_{\langle Na, Nb \rangle}$$

Fig. 1. NSPK++: the NSPK protocol terminated with the completion steps

Figure 2 portrays Lowe's attack [6]. The attacker C masquerades as A with B to carry out an illegal money transfer at B from A's account to C's. Lowe suggests to interpret B as a bank to better appreciate the attack. At present, B can also be interpreted as an e-bay principal or, more generally, as a participant in an electronic market where purchases are conducted by exchanging various forms of e-coins (tokens, credits, etc.). Each principal can buy as well as sell goods, and hence anyone may naturally be an attacker. In consequence, this scenario is worth studying under the GA threat model.

1. $A \to C : \{Na, A\}_{Kc}$

   1'. $C(A) \to B : \{Na, A\}_{Kb}$
   2'. $B \to A : \{Na, Nb\}_{Ka}$

2. $C \to A : \{Na, Nb\}_{Ka}$
3. $A \to C : \{Nb\}_{Kc}$

   3'. $C(A) \to B : \{Nb\}_{Kb}$

4a'. $C(A) \to B : \{$"Transfer 1000€ from A's account to C's"$\}_{\langle Na, Nb\rangle}$

Fig. 2. Lowe's attack to the NSPK++ protocol

3   Analysis under the General Attacker Threat Model

An important premise is that knowledge of the traffic in GA means knowledge of all messages that ever traversed the network, but no attacker can observe the real sender of each such message. This is in common with the standard implementations of DY, such as in CSP [7] or in the Inductive Method [8]. In a stronger model where the association of a network message to its sender were possible for anyone, Lowe's scenario would not exist: A would observe B's (induced) replication of nonce Na in 2' and would therefore quit.

It is known that Lowe's attack succeeds because C learns Nb. It is perhaps less popular that there is a second nonce whose confidentiality is violated— by B, not by C—in this scenario: it is Na. Although it is invented by A to be only shared with C, also B learns it. This does not seem to be an issue in the DY model, where all principals except C follow the protocol like soldiers follow orders. By contrast, in GA principal B may exploit his knowledge of Na for his own profit. And it is also worth investigating whether principal C may at all become a victim.

These questions are relevant today, when hackers routinely attack each other, and can be formally answered in the GA threat model. We proceed informally but systematically by analysing the six permutations of the three principals involved. They will reveal who can attack whom using an appropriate instance of the protocol messages 4a or 4b.

The first move is to state the beliefs of principals upon the pair of nonces (that form a session key) at the end of Lowe's scenario, that is after the trace $1, 1', 2', 2, 3, 3'$.

Belief i. B believes that the nonce pair is shared with A and not with C. Indeed, B replied to a session apparently with A and completed the protocol successfully.

Belief ii. A believes that the nonce pair is shared with C and not with B. Indeed, A chose to initiate a session with C and noticed no irregularity.

Belief iii. C believes that the nonce pair is shared with A *and* with B. Indeed, C knows the threat model—see below.

The first two beliefs are rather obvious. The third means that C assumes the worst case that everyone will attempt exploitation of his own knowledge for personal profit. In particular, C himself handed the nonce pair over to B, and therefore knows that B may attempt to exploit such a knowledge in every possible way.

We are now ready for the second move, a systematic analysis. Here are the six possible attack attempts that may follow Lowe's scenario. They are obtained by permuting the three involved principals.

Attempt I. $C(A) \rightarrow B$: {Dear B, move 1000€ from A's account to C's}$_{\langle Na, Nb \rangle}$

Attempt II. $B(C) \rightarrow A$: {Dear A, move 1000€ from C's account to B's}$_{\langle Na, Nb \rangle}$

Attempt III. $A(C) \rightarrow B$: {Dear B, move 1000€ from C's account to A's}$_{\langle Na, Nb \rangle}$

Attempt IV. $B(A) \rightarrow C$: {Dear C, move 1000€ from A's account to B's}$_{\langle Na, Nb \rangle}$

Attempt V. $C(B) \rightarrow A$: {Dear A, move 1000€ from B's account to C's}$_{\langle Na, Nb \rangle}$

Attempt VI. $A(B) \rightarrow C$: {Dear C, move 1000€ from B's account to A's}$_{\langle Na, Nb \rangle}$

The concluding move is a number of propositions that establish whether the mentioned attempts succeeds as attacks or not. Because C is the only principal who acted illegally until the end of Lowe's scenario, our analysis begins with C's attack and the corresponding retaliation. It is useful to recall that given an attack, we can define its direct retaliation attack, as carried out by the former victim against the former attacker, and its indirect retaliation attack, as carried out by some former third party against the former attacker [5].

Proposition 1. *Attempt I succeeds as an attack—it is Lowe's attack [6].*

Proof. By Belief i.

Proposition 2. *Attempt II succeeds as an attack—it is a published indirect retaliation attack of Lowe's attack [5].*

Proof. By Belief ii.

Proposition 3. *Attempt III does not succeed as an attack—it remains an attempt at direct retaliation of Lowe's attack.*

Proof. By Belief i.

Proposition 4. *Attempt IV succeeds as an attack—it is an unpublished attack that we name "our attack".*

Proof. By Belief iii, C cannot discern the real sender.

Proposition 5. *Attempt V does not succeed as an attack—it remains an attempt at indirect retaliation of our attack.*

Proof. By Belief ii.

Proposition 6. *Attempt VI succeeds as an attack—it is an unpublished direct retaliation attack of our attack.*

Proof. By Belief iii, C cannot discern the real sender.

4   A Glimpse at Automatic Validation

We have used one of the AVISPA [9] backends to perform our experiments: the SAT-based model checker SATMC. This tool has successfully tackled the problem of determining whether the concurrent execution of a finite number of sessions of a protocol enjoys certain security properties, expressed in Linear Temporal Logic (LTL), in spite of the DY attacker [10]. Leveraging on that work, we have relaxed the assumption of a single, super-potent attacker in order to specify the GA threat model, where principals can even compete each other.

Assuming that the reader is familiar with the basics of SAT-based model checking, the main task is to extend the account on the attacker's knowledge in DY as a general account on principals' knowledge in GA. In practice, what was the `ik` (abbreviation of "intruder knows") fact to represent the DY attacker knowledge is now replaced by `ak` (abbreviation of "agent knows"), which has as an extra parameter the principal's identity whose knowledge is being defined.

Here is the self-explaining definition of `ak`, written in IF language, which can be used to specify inputs to SATMC. The definition is composed of four rewrite rules, labelled `encrypt`, `decrypt`, `pairing` and `decompose`:

$$\text{ak}(a, m) \cdot \text{ak}(a, k) \xrightarrow{\text{encrypt}(VARS(a,k,m))} \text{ak}(a, \{m\}_k) \cdot LHS$$

$$\text{ak}(a, \{m\}_k) \cdot \text{ak}(a, \overline{k}) \xrightarrow{\text{decrypt}(VARS(a,\overline{k},m))} \text{ak}(a, m) \cdot LHS$$

$$\text{ak}(a, m_1) \cdot \text{ak}(a, m_2) \xrightarrow{\text{pairing}(VARS(a,m_1,m_2))} \text{ak}(a, \langle m_1, m_2 \rangle) \cdot LHS$$

$$\text{ak}(a, \langle m_1, m_2 \rangle) \xrightarrow{\text{decompose}(VARS(a,m_1,m_2))} \text{ak}(a, m_1) \cdot \text{ak}(a, m_2) \cdot LHS$$

where $VARS(t_1, \ldots, t_h)$ abbreviates all IF variables occurring in the IF terms represented by $t_1, \ldots, t_h$, and LHS abbreviates the set of facts occurring in the left hand side of the rule. Also, k and $\overline{k}$ are the inverse keys of one another.

Let us consider a meta-predicate $attack()$ to instantiate with the specific attack under study (e.g., illegal money transfers in NSPK++ i.e., those successful transfers that are not requested by the account holder). Direct and indirect retaliation can then be modelled in LTL as the following meta-predicates respectively:

$$direct\_retaliation(a, c) = \mathbf{F}(\ attack(c, a, b1) \wedge \mathbf{X}\,\mathbf{F}\ attack(a, c, b2)\ ) \quad (1)$$

$$indirect\_retaliation(a, c, b) = \mathbf{F}(\ attack(c, a, b) \wedge \mathbf{X}\,\mathbf{F}\ attack(b, c, a)\ ) \quad (2)$$

It can be seen that the LTL formula introduced by Definition (1) is valid on those traces where an attacker hits a victim who hits the attacker back. Each attack can be carried out with the help of potentially different supporters $b1$ and $b2$. By contrast, the formula in Definition (2) of indirect retaliation shows that who hits the attacker back is not the victim but some supporter (who perhaps realises what he has just done and decides to rebel against the attacker).

As an example of detection of a retaliation attack, SATMC can be launched on a significant property such as $indirect\_retaliation(a, c, b)$. It returns a counterexample trace that can be automatically translated in the user-friendly message exchange of Figure 3.

1. $a \rightarrow c : \{na, a\}_{kc}$
2. $c(a) \rightarrow b : \{na, a\}_{kb}$
3. $b(c) \rightarrow a : \{na, nb\}_{ka}$
4. $a \rightarrow c : \{nb\}_{kc}$
5. $c(a) \rightarrow b : \{nb\}_{kb}$
6. $c(a) \rightarrow b : \{$Dear b, move 1K€ from a's account to c's$\}_{\langle na, nb \rangle}$
7. $b(c) \rightarrow a : \{$Dear a, move 2K€ from c's account to b's$\}_{\langle na, nb \rangle}$

Fig. 3. Trace of NSPK++ featuring Lowe's attack and b's indirect retaliation

A sheer look at the attack convinces us that both b and c are acting illegally in this trace, a development that cannot be observed by previous analyses under DY. Elements 3 and 4 show that b is impersonating c with a, who naively replies to c. The next element confirms c's attempt at fooling b. Now c can finalise his attack as in elements 6, which makes $attack(c, a, b)$ hold (under the identity of a, c convinces b to transfers money from a's account to c). The last element witnesses b's retaliation attack by making $attack(b, c, a)$ hold. Therefore, by Definition 2, the property $indirect\_retaliation(a, c, b)$ holds, indicating that the tool reports Lowe's attack and its indirect retaliation attack confirmed by Proposition 1 and Proposition 2 respectively.

5 Conclusions

Any principal may easily be an attacker today: hardware is inexpensive, security-offensive abilities are inexpensive to get from the Internet, and malicious exploits are easily downloadable for naive surfers to try. In this setting, the DY threat model, which formalises all malicious principals colluding and sharing knowledge for a common, illegal aim, is inappropriate. By contrast, in the General Attacker threat model, each principal monitors the network, minds his own private information, may play with messages as he wants except performing cryptanalysis, and aims at his own personal interests.

Building on a well-known, paradigmatic scenario, we have demonstrated how anyone in the novel threat model can profitably exploit any information not meant for him. If a principal initiates anything that deviates from the underlying protocol, then principals may end up attacking each other. Mechanical machine support appears to scale up to the new model at a negligible effort, and the field of formal protocol analysis does not seem anywhere near an end.

References

1. Bellare, M., Rogaway, P.: Provably secure session key distribution– the three party case. In: Proceedings 27th Annual Symposium on the Theory of Computing, pp. 57–66. ACM (1995)
2. Abadi, M., Rogaway, P.: Reconciling Two Views of Cryptography (The Computational Soundness of Formal Encryption). In: Watanabe, O., Hagiya, M., Ito, T., van Leeuwen, J., Mosses, P.D. (eds.) TCS 2000. LNCS, vol. 1872, pp. 3–22. Springer, Heidelberg (2000)
3. Gollmann, D.: On the verification of cryptographic protocols — a tale of two committees. In: Proc. of the Workshop on Secure Architectures and Information Flow. ENTCS, vol. 32. Elsevier Science (2000)
4. Backes, M., Pfitzmann, B.: Relating symbolic and cryptographic secrecy. In: IEEE Symposium on Security and Privacy (2005)
5. Bella, G., Bistarelli, S., Massacci, F.: Retaliation: Can we live with flaws? In: Essaidi, M., Thomas, J. (eds.) Proc. of the Nato Advanced Research Workshop on Information Security Assurance and Security. Nato through Science, vol. 6, pp. 3–14. IOS Press (2006),
   http://www.iospress.nl/loadtop/load.php?isbn=9781586036782
6. Lowe, G.: Breaking and Fixing the Needham-Shroeder Public-Key Protocol Using FDR. In: Margaria, T., Steffen, B. (eds.) TACAS 1996. LNCS, vol. 1055, pp. 147–166. Springer, Heidelberg (1996)
7. Ryan, P.Y.A., Schneider, S., Goldsmith, M., Lowe, G., Roscoe, A.W.: Modelling and Analysis of Security Protocols. AW (2001)
8. Bella, G.: Formal Correctness of Security Protocols. Information Security and Cryptography. Springer (2007)
9. Armando, A., Basin, D., Boichut, Y., Chevalier, Y., Compagna, L., Cuellar, J., Drielsma, P.H., Heám, P.C., Kouchnarenko, O., Mantovani, J., Mödersheim, S., von Oheimb, D., Rusinowitch, M., Santiago, J., Turuani, M., Viganò, L., Vigneron, L.: The AVISPA Tool for the Automated Validation of Internet Security Protocols and Applications. In: Etessami, K., Rajamani, S.K. (eds.) CAV 2005. LNCS, vol. 3576, pp. 281–285. Springer, Heidelberg (2005)
10. Armando, A., Carbone, R., Compagna, L.: LTL Model Checking for Security Protocols. In: Proceedings of the 20th IEEE Computer Security Foundations Symposium, CSF20, Venice, Italy, July 6-8. IEEE Computer Society (2007)

Attacking Each Other
(Transcript of Discussion)

Xavier Chantry

SAP Research Labs

The main idea behind this talk is an idea of Giampaolo Bella from the University of Catania. The general picture nowadays is that each transfer has just one precise short-lived goal, such as for an eBay purchase, and each transfer may attempt malice aiming for personal benefit to them of money, or any kind of purchases. In the context of brief encounters, each transfer can just quickly leave one context and join another. If each may choose transfers, they can really collude towards the same malicious goal, and if they want to share the greater knowledge. But it's more realistic, that each malicious transfer will act for his own sake, and just use the resources at his disposal, and try to attack on his own.

The question is, what is the right threat model to analyse this kind of scenario? Is a Dolev-Yao threat model which attempts collusion on chain of proof of knowledge really appropriate? And so we are wondering if these transfers can really have a static state regarding which transfer is honest, which transfer is dishonest, and if we don't, whether we need a more innovative model where every transfer can switch from a dishonest behaviour to an honest behaviour, or vice-versa.

It might be a bit embarrassing to work on the NSPK protocol[1] again and again, but what we need is a known protocol and a known attack that everyone understands perfectly, and we shall show a known attack that is expressed in the Dolev-Yao model, and we are wondering, what could done in a new threat model?

Our new threat model is where every transfer can attack each other. In the general attacker threat model, each transfer may act as a Dolev-Yao attacker. But an important point is that there is no collusion or no sharing of knowledge otherwise this malicious Dolev-Yao attacker will just be seen as one global Dolev-Yao attacker, and it will not be able to model scenarios where attackers are attacking each other. So this threat model might be more appropriate to an analysis of privacy in the context of brief encounters, collusion may not be practical, because there is no time to join forces, and so maybe a general attacker is more appropriate. This model is a simplification of the threat model which was introduced by Giampaolo in 2003 so this is the threat model, we have static partitioning of principals between bad transfers, weak transfers and good transfers. The bad were the attackers, the good were doing transfers following the protocols just as they are written there, and the weak are bits in-between, which means they didn't launch attacks, didn't participate in attacks actively but maybe passively. And maybe this threat model where each transfer may

---

[1] Needham & Schroeder: "Using encryption for authentication in large networks of computers." Communications of the ACM, December 1978.

B. Christianson et al. (Eds.): Security Protocols 2009, LNCS 7028, pp. 48–50, 2013.
© Springer-Verlag Berlin Heidelberg 2013

attack each other is realistic because now it's becoming easier for everyone to just attempt to launch an attack, for example, from the web. So we completed each of the NSPK protocols with the computation set. So in this protocol the man-in-the-middle attack proves that the nonce there is shared, and is a transfer, and so this gives the possibility to pretty much make each transfer have the ability to attack each other, or at least to try. And of course the NSPK is a very basic protocol, so we assume there was a known attack on the protocol, and we are interested in helping the original attacker to that scenario.

We also want to automate the way we validate a protocol in the new threat model. We adapted SATMC, which is a type of model checker, to capture the GA threat model and used that tool to run this experiment.

So now a quick look at the modelling. We reduce the problem of finding an attack on the protocol to a model checking problem. The property we want to check, for example, can be one of the previous attacks. And so the status of the transitions needs to be modified to support the new threat model of the attacker. We could just track the knowledge of one Dolev-Yao there, where now we want to trust the knowledge of every transfer.

Bruce Christianson: What does not trustworthy mean in that context?

Reply: Actually for the General Attacker model we suppose that anyone is not trustworthy, so this means that anyone may act as a Dolev-Yao attacker, but in the model there we give more precise definitions. So for example, we have a provision that an agent is known as trustworthy, which for our model, we just describe any transfers and non trustworthy transfers about to fake or intercept messages, as any transfers about to infer some new knowledge by either encrypting, decrypting or composing without the proper nonce.

And so in conclusion, this new threat model seems appropriate to find interesting properties in protocols, such as situations where transfers attack each other or may retaliate against each other. So we were able to express a new threat model, and to return the results that we expected from our analysis. And are doing more protocols, such as Google's SAML protocol. So in these situations, we have clients, in this protocol we have a client who wants access to some service from a service provider; for doing that he transmits to authenticate with a supervisor, so the client receives a notification from an identity provider, and then can provide it to a service provider to access the service. So the conclusion is that the Google version of this protocol was good, and there is an authentication but it was too general to generate, for example, this authentication here can be replayed. So, for example, a service provider could just replay, if a malicious service provider managed to convince a client to authenticate and to access his service, he was able to replay authentication of the clients, and to, for example, accept the notification of this provider in the name of the client. And so we are wondering what this general attacker can bring to this scenario, for example, since we suppose that anyone is malicious, we could imagine that it could be the service provider itself which makes this transition from the clients, and their service provider, and so accessing information from the client.

Andy Gordon: These kinds of issues are certainly worth studying but you know Google might turn out to be malicious for example, in that particular protocol. Maybe Dolev-Yao in the original paper didn't speak about this, but in the tradition of Dolev-Yao formal models of protocols you consider that some events might occur, and any principal in any role might give up his keys to the attacker, and then the attacker can act maliciously on behalf of that principal.

Reply: Yes, but that's what we want, we want to have no sharing of previous knowledge, so each transfer acts on his own right through to getting something like his keys.

Andy Gordon: But what would that mean? In the standard model, a bunch of principals within the roles might get compromised, and they could act on their own without sharing knowledge. So anything within this GA model could happen in the standard model, and in the standard model additionally the principals could share messages. So I don't understand what you're gaining by saying that compromised principals can share information with one another.

Paul Syverson: One answer, a partial answer I suppose, Cathy and I had a paper back in 2000[2], where we were considering, suppose you have intruders which are self-interested. If you're looking at it as compromised clients, it doesn't make any sense, but if you're thinking about it as actually they're malicious people, bad guys, it's not like honour among thieves, they don't want to give their key off to some other guy, they don't trust him either. So we were exploring in that model, how much the kinds of attacks that you could get in Dolev-Yao you could also get if people weren't willing to do that. And the answer as I recall turned out to be quite a lot, I don't remember exactly what our results were, it's too long ago, do you remember Cathy?

Cathy Meadows: Yes, I don't remember exactly, the whole point I guess was that if you were willing to countenance the Machiavellian intruder, it seemed to be somewhat paradoxical that if you didn't give up your keys, there were certain assumptions you had to make on the protocol (I don't remember what they were), so that even if you didn't give up your keys, the attacker didn't lose anything.

Paul Syverson: So, I don't remember what we accomplished, but we did something, and the point is that there is some value I think to looking at things in this model, yes, it's weaker than the Dolev-Yao model, but in some sense it's realistic. And like the stuff Matt was talking about this morning[3], this is a somewhat more realistic, at least in some settings, threat, because you know, unless they're compromised bad guys are not going to give up keys just in order to do whatever they can. So maybe that's one partial answer, and that's why it's worth exploring questions like this.

---

[2] "Dolev-Yao is no better than Machiavelli" by Paul Syverson, Catherine Meadows and Iliano Cervesato: First Workshop on Issues in the Theory of Security.

[3] Blaze, these proceedings.

Bringing Zero-Knowledge Proofs
of Knowledge to Practice

Endre Bangerter[1], Stefania Barzan[2], Stephan Krenn[2],
Ahmad-Reza Sadeghi[3], Thomas Schneider[3], and Joe-Kai Tsay[4,*]

[1] Security Engineering Lab, Bern University of Applied Sciences, Switzerland
endre.bangerter@bfh.ch
[2] Security Engineering Lab, Bern University of Applied Sciences, Switzerland,
and University of Fribourg, Switzerland
{stefania.barzan,stephan.krenn}@bfh.ch
[3] Horst Görtz Institute for IT-Security, Ruhr-University Bochum, Germany
{ahmad.sadeghi,thomas.schneider}@trust.rub.de
[4] LSV, École Normale Supérieure de Cachan, France, and
CNRS, France, and INRIA, France
tsay@lsv.ens-cachan.fr

Abstract. Efficient zero-knowledge proofs of knowledge (ZK-PoK) are
basic building blocks of many practical cryptographic applications such
as identification schemes, group signatures, and secure multiparty computation. Currently, first applications that critically rely on ZK-PoKs
are being deployed in the real world. The most prominent example is Direct Anonymous Attestation (DAA), which was adopted by the Trusted
Computing Group (TCG) and implemented as one of the functionalities
of the cryptographic Trusted Platform Module (TPM) chip.

Implementing systems using ZK-PoK turns out to be challenging, since
ZK-PoK are, loosely speaking, significantly more complex than standard
crypto primitives, such as encryption and signature schemes. As a result,
implementation cycles of ZK-PoK are time-consuming and error-prone, in
particular for developers with minor or no cryptographic skills.

In this paper we report on our ongoing and future research vision
with the goal to bring ZK-PoK to practice by making them accessible to
crypto and security engineers. To this end we are developing compilers
and related tools that support and partially automate the design, implementation, verification and secure implementation of ZK-PoK protocols.

1 Introduction

A zero-knowledge proof of knowledge (ZK-PoK) is a two-party protocol between
a prover and a verifier, which allows the prover to convince the verifier that he
knows a secret value that satisfies a given relation (*proof of knowledge property*),
without the verifier being able to learn anything about the secret (*zero-knowledge*

---

* This work is being performed within the FP7 EU project CACE (Computer Aided
Cryptography Engineering). This work was done while Tsay was at the Chair for
System Security at Ruhr-University Bochum.

B. Christianson et al. (Eds.): Security Protocols 2009, LNCS 7028, pp. 51–62, 2013.

property). For a formal definition we refer to [1]. There are fundamental results showing that all relations in NP have ZK-PoK [2–5]. The corresponding protocols are of theoretical relevance, but are much too inefficient to be used in practical applications.

In contrast to these generic, but practically useless protocols, there are various protocols which are efficient enough for real world use. Essentially, all ZK-PoK protocols being used in practice today are based on so called Σ-protocols. What is typically being proved using basic Σ-protocols is the knowledge of a preimage under a homomorphism (e.g., a secret discrete logarithm). Yet, there are numerous considerably more complex variations of these preimage proofs. These ZK-PoK proof techniques play an important role in applied cryptography. In fact, many practically oriented applications use such proofs as basic building blocks. Examples include identification schemes [6], interactive verifiable computation [7], group signatures [8], secure watermark detection [9], and efficient secure multiparty computation [10] – just to name a few.

While many of these applications typically only exist on a specification level, a direction of applied research has produced first applications using ZK-PoKs that are deployed in the real world. The probably most prominent example is Direct Anonymous Attestation (DAA) [11], which was adopted by the Trusted Computing Group (TCG), an industry consortium of many IT enterprises, as a privacy enhancing mechanism for remote authentication of computing platforms.

Another example is the *identity mixer* anonymous credential system [12], which was released by IBM into the Eclipse Higgins project, an open source effort dedicated to developing software for user-centric identity management. Identity mixer is probably one of the most advanced protocol suites supporting the "transient relationship paradigm".

Up to now, design, implementation and verification of the formal cryptographic security properties (i.e., zero-knowledge and proof of knowledge property) as well as code security properties (e.g., security against buffer overflows, race conditions, side channel vulnerabilities) is done "by hand". In fact, past experiences, e.g., during the design and implementation of the preceding two examples, have shown that this is a time consuming and error prone task. This has certainly to do with the fact that ZK-PoK are considerably more complex than other crypto primitives such as signature- and encryption schemes or hash functions.

The goal of our ongoing and future research is to bring ZK-PoK to practice by making them accessible to crypto and security engineers. To this end we are working on compilers and related tools that support and partially automate the design, implementation, verification, and secure implementation of ZK-PoK protocols. For instance the compiler which is part of our toolbox, will take as input a high-level specification of the goals of a ZK-PoK, automatically find a corresponding protocol, and output its implementation in, e.g., Java or C code. We have already developed and implemented a language and compiler that automates the latter step from protocol specification to code generation. Finding a protocol from a high-level specification is subject of ongoing research. Also, we are working on tool-based support for the verification of the security properties of ZK-PoK.

In the following we describe the challenges pertaining to using ZK-PoK in practice in Sec. 2 and give an overview of a solution blueprint and first results on solving these challenges in Sec. 3.

1.1 Related Work

ZK-PoK were introduced in [15], and the first efficient protocols for preimage proofs in groups of known order were given in [6, 16]. Unified frameworks for preimage proofs in known order groups were given in the following by [17–20]. A profound analysis of the Σ^Φ-protocol was performed by Cramer [21].

The first efficient solution for proofs in unknown order groups was given in [22] and has been corrected by Damgård and Fujisaki [23]. Subsequently, other variants overcoming some of their restrictions have been proposed. In very recent work, a long overdue unified framework for exponentiation homomorphisms in arbitrary groups was given by Camenisch et al. [24].

An efficient way to combine arbitrary Σ-protocols was described by Cramer et al. [17].

To bridge the gap between theory and practice, a first prototype of a zero-knowledge compiler was started in [25, 26], and was later extended in [27]. Yet, its authors state explicitly that it was designed as a proof of concept prototype only. This prototype handles proofs in known order groups only, and includes neither a verification tool nor extensions to achieve concurrent ZK or non-interactivity. Unfortunately, multiple proofs are combined in a very inefficient way only. Furthermore, the input language of this compiler is less intuitive than ours.

Our input language was inspired by the commonly used notation of Camenisch and Stadler [28]. Yet, this is an inprecise and ambiguous notation. Therefore we augment it by the missing parts such as group descriptions, etc.

As basic building blocks we apply the techniques from [6, 16, 21] in known order groups, proofs in unknown order groups are done by applying those from [23, 27]. Predicates are combined using the method described in [17] instantiated with Shamir's secret sharing scheme [29]. To obtain non-interactive ZK and concurrent ZK we use the Fiat-Shamir heuristic [30].

Similar work to ours performed in the field of secure function evaluation [31, 32]. Their compilers allow to specify the function to be evaluated in a high-level language, and output executable code. In principle, zero-knowledge proofs could be realized by secure function evaluations. Yet, the resulting protocols are significantly less efficient than those generated by our compiler.

Compiler support for an efficient and secure low-level implementation of cryptographic primitives resistant against software side-channels [33] and applications to elliptic curve cryptography [34] is provided by Cryptography Aware language and cOmpiler (CAO) [35].

2   Challenges

In the following paragraphs we will describe the main challenges that ZK-PoK pose to crypto engineers and protocol designers, which we aim to tackle with our compiler suite.

Let us introduce some notation first. By the *semantic goal* of a ZK-PoK we refer to *what a prover wants to demonstrate in zero-knowledge*. For instance, the semantic goal can be to prove knowledge of a discrete logarithm of a group element with respect to another group element. A more complex goal is to prove that a given cipher-text encrypts a valid (with respect to some given public key) signature on a specific message. By a ZK-PoK *protocol (specification)* we refer to the actual description of a protocol (i.e., the operations of prover and verifier and the messages being exchanged). For instance, the well known Schnorr protocol [6] realizes the first semantic goal mentioned above, and verifiable encryption protocols [36] realize the latter. It is important to note that given a semantic goal, there can be many different protocols realizing that goal; also sometimes one does not know how to construct an efficient protocol realizing a goal (which does not mean that there is no better protocol than using a generic protocols for NP statements). Finally, by a *(protocol) implementation* we refer to actual code (e.g., in C or Java) realizing a specification.

Now, let us turn to the challenges mentioned above.

Designing ZK-PoK. On a conceptual level ZK-PoK are easy to grasp and intuitive: formulating the semantic goal of a ZK-PoK is an easy task for a protocol designer. It essentially boils down to formulating the requirements of a ZK-PoK. Yet, finding a protocol specification realizing a semantic goal is in many cases difficult or impossible for people who don't have extensive expertise in the field. As a result, we believe that unlike other, less complex crypto primitives (such as encryption, signatures, etc.), ZK-PoK are not part of the toolbox of many crypto engineers. This in turn lets us conjecture that the potential of novel applications that can be built using ZK-PoK is only poorly exploited.

Why is it actually often hard to find a ZK-PoK protocol meeting a semantic specification? The main problem is the lack of a unified, modular, and easy to understand theoretical framework underlying the various ZK-PoK protocols and proof techniques. As a result there is no methodological formal way to guide cryptographic protocol designers. In fact, there is a large number of tricks and techniques "to prove this and that", yet combining various tricks and preserving the security properties (i.e., the ZK and PoK properties) is not straightforward and is non-modular. The composition of techniques often needs intricate knowledge of the technique at hand, and may also require modification of the technique. For instance some techniques only work under certain algebraic assumptions and preconditions. These can be conditions on the order of the algebraic group and group elements being used, conditions on whether the prover knows the factorization of a composite integer, distributions of protocol inputs etc. The algebraic conditions in turn require tuning protocol parameters. As a result, finding and designing ZK-PoK protocols is a heuristic process based on experience and a detailed understanding of the techniques being used. In contrast, encryption and signature schemes and other primitives can be composed in a modular way and are easily accessible to designers.

Efficiency of implementation process. The step going from the protocol specification of a ZK-PoK to its protocol implementation is often considered to be
trivial from a conceptual point of view. Yet in practice it is not. In fact, experiences made while implementing, e.g., a prototype of the identity mixer [12, 37]
protocols have shown that a manual implementation can be tedious and error
prone and easily takes person weeks. Moreover, protocol specifications are often
written by cryptographers while the implementation is done by SW engineers.
This "skill gap" may lead to implementation errors. The former often don't care
sufficiently or don't have the skills to cope with implementation issues and their
specifications may be slightly incomplete; the latter may have a hard time to
assess implementation decisions, which depend on cryptographic subtleties.

Additionally, minor changes in the semantic goal often result in fundamental
changes of the resulting protocol.

Efficiency of code. Getting efficient code, in terms of computation time, memory
usage, size of messages sent over the network, number of message exchanged
etc., can be of great concern when using ZK-PoK. The choice of the resource to
optimize may greatly differ depending on the actual device on which the code
is run. For instance, parts of the prover's algorithm in the DAA protocol [11]
are run inside a relatively simple and low cost TPM chip while the verifier's
algorithm may run on a powerful computer.

There are at least two places where one can optimize ZK-PoK. On a high-
level, there is potential for optimization by finding the most efficient protocol
specification realizing a given semantic goal (this type of optimization is closely
related to the "designing ZK-PoK" issue described above). On a lower level one
can optimize the code implementing a given protocol, much like the optimization
performed by compilers for conventional programming languages like C, Java
etc., whereas one should specially focus on the optimization of crypto operations.

Optimization in general, requires substantial experience and an intricate understanding of the runtime environment.

Correctness and security of implementations. The correctness and security of
the protocol implementations is primordial. One can distinguish two classes of
correctness and security properties. One are the cryptographic security properties, which are formalized mathematically and are present already on a protocol
specification level. These properties are: correctness (the protocol works when
prover and verifier are honest), zero-knowledge and proof of knowledge. At the
current state of the art, the crypto community will not accept a ZK-PoK protocol, unless these properties are formally proven on a specification level. These
proofs are often non-trivial and certainly tedious and time consuming, and as a
result there exist various published protocols that contain flaws in their security
analysis. For instance the security proof in [22] was incomplete as outlined and
corrected in [23].

Of course one also needs to assert that those security properties are indeed
assured by the implementation of the protocol (i.e., that an implementation
correctly reflects the specification).

Of equal importance are security issues that occur at an implementation level. These include security against generic implementation errors like buffer overflows, race conditions etc., but also crypto specific code problems, such as side-channel vulnerabilities. Getting these code security issues right requires substantial know-how, which is often not part of the skill set of developers.

3   Solution Blueprint and Results

In the following we give a brief description of our compiler suite (see Fig. 1), and sketch how it can be used for resolving the challenges explained above. Also first results achieved for each of these challenges will be described.

From a usage perspective, our compiler suite takes a description of the semantic goal in a *high-level language*, and outputs a protocol implementation together with a formal proof of its correctness. From a technical point of view, the compiler is divided into three parts, which we want to discuss briefly now:

- The compiler will take a description of the semantic goal in a *high-level language* as input, and translate it into a *protocol specification* in a first compiler step (the *high-level compiler*) by choosing the most appropriate techniques to meet the user's requirements. This protocol specification describes a unique protocol, without containing the exact algorithms or single messages to be exchanged, etc.
- In a second step, the *protocol compiler* will expand this protocol specification into C or Java code, as well as LATEX-code for documentation purposes.
- Both compiler steps will add annotations, including information about decisions made, to their output. The semantic goal, the protocol specification and its implementation will be given to the *protocol verification toolbox*, which using those annotations will formally verify that the implementation indeed realizes the semantic goal in a secure way.

Let us now turn to how we plan to tackle the problems stated in Sec. 2.

The "efficiency of implementation process" and "efficiency of code" challenges are equally important but less difficult to achieve than the two others; we therefore only discuss them briefly.

Efficiency of implementation process. This goal is achieved inherently by our compiler based approach, as the implementation is automatized. Our first prototype runs within less than one second, and we expect the final version to run within a couple of seconds. To ease usage of our compiler suite, a tool-chain with a consistent user interface could be given to our compiler. This could be based on an IDE such as Eclipse and support the developer by syntax highlighting, performance testing, etc.

The input language is inspired by the notation introduced in [28]. Yet, to remove unambiguities, some more information has to be added to this language.

Let us consider the following example:

$$ZKPoK\Big[(\chi) : y = g^{\chi}\Big]$$

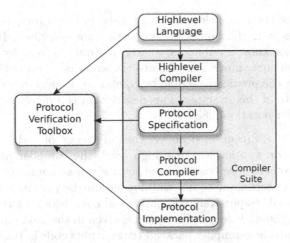

Fig. 1. Architecture of our framework for automatic generation and verification of ZK-PoK protocols

specifies a proof of knowledge of the discrete logarithm $x \in G$ of $y \in H$ in base $g \in H$. This notation does not contain any information about the groups G, H, the order of g, y, or the knowledge error that has to be achieved.

Still, from having the above protocol description and knowledge about the groups, etc., it's straightforward to obtain the input of our compiler, such as:

```
01:  Declaration{
02:     Prime(1024) p;
03:     Prime(160) q;
04:     G=Zmod+(q) x;
05:     H=Zmod*(p) g, y;
06:  }
07:
08:  ProtocolInputs{
09:     ProverPrivate  := x;
10:     ProverPublic   := p,q,g,y;
11:     VerifierPublic := p,q,g,y;
12:  }
13:
14:  ProtocolProperties{
15:     KnowledgeError    := 80;
16:     ProtocolComposition := P_1;
17:  }
18:
19:  SigmaPhi P_1 {
20:     Homomorphism (phi : G -> H : (a) |-> (g^a));
21:     ChallengeLength := 80;
22:     Relation ((y) = phi(x));
23:  }
```

Lines 01-06 declare the group elements being used in the subsequently described protocol. In lines 08-12 the inputs of the parties are described. If for example the verifier did not know a public parameter, it would be sent by the prover in a synchronization step. Lines 14-17 declare the knowledge error that has to be reached, and how the predicates should be composed. Finally, lines 18-23 describe the only predicate in this example. This description is a direct analogon to the Camenisch-Stadler notation [28].

Efficiency of code. As mentioned above, the "efficiency of code" challenge has to be dealt with on two levels. On a high level, the compiler has to find the most efficient protocol specification meeting a given semantic proof goal. The choice of the proof technique to use will depend on the priorities the user gives to communicational- respectively computational complexity, as there is often a tradeoff between those. A deeper discussion is given in the next paragraph. On a low level, we'll provide a compiler backend that outputs code in the CAO ("Cryptography Aware language and cOmpiler") language [35]. This is a language and a compiler geared towards the generation of an efficient and secure low-level implementation of cryptographic primitives; CAO is also being developed within the CACE project.

Let us discuss the remaining challenges in more detail.

Designing ZK-PoK. At the moment we are designing a high-level language in which the semantic goal of a ZK-PoK together with its non-functional properties can be formulated in a user-friendly way. The language is inspired by the well-known Camenisch-Stadler notation [28] which is used to formulate the intended semantic goal. We enrich this with non-functional properties which allow to specify optimization goals (e.g., optimize computational or communicational complexity) and the security level (e.g., knowledge error, tightness of the statistical zero-knowledge property, etc.) of the protocol being generated. In this high-level language, we abstract away as many technical details as possible to ease design and usage of ZK-PoK for non-experts.

In our architecture (cf. Fig. 1) the high-level compiler is responsible for finding a protocol specification that realizes the semantic proof goal and simultaneously takes into consideration the user's non-functional specifications. To enable the compiler to make "good" decisions, the compiler backend reports the costs on a specific target platform upwards to the high-level compiler. For example efficient interval proofs can be realized either with the techniques of [38] or [39] with different costs.

To be able to actually build a compiler for the semantics of that high-level language we are currently working on a unified theoretical framework for the various ZK-PoK techniques. For this, we extend the existing theory for zero-knowledge proofs which by now mainly deals with known order groups [17, 19–21]. Our extended theoretical framework is capable to cope with arbitrary combinations of protocols in hidden order groups (e.g., RSA groups) as well [14, 23, 24]. To this end, we have conceived the new Σ^{exp} protocol [27], which yields efficient ZK-PoK in a more modular manner than the existing protocols [14, 23, 24].

A first prototype of our compiler and semantic language [27, 40] implements a subset of the envisaged compiler framework. It already supports the generation of various crypto-systems such as Pedersen commitments/verifiable secret sharing [41], Schnorr authentication/signatures [6], electronic cash [42–44], group signatures [45], or ring signatures [17].

Correctness and security of implementations. One of our main goals concerning the security of the code output by the compiler, is to formally verify the zero-knowledge and proof of knowledge properties. To this end we are developing a protocol verification toolbox as part of our compiler framework (see Fig. 1). Its task is to accomplish a semi- or (ideally) fully automatic formal verification of these properties.

We currently focus on the proof of knowledge property. The toolbox takes as input the user's description of the semantic goal and the protocol implementation (output by the compiler). It then interprets this information in order to assemble a proof goal for the Isabelle/HOL theorem prover [46]. The theorem prover then formally verifies whether the protocol is indeed a proof of knowledge for the given goal (by constructing a knowledge extractor).

One step towards automating this verification process is to consider the most relevant proof strategies used in existing published proofs and to develop corresponding proof tactics for the theorem prover. Also, to facilitate this automated verification, the different parts of our compiler (i.e., the high-level compiler respectively the protocol compiler) annotate helper data to the code they output.

We have already formally verified the proof of knowledge property for basic protocols such as those in [6, 23] and generic AND– and OR– compositions among those. Currently, we are tackling more complex protocols.

Last but not least, also to assert code security properties (e.g., against buffer overflows and side channel attacks) we rely on the verified compiler backend to output CAO-code [35] (see above). The CAO language is designed to automatically generate secure implementations resistant against software side-channels.

References

1. Bellare, M., Goldreich, O.: On Defining Proofs of Knowledge. In: Brickell, E.F. (ed.) CRYPTO 1992. LNCS, vol. 740, pp. 390–420. Springer, Heidelberg (1993)
2. Dwork, C., Feige, U., Kilian, J., Naor, M., Safra, M.: Low Communication 2-Prover Zero-Knowledge Proofs for NP. In: Brickell, E.F. (ed.) CRYPTO 1992. LNCS, vol. 740, pp. 215–227. Springer, Heidelberg (1993)
3. Goldreich, O., Micali, S., Wigderson, A.: Proofs that yield nothing but their validity or all languages in NP have zero knowledge proof systems. Journal of the ACM 38(1), 691–729 (1991); Preliminary version in 27th FOCS (1986)
4. Ishai, Y., Kushilevitz, E., Ostrovsky, R., Sahai, A.: Zero-knowledge from secure multiparty computation. In: ACM Symposium on Theory of Computing – STOC 2007, pp. 21–30. ACM Press, New York (2007)
5. Prabhakaran, M., Rosen, A., Sahai, A.: Concurrent zero knowledge with logarithmic round-complexity. In: IEEE Symposium on Foundations of Computer Science – FOCS 2002, pp. 366–375. IEEE Computer Society, Washington, DC (2002)

6. Schnorr, C.: Efficient signature generation by smart cards. Journal of Cryptology 4(3), 161–174 (1991)

7. Camenisch, J., Michels, M.: Proving in Zero-Knowledge that a Number Is the Product of Two Safe Primes. In: Stern, J. (ed.) EUROCRYPT 1999. LNCS, vol. 1592, pp. 107–122. Springer, Heidelberg (1999)

8. Camenisch, J.: Group Signature Schemes and Payment Systems Based on the Discrete Logarithm Problem. PhD thesis, ETH Zurich, Konstanz (1998)

9. Adelsbach, A., Rohe, M., Sadeghi, A.R.: Complementing zero-knowledge watermark detection: Proving properties of embedded information without revealing it. Multimedia Systems 11(2), 143–158 (2005)

10. Lindell, Y., Pinkas, B., Smart, N.P.: Implementing Two-Party Computation Efficiently with Security Against Malicious Adversaries. In: Ostrovsky, R., De Prisco, R., Visconti, I. (eds.) SCN 2008. LNCS, vol. 5229, pp. 2–20. Springer, Heidelberg (2008)

11. Brickell, E., Camenisch, J., Chen, L.: Direct anonymous attestation. In: Atluri, V., Backes, M., Basin, D.A., Waidner, M. (eds.) ACM Conference on Computer and Communications Security – CCS 2004, pp. 132–145. ACM Press (2004)

12. Camenisch, J., Herreweghen, E.V.: Design and implementation of the idemix anonymous credential system. In: Atluri, V. (ed.) ACM Conference on Computer and Communications Security – CCS 2002, pp. 21–30. ACM Press (2002), http://www.zurich.ibm.com/security/idemix/

13. Bangerter, E.: Efficient Zero-Knowledge Proofs of Knowledge for Homomorphisms. PhD thesis, Ruhr-University Bochum (2005)

14. Bangerter, E., Camenisch, J., Maurer, U.: Efficient Proofs of Knowledge of Discrete Logarithms and Representations in Groups with Hidden Order. In: Vaudenay, S. (ed.) PKC 2005. LNCS, vol. 3386, pp. 154–171. Springer, Heidelberg (2005)

15. Goldwasser, S., Micali, S., Rackoff, C.: The knowledge complexity of interactive proof-systems. In: ACM Symposium on Theory of Computing – STOC 1985, pp. 291–304. ACM Press, New York (1985)

16. Guillou, L.C., Quisquater, J.-J.: A "Paradoxical" Identity-Based Signature Scheme Resulting from Zero-Knowledge. In: Goldwasser, S. (ed.) CRYPTO 1988. LNCS, vol. 403, pp. 216–231. Springer, Heidelberg (1990)

17. Cramer, R., Damgård, I., Schoenmakers, B.: Proof of Partial Knowledge and Simplified Design of Witness Hiding Protocols. In: Desmedt, Y.G. (ed.) CRYPTO 1994. LNCS, vol. 839, pp. 174–187. Springer, Heidelberg (1994)

18. Camenisch, J., Stadler, M.: Proof systems for general statements about discrete logarithms. Technical Report 260, Institute for Theoretical Computer Science, ETH Zürich (1997)

19. Brands, S.: Rapid Demonstration of Linear Relations Connected by Boolean Operators. In: Fumy, W. (ed.) EUROCRYPT 1997. LNCS, vol. 1233, pp. 318–333. Springer, Heidelberg (1997)

20. Bresson, E., Stern, J.: Proofs of Knowledge for Non-monotone Discrete-Log Formulae and Applications. In: Chan, A.H., Gligor, V.D. (eds.) ISC 2002. LNCS, vol. 2433, pp. 272–288. Springer, Heidelberg (2002)

21. Cramer, R.: Modular Design of Secure yet Practical Cryptographic Protocols. PhD thesis, CWI and University of Amsterdam (1997)

22. Fujisaki, E., Okamoto, T.: Statistical Zero Knowledge Protocols to Prove Modular Polynomial Relations. In: Kaliski Jr., B.S. (ed.) CRYPTO 1997. LNCS, vol. 1294, pp. 16–30. Springer, Heidelberg (1997)

23. Damgård, I., Fujisaki, E.: A Statistically-Hiding Integer Commitment Scheme Based on Groups with Hidden Order. In: Zheng, Y. (ed.) ASIACRYPT 2002. LNCS, vol. 2501, pp. 125–142. Springer, Heidelberg (2002)
24. Camenisch, J., Kiayias, A., Yung, M.: On the Portability of Generalized Schnorr Proofs. In: Joux, A. (ed.) EUROCRYPT 2009. LNCS, vol. 5479, pp. 425–442. Springer, Heidelberg (2009)
25. Briner, T.: Compiler for zero-knowledge proof-of-knowledge protocols. Master's thesis, ETH Zurich (2004)
26. Camenisch, J., Rohe, M., Sadeghi, A.R.: Sokrates - a compiler framework for zero-knowledge protocols. In: Western European Workshop on Research in Cryptology – WEWoRC 2005 (2005)
27. Bangerter, E., Camenisch, J., Krenn, S., Sadeghi, A.R., Schneider, T.: Automatic generation of sound zero-knowledge protocols. Cryptology ePrint Archive, Report 2008/471 (2008), http://eprint.iacr.org/, Poster Session of EUROCRYPT 2009
28. Camenisch, J.L., Stadler, M.A.: Efficient Group Signature Schemes for Large Groups (Extended Abstract). In: Kaliski Jr., B.S. (ed.) CRYPTO 1997. LNCS, vol. 1294, pp. 410–424. Springer, Heidelberg (1997)
29. Shamir, A.: How to share a secret. Communications of the ACM 22(11), 612–613 (1979)
30. Fiat, A., Shamir, A.: How to Prove Yourself: Practical Solutions to Identification and Signature Problems. In: Odlyzko, A.M. (ed.) CRYPTO 1986. LNCS, vol. 263, pp. 186–194. Springer, Heidelberg (1987)
31. MacKenzie, P., Oprea, A., Reiter, M.K.: Automatic generation of two-party computations. In: Jajodia, S., Atluri, V., Jaeger, T. (eds.) ACM Conference on Computer and Communications Security – CCS 2003, pp. 210–219. ACM Press (2003)
32. Malkhi, D., Nisan, N., Pinkas, B., Sella, Y.: Fairplay – a secure two-party computation system. In: Proceedings of the 13th Conference on USENIX Security Symposium – SSYM 2004 (2004), http://www.cs.huji.ac.il/project/Fairplay/fairplay.html
33. Barbosa, M., Page, D.: On the automatic construction of indistinguishable operations. Cryptology ePrint Archive, Report 2005/174 (2005), http://eprint.iacr.org/
34. Barbosa, M., Moss, A., Page, D.: Compiler Assisted Elliptic Curve Cryptography. In: Meersman, R. (ed.) OTM 2007, Part II. LNCS, vol. 4804, pp. 1785–1802. Springer, Heidelberg (2007)
35. Barbosa, M., Noad, R., Page, D., Smart, N.P.: First steps toward a cryptography-aware language and compiler. Cryptology ePrint Archive, Report 2005/160 (2005), http://eprint.iacr.org/
36. Ateniese, G.: Verifiable encryption of digital signatures and applications. ACM Transactions on Information and System Security 7(1), 1–20 (2004)
37. Camenisch, J.L., Lysyanskaya, A.: An Efficient System for Non-transferable Anonymous Credentials with Optional Anonymity Revocation. In: Pfitzmann, B. (ed.) EUROCRYPT 2001. LNCS, vol. 2045, pp. 93–118. Springer, Heidelberg (2001)
38. Boudot, F.: Efficient Proofs that a Committed Number Lies in an Interval. In: Preneel, B. (ed.) EUROCRYPT 2000. LNCS, vol. 1807, pp. 431–444. Springer, Heidelberg (2000)
39. Lipmaa, H.: On Diophantine Complexity and Statistical Zero-Knowledge Arguments. In: Laih, C.-S. (ed.) ASIACRYPT 2003. LNCS, vol. 2894, pp. 398–415. Springer, Heidelberg (2003)

40. Bangerter, E., Briner, T., Henecka, W., Krenn, S., Sadeghi, A.-R., Schneider, T.: Automatic Generation of Sigma-Protocols. In: Martinelli, F., Preneel, B. (eds.) EuroPKI 2009. LNCS, vol. 6391, pp. 67–82. Springer, Heidelberg (2010)

41. Pedersen, T.P.: Non-interactive and Information-Theoretic Secure Verifiable Secret Sharing. In: Feigenbaum, J. (ed.) CRYPTO 1991. LNCS, vol. 576, pp. 129–140. Springer, Heidelberg (1992)

42. Brands, S.: Untraceable Off-Line Cash in Wallets with Observers. In: Stinson, D.R. (ed.) CRYPTO 1993. LNCS, vol. 773, pp. 302–318. Springer, Heidelberg (1994)

43. Chan, A., Frankel, Y., Tsiounis, Y.: Easy come - easy go divisible cash. Technical Report TR-0371-05-98-582, GTE (1998), Updated version with corrections

44. Okamoto, T.: An Efficient Divisible Electronic Cash Scheme. In: Coppersmith, D. (ed.) CRYPTO 1995. LNCS, vol. 963, pp. 438–451. Springer, Heidelberg (1995)

45. Camenisch, J., Lysyanskaya, A.: Signature Schemes and Anonymous Credentials from Bilinear Maps. In: Franklin, M. (ed.) CRYPTO 2004. LNCS, vol. 3152, pp. 56–72. Springer, Heidelberg (2004)

46. Paulson, L.C.: Isabelle. LNCS, vol. 828. Springer, Heidelberg (1994)

Bringing Zero-Knowledge Proofs of Knowledge to Practice

(Transcript of Discussion)

Stephan Krenn

Bern University of Applied Sciences

This is the joint work of several people of whom only Joe-Kai is here today. The whole work is still open research and, as the title indicates, aims to facilitate the secure and efficient usage of non-standard crypto primitives, especially for software engineers.

Let's start with the very informal definition of zero-knowledge proofs. They are a two-party protocol between a prover and a verifier where the prover claims to know some secret value, for example, login credentials or something, and he has to convince the verifier that he actually does, and this means that the prover has the possibility to cheat, of course, but on the other hand, the verifier would not be able to gain any information about the secret; this is the zero-knowledge property.

Two examples: the first one is idemix, or Identity Mixer[1], which was designed and implemented by IBM some years ago. It's an anonymous credential system which allows organisations to issue credentials to clients in a way that is secure for both parties. And if the clients collude, they are not able to gain credentials, one of them would not have got them, and on the other hand, the organisations only get the information they really need to issue a credential. This also means that organisations are not able to leak information they know about a specific user. And only in the case of malicious client it is possible to revoke this anonymity.

The second example is not about the identity of the user but about the identity of the machine, it's Direct Anonymous Attestation, or DAA[2], which was adopted by the Trusted Computer Group and is implemented in TPMs in most of today's laptops. It allows us to remote authenticate the TPM without revealing the identity of the machine itself.

From our point of view there are at least four main challenges of executing such protocols. The first one is, it's very easy to write down the proof goal, I want to prove this number is an RSA modulus for example, but it's not clear how to get a protocol for this proof goal. There are proof techniques to prove this and that, but it's not clear how to put them together, especially when you want to optimise a protocol for given architecture.

The second problem is that the implementation process is quite time-consuming, because the protocol designers often don't have enough programming skills to do the implementation themselves, and the programmers often don't have the cryptographic skills to do the design of the protocol. And even

---

[1] http://www.zurich.ibm.com/security/idemix/
[2] http://www.zurich.ibm.com/security/daa/

B. Christianson et al. (Eds.): Security Protocols 2009, LNCS 7028, pp. 63–68, 2013.
© Springer-Verlag Berlin Heidelberg 2013

if you are able to compose the implementation and the design it's still time-consuming because as soon as you do a tiny change to the proof goal, you must start again from the very beginning.

Now the third problem is related to the last one, it's about the security of the implementation itself. You should avoid insecurities in the implementation, so the C code, for example, should avoid buffer overflows, etc. (and it should be optimised for a given architecture).

And the very last challenge from our point of view, is the reputation of the protocols. I mean, you can write down a C program and say that it realises a given proof goal, but it's not easy to formally prove that the program implements this proof goal. Especially if you are a non-expert you would have a quite hard time and if you are an expert on the subject then it's at least very time-consuming and a bit boring.

So the question is, is it possible to optimise the whole idea, and that's our approach, we want to build a compiler that takes an abstract description of the proof goal as an input, and output three parts. The first part is the C, or Java implementation of the given proof goal. The second part is a documentation, and the third one is formal proof, that this implementation really realises the proof goal.

Well let's look at this zero-knowledge compiler box a bit closer. The user will give a high level description of the proof goal, and the first step, the proof techniques will be chosen and the protocols will be defined for the proof goal, and the protocol specification will be output, that's an abstract description, which describes a unique protocol but abstracts away all the information that's not really relevant. Then the protocol compiler compiles this protocol specification to C or Java code, or whatever. And both parts of the compiler will add annotations to the code containing information about group orders, or whatever information is known to the prover, if this information is known to the verifier. Now this information will go into protocol verification, which is based on the prover, and will hopefully output the formal proof of the correctness of this implementation.

At the moment we have the protocol compiler more or less done, the high-level compiler is only started, it's under construction, and for the protocol verification toolbox we are currently thinking how to automise the proofs.

At the beginning I said something about the mission of this project. At the moment if you are a software engineer and you think about the cryptographic primitives you might use for implementation you think of hash functions, of signature schemes, of encryption schemes, and essentially that's it. The goal of the project is to enrich this by zero-knowledge proof of knowledge.

Sören Preibusch: It seems then to me the limits of the protocol design will be the expressiveness of the high-level specification language that the compiler can handle.

Reply: Exactly.

Sören Preibusch: So if you want a not-off-the-shelf protocol then you can't use your compiler.

Reply: Well the idea is that you can, the high level language makes it possible to describe abstract proof goals in this other language, and for all proof goals that you can describe inside of the language, the compiler can . . . .

Sören Preibusch: Sorry, I meant that the high level things you want to describe may be very diverse.

Reply: Of course, it depends on how abstract you design this high level to be. You can write a sentence about the proof model there, but yes, that's not realistic. So we are not sure how abstract this, we don't know yet.

Sören Preibusch: And how can you cope with things like that an implementation may no longer implement the specification as the attacker gains more capabilities as time goes by. Like if you say, I want to have a secure key, then your compiler says, OK, I'll take 512 bits, that may be true some years ago, but some years later it no longer meets the specification; by then it is equivalent to 160 bits which is low level security.

Simon Foley: You're generating your implementation from the high-level specification, so how would you then target the implementation to whatever the final system is going to be? If you've got two systems reporting to each other, surely your implementation would be modified and changed, so the generated implementation would be modified and changed in order to deploy it to whatever situation it's going to be used in? So if you're generating say high-level C code, which implements the protocol, surely depending on your application system you're going to have different kinds of implementation interacting in different ways, so although the high-level protocols are the same, in terms of the final target code, surely you're going to have to make changes to the protocol implementation.

Reply: This protocol compiler is relatively modular, which means that you can specify, OK, I want to use this maths library, for example, and I want to use this library for communication, etc. Well the goal is that you have the possibility to choose which libraries you want to use, which are available.

George Danezis: Why do you write the language if you cannot express the requirement except with a specification that you believe you already have a protocol for, why don't you just provide the protocol?

Reply: The idea is that this high level compiler has been especially optimised for the architecture. You can say, for example, I want to use subtle proof knowledge for it to be effective, or I want to use the signature proof of knowledge with the number of communication routes, for example, to be minimised.

George Danezis: Yes, but what I'm suggesting is, there could be a set number of things like that you can do and that your compiler will interpret them. Why not just provide the library that does this stuff, instead of a language, since the expressiveness of the language is somehow limited to what the compiler will do something clever about.

Reply: There's a number of primitives that you can use for different proofs, depending on what you want. To prove some relations among privacies, for example, the compiler hopefully will choose the correct techniques to find the protocol that this proof needs, otherwise the network would have to provide a technique for specific relations of this specification.

Joe-Kai Tsay: The compiler will compose certain protocols, I mean, if you want to prove something like knowledge of some secret exponents, just with a library, you would already have to have in the library every possible kind of proof goal, or protocols for any possible proofs or proof goals that someone might ask for.

George Danezis: Yes, but this is the point of having a compiler, so with a set of proofs which enjoy composition related properties, they can combine different statements with conjunction. Some zero-knowledge proofs don't combine for free, but if I choose them correctly, and set up the parameters correctly, then I could have such a combination provided by the compiler?

Matteo Maffei: What kind of zero-knowledge proofs do you deal with precisely, are some interactive and do the protocols include an on-line verifier?

Reply: Well the basic protocols would give us non-interactive protocols, and some will be implemented to take account of zero-knowledge. But the basic protocol is always a single one.

Matteo Maffei: Do you think it would be possible to have a more high-level language, where it can just write statements of the following form: I know that these messages are encryption over some other messages, and I hide some of these messages in the statement, and then I choose some proof of the encryption scheme, and use this statement to prove knowledge of the statement. Do you think it would be possible? It would give the user an even higher level interface, something understandable, and the zero-knowledge proof will be automatically generated by hiding away the case of the proof.

Joe-Kai Tsay: The level you describe is I think exactly what is realistic because you could say, OK, I want to prove the note, the content of the ciphertext.

Matteo Maffei: And who checks that the user doesn't screw up the parameters in the high level language, because I guess that the correctness of the proof depends on the values that the user chooses, if it's got another language, so do you have a way to check that the proof that was generated is zero-knowledge?

Joe-Kai Tsay: Not yet.

Reply: The verification toolbox may try to do something on the protocol level, but not like Xavier's C code[3].

Joe-Kai Tsay: There's a difference between that and this scheme. Secure zero-knowledge just means that for the protocol to run the high-level compiler

---

[3] Chantry, these proceedings.

hopefully chooses this parameter so the user should not be able to do something else. But it's the goal that we want to reach.

Sören Preibusch: I think the problem is that we don't know yet how refinement really works, and how we can optimise it, and what you're doing is protocol refinement. I think it's two questions at one time; you have a problem with protocols, we don't know how to engineer protocols, and you make a refinement of high-level to more fine-grained implementation, and that's refinement, but we also don't know how refinement works. So I think it's very hard to achieve this goal.

Reply: Yes, you're right, it's hard, realistically to abstract a level of how we describe it, it depends on the structure.

Andy Gordon: But in defence of this approach, this seems a very cool work in synthesising crypto protocols from high-level descriptions. In Paris, they've got this language where the top is very much this structure, it's not about zero-knowledge proofs, not the same thing that we see here, but the input is a description of the message flow you want between multiple parties, and you say nothing about cryptography. So you may want to say that parts of the messages have been kept secret, and you certainly want guarantees that you if think the message came from somebody, did it actually come from them, and all that is implicit in the graph that you build and then you synthesise protocol code from that. And they can prove with their setup that the refinement is correct, that you do get accepted security guarantees. So something like this, but that's done with zero-knowledge, is possible.

Jean Martina: I would like to understand better how the protocol verification toolbox works, because you were saying that a protocol designer should be able to prove something in Isabelle. Isabelle is a nightmare; I can tell you, because I work with it every day.

Reply: No, our goal is to prove this automatically.

Jean Martina: But in Isabelle there is no automation. Composition is something that is not meant to be implemented in Isabelle; you can derive things, but if you give it some very minor variation, the proof needs to be redone completely. Maybe if you go to another prover, something like an automatic one, a first order logic, maybe it's worth it, but with Isabelle, I know it would be wonderful but Isabelle is not supposed to do composition of proofs.

Joe-Kai Tsay: Not even if people generate your initial goals?

Reply: Yes you can teach Isabelle, the proofs which it should use, and then you can teach a different situation like this, use this proof, try these proofs.

Jean Martina: Yes, but reusability of proof strategies is really, really difficult, and involves very deep knowledge on how the simplifier works in Isabelle. I don't know, I am a sceptic on seeing things being done automatically in Isabelle, I have been working with it for two years, and every day there is still no automation. The results are good, and you produced very nice results, and insights of how to do things, but to prove something like a protocol with six lines takes two months, so that's...

Peter Ryan: Are you feeling better getting all this off your chest? Larry has given talks in the past, and I think he claimed that he did the proof in a few days.

Jean Martina: But then Larry is on a different level than other people with Isabelle.

Bruce Christianson: Yes, that's like breaking RSA using a quantum processor.

Michael Roe: There's an economy of scale when you've already done lots of proofs, the marginal cost of doing one more is low.

Simon Foley: Well hopefully that's something you would get here, because hopefully the compiler is going to generate protocols that are similar to the one another, so it is possible to generate different things that work.

Michael Roe: But it's a matter of whether the human being needs to do something. If it's something like type safety, you can get it so the compiler is automatically churning out a proof that these types are being checked, and because of the nature of the thing you're trying to prove, you can do that with no human intervention whatsoever. But otherwise, if the program really isn't typesafe, you've got to fix your program. But I think security protocols might not be like that; you could have a protocol that was actually a correct protocol, but the prover can't find the proof.

Bruce Christianson: It's much harder to spot the invariant.

Michael Roe: So I'm wondering whether you can, even in principle.

Bruce Christianson: Well once again, we're ending on a pessimistic note; thank you very much.

Towards a Verified Reference Implementation of a Trusted Platform Module

Aybek Mukhamedov[1,2], Andrew D. Gordon[1], and Mark Ryan[2]

[1] Microsoft Research
[2] University of Birmingham

Abstract. We develop a reference implementation for a fragment of the API for a Trusted Platform Module. Our code is written in a functional language, suitable for verification with various tools, but is automatically translated to a subset of C, suitable for interoperability testing with production code, and for inclusion in a specification or standard for the API. One version of our code corresponds to the widely deployed TPM 1.2 specification, and is vulnerable to a recently discovered dictionary attack; verification of secrecy properties of this version fails producing an attack trace and highlights an ambiguity in the specification that has security implications. Another version of our code corresponds to a suggested amendment to the TPM 1.2 specification; verification of this version succeeds. From this case study we conclude that recent advances in tools for verifying implementation code for cryptographic APIs are reaching the point where it is viable to develop verified reference implementations. Moreover, the published code can be in a widely understood language like C, rather than one of the specialist formalisms aimed at modelling cryptographic protocols.

1 Introduction

The Trusted Platform Module (TPM) is designed to enable trustworthy computation and communication over open networks by realizing robust platform integrity measurement and reporting, secure platform attestation, secure storage and other security mechanisms. TPM is part of the Trusted Computing Base and interacts with applications via a pre-defined set of commands (an API). To guarantee its reliability it is important that the TPM commands are defined unambiguously and do not give rise to subtle interactions and functionality unforeseen by its designers. Design failures can lead to expensive recalls of computers and costly replacements of the embedded TPMs.

Since the TPM 1.2 specification defines more than 90 commands (and the next version is expected to have even more functionality), it is not feasible to reliably check the API for the absence of such issues by manual inspection alone. Indeed, several security vulnerabilities have already been identified in the literature [1–4]. The API's security analysis needs to be automated with computer-aided verification techniques. Formal methods from the security protocols verification domain appear appropriate.

B. Christianson et al. (Eds.): Security Protocols 2009, LNCS 7028, pp. 69–81, 2013.

The underlying motivation for employing formal security protocols analysis methods is that security APIs such as that of the TPM can be seen as two-party protocols between a user and the security module. The aim of the attacker is to compose a sequence of messages that breaks the expected security property (e.g. divulges a secret data stored in the module). However, analysis of security APIs is different from that of standard protocols, as security modules maintain mutable states across sessions and may exhibit subtle interactions via error messages and conditions.

We have developed a reference implementation for the TPM's authorization and encrypted transport session protocols in the F# programming language [5]. Our implementation is based on data structures and command instructions taken from the specification of the TPM commands [6]. We subsequently performed formal verification of the protocols using the verification toolchain FS2PV [7] and ProVerif [8], for the secrecy of weak authorization data (authdata). The analysis captured the weak authdata attacks on the authorization protocols recently uncovered by Chen and Ryan [4] and highlighted an ambiguity in the specification of the encrypted transport session protocol that has security implications. Our analysis also pointed us towards a simple amendment to the encrypted transport session protocol that allows it to protect authorization protocols against weak authdata attacks. Lastly, we have implemented a translator that converts TPM commands and data structure specification written in an F# fragment into executable C code. We have coded up a sample TPM client in C++ in order to demonstrate executability of the generated C specification.

Our contributions. In summary, the contributions of this work are:

- A reference implementation of the TPM's authorization and encrypted transport session protocols in the F# programming language.
- A formal analysis of the implementation code with the FS2PV/ProVerif toolchain against weak authdata secret attacks, that captures a known attack [4], highlights an ambiguity in the specification document [6], and proves correctness of our proposed amendment.
- A translator F2C that generates executable C code from an implementation written in a functional fragment of F#.

Related work. The research into API security analysis has been instigated by Bond et al. [9, 10], who thoroughly examined interfaces of several security devices, including IBM's 4758 hardware security module (HSM) and uncovered many pernicious attacks. Although fruitful, the analysis was ad hoc and consisted only of manual API inspection. Such an approach clearly can neither guarantee that all attacks are discovered nor prove the absence of them. A similar study by Berkman et al. [11] uncovered PIN derivation attacks on financial PIN processing APIs.

Subsequently, a joint MIT/Cambridge research group attempted to perform a formal analysis of 4758 API with general purpose verification tools: the theorem prover Otter [12] and the model checker Failures-Divergence Refinement (FDR) [13]. They were able to uncover some unknown attacks with Otter (with human guidance) [3], but analysis with FDR did not prove to be so fruitful.

In another approach Steel et al. [14] performed a formal analysis of the revised IBM 4758 HSM with a model checker CL-AtSe from the AVISPA tool set [15]. They found a weakness in a symmetric key importing operation, and proved correctness of other revisions. The authors also proposed a class of protocols that includes the IBM HSM API, in which they showed secrecy to be decidable for an unbounded number of sessions, and developed an ad hoc decision procedure that can perform such analysis. More recently, Steel et al. [16] utilized the NuSMV model checker to perform the first verification of the PKCS#11 API that accounts for mutable states, albeit with a bounded number of nonces and other restrictions.

Contents of this Paper. Section 2 gives an overview of the TPM architecture, its authorisation mechanisms, a recent vulnerability (due to Chen and Ryan [4]) that we use as motivation for this work, and a brief overview of the FS2PV framework we use in our formal analysis. Section 3 explains our reference implementation of a fragment of the TPM API, its formal analysis and C code generation. Our verification tools confirm the Chen/Ryan vulnerability, and verify a potential amendment to the API. Section 4 concludes and sketches some potential future work.

2   Background

2.1   TPM Overview

The Trusted Platform Module (TPM) specification is an international standard coordinated by the Trusted Computing Group (TCG), for realizing the Trusted Platform in commodity hardware [6, 17, 18]. TPMs are chips that aim to enable computers to achieve greater levels of security than is possible in software alone. There are over 100 million TPMs currently in existence, mostly in high-end laptops. Application software such as Microsoft BitLocker and HP ProtectTools use the TPM in order to guarantee security properties.

The Trusted Platform provides three features: protected storage, platform integrity measurement and integrity reporting. Security guarantees that these features provide rely on three components that implement critical operations of the trusted platform. They are called *roots of trust* and they must be trusted to function correctly: Root of Trust for Measurement (RTM), Root of Trust for Reporting (RTR) and Root of Trust for Storage (RTS). In the current implementations, the TPM acts as RTR and RTS.

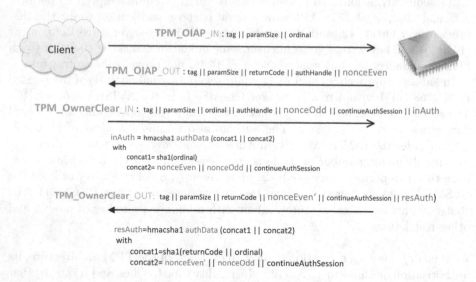

Fig. 1. TPM_OwnerClear executed in a session initiated using Object Independent Authorisation Protocol (OIAP)

Authorization. TPM objects that do not allow "public" access have authorisation data, *authdata* for short, associated with them (such objects include TPM keys, encrypted blobs and owner privileged commands). Authdata is a 20 byte secret that may be thought of as a password required to access such TPM objects. A process requesting access needs to demonstrate that it knows the relevant authdata. This is realized via authorization protocols, where a TPM command is accompanied with an HMAC [19] keyed on the authdata or on a shared secret derived from the authdata. When a new object is created the client chooses its authdata, which ideally should be a high-entropy value.

The TPM provides two kinds of authorisation protocols, called *object independent authorisation protocol* (OIAP) and *object specific authorisation protocol* (OSAP). OIAP allows multiple objects to be used within the same session, but it does not allow commands that introduce new authdata, and it does not allow authdata for an object to be cached for use over several commands. An OSAP session is restricted to a single object, but it does allow new authdata to be introduced and it creates a session secret to securely cache authorisation over several commands. Figures 1 and 2 below demonstrate sample message flows in OIAP and OSAP executions with TPM_OwnerClear command, which resets the TPM to un-initialized and un-owned state and clears its internal secret values (ownerAuth, tpmProof, SRK, etc.).

2.2 Weak Secrecy

Weak secrets are secret values that have low entropy, such as those derived from memorable passwords and short PIN numbers. The domain that such secrets

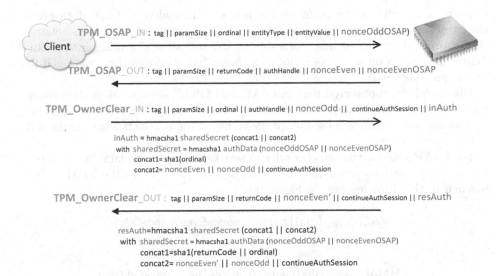

Fig. 2. TPM_OwnerClear executed in a session initiated using Object Specific Authorisation Protocol (OSAP)

are chosen from can be efficiently enumerated by the attacker and therefore protocols that make use of weak secrets need to ensure they are obfuscated with high entropy values when sent in messages on the open network.

Guessing attacks on weak secrets can be either on-line or off-line. In the former case, the attacker is able to interact with other agents to verify all their guesses. On-line guessing attacks can be mitigated, for example, by limiting the number of successive failures allowed in protocol execution. Such mechanism, in particular, needs to be employed by the TPM as stated in the specification documents (the details are manufacturer specific). In off-line guessing attacks, the attacker tries to verify their guesses with the help of intercepted messages sent between protocol participants.

In this paper we are concerned with weak secrecy analysis against off-line attacks. Such secrecy has been defined by Blanchet, Abadi and Fournet in [8], which informally can be stated as follows.

Definition 1 (Weak secrecy). *A protocol prevents off-line guessing attacks against the weak secret w, if after the execution of the protocol the attacker cannot distinguish w used in the protocol from an unrelated fresh value.*

Off-Line Weak Authdata Attack. A vulnerability was uncovered by Chen and Ryan [4], which allows the attacker to recover low-entropy authdata secrets by off-line dictionary attack on messages exchanged between a legitimate user and the TPM. The attacker can access the messages either by tapping the TPM's databus, compromising the software stack that manages communication of the user with the TPM, or in case of a remote user, by listening in on the unprotected traffic at any point on the network. Knowledge of authdata gives the attacker unrestricted access to the TPM object with which it is associated (for example, knowing authdata of a signing key will allow the attacker to create digital signatures on messages of its own choice based on that key, via a call to TPM_Sign command).

Chen and Ryan observed that in OIAP and OSAP sessions all high entropy message components (nonces) are sent out in the clear, and therefore, do not obfuscate the weak authdata used as an HMAC key value in constructing command authorization digests.

For OIAP sessions the attacker tries to test their guess authdata' by attempting to reconstruct the authorization digest sent by the user to the TPM (value inAuth in the third message in Figure 1):

$$\mathsf{HMAC_{authdata'}}(\mathsf{sha1}(param), \mathsf{nonceEven}, \mathsf{nonceOdd})$$

$$? =$$

$$\mathsf{HMAC_{authdata}}(\mathsf{sha1}(param), \mathsf{nonceEven}, \mathsf{nonceOdd})$$

where param is a concatenation of command parameters, and both nonceEven and nonceOdd are rolling session nonces. All of those message components are available to the attacker as they are sent in clear over the network.

Similarly for OSAP sessions, the attacker tries to test their guesses by reconstructing authorization digest sent by the user to the TPM (value inAuth in Figure 2).

2.3   Encrypted Transport Protocol

TPM supports encrypted transport protocol to allow logging and encryption of commands using a transport session. We studied the protocol to ascertain whether this readily available TPM facility can protect authorization sessions against the weak authdata attacks mentioned above.

Transport sessions can intuitively be thought of as a wrapper for other commands. They proceed by establishing a shared secret that is subsequently used to authorize and encrypt relevant commands sent and received by the TPM. The user of the transport session can execute any command within a transport sessions, except for a command that creates another transport session.

Transport sessions are initiated with the TPM_EstablishTransport command, which exchanges transport session nonces and a secret generated by the user. The secret is used later as an HMAC key to generate authorization digests and as a part of the symmetric encryption key for wrapped commands. TPM_ExecuteTransport delivers a wrapped command to the TPM and its output returns the result of the execution back to the user.

Transport sessions do not encrypt all components of the wrapped commands and some commands stipulate further exceptions as to the encryption of their parameters [6]. A schematic presentation of a transport session is given in Figure 3. DATAw in the figure denotes encryption of the components of the wrapped command with transEncKey, and Enc{secret,pk(K_{TS})} stands for asymmetric encryption of the transport session secret by the public key whose corresponding private key is K_{TS}.

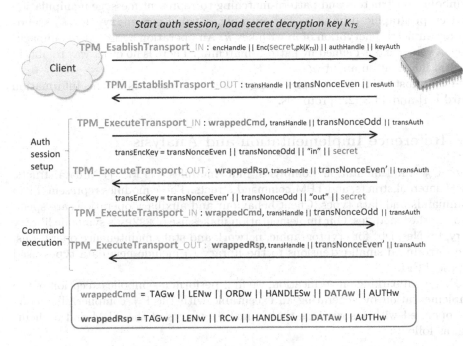

Fig. 3. Encrypted transport session execution

2.4 FS2PV **Verification Framework**

We utilize the FS2PV toolkit developed by Bhargavan et al. [7] for the verification of our F# implementation. FS2PV accepts programs written in a first-order subset of F# and outputs a model that can be analyzed with the automated theorem prover ProVerif [8].

The toolkit provides cryptographic, communication and other auxiliary libraries that programs need to use for cryptography, network communication, message composition and other operations. Each operation provided by the framework has dual *concrete* and *symbolic* implementations. Concrete libraries are used for compilation of an executable of the protocol, whereas the symbolic counterparts are employed in the ProVerif model extraction. In this work, we only utilize FS2PV's symbolic library and generate executable code with our F2C translator.

FS2PV's symbolic implementation of cryptographic and network operations encodes strong black-box assumptions on cryptography, which are assumed to be safe abstractions (in the style of Dolev and Yao [20]). To model cryptographically constructed byte arrays there is an algebraic datatype bytes equipped with symbolic constructors and pattern-matching to represent message manipulation and cryptographic primitives. For example, a value sym_encrypt(m, k) stands for a symmetric encryption of m with key k. An operation sym_decrypt unpacks such a value, and is defined by pattern-matching. There is no other way to obtain partial information about m.

Two substantial case studies using FS2PV are analyses of the Information Card [21] and TLS [22] protocols.

3   Reference Implementation and Analysis

Our F# implementation comprises four modules: TPM, TPM_data_structs, TPM_internal_structs, and TPM_command_structs. These modules represent TPM commands and data types. Client behaviour and auxiliary operations are specified in other modules. Our implementation makes use of FS2PV's symbolic library (Crypto, Net, Db) for cryptographic, network and state maintenance operations. We introduced small extensions to the library to include new data types used by the TPM.

Before embarking on verification, we first perform a symbolic execution of the implementation by generating an executable with the F# compiler. The code is appended with instructions that launch instances of the TPM and a client, e.g. as follows:

```
do Pi.fork(fun() -> Client())
do TPM()
```

Symbolic execution pretty-prints messages exchanged between the parties in the console. We found this facility of FS2PV invaluable in debugging the implementation code, as well as making sure that the formal verification is not carried out on vacuous models (that is, models that are trivially secure because no messages are accepted).

3.1   Formal Analysis

We use the FS2PV/ProVerif toolchain to verify our reference implementation for authorization protocols OIAP and OSAP, and for the encrypted transport session protocol.

In our threat model, we assume there is an active attacker on the network between the client and the TPM that can intercept, manipulate and inject new messages constrained by the perfect cryptography assumption [20]. FS2PV framework formalizes the attacker as an arbitrary program that is able to call interfaces defined by our implementation code and the symbolic libraries.

The TPM and a client maintain state during authorization and transport sessions protocols, which stores latest session nonces, shared secrets, handles and other information. In our implementation of authorization sessions we have used databases from FS2PV's Db module to store the state data, which FS2PV translates into message passing over private channels.

The underlying verification engine ProVerif, however, encountered difficulties verifying and reconstructing attack traces for larger models that make use of private channels, so we had to tweak our handling of state information and the client code. In the encrypted transport session protocols, instead of using Db, we have extended the datatype bytes with private data constructors TSD and CSD to store the session state. In this approximation, the state data is wrapped with these constructors that the attacker cannot deconstruct and the state is output into and read in from the open network. This allowed ProVerif to reconstruct non-trivial attack traces. The verification of the corrected version of the encrypted transport session protocols, however, still did not succeed causing ProVerif to run out of memory (2GB) due to the amount of state information. We further approximated our model by allowing the attacker to access the client's state information, removing some of the client's integrity checks, and allowing transport session nonce generation function used by the TPM to produce free names instead of fresh ones (this is akin to having a faulty random number generator that produces known values). This allowed us to prove correctness of the fixed version of the encrypted transport session protocol, which implies correctness of the fix without such approximations.

We have expressed secrecy of weak authdata in the following form, so that the name used for authdata in the query file and the source code is propagated into ProVerif script generated by FS2PV:

```
(*** Declaration in an implementation file ***)
let ownerAuthData = Pi.name "broccoli"
let fOwnerAuthData = Fresh ownerAuthData

(*** Query file ***)
weaksecret ownerAuthData.

(*** Resulting declaration in the ProVerif script generated by fs2pv ***)
private free ownerAuthData.
...
weaksecret ownerAuthData.
```

Authorization Sessions. Our verification of authorization protocols (OSAP and OIAP) found Chen and Ryan's attacks on the secrecy of weak authdata and produced attack traces.

Encrypted Transport Sessions. We have written a concrete F# implementation of the transport session protocol with the aim of formally verifying whether it can protect authorization sessions OIAP and OSAP against weak authdata attacks. The analysis highlighted an ambiguity in TPM_ExecuteTransport command's specification that had security implications in our analysis.

The specification of TPM_ExecuteTransport command states that for authorization session initiation commands TPM_OSAP, TPM_OIAP no parameters are encrypted in the request sent from the client, but it does not specify any caveats for the output sent back to the client. Therefore, following the specification of the command, the responses of TPM_OSAP and TPM_OIAP are sent back in encrypted form. Our analysis showed that in this case weak authdata leak is prevented for OSAP sessions, but not for OIAP sessions. Intuitively, OIAP sessions are not protected, since each command executed within OIAP produces an HMAC digest keyed on authdata, and all other data included in the digest are sent out in clear.

The specification of TPM_OIAP and TPM_OSAP commands, however, stipulates that no input or output parameters are encrypted when wrapped in a transport session. In this case, clearly wrapping OSAP sessions with encrypted transport protocol does not stop weak authdata leaks.

Our verification highlighted the following simple amendments to the encrypted transport protocol that will protect the weak authdata:

- for the wrapped OSAP session, encrypt nonceEvenOSAP sent to the client in the response of TPM_OSAP command;
- for the wrapped OIAP session, encrypt the rolling nonceEven in each response of a command executed in the session.

These amendments correspond to including nonces in the DATAw component in Figure 3, instead of sending them out in clear as part of **AUTHw**. The verification proved correctness of these fixes.

Our analysis also revealed a potential weakness in the encrypted transport protocol when a key of type TPM_KEY_LEGACY is used as an encryption key for the transport session's secret. If such key is not used with RSA OAEP encryption scheme and has a weak authdata associated with it, then an attacker can acquire the transport session secret by invoking the TPM_UnBind command, which decrypts the secret without checking decrypted message structure. To avoid this weakness, a client needs to ensure that a high-entropy authdata is chosen for the transport secret encryption key, or choose a key that is either a storage key (TPM_KEY_STORAGE) or is used with RSA OAEP encryption. The TPM commands specification states that use of the key type TPM_KEY_LEGACY in general is not recommended, and our finding corroborates the recommendation.

3.2   F2C: Translation into an Executable C Specification

We have implemented a tool that generates executable C code from the TPM implementation written in an F# fragment. It is developed on top of FS2PV's library that builds the AST of the F# input code. We apply the translator to TPM, TPM_data_structs, TPM_internal_structs, TPM_command_structs modules to generate executable C code for commands and data structures of the TPM.

Figure 5 below shows a sample C code generated from the corresponding F# code in Figure 4.

```
let TPM_OSAP (input:TPM_OSAP_IN) : TPM_OSAP_OUT =
    if (input.tag_osapIn = TPM_TAG_RQU_COMMAND) then
        if (input.ordinal_osapIn = TPM_ORD_OSAP) then begin
            let nonceEven : TPM_NONCE = mkNonce() in
            let nonceEvenOSAP : TPM_NONCE = mkNonce() in
            let xNonceOddOSAP : TPM_NONCE = input.nonceOddOSAP_osapIn in
            let hmac_data : BYTES = dconcatSK xNonceOddOSAP in
            let handle : TPM_AUTHHANDLE = allocHandle() in
            let entityType : TPM_ENTITY_TYPE = input.entityType_osapIn in
            if (entityType=TPM_ET_OWNER) then begin
                let pd : TPM_PERMANENT_DATA = loadPermData() in
                let authData : TPM_SECRET = pd.ownerAuth in
                let tsharedSecret : TPM_HMAC =
                    tpm_hmacsha1((key authData.digest),hmac_data,sizeof(hmac_data)) in
                let s1:TPM_SESSION_DATA = {
                    sHandle=handle;
                    pid=TPM_PID_OSAP;
                    nonceEven=nonceEven;
                    sharedSecret=tsharedSecret;
                    entityValue = input.entityValue_osapIn
                } in saveState s1;
                let res : TPM_OSAP_OUT = {
                    tag_osapOut = TPM_TAG_RSP_COMMAND;
                    paramSize_osapOut = UINT32 0;
                    returnCode_osapOut = TPM_SUCCESS;
                    authHandle_osapOut = handle;
                    nonceEven_osapOut = nonceEven;
                    nonceEvenOSAP_osapOut = nonceEvenOSAP } in
                setSize(res,res.paramSize_osapOut); res
            end else failwith (string TPM_FAIL);
        end else failwith (string TPM_BAD_ORDINAL)
    else failwith (string TPM_FAIL)
```

Fig. 4. Sample TPM command code (fTPM.fs)

```
TPM_OSAP_OUT TPM_OSAP (TPM_OSAP_IN input) {
    if (input.tag_osapIn == TPM_TAG_RQU_COMMAND) {
        if (input.ordinal_osapIn == TPM_ORD_OSAP) {
            TPM_NONCE nonceEven = mkNonce();
            TPM_NONCE nonceEvenOSAP = mkNonce();
            TPM_NONCE xNonceOddOSAP = input.nonceOddOSAP_osapIn;
            struct {TPM_NONCE nonceEvenOSAP_sf; TPM_NONCE xNonceOddOSAP_sf;}
                hmac_data_st={nonceEvenOSAP, xNonceOddOSAP};
            BYTES hmac_data = (BYTE*)& hmac_data_st;
            TPM_AUTHHANDLE handle = allocHandle();
            TPM_ENTITY_TYPE entityType = input.entityType_osapIn;
            if (entityType == TPM_ET_OWNER) {
                TPM_PERMANENT_DATA pd = loadPermData();
                TPM_SECRET authData = pd.ownerAuth;
                TPM_HMAC tsharedSecret =
                    tpm_hmacsha1(authData.digest,hmac_data,sizeof(hmac_data_st));
                TPM_SESSION_DATA s1 = {0,nonceEven,TPM_PID_OSAP,handle,tsharedSecret};
                saveState(s1);
                TPM_OSAP_OUT res =
                    {handle,nonceEvenOSAP,nonceEven,0,TPM_SUCCESS,TPM_TAG_RSP_COMMAND};
                res.paramSize_osapOut=sizeof(res);
                return res;
            } else {mkErrorReturn_TPM_OSAP(TPM_FAIL);}
        } else {mkErrorReturn_TPM_OSAP(TPM_BAD_ORDINAL);}
    } else {mkErrorReturn_TPM_OSAP(TPM_FAIL);}
}
```

Fig. 5. Generated sample C code

Table 1. Summary of the verification results

	LoC F#	C	Verification of the secrecy of weak authdata
OIAP session	250	260	attack found
OSAP session	265	275	attack found
OIAP wrapped in an encrypted transport session	780	660	attack found
OSAP wrapped in an encrypted transport session	800	680	attack found if TPM_OSAP command response is not encrypted
OIAP, OSAP wrapped in the amended encrypted transport session	800	680	correctness proved

4   Conclusion and Future Work

We have implemented concrete F# specifications for OIAP, OSAP and encrypted transport session protocols and were able to perform their formal verification using FS2PV, as well as to generate corresponding C specification with F2C. For authorization protocols, we have implemented a TPM client in C++ to demonstrate executability of the generated C specification. In our formal analysis, we have captured the weak authdata attacks on the authorization sessions and verified that our enhancements to the encrypted transport sessions thwart such attacks.

It would be desirable to demonstrate interoperability between our reference implementation and existing software for communicating with a TPM; this has not yet been attempted. Another future direction is to develop our tools to the point where they could be used to define a reference implementation for the whole TPM or some other cryptographic token. Our results so far suggest this goal is probably within reach with the current generation of verification tools.

Acknowledgements. The research described in this paper was performed during Aybek Mukhamedov's internship at Microsoft Research. We thank Karthik Bhargavan, Johannes Borgström, and Cédric Fournet for useful discussions about this work. We also thank Paul England and David Wooten, Microsoft representatives on the Trusted Computing Group, for their support and advice.

References

1. Bruschi, D., Cavallaro, L., Lanzi, A., Monga, M.: Replay attack in TCG specification and solution. In: ACSAC 2005: Proceedings of the 21st Annual Computer Security Applications Conference, pp. 127–137. IEEE Computer Society, Washington, DC (2005)
2. Gürgens, S., Rudolph, C., Scheuermann, D., Atts, M., Plaga, R.: Security Evaluation of Scenarios Based on the TCG's TPM Specification. In: Biskup, J., López, J. (eds.) ESORICS 2007. LNCS, vol. 4734, pp. 438–453. Springer, Heidelberg (2007)
3. Lin, A.H.: Automated Analysis of Security APIs. Master's thesis. MIT (2005), http://sdg.csail.mit.edu/pubs/theses/amerson-masters.pdf

4. Chen, L., Ryan, M.D.: Offline dictionary attack on TCG TPM weak authorisation data, and solution. In: Grawrock, D., Reimer, H., Sadeghi, A., Vishik, C. (eds.) Future of Trust in Computing. Vieweg & Teubner (2008)
5. Syme, D., Granicz, A., Cisternino, A.: Expert F#. Apress (2007)
6. Trusted Computing Group: TPM Specification version 1.2. Parts 1-3 (2007), www.trustedcomputinggroup.org/specs/TPM/
7. Bhargavan, K., Fournet, C., Gordon, A.D., Tse, S.: Verified interoperable implementations of security protocols. In: IEEE Computer Security Foundations Workshop, CSFW 2006, pp. 139–152 (2006)
8. Blanchet, B., Abadi, M., Fournet, C.: Automated verification of selected equivalences for security protocols. Journal of Logic and Algebraic Programming 75(1), 3–51 (2008)
9. Bond, M., Anderson, R.: API-level attacks on embedded systems. Computer 34(10), 67–75 (2001)
10. Bond, M.: Understanding Security APIs. PhD thesis. University of Cambridge (2005)
11. Berkman, O., Ostrovsky, O.M.: The Unbearable Lightness of PIN Cracking. In: Dietrich, S., Dhamija, R. (eds.) FC 2007 and USEC 2007. LNCS, vol. 4886, pp. 224–238. Springer, Heidelberg (2007)
12. McCune, W.: OTTER 3.3 Reference Manual. Aragonne National Laboratory (2003)
13. Goldsmith, M.: FDR2 User's Manual version 2.82. Formal Systems (Europe) Ltd. (2005)
14. Cortier, V., Keighren, G., Steel, G.: Automatic Analysis of the Security of XOR-Based Key Management Schemes. In: Grumberg, O., Huth, M. (eds.) TACAS 2007. LNCS, vol. 4424, pp. 538–552. Springer, Heidelberg (2007)
15. AVISPA Tool Set, http://www.avispa-project.org/
16. Delaune, S., Kremer, S., Steel, G.: Formal analysis of PKCS#11. In: CSF, pp. 331–344. IEEE Computer Society (2008)
17. ISO/IEC PAS DIS 11889: Information technology – Security techniques – Trusted platform module
18. Anderson, R.: Trusted Computing FAQ (2003), http://www.cl.cam.ac.uk/rja14/tcpa-faq.html
19. ISO/IEC 9797-2: Information technology – Security techniques – Message authentication codes (MACs) – Part 2: Mechanisms using a dedicated hash-function
20. Dolev, D., Yao, A.: On the security of public key protocols. IEEE Transactions on Information Theory IT-29(2), 198–208 (1983)
21. Bhargavan, K., Fournet, C., Gordon, A.D., Swamy, N.: Verified implementations of the Information Card federated identity-management protocol. In: ASIACCS 2008 (2008)
22. Bhargavan, K., Fournet, C., Corin, R., Zalinescu, E.: Cryptographically verified implementations for TLS. In: CCS 2008 (2008)

Towards a Verified Reference Implementation of a Trusted Platform Module
(Transcript of Discussion)

Aybek Mukhamedov

University of Birmingham

This work was done jointly with Andrew Gordon and Mark Ryan. A TPM is a trusted platform module. The trusted platform is supposed to provide two main functions: integrity measurement, report and storage. And the trusted platform relies on a security chip called a TPM to realise two of those functions, trusted storage and reporting. The TPM defines more than 90 commands with its API. Manual inspection of them is not feasible, and clearly product recalls are expensive because TPM is bound to the computer. So there's a need for formal analysis of the API, and protocol verification tools seem to be suitable for the task.

There are a number of successful frameworks for protocol verification, for example, specialised ones like ProVerif, or general purpose tools like FDR. There has been an effort to do an API analysis previously, but a common feature of the previous work was that it did the analysis of the abstract model, and there was no clear connection between the verified model and the implementation.

FS2PV is one of the frameworks that does analysis of the implementation written in F# code, it's developed at MSR Cambridge by Andy Gordon and his team, and we used the tool to do the analysis of the TPMs.

FS2PV is part of a larger cryptographic verification kit, which includes a few more tools like FS2CV, that does computational crypto proofs based on CryptoVerif. That work was done jointly by MSR Cambridge and MSR INRIA. There have been several big case studies done by those teams that focused on TLS protocol and on web services. In our work we used the FS2PV tool. It takes F# code and then writes a ProVerif model, which can be analysed to prove security properties or find counterexamples. In our analysis we focused on the authorisation protocols, and that's an important part of the TPM, as many commands depend on that, and because there was recently a weakness pointed out by Chen and Ryan, which showed that the weak secrets can lead to weak secret offline attacks.

Sören Preibusch: I have no idea what the weak secret offline attack means.

Reply: Oh right, so you have a secret, and if it happens to be low entropy data, then an attacker observing the messages exchanged between the user and the TPM can deduce that secret by brute force attack, that's the weak offline attack.

We need a complete implementation of the authorisation protocol in F# together with the encrypted trusted sessions that the TPM supports to see if that facility can prevent the weak authdata attacks. And well, we did the analysis with FS2PV and we found that the transport sessions don't protect the weak

B. Christianson et al. (Eds.): Security Protocols 2009, LNCS 7028, pp. 82–86, 2013.
© Springer-Verlag Berlin Heidelberg 2013

authdata links, and we proposed fixes and proved their correctness. And lastly we developed this small tool as an add-on to the FS2PV, that does automatic translation of F# into executable C.

So, authorisation data. Most of our TPM commands and objects require authorisation, and that's realised by a shared secret called authdata. That's just a 25 bit string, and is chosen by a client. Ideally it's a secret plus some high entropy data.

So there have been some analyses. The analysis by Chen and Ryan found this offline attack on the low entropy data, authdata, and we wanted to see if our tool can capture those type of leaks.

There are two types of authorisation protocol the TPM supports. One is object independent authorisation protocol, which is one that can authorise several entities within a session, and the authorisation is done by the HMAC digest, which is keyed on the authdata. There is also object specific authorisation protocol, which is tied to a particular entity like a single key, and there authorisation is done by HMAC digest keyed on a secret derived from authdata, but that also acts as a session key to encrypt the secret passed onto the TPM when, for example, creating a new key or sharing new data. Most commands allow either protocol, but those that introduce new authdata have to use object specific authorisation. That's the representation of the OAIP protocol, the object independent protocol, and there you see, you basically have four messages, those two just exchange the parameters, in the second one TPM generates a nonce, and these two correspond to the actual execution of the command.

The observation of Chen and Ryan was that all the high entropy components of this digest are sent out in the clear. These are the red ones here, the nonces, so therefore the attacker who can observe those messages can by brute force find out what the authdata is.

The second protocol, the OSAP is slightly different in that the HMAC digest is keyed on the shared secret, and the shared secret is derived from authdata together with the nonces shared between the TPM and the user. But in this case also they saw that all the nonces' high entropy components are sent out in the clear, therefore it doesn't help that the authorisation digest is keyed on a temporary secret. And in this case also the attacker could derive the authdata.

So these are the two protocols, and we also wanted to look at the encrypted transport sessions that the TPM supports to see if one could use that to prevent these type of leaks.

The encrypted transport protection just acts as a facility to wrap the other commands that the TPM supports within a session, and this wrapped CMB corresponds to the command you want to execute within the transport session. Part of this wrapped CMB is encrypted, which is in red, and the idea is that that should provide more confidentiality, and we wanted to check whether using the transport sessions would prevent the weak data, if you executed commands within this protocol.

So we wrote down the complete specification in F# for both protocols; that's just a snippet of the code. We define symbolic libraries for cryptography, for data, for network operations, and the database library. In this framework we have the device defined as a type that consists of components, and the operations that are performed on those components are modelled, for example, by pattern matching, that represents the black box abstraction of the cryptography, so you can decrypt only if you have the right key, and you can't reverse or derive any information from the hash. FS2PV has to generates a ProVerif model, which is verified against any number of TPM client runs and the transactions.

So in our verification results we found the reported witnesses, and also found out that the transport sessions do not really protect against that leak. And we also proposed some simple amendments to the transport protection protocol, and proved that if you do that, then that will protect against this type of attack. We also implemented this tool that does the translation of F# code into C, because F# is not widely adopted yet, and relies on Dot Net. The tool translates the verified code of the TPM into executable C implementation, so we take the TPM commands and this data structure defined in F#, and generate C code. It's built on top of the FS2PV library. We also wrote down a sample of clients for the TPM and crypto functions library in C++ that rely on the Microsoft API, just to demonstrate that the generated code is executed and works with the client. So that's the snapshot of the run of the generated C code, so you can see an interaction of the client with the TPM, so the four messages are exchanged, and the message from the client to TPM, from TPM to client.

So, conclusions. This was very interesting work. We verified a complete implementation of the TPM API fragment. We captured a number of known attacks, found some problems with the transport encryption, and we got some little fixes and showed that the fixes were correct. And we also did this tool that generates C code. But the future work is that there's many more commands to cover, and we haven't tested the interoperability of the generated C code. We also need to account for mutable state in our analysis. At the moment it's approximated, but this was enough to do the analysis for this authdata. And we eventually want to do verification directly of the C code, and do translations into F#, and use one of the tools from the cryptographic architecture.

So the overall message of this work was that a verified reference implementation of the whole API seems to be within reach.

Michael Roe: When you say the authdata is chosen by a client of the TPM, do you mean a program or the human beings using it?

Reply: Oh, just any user of the TPM. It could be a human, and a password and dialup box. If it's a program then there's hope that there would be a better password chosen.

Frank Stajano: But who's supposed to have the high entropy data?

Reply: The authdata is chosen by the user of the TPM.

Michael Roe: A question about your threat model. You're treating this like it's a networking equivalent attack or eavesdropping, but it's not a traditional setting at all. This is performed on the motherboard of your computer, the

PC. It's transactions within the same machine. If the attacker can put a logic analyser on the bus, then he can possibly use the analyser to get at the state of the program that's sending these messages. So it's not clear that crypto helps you in the same way that it would you would if this was over a network. And I was wondering if you could justify your assumptions some more here.

Reply: Yes, in our threat model we assume an active attack.

Chris Mitchell: You said there were many more commands to cover. I think that's an understatement if anything. And these commands do a whole raft of different things, and there's all kinds of different functionality, so from my rather naïve perspective, the idea that you could ever prove that everything is OK is beyond the realms of possibility. But obviously it ought to be possible to prove certain specific things. What kinds of things would be near the top of your list of priorities to try and prove? I mean, would it be to do with the secrecy of keys?

Reply: Yes, the next thing we want to look at is key management, key migration and secrecy of the generated keys, and the attacks for example that Ron Rivest's student recently identified.

Andy Gordon: Also the instruction set is not totally arbitrary. Much of it is defined by tables, with different modes of authorisation, and so on. For each instructions there is a little bit of instruction specific logic. We spoke about this to the guys at Redmond, and they already had spreadsheets that describe a lot of the functionality of the TPM. One thing we're considering is taking that spreadsheet and generating the F# input from it. So although what we've done in this paper is only a few instructions, and there are, I don't know, maybe an order of magnitude more instructions in the whole thing, it doesn't seem such a leap.

Chris Mitchell: It's not so much you couldn't capture it, but what do you want to prove when you have captured it? That seems like a difficult question to answer.

Michael Roe: Your concern would be that out of the hundreds of those transactions there's one that breaks some obvious property you want, like with the IBM 4758. You could write down two or three top properties and then look at hundreds of transactions and make sure there's no complicated chain of transactions that breaks them.

Andy Gordon: Also we think it's more likely there will be bugs in the cryptographic operations than in the translation to C. So we want to focus attention on verifying the F# model, whereas going from F# to C is a relatively standard bit of work, so it's less likely there will be bugs there.

Matteo Maffei: Did you have any problems with the tools? Did you have problems with termination, for example?

Reply: The problem with ProVerif is that verification doesn't always terminate, so you need to understand how the verification works.

Michael Roe: What are your assumptions about what the attacker can do in this setting? Because I'm really puzzled under what situation you would have an attacker that can monitor what's going across the bus of a TPM within the same machine but can't see other memory accesses.

Andy Gordon: Yes, there's some controversy about that. They're thinking about some sort of virus, or something. So you don't have attestations but you're still talking to the TPM, so you could have some kind of virus in the CPU that can see this traffic, but that perhaps doesn't have complete control the of machine, so it can't see all the memory in other processes. Like I said, I don't want to push that too hard. I mean, Chen and Ryan came up with this attack and this really spooked the TPM committee because this is an unexpected situation. As far as they were concerned they'd got the design of the instruction set correct, and so they wanted to have some kind of work like that we're doing on verifying it. I'm not sure how they see that attack. We looked into this and in fact there's very few applications that actually use the TPM. Bitlocker is one, but Bitlocker doesn't seem to be vulnerable to this particular attack. So yes, at the moment I would say that we don't have any specific instances where this attack could be used on actual deployed systems, so I don't want to press that too highly. But it's a kind of unexpected artefact that alarmed the designers, so they want to have confidence that this sort of thing doesn't come up. I mean, this kind of attack maybe isn't exploitable at present, and it's controversial, but others might be so we want to make sure that there aren't others.

Michael Roe: If I was talking about Bitlocker I would have a completely different model for what the attacker is. You could say, OK my system initially has integrity, it's running the right software, then it forgets the key: I power off my laptop, I leave it in a taxi, at that point some attacker gets hold of it, but doesn't know the user data. Given I own the laptop I'm the only person who knows that. But then the attacker can boot up into Linux and send whatever transactions they like to the TPM, and what you want to prove is they can't decrypt the hard disk. But that's a very different property from the one you're proving. Because, for example, the attacker in that case doesn't have a log of the messages that were sent to the TPM beforehand.

Andy Gordon: Previously?

Michael Roe: Before the point where your laptop was left on the bus or whatever.

Andy Gordon: Right.

Michael Roe: The other threat model where it might make sense is where you've got isolated execution, so the idea is on your machine you're running a thoroughly malicious hypervisor that has been written by some guy who is deliberately trying to break these guarantees, you also have running in some hardware protected mode on that same CPU an applet talking to the TPM, and the hypervisor is acting as the man-in-the-middle.

Bruce Christianson: The other case is where you want to have two different TPMs belonging to two different domains on the same hardware.

The Least Privacy-Damaging Centralised Traffic Data Retention Architecture

(Extended Abstract)

George Danezis

Microsoft Research Cambridge,
Roger Needham Building,
7 J J Thomson Avenue,
Cambridge, CB3 0FB, U.K.
gdane@microsoft.com

Abstract. We present a protocol that can be used by service providers to store traffic records centrally, while only making them readable to law enforcement after a proper authorisation has been issued and logged. Despite the system's best efforts to prevent mass profiling and surveillance, we discuss how it is inherently fragile.

1 Introduction

On 15 March 2006 the European Union adopted Directive 2006/24/EC requiring member states to ensure traffic data is retained and made available to law enforcement for periods ranging from 6 months to 2 years after they were generated[1]. The classes of traffic data to be retained are rather specific, and include means to identify the communicating parties, the duration and time of a communication, the devices used and their location. The directive was fiercely opposed by privacy advocates and a couple of countries are challenging it at the European Court of Justice.

Unsurprisingly [1,2], the UK government is considering the option of implementing a centralised repository of traffic data, to hold the records currently stored and managed at telecommunications and internet service providers. The cost of this project is rumoured to be tens of billions of pounds[2], and is justified on the basis of faster response times to law enforcement requests, reduced costs for service providers, and more efficient operations overall.

Traffic data retention itself, and the centralisation of traffic data are already creating systemic and large scale risks when it comes to the privacy of communication. To add to this problem, a naive implementation of a centralised scheme, where data would simply be stored on a data centre with a simple reference

---

[1] "Telecommunications Data Retention", Wikipedia,
http://en.wikipedia.org/wiki/Telecommunications_data_retention
[2] "UK.gov to spend hundreds of millions on snooping silo", The Register,
http://www.theregister.co.uk/2008/08/19/ukgov_uber_database/

B. Christianson et al. (Eds.): Security Protocols 2009, LNCS 7028, pp. 87–92, 2013.

monitor authorising and servicing requests, would enable wide spread abuse of the stored data.

The aim of this work is to propose an architecture that would minimise the potential for large scale abuse and data-mining operations of a centralised traffic data store. It also enables some auditing of the uses made of the database, without increasing, for technical reasons, the delays necessary to serve requests for data. Even our approach has drawback, and it does not totally neutralise the risks inherent in blanket centralised retention of traffic data.

The design philosophy behind our architecture is that *technical bottlenecks* that slow down the servicing of law enforcement requests, are removed by maintaining a central store of traffic data. This cuts down on the storage, retrieval and transfer costs of the service providers, and ensure the records are present when needed by law enforcement. On the other hand the procedure requiring the *collaboration of service providers* for the data to become legible are maintained in place, and augmented to ensure that a proper audit trail of accesses can be reconstructed. This approach somehow "balances" the need for high integrity and availability of the data for LE, reduced costs for service providers, and some privacy guarantees against blanket surveillance and data mining for users.

As we discuss, even the proposed scheme is easier to abuse than a decentralised data retention regime, or even better a data preservation regime. Another drawback, is its higher cost over a solution that does not protect privacy using cryptography, but only though procedural control, that are trivial for insiders to bypass. The fraction of the budget devoted to increasing surveillance versus ensuring privacy will be a lasting testament to the relative importance policy makers attach to these two features of the system.

2 A Secure Remote Record Storage Scheme

The architecture proposed for the safe centralised storage of traffic data is based on the literature on secure logging [3] as well as secure remote storage [4,5]. The principle behind our design is that a central store of encrypted data is maintained centrally, yet the keys to identify or decode particular records are derivable only by the service provider. Furthermore the key derivation requires the LE to disclose some information about the target and the scope of the data being accessed, that can be logged.

The storage and retrieval protocol works in 3 stages:

1. **Storage.** The service provider creates a record, derives a key, and sends the encrypted record as well as an index to the central repository of traffic data.
2. **Request.** The law enforcement authority makes a request to the service provider, to get access to records with a particular target identifier, time window and type.
3. **Response.** After logging the request the service provider derives the keys necessary to locate and decode the records and sends them to the law enforcement authority.

We first describe the key hierarchy used to encrypt and identify each record, and then the protocols necessary to reveal parts of it to law enforcement.

2.1   A Key Hierarchy for Traffic Data Records

We assume that each service provider has an identity and generates a set of traffic data records $R = \{R_0, \ldots, R_i, \ldots\}$. We are not overly concerned with the structure of each record R_i but we assume there are some deterministic procedures to extract information from each of them:

- provider(R_i), extract the identity of the provider that generated the record.
- type(R_i), extracts a set of types for the record.
- subject(R_i), extracts a set of network identifiers that the record relates to, annotated by their protocols.
- time(R_i), extracts a set of time periods related to the record. It is up to the system designers to decide the granularity of the time period, but in this work we assume to have a resolution of about a day.

Each provider has a sequence of symmetric master secret keys associated with the tuple of provider ID and time, that we denote $\mathcal{K}_{P \times t}$, where $\mathcal{P}$ is the provider and t is the time window. Given a record R_i we extract the four-tuples consisting of the Cartesian product of its provider, types, subjects and times, that we denote as:

$$L \equiv (P_j, T_j, S_j, t_j) \equiv \{\text{provider}(R_i)\} \times \text{type}(R_i) \times \text{subject}(R_i) \times \text{time}(R_i). \quad (1)$$

We assume that the function $H(\cdot)$ acts as a perfect hash function and random oracle. Given the set L of four-tupes for a record K_i we derive $|L|$ separate keys for each combination of attributes. Symmetric key $K_j = H(K_{P_j, t_j}, P_j, T_j, S_j, t_j)$ corresponds to the four-tuple (P_j, T_j, S_j, t_j). Furthermore multiple symmetric keys can be associated with each unique combination of attributes, by using a counter and deriving a further key $K_{jk} = H(K_j, k)$, where $k = 0, 1, 2, \ldots$

   We denote as keys(R_i) a function that given a record R_i extracts all its relevant attributes (P_j, T_j, S_j, t_j), and returns all corresponding keys K_{jk}.

2.2   Cryptographic Packaging of Records

Each record is encrypted and tagged individually as soon as it is created. The encryption ensures that a key is necessary to recover the record in full, and the ID tag facilitates the recovery of specific records within a database. We assume a secure randomised symmetric encryption method that we denote as $E_K(\cdot)$, where K is the symmetric key. The corresponding decryption operation is denoted as $D_K(\cdot)$.

   Given a record R_i we extract all keys corresponding to its combination of attributes K_j as described in the previous section. The sequence number k is chosen such that no other record was encrypted under the same k, the key $K_{jk} = H(K_j, k)$ is derived and the counter k is increased.

The encrypted record takes the form:

$$\mathrm{ID}_{R_j} \equiv H(\text{“ID”}, K_{jk}); \mathrm{BODY}_{R_j} \equiv E_{K_{jk}}(R_j) \tag{2}$$

The first component ID_{R_j} is the tag of the record, and the second component BODY_{R_j} is the body.

Given a database of N tuples of tags and bodies, as well as a key K_j it is possible to locate all records in time proportional to $\mathcal{O}(k \cdot \log N)$. The sequence of keys K_{jk}, starting with key $k = 0$ is generated, and for each ID $H(\text{“ID”}, K_{jk})$ a $\mathcal{O}(\log N)$ algorithm can be used to look-up the corresponding record. When the first k is tried for which the record does not exist, the search terminates.

It is worth noting some security properties afforded by this encoding:

- Trivially, given an encrypted record it is unfeasible to decrypt it without the appropriate key.
- Given two encrypted records it is unfeasible to tell whether they have been encrypted under the same key K_j or not, unless that key is known. The IDs are computed using the derived keys K_{jk} containing a different value of k.
- Given a key K_j it is easy $(k \cdot \mathcal{O}(\log N))$ to locate all records encrypted with this key.

These properties are important in designing the protocol to securely store and efficiently decode the encrypted records.

2.3   A Remote Storage and Logged Access Protocol

The justification for centralised data retention is speed of access, and completeness of the data held. We design a protocol to ensure the data can be accessed quickly, as soon as an authorisation has been logged, while at the same time preventing access without authorisation and logging. In particular our scheme prevents the traffic data store from performing fishing expeditions, or profile without authorisation. Two simple protocols are needed for this: a *storage* protocol and an *access* protocol, executed between the service provider (SP) and a central data store (CDS).

Storage. The storage protocol simply consists of the service provider (SP) encrypting each new record R_i, as it is generated with all keys keys(R_j), and sending the resulting ciphertexts to the central data store (CDS).

Access (request-response). The authority managing the central data store can request access to some of the stored records. To do this it has to decide the criteria for selecting the records to access: namely a window of time as a set of periods t_{CDS}, the set of service providers concerned P_{CDS}, the set of subjects concerned S_{CDS}, and the types of records required T_{CDS}.

The central data store then sends the four sets $(P_{\mathrm{CDS}}, T_{\mathrm{CDS}}, S_{\mathrm{CDS}}, t_{\mathrm{CDS}})$ to all service providers in the set P_{CDS}, with any material authorising them to retrieve records, requesting the keys necessary for decryption. Upon receiving the sets, the *request is checked and logged*, and the keys necessary to decrypt any records of this description are released. For all four-tuples in the Cartesian product of the sets $L_{all} \equiv P_{CDS} \times T_{CDS} \times S_{CDS} \times t_{CDS}$ the corresponding key is released, namely $\forall (P_j, T_j, S_j, t_j) \in L_{all}.K_j \equiv H(K_{P_j,t_j}, P_j, T_j, S_j, t_j)$.

The "raw" keys are released that allow the data store to detect and retrieve multiple records that fulfill the same criteria by simply looking for all IDs such that $ID_{R_j} \equiv H("ID", H(K_j, k))$ for $k \geq 0$. Once these records are located they can be decrypted with the corresponding key $K_{jk} = H(K_j, k)$.

The combined effect of these two protocols is that records are remotely stored, lessening the cost on the service providers and speeding the access speed for the authorities. On the other hand the administrative decisions on whether proper authority exists to access the records, as well as the logging of the criteria with which records are accessed is safeguarded. This might increase the time necessary to access records, but it is a vital safeguard against abuse.

3   Why Is This Not Good Enough?

There are several problems associated with this protocol and traffic data retention in general, that make it inherently less safe than a speedy data preservation regime, from the point of view of privacy:

- It is very difficult to ensure that data is ever deleted. Encrypted records can be stored beyond the period permitted by law, or indefinitely. More seriously decrypted records, and released key material can be saved forever. It is difficult to design a cheap system to remedy that. Note that the encryption of the records makes it easier on the side of the service provider to destroy records, by simply forgetting the session keys.
- The scheme relies on service providers maintaining few symmetric keys associated with a time period, that we have denoted K_{P_j,t_j}. This makes the scheme inherently fragile: a small leak of keys gives access to a very large volume of information. Even a temporary compromise of these keys might result in mass surveillance becoming possible [6].
- Since the symmetric keys have to be available on request to derive further specialised keys to decrypt records, they are exposed to abuse. Secure hardware can be used to store them and protect them, and ensure they only get released if a log entry was created. Even then the manufacturer of the hardware has to be trusted to not compromise it.
- Many jurisdiction's do not hesitate to simply seize material when it is needed in an investigation. There is nothing preventing a police force from raiding the key server of a service provider and be able to decode all previous traffic. Some jurisdiction, like the UK may ever force parties to make keys available under a gag order, which could include preventing a log entry being created.
- It is not clear how the service providers should react to authorisations that seem disproportionate (like for all users) but are none the less authorised properly. Unless an effective oversight mechanism exists this is a fundamental problem with this approach. It is not clear that such oversight regimes are possible.

In general the efficiency with which the storage and decoding process proceeds makes it all more fragile to abuse.

4 Conclusions

We presented an architecture that fulfils the stated requirements for centralised traffic data retention, namely efficiency of delivery and low cost, while at the same time limiting the potential for mass surveillance. The authorities still have to trust the service providers to truthfully package and send records, as it is the case today, but privacy is protected by a robust logging mechanisms implemented as a dual-control policy.

Even this approach has limitations, since the two parties involved in the protocols have fundamentally different powers: law enforcement comes with legal authority, massive state funding and a long history of subversion and clandestine operations, while the service providers have limited resources, are bound by commercial necessities and heavily regulated – most importantly they only have a peripheral interest in their customer's privacy.

References

1. Escudero-Pascual, A., Hosein, I.: Questioning lawful access to traffic data. Communications of the ACM 47(3), 77–82 (2004)
2. Taylor, M.: The EU Data Retention Directive. Computer Law & Security Report 22(4), 309–312 (2006)
3. Schneier, B., Kelsey, J.: Secure audit logs to support computer forensics. ACM Trans. Inf. Syst. Secur. 2(2), 159–176 (1999)
4. Goh, E.J., Shacham, H., Modadugu, N., Boneh, D.: Sirius: Securing remote untrusted storage. In: NDSS. The Internet Society (2003)
5. Li, J., Krohn, M.N., Mazières, D., Shasha, D.: Secure untrusted data repository (sundr). In: OSDI, pp. 121–136 (2004)
6. Danezis, G., Wittneben, B.: The Economics of Mass Surveillance and the Questionable Value of Anonymous Communications. In: Proceedings of the 5th Workshop on The Economics of Information Security, WEIS 2006 (June 2006)

The Least Privacy-Damaging Centralised Traffic Data Retention Architecture

(Transcript of Discussion)

George Danezis

Microsoft Research

Good afternoon everybody! It feels like today there hasn't been a lot of controversy that would interrupt the talks in the first five minutes, so I thought that I should inject a bit more. So I will make slightly more extreme comments about everything I'm going to be talking about than I intended to, just to inject a bit of energy in the room at this late hour.

The subject of my talk today is coming from experience. I talk to a lot of people who are working in policy and technology, and they told me all our nightmares are actually going to come true – we always thought that but now we actually have a confirmation – and the UK government is actually planning not only to retain all traffic data that goes to service providers, but also to centrally store it, and to do who knows what else. So I was thinking about this issue from a technology perspective and today I hope we can have a discussion about the technology issues around this more general policy problem.

I make an assumption here that most of you already know a lot of things about traffic data retention. It has been a big policy hotspot on both sides of the Atlantic, particularly in the EU but also I believe in the US (our colleagues from there can correct me). The idea is rather simple. Law enforcement requires some data in order to do its business online, in order to catch the bad guys. This data is right now not guaranteed to be there, mostly in Europe because of data protection issues, so they're worried that it's going to start getting deleted. There is nothing to substantiate this, as far as I'm concerned everybody keeps data forever. But somehow they wanted to be sure that the data will be available. They made some kind of fantasy distinction between traffic data and content data, and they decided that telling people that the content of their phone calls is going to be retained is not going to be very popular so they decided to retain just the traffic data, which is who's calling whom, for how long, when, from which location, and so forth. And the idea is that all this data should be kept in a mandatory way for some period of time, to allow investigations to look at it into the past and find out who has been talking to whom in order to facilitate catching bad guys.

As I mentioned, this comes down from an EU Directive that was voted in about 2006. Voted is a loose term when it comes to EU policy making.

Matt Blaze: Voting is a loose term, period.

Reply: As we know, yes.

B. Christianson et al. (Eds.): Security Protocols 2009, LNCS 7028, pp. 93–110, 2013.
© Springer-Verlag Berlin Heidelberg 2013

It's really interesting to understand how this has been sold to a lot of people, including some people from our community. The technical community has been told about a fantasy implementation, namely that, well what's the big deal, you used to keep this data on backup tapes for like six months, a year, you used to never delete it actually, so now you're just going to keep your backup tapes for a bit longer. I mean, what do you need, you just need a bigger storage room effectively to keep this data. It's not a big deal, right?

Now very early on I was involved in this debate and there were some key facts about the techniques that will be necessary and economic to implement traffic data retention that really popped out. First of all, the important thing is that a lot of the cost associated with traffic data retention has to do with actually fulfilling requests, like getting the requests from law enforcement and giving back the data: trawling through the data, packaging it, making sure that the timestamps match, and giving it away. So the economics of traffic data retention really point to the fact that this stuff is not going to be stored on tapes – then you would have to go through the tape library and put every tape in the tape reader to read it serially and find the records you want. It's quite obvious that this stuff is going to be kept on live random access spinning media so that they can just read it off a hard disk rather than read it literally from a tape.

The second thing is that it is very likely that the economics will point to pre-indexing all this as we write it on the spinning media, so that when the query comes it can be answered in order log n time rather than order n time, as you do for a search engine or whatever. And the third point where the economics of actually serving this request points us to: this is unlikely to be on some kind of separate system that is separated by an air gap from the rest of the world, because it has to keep receiving the data, and it has to answer requests. Therefore it is very likely that these systems are going to be networked, and you should be able to access this data from quite a few places around your enterprise or your system provider.

Now this is quite a complex operation, and what do companies do when they're faced with a complex operation that is not their core business model? They outsource. That's what you do, you don't want to be doing your own cleaning, because you don't want to be keeping up with the latest cleaning technology, and so forth.

Matt Blaze: So just to clarify, these regulations are aimed at generic ISPs?

Reply: It depends, but yes, mainly telecommunication providers and ISPs. There are huge grey areas, like if I run an anonymity service, am I a communications provider? The Germans say yes, everybody else says maybe. I say no. You know, it's up for grabs.

Joseph Bonneau: There is also a comment that it would extend to online communications providers like social networks and Windows Live Messenger.

Reply: Yes, and we'll come back to that in a second.

Sören Preibusch: And also companies are believed to be telecommunication service providers if they allow private emailing.

Reply: A Directive gives a framework, and different countries have adopted slightly different definitions, which doesn't make anything easier or better for trans-national police operations, because you don't quite know what's going to be available in the country next to you.

Matt Blaze: And similarly, is it anywhere defined what constitutes a communication?

Reply: That's also not concrete, although the Directive at the back, unhelpfully rather than helpfully, contains a list of items that have to be retained. That makes things worse in many ways, because the items retained automatically provide you good linkability, but still basically violate a lot of privacy, so you get the worst of both worlds by being specific there.

Cathy Meadows: And it's the ETSI[1] protocols that they're using for this?

Reply: Different providers use different protocols. The ETSI protocols are again a fantasy. No-one implements the ETSI protocols.

Cathy Meadows: Or the equivalent of CALEA[2]?

Reply: Yes, the equivalent of the CALEA interface is probably going to be used for Telco equipment. It's not clear these are going to be used for ISP equipment. RADIUS logs are going to be used for ISP equipment, and SMTP logs, and HTTP logs. That's more likely to be at the level these guys are looking for, they're not tracing UDP or TCP.

Matt Blaze: So the obvious difficulty here is routers don't have storage.

Reply: It's not quite at the granularity of TCP, it's at the granularity of SMTP, HTTP.

Ben Laurie: Which allows you to poke inside the packets and say that some of what's inside the packets is traffic data and some is communications data.

Reply: Right, so this is what I'm talking about, this fantasy of content versus traffic data, because you have to look through layers and make a guess about what is what.

We thought, all of that will lead to outsourcing, which will lead to centralisation. There are going to be a few companies that create silos of data serving lots of customers and managing this whole process. And our overarching feeling is that this is bad, OK, because whereas before our fantasy was some tapes in some basement with a big strong door, now we suddenly have an online decentralised surveillance infrastructure.

---

[1] European Telecommunications Standards Institute.
[2] Communications Assistance for Law Enforcement Act.

Matt Blaze: In fact you don't need speculation there, if you look at the experience of CALEA in the United States, an entire outsourcing industry has emerged.

Reply: Indeed. So this is not crazy stuff, I mean, the economics are pointing there, therefore a rational actor will do that.

Now, our idea as privacy-friendly people was that this was all bad for privacy. The UK government seems to want to do even more of that. So now there is a new policy being decided which is called the Interception Modernisation Programme. Nothing is really set in concrete yet; we only know things through ministers talking to the press, and leaking some things, and hinting at other things, and all that stuff. So first of all, the Interception Modernisation Programme has provisions for having a centralised repository of traffic data. The idea is that all the data that is gathered right now and stored in these miraculous caves is going to be centralised. It has other provisions which are not quite of so much interest to us such as online interception, *à la* Carnivore, but a bit more Web 2.0 style, so you can probably upload an applet on your Carnivore box and it will do cool stuff: decode the protocol of the day or something. And some articles have appeared in the media saying that in the same framework they would like to get all the Facebook data and all that stuff. It's not quite clear if that means intercepting on the wire, or getting traffic data, it's a bit in flux right now.

But basically they're saying, we want centralised repositories of traffic data. Why do we want that? Because first of all you cut costs, you don't have replication. That's the argument for why you will have centralisation and outsourcing, so this argument is actually quite a reasonable one. Secondly they say, well you know, we're not quite sure there are equally good ways for the ISPs to gather all this data and keep it forever, and we're not really sure if their tapes are going to work in a year's time, so we will have a consistent quality controlled system which will be better. Now the weirdest argument that I've heard is that this will be better for security and privacy. If I had submitted a paper with that thesis in a workshop, or in a conference of our community, I would have a very hard time to go through explaining how that works, but I will try to do that in a second. And the final argument is that it will provide an agility and adaptability, particularly intercepting on the wire with some kind of applets marshalling different protocols.

Now what is most shocking to me was the argument that somehow this centralised architecture will provide better security and privacy.

Vaclav Matyas: George, do you show us the key arguments directed towards inside of the government or towards the public?

Reply: I can only tell you what's towards the public because I'm not inside the government. I will speculate about that later though.

So I decided that the best way of actually testing this is trying to find out, what kind of architecture would you implement that would make security and privacy better, that is centralised? And this is really the exercise that I did. I'm trying to find the least privacy-invasive way of doing traffic data retention in a centralised manner.

So "better for security and privacy". Let's try to understand this argument a bit more, even though it is pretty twisted. First of all, there is a different threat model from the people inside the government, as Vaschek says, than from the people outside the government. Outside the government, the obvious threat model we all have in our minds when a government says, we'll just take all the traffic data and sit on it, is that, well we'll need to have some ways of protecting this data from unauthorised access, including systematic insider attacks. So if my government at some point decides that they would like to just look at it all, and run profiling, and find out who should be sent to the Commission on UnAmerican Activities, that should not really be allowed, and somehow we need to have protections against this. The government has a slightly different threat model. They accept very well that unauthorised access has to be prohibited, they also accept that insiders might be present in ISPs and so forth. They also assume that there might be some abuse within the system, but they never, ever believe that this abuse will be systematic enough for the whole system effectively to be geared towards mass surveillance, rather than serving legitimate requests. And therefore there is a kind of impedance mismatch every time people say, "we will provide a system with better security and privacy", because if you take out this threat, i.e. that of the very motivated and systematic adversary, then it all comes down to making sure that the right people have the right permissions, and they don't forget their passwords, and so forth. So really there is a bit of a mismatch, and when I propose a system I will propose it in the first threat model, which is the strong one.

The second problem that confuses things, is that it seems that we have two opposing forces when it comes to security engineering. The first one says, do not aggregate your targets, it's a bad idea to put a lot of high value stuff in one place, because then the adversary is more motivated to spend a lot of effort to attack this place, and this would basically seem to say you should not have a centralised database. On the other side we have another principle which says, you should minimise the attack surface, and that says basically that if you have a million databases around the country then some of them will be compromised because you have to protect a million things. If you only have one place and you have a really tight API to access it and so forth, you have a better chance to prove things about it, and use really high quality secure hardware, and therefore you stand a better chance of protecting it, which means that you should centralise.

Ross Anderson: But this is not new. There were several arguments about whether you should have medical records in 11,000 document offices or one NHS database.

Reply: That is indeed exactly the same argument. So, it's very difficult to give a clear-cut balance because people can use these arguments to push one way or the other. So I did this exercise in futility. I propose to try to design a secure centralised tracking database, and there is a very strict threat model that insiders should not be able to do mass surveillance, and it should fulfil all the properties that the government says that it should fulfil, except that it should also prevent them from doing mass surveillance. And the privacy goal really comes down to an extremely weak property, which is that if a record is accessed there should be a secure log record, not in the hands of the government, that says that record has been accessed with these properties. It's not even that anyone is prevented from accessing things, providing they are required to have some secure login.

Now why do I say this is a futile exercise? That comes back to Vashek's point. First of all, I've tried as much as I can to take all the stated requirements, but I do believe that there are unstated requirements, namely that the government will be able to sit on this huge database and do whatever they want with it. So even if my protocol is perfect in fulfilling the stated requirements, I still think it's not going to be very popular when I try to sell it to the government, because it's quite nice to sit on a bunch of data. You know, it's got value.

The second thing is that my protocol has a very high complexity: it contains cryptography and all that stuff, versus the protocol of the government, which is, give us all your data, we'll put it on a database, and the Oracle database access control system will take care of the security. Which is effectively impossible to ensure, because those systems have not been designed to protect against very strong adversaries.

These guys never really provide a security design that is as robust as the security designs we're looking for, but it seems that their security comes at no extra cost, whereas our cryptographically based systems come at a very high added cost. Of course, I'm talking about the visible cost and complexity, because the invisible cost is that it's basically impossible to secure their architecture.

Matt Blaze: OK, so let me quibble with that. Recalling the key escrow headache of the 1990s, one of the arguments that the government repeatedly made about why trust is not an issue is, we are building systems with the same engineering principles used to protect nuclear access codes. You heard that a lot. Of course that's absurdly expensive, and nuclear weapons still proliferate in spite of that, so in fact it's not a very convincing argument on either the effectiveness or the cost side.

Reply: But the question is, what kind of incentives has the person who will put in the investment to protect the system? When you have nuclear launch codes you would hope the government has the correct incentives to protect the codes. When the government is holding onto your data, and some parts of the government have incentives to get access to it, other parts of the government have no incentive to spend a big budget to protect it effectively. I mean, there is a kind of an investment balance there.

Bruce Christianson: The obvious incentive is to salt a few real launch codes in the database and see if the bad guys can find them.

Matt Blaze: This is Whit Diffie's idea of hiring some comedians and have them write original jokes.

Sören Preibusch: Traditionally government has achieved privacy by installing legal safeguards. For instance, the police have all technical means to eavesdrop your phone, but to do so they need authorization.

Reply: Right. I think one can engage with what you said at two levels. The first level is, yes, this is right, of course they usually have an authorisation that is independent from the actual person who's going to do the surveillance, either through the judiciary, or through the ISPs these days, that have to see the proper paperwork to enable the wiretap. So there is this kind of double check effectively, in that the ISP to activate a wiretap will have to see some kind of legal authorisation. At another level I would say, yes, I agree with you, this has been the traditional way of protecting against illegal wiretapping, and it has been so poor that every year we have interception scandals. So I wouldn't want to say, what we need is to go back to this golden era of privacy of the 70s, the 80s, the 90s, or the noughties, because that would actually be a very poor state to aspire to.

Sören Preibusch: My main argument is that governments are not looking for technical solutions.

Reply: Yes, they're not looking for technical solutions. I believe this is why we have been in such a poor state in the past as well.

So the idea here is very simple and it starts from the premise of centralised traffic data management. We have a happy user browsing here, and they browse through a service provider, and the government's idea is that this service provider is also going to be sending the records to a central repository somewhere or other. The only difference is that instead of the record being sent in clear the record is encoded cryptographically under a particular key K, and we'll see what that is in a minute. And effectively what the service provider does, in the terminology of our community, is secure remote storage on an untrusted store. So effectively the service provider uses the reliability and cheapness of the storage, and all that stuff, but does not actually assume that this is a secure hard disk[3]. And then there is a secondary protocol between the repository of whoever has authority to perform queries and the service provider, that allows them to get the key for the identification of the records and the decryption of particular records.

Conceptually it's very simple, and the only aim of this protocol is to allow the authorisation here to be decoupled from the actual bit transfer and storage.

Frank Stajano: So what's the granularity of this K? Is there a K for every piece of data that gets stored?

Reply: Excellent, so that question leads us to the key hierarchy, and how we derive this magic K. The idea is that we cannot really be very restrictive on what is a record, because we will have to store in the same database SMTP logs, HTTP logs, RADIUS logs, whatever. So we assume that we have some record that is free form, and the only thing we care about this record is that we can apply four functions to it: to extract who the provider is, i.e. who the ISP who

---

[3] The assumption is that the attacker can read it, but not overwrite it.

holds it is; the type of the record – an SMTP record, or whatever – so that we have some type information; the subjects involved, if George sends to Frank this would be George and Frank; and the time period in which it was generated, at some granularity.

Ross Anderson: But how do you know in advance what attributes government will decide it wants to search on? What if it suddenly decides it wants to search geographically?

Reply: For any requirements that the government is happy to share with us, we can produce a solution that allows them to query securely and privately.

Ross Anderson: But their requirement will be that they want flexibility.

Reply: If the requirement is, we would like to decide tomorrow what to do, then that's tough luck basically, because it means we cannot provide a privacy preserving system.

Frank Stajano: It might, in theory, be possible for the government to change their mind about the specs and then for everything to be re-encrypted in the way you say.

Reply: Right, you could do that, but it would take a linear time over the databases.

We create for each record a set of labels, that is a couple of tags that characterise the record, and then we use a key derivation scheme that takes a master secret according to the provider and the time period – so that we can change the keys periodically – and combines this with all the sets of attributes of a particular record, to derive a key for that particular record type according to its attributes. And then – because many records might actually have all these attributes being the same, namely the type, the subject, and the time – we actually create many keys, a whole family of keys, just by using an index j to derive the key K_j.

And how do we encode the records? We take the record, R_j, we create the keys K_j, and then we hash it with the string ID to get an ID for that record, and we encrypt it using some secure encryption procedure to get the encrypted body of that record.

Now, what are the properties of this simple key hierarchy? First of all, we can show that you cannot decrypt the body or the ID without the key. That's cool, that's the basis of securite remote storage.

Furthermore, we have some interesting privacy properties: if you have two records then you really cannot tell whether they have been encrypted under the same key or different keys, because if you could then you could infer something about the labels of the records. Since we're talking about traffic data, the labels contain a lot of information about the records, so that's a nice privacy property. Finally, and this is really the key selling point for my government client, given that you actually have the master key K_j for the record, or for the type of query you are doing, you can retrieve all the records with these labels in log n time. If you think about it it's quite simple, you just need to index those IDs that are only dependent effectively on K_j. When you do a query and get one of those K_js then you try with index zero, and that takes you log n time to look through your index to find the record, then K_1, K_2, K_3, until you don't find any more.

Virgil Gligor: You cannot tell if two records are encrypted with the same key by looking at the ciphertexts. What about more than two?

Reply: That scales, because all the keys are different, and you never encrypt under the same key.

The central store sends the provider some labels that describe what type of data they want, about what subjects, and for what time period–which is what a request usually looks like I am told, that's pretty straightforward. Actually 90% of the requests are just subscriber information, so you would send a provider, I would like some subscriber information on a phone-line.

Matt Blaze: So I'm just curious, when you say 90% of these requests are subscriber requests, is there actually data on that?

Reply: Richard Clayton is working with a major UK ISP and has this kind of data. A lot it is just subscriber data, like I have this number, which door do I go to?

Matt Blaze: I've heard those kinds of statistics before, but I've never seen an authoritative citation for it.

Reply: The report from the Interception Commissioner might actually confirm some of that data, and it's made public every year, so that might be a place to look for it[4].

So when we receive this query, it logs and audits, it logs actually, the audit is possible later, but it's not clear it's ever going to happen, and then it constructs the key according to these labels K_j that will allow you to decrypt any records under these labels, and then you as a provider send a list to the central store, the provider uses a counter from zero to the last record they find to get the keys, and then they decrypt the records they find, and they have the records that match these labels, and that's that.

Andy Gordon: If there was traffic between multiple parties, would you have a record for each party? I mean, if I was wanting to see the subjects that get encrypted by the pair of George and Frank?

Reply: No, there's George and separately another record is made for Frank.

This way you can have flexible queries, where you can retrieve all records that concern Frank, because that's actually quite a usual way of phrasing these queries: Frank is under suspicion, give me everything about Frank from January to May, and then you get all the stuff that Frank has sent and received. So that's the idea of not just using pairs as identifiers, yes.

---

[4] See e.g. the 2010 Annual Report of the Interception of Communications Commissioner, p32, and contrast pp41, 45, 46. ISBN: 978-0-102974072;
http://www.official-documents.gov.uk/document/hc1012/hc12/1239/1239.pdf

James Malcolm: How many keys does the ISP need to keep secret? I mean, most of these are generated keys aren't they, is there a master key?

Reply: Ah, that's right, the master key of the ISP is just the key of the provider and a time period, so effectively the ISP has to refresh their keys every time period. But everything else just follows from that. And of course you can have some kind of system in order to generate the time period key from a master key as well.

But this actually leads us to the problem, why this protocol is not good enough. First of all, it's impossible to tell if the data is ever deleted once it is decrypted. Once a record is decrypted, and is in clear in the hands of whoever in law enforcement, how do you ever tell if it is eventually deleted? That's a limitation that I can't really do anything to help with, but it's a limitation of the systems used today as well.

Frank Stajano: Is there any technical way of ever doing that?

Reply: I don't know. I don't know of any, I don't think there is, and I think under some models you can prove that you can't do this.

Cathy Meadows: Some of the law enforcement equipment that we've looked at, that we'd gotten from eBay and places like that, still had the data on it.

Reply: Excellent!

Now the second problem relates to these master keys. We have reduced the whole security of this scheme to a few master keys in the hands of the ISP. Now the ISP, as we said, is not in the business of protecting your privacy, it's not in the business of protecting high value keys or anything like that. So why do we make this assumption that the ISP is capable, or even willing, to hold onto these keys and only perform this protocol correctly? Even a very small covert channel out of the ISP will allow you to leak a few hundred bits. So no matter what we do, against a powerful adversary any protocol like this will be weaker than not having a central tracking data regime, because that would require the covert channel to be huge to track all the data.

Matt Blaze: Just use a public key and that solves that, right, keys have to be live to encrypt records. You can use public keys if you're willing to spend more.

Reply: Then you need to spend more on hardware to actually do that at the rate logs are written, yes, that is very true.

Legal compulsion is a problem. You might have a fantastic system where all the ISPs keep keys and play the game, and then at some point they receive a notice from a court that says, now can we please have all the keys, and there is nothing in the UK that could stop a judge from doing that. You would have to go all the way up to the European Court of Human Rights before it decided about proportionality.

Jonathan Anderson: Maybe you should have another kind of centralisation and all the data would be stored at Cheltenham and all the keys be stored with the Privacy Commissioner, or something like that.

Reply: Right, that's another aggregate targets or not argument.

Joseph Bonneau: The ISP is generating all these records, and you want to get them to the central database without the central database knowing what time they were generated. So you could push them every month or so, but that approach pushes the intermediate storage problem back to the ISP. But if you stream them live, then the central repository can just tag them as they come in and you've lost privacy in doing that. So is there a way to deal with the time problem?

Reply: No.

Ross Anderson: There's a very important incentive at work, which is that to get retained data the police typically pay the ISP £500. Once you centralise it, the government pays £15 billion once, and then the marginal cost is effectively zero. So there is an enormous incentive for them then to find new ways of using it to (ahem) serve the public.

Bruce Christianson: If you put the keys in one secure place and the encrypted data in another, there's then no longer an incentive to aggregate your target, because the attacker needs both the key and the encrypted data. The usual arguments about don't aggregate and don't increase the attack surface are now working in harmony, instead of against each other, because the attacker has got to succeed in all the attacks, rather than just one.

Reply: Right, yes OK, that's very true. But I'm going to say that I didn't even dare call this system privacy enhancement, or privacy preserving, because these problems are so fundamental given a realistic threat model. It's really going to be pretty privacy damaging, given this state is not good enough to protect against systematic attack under the use of this kind of database. It's a sad state of affairs but I can't really find a way of providing a system like that.

Matt Blaze: I live in this country where we've had a problem with systematic state use of wiretap laws. One of the problems is that what *we* consider abuse gets defined as not being abuse, and that's how databases work.

Reply: Right, and it really points to this issue, who does the authorisation? And this is really a political question, who does the authorisation and what criteria they use to say whether it is legitimate or not legitimate. So if you have a conspiracy at high levels about this, then it's very difficult to protect any kind of centralised system in that aspect. And self-authorisation is as good as an authorisation, and this is really the model that the UK police are really keen on at this point.

But the interesting exercise is not quite so futile, because now I hope that the Home Office does put out an application to tender for contracts and all that stuff, and that they are pointed at this paper, and tough questions are asked exactly about what kind of architecture is going to be used in order to implement their retention scheme.

Luke Church: It seems to me that you said, here's a social context, here are a bunch of properties that I would like to support, and look, I can indeed do all the technical protocol munging to support those properties, but actually all of those properties are irrelevant because the social context can shift arbitrarily. Why are we trying to have a debate about social properties in a technical domain?

Reply: Because one of the key reasons why centralisation is pushed is the claim that it is better for security, and this is exactly the argument that I am trying to investigate. Is it the case that a centralised system will be technically better for security? Of course, there are also many other arguments about why this is a good idea or not.

Luke Church: But the real threat is not whether it's technically better for security, it's whether it's socially better for security. So the word is being used in two different discourses, and arguments about protocols aren't going to persuade government purchasers.

Reply: No, but if these guys go for this centralised architecture then I want them to buy mine.

Alastair Beresford: This idea of separating the keys from data is very similar to the government proposal for managing congestion charging on the road network, where they proposed a very similar scheme. In fact the Department of Transport had a big proposal which had an architecture that was quite similar. That might be a useful leverage point.

Reply: Oh, I'm very pleased to hear that, I didn't realise.

Alastair Beresford: I know a department has already proposed a protocol for this, which of course is now dead in the water because they've decided not to do congestion charging.

Paul Syverson: You have this simple query protocol but are they putting out queries that say, give me all of Matt Blaze's communications for January, or is it a central repository of all the data? I thought you were saying there's queries from the repository to the service providers, but you also seemed to be implying that the repository has everything in it.

Reply: The repository has everything in it in an encrypted form. The queries allow you to retrieve the keys that allow you to locate the record and decode the records.

Paul Syverson: I see, so the service providers are effectively going to be the guardians of the keys. It seems strange to me that you make the service providers those guardians.

Reply: Of keys rather than records, yes. It is very strange, and it would be better to have someone else, but I can't think of anyone else who's naturally in the pipeline.

Paul Syverson: The other thing that comes to mind is that, where people are actually trying to design systems like this, like in the US, and especially if they want it to be centralised, I find it implausible that, when they put out the query, they actually want to reveal to the service provider that they want Matt Blaze's stuff. I think that's got to be a security violation right there. But that's what people are designing?

Reply: That is the current model, that is exactly what is happening today, and this is not one of the arguments that is being used in order to push for centralisation. I agree that it may be a hidden requirement

Paul Syverson: But, there are funded programmes to do Private Information Retrieval to manage this.

Sandy Clark: But they are not being used. I can give you some documentation from a third-party service provider, that shows exactly the request it sent, and then the things that the system administrator is supposed to fill out when they get the warrant, so it's not hidden at all.

Paul Syverson: Yes, but you're talking about how it's done now, and George is talking about designing a future system.

Matt Blaze: Right, but I also think you guys are slightly at cross purposes. Sandy is speaking specifically about US law enforcement requirements, and Paul is talking about national security requirements, which are different, right, under US law.

Paul Syverson: Yes, and that's something that the security people care a lot about, they're working very hard to separate those issues, and (at least some of them) try hard not to cross those lines.

Matt Blaze: The lines are getting blurry though. One of the arguments in the key escrow debate, which ultimately was one of the strong ones that carried the day I think, was that key escrow is bad, because it is dealing with a fast moving area of computing technology and communications, and it essentially took away a simple and inherently cheap technology and turned it into an inherently expensive technology.

Crypto is something you can do offline, it's cheap, you can do it in software, whereas key escrow required maybe hardware, or maybe expensive online stuff, so there was this argument that requiring this sort of thing is going to stifle development of low-end technology. Well it seems that we have the same problem with what's being proposed here, that because we don't know what the communications infrastructure five years from now is going to look like, the need to create this kind of record in this kind of database may be stifling. If 90% of the cost of providing a communication service is complying with this data retention requirement, that becomes a non-viable service.

Paul Syverson: Are you saying they could use this to squash that Skype thing that's now giving them such a headache?

Matt Blaze: Yes, I wonder, do you address that argument?

Reply: No, because this is an argument that from a policy point of view has already been lost. We're not discussing here about whether there is going to be traffic data retention which has all the problems you described, we're now just talking about where the < expletive deleted > records are going to be residing. But I agree totally with your arguments, I think that at a policy level it is misguided to do it at all.

Matt Blaze: But in fact this largely exacerbates that.

Reply: Yes, it makes the problem that you described slightly worse and slightly more expensive. They try to optimise it to make it less expensive, but it is inherently a very expensive and ill thought thing to do.

Ross Anderson: We should call this data escrow, because we already in Britain have a law that says that the government doesn't escrow keys centrally but you must hand them over if the police ask.

Reply: That is basically key escrow by request, and this is data escrow by request.

Ross Anderson: But it's not really escrow, it's key handover, basically at present we have data handover by ISPs.

Sandy Clark: So how is the log protected, and what's logged? Because couldn't you reverse engineer all of the keys you're looking for from looking at the log?

Paul Syverson: The log of what?

Reply: The log of accesses. Yes, there is actually a confidentiality property that we need too, because (following Paul's argument) you don't want a crook to be able to find out if they're being intercepted.

Ben Laurie: You can store it in a central database so the government can delete the log.

Reply: Right, so how can you do reliable integrity-protected and confidential login for this is interesting as well. Schneier and someone else has a protocol that does some of that stuff, again under the assumption that the keys are secure. If your keys are not secure then you have problems.

Joseph Bonneau: You mention that you don't like the ISPs holding all these keys but you can't think of anyone else to do it. I'm wondering if there's some precedent for government setting up quasi-government organisations to do some really specific tasks that we don't trust the government to do.

Sören Preibusch: Yes, they are called banks.

Joseph Bonneau: Actually, in the US we have the Federal Reserve which doesn't really work that well, but we also have the Supreme Court whose job is to be the referee when the constitution is being flagrantly violated, they're supposed to stand up.

Reply: I have a very standard story about this kind of division of power when it comes to cryptography. Lots of people proposed escrow systems, or whatever, they have this kind of abstract quorum of authorisation entities, that authorise bypassing a security property, and I have never actually seen a real entity like this, and there is a very good reason for this. If you say these entities are going to be, for example, the judiciary, the judiciary are used to doing some things and not others, they're really used to sitting in a court with other judges and making a decision about what a reasonable man would expect or not, but they are not used to handling cryptographic keys. They're very nice people, I trust them to make legal decisions, I do not trust them to actually be able to keep a bit string secure. So what is going to happen if you give the judiciary the role of maintaining the key? They will go to the branch of government that is in the business of protecting keys, this is going to be CESG in the UK, which in fact are a branch of GCHQ, but there are equivalent ones everywhere else, and they will have to provide the judges with boxes in which these keys are effectively going to reside, and with the protocols that they are going to use in order to let the keys go out if they authorise them. Now the main adversary you're worried about in this scenario is GCHQ itself, that they're going to somehow find their way through the government chain to be the ones that construct the systems that are meant to protect against them. It's very difficult to actually balance this out, and I haven't really seen any kind of workable constitutional solution that doesn't at the end leak the keys to the NSA, or the branch of government that is in charge of keeping secrets.

Joseph Bonneau: The goal is to get somebody who will be more independent than ISPs. There's a whole lot of reasons why governments can exert pressure on ISPs if they don't go along with this scheme, so I'm just wondering if it's possible to create some council of crypto elders who would ...

Ross Anderson: I don't believe that much in quorum systems, and the reason is that if you send an email to six people none of them will reply, if you send emails to six individual people all of them will reply, this is a well-known fact. If you think that six people make things more dependable, we all look up back at case history where a US B-52 carried half a dozen cruise missiles with live hydrogen bomb warheads, that was not supposed to happen. There were six people supposed to check that the cruise missiles had got no live nuke in it before it was loaded on board, and everyone of those six people trusted all the other five would do the job.

Joseph Bonneau: I'm not arguing for a threshold, it can be one, we can say Ross is the manager of the UK's crypto keys. My point is that instead of the ISPs having to manage all these keys, we can have somebody else do it, without changing George's protocol

Ross Anderson: But I'll end up owning the big house on the hill.

Paul Syverson: Actually, this is quite hopeful, because already now, without any of these issues, the black ops people never talk to one another, so you've already got that separation in place.

Jonathan Anderson: Even if you don't believe that there could be a separation within the UK government, there might be scope for a European Privacy Commissioner approach. At the very least it would be hard to get their friends in Germany to agree that the UK police really need to get at this though they're not supposed to be able to.

Reply: Doing the crypto is difficult enough, I'm not in the business of international relations.

Ross Anderson: One of the things that helped to kill key escrow in Europe, was the question that if you got somebody who is a Brit and he buys a phone in France and has a SIM card from Germany, and he stands in Helsinki when he makes a phone call to somebody in Stockholm, which of the police forces of these countries should have access to the traffic, and how do you engineer that.

Matt Blaze: I think George's last bullet point is a very important contribution, I mean, since they never follow our advice there's no reason to believe they're going to follow it this time.

Reply: Yes, I'd be a bit suspicious if they did.

Matt Blaze: But it would be interesting to compare your architecture with the architecture of Verisign's lawful intercept service in the US, which most of the ISPs and law enforcement agencies subscribe to. It's specifically for phone calls, but essentially it aggregates the data coming from Telcos so it can get to law enforcement agencies easily. There's no data retention there, it's a live interface, but it's similar enough that it would be interesting compare that with the protocols that you've designed.

Paul Syverson: Last year we were solving a similar problem for logs from a system, and we came up with a quite similar protocol, one difference was that the key on the provider side in ours is stored inside a Smartcard.

we chose to use a deliberately a slow protocol; it takes one minute to retrieve they key for one set of records, which limits the number of queries.

And we were afraid of government trying to ask for data outside the data retention period, so the Smartcard contacts a trusted time server and retrieves the time, so it is able to decide if the request is correct or not.

Reply: I discuss the limitations of secure hardware in this last section. Secure hardware gives the impression that somehow you have a secure computer, a trusted computing base there, but effectively what you trust is the provider of the secure hardware, and the software manufacturer of the software that runs inside the trusted hardware, and you need to have some ways of updating, and some ways of recommissioning the trust. So it's not just a kind of bullet-proof thing. You just end up trusting another entity, which is IBM, let's say, that makes a crypto-processor, or GemPlus that does the card, or whoever does the software. Effectively some of them will have to be trusted. And rather than the manufacturer of the equipment, I actually preferred having my trusted entities being like the ISP, the judge, whatever, because they really have no incentive to play games to protect the good reputation of their brand of security protocols.

Paul Syverson: I perfectly agree with you. I'm not saying that Smartcards are trustworthy, but you can employ several Smartcards.

Reply: As a general rule, since we don't have a good candidate for who should be holding the keys, anyone is as good as any other at this point. There are so many problems with the ISPs doing this business, because it's not their business.

Paul Syverson: In regard to the other point, can law enforcement agency force you to change your implementation of the key retrieval system because it's too slow, for example? If it takes one minute for each record, and this is too slow for them, can they force you to change?

Sören Preibusch: It comes down to the requirements in the law.

Paul Syverson: But these tend to be like, in a reasonable time, or something like that, rather than saying that you should answer 1000 requests per day or something specific like that.

Sören Preibusch: And usually when it's required by authorities that are non-government, it's just guidelines.

Ross Anderson: Well the issues of costs and so on become salient here. So long as each request costs £500, so long as all requests made by the police in the context of criminal cases must be disclosed to the defence, there's a check there. There's another existing tension that might be brought over by systems like this, which is the traditional enmity and hatred between the intelligence people and the police. I was speaking to a retired senior GCHQ sort of person and from his point of view what's gotten broken within the past ten years is that the ops intel divide between the people who gets access to intelligence, and the police who never used to, has become blurred, which he reckons is going to lead to disaster because the police haven't had the three year training to deal with intelligence that people who work for GCHQ have. As soon as they come across evidence of criminal wrongdoing they'll rush out with their blue lights flashing, arrest somebody, and completely destroy all channels of intelligence.

So it would be nice to come up with some approach that instead of papering over the cracks between the spooks and the cops, somehow exacerbated them. In a world in which GCHQ had access to traffic data from its own database, but in which the police had to go cap in hand to the ISPs and pay £500, we would still have some of the traditional controls, the spooks would be able to watch everybody all the time, but the police would only be able to watch anybody at any time, and so from the point of view of the actions of a large slice of the state we would still have something like the traditional privacy controls.

Reply: Allow me to reiterate my worry every time I hear this concept of traditional controls. Lawful interception has a long history and I don't ever think there was ever a golden privacy period, from the moment we invented telegraph on down the line. I agree with you that there have been tensions and inefficiencies, and some people think they are good, some other people think they are bad, this is why I think the government is pushing for this stuff, but I don't think that there are good enough privacy safeguards per se. I would prefer actually to see the constitutional safeguards that we talked about (although they're not very good either by the way), and then also technical safeguards.

But fundamentally I think that as a society we have to decide what kind of level of risk we're happy to work with, in order to maintain effectively some of the civil liberties we're used to.

Ross Anderson: I do agree that we need both technical controls and legal controls. We've seen what happens when, for example, medical records moved to one big monster database from being scattered in tens of millions of brown paper envelopes, you can't do that without bringing in more controls, we've now learned the hard way. And similarly, if we're going to make all the traffic data available at the flick of a switch, then the police will become used to doing snowball searches, and all sorts of weird data mining.

Reply: They will get effectively addicted to the feed, that's a key problem. I was reading the public order manual about the use of tear gas and I found a very interesting note there, which I think is the same here, that using tear gas in a public order situation creates an addiction on the police on using tear gas, they forget about how to handle situations in any other way. So I think it's a very real risk here that providing a feed of data creates an addiction on that stuff at the detriment of other techniques to do investigations that might be more appropriate.

Pretty Good Democracy

Peter Y.A. Ryan[1] and Vanessa Teague[2]

[1] Dept. Computer Science and Communications
University of Luxembourg
peter.ryan@uni.lu

[2] Dept. Computer Science and Software Engineering
University of Melbourne
vteague@csse.unimelb.edu.au

Abstract. *Code voting* seeks to address the issues of privacy and integrity for Remote Internet Voting. It sidesteps many of the inherent vulnerabilities of the Internet and client platforms but it does not provide *end-to-end* verification that votes are counted as cast. In this paper, we propose a simple technique to enhance the verifiability of code voting by ensuring that the Vote Server can only access the acknowledgement codes if the vote code is correctly registered by a threshold set of Trustees. The mechanism proposed here therefore adds an extra level of verifiability in registering and counting the vote. Voter-verification is simple and direct: the voters need only check that the acknowledgement code returned to them agrees with the value on their code sheet. To ensure receipt-freeness we propose the use of a single acknowledgement code per code sheet, rather than individual acknowledgement codes for each candidate with usual code voting.

1 Introduction

Internet Voting is highly controversial. The inherent insecurity and unreliability of the Internet as infrastructure, and of home or office PCs as voting platforms, present severe obstacles to its usage. The dangers of vote buying and coercion are especially problematic for remote Internet voting. Nonetheless, there appear to be contexts in which such threats are mild enough to consider Internet voting as viable, such as elections for student bodies, professional societies, university officeholders [AdMPQ09] *etc.* This paper advances techniques for side-stepping many of the vulnerabilities of the Internet, though we would not claim our scheme is secure enough for use in national or regional elections.

Our scheme is based on *Code voting*, which aims to avoid requiring the voter to trust any computational device or digital signature in order to vote. Instead, code sheets are sent out to the voters via ordinary mail or other supposedly secure channel. These code sheets have random vote codes against each candidate. In effect, they serve as private code books to enable the voters to communicate securely with the voter server. Chaum's SureVote, [Cha01], appears as the first place that such an approach is presented. Typically these code sheets include acknowledgment codes (ack codes for short) that the server returns to the voter

B. Christianson et al. (Eds.): Security Protocols 2009, LNCS 7028, pp. 111–130, 2013.
© Springer-Verlag Berlin Heidelberg 2013

after receiving valid codes from the voter. These ack codes serve a dual role: to assure voters that their code was correctly received and to authenticate the voting system to the voter. However, receipt of the correct ack code does not give any assurance that the vote will subsequently be correctly included in the overall count. Such schemes are therefore not *end-to-end*, that is, there is no guarantee that votes make it all the way from being cast to being counted.

Our objective is to provide a mechanism such that on receipt of the correct ack code during the voting session, the voter can be confident that her vote will be accurately included in the election outcome.

Like other *end-to-end* verifiable election schemes, we make use of a public *Bulletin Board*, which is an authenticated broadcast channel with memory. (This could be implemented as a website which provides some added assurance that everyone is served the same data.) We describe a mechanism whereby the Voting Server can only recover the correct Acknowledgement Code with the cooperation of a threshold set of Trustees. In the absence of a large-scale collusion between the Trustees or the leaking of information about their codes, the fact that a voter gets the correct ack code back from the vote server ensures that their vote code is accurately registered on the Bulletin Board. Standard techniques such as the robust anonymising mixes described in [Rya08] [Adi06] can then be used to ensure the codes recorded on the Bulletin Board are correctly translated into votes in the final tally.

In contrast to most verifiable schemes, that require the voter to subsequently visit the Bulletin Board and confirm their receipt is correctly posted, our scheme simplifies the procedure for the voter. All the voter needs to do is to verify the received ack code during the voting session. It is hoped that this simpler, more immediate check will encourage a higher proportion of voters to participate in the verification process. Optionally, voters, or proxies acting on their behalf, can also subsequently visit the Bulletin Board and confirm the registration of their vote.

Another problem of remote voting in general and *Code Voting* in particular is its vulnerability to vote selling, that is, a voter simply sells her code sheet to a coercer or vote buyer. The present scheme does not as it stands address this problem but it could be enhanced by adding, for example, multiple casting [VG06] or *tokens* [JCJ05]. The idea is allow the voter to appear to sell their code sheet to the coercer, while actually retaining the opportunity to vote.

Our scheme is however receipt-free due to the use of a single acknowledgement code for each ballot rather than a distinct ack code for each candidate as usual for code voting. Thus, the fact that the ack codes are publicly available does not allow an adversary to identify the vote cast. It does of course demonstrate that a vote was cast with that code sheet, so opening up the possibility of forced abstention attacks.

Although at first glance the single ack seems to reduce the voter's opportunity to verify that the *correct* code was received, we do not believe that this is true. With either single or multiple ack codes, the voter's guarantee of integrity depends upon the secrecy of their (vote and ack) codes. An adversary who could learn a voter's codes and intercept their communications could substitute the individual ack that the voter expected just as easily as it could send a substituted vote code to the server. One the other hand, it may be that receiving a distinct ack code corresponding to their choice of candidate may give the voter an additional sense of confidence. It might make sense to return distinct ack codes during the voting session but not post them on the bulletin board. We will return to this point in Section 9.3.

Related Work is described in following section, then in Section 3 we explain the security properties of our contribution. Section 4 describes Code Voting. Our enhanced code voting scheme, PGD, is presented in Sections 5 to 8, with some further enhancements in Section 9.

2   Related Work

Similarly in its goal, Peters in [Pet05] describes a scheme for a secure Web Bulletin Board that prevents the corruption of a few parties from endangering the security goals of the entire election. To do so he uses threshold signatures. If the user receives such a signature and is able to verify it, they get the assurance that their vote is included on the board. The drawback of this approach is that the voter needs to rely on some computational capabilities on their computer.

Oppliger et al. evaluate the pros and cons of using multiple casts, multiple code sheets, and voting credentials [OSH08]. As an alternative Helbach et al. mentions linkable group signatures in combination with multiple casts [HSS08]. While preventing vote selling attacks these mechanisms cannot prevent coercion except for allowing a voter to update an influenced vote.

The scheme presented here has some points of contact with Chaum et al's Scantegrity II, [CCC+08]. While PGD and Scantegrity II are very different, in particular Scantegrity II is a supervised scheme while PGD is a remote scheme, there is some commonality in the use of random codes. Both schemes use such codes and in both it is important that certain players learn only one of the full set of codes per ballot, but for quite different reasons. In Scantegrity II, it is the voter who should only learn the selected code. This is done using invisible ink on optical scan type ballots to reveal only the code against the chosen candidate. Revealing more than one code per ballot invalidates the ballot. This is because the voter does not get a receipt but just notes the code revealed when making her selection. The fact that she should learn only the chosen code protects the voter against being accused of presenting fake codes. In PGD, it is the Vote Server that should only learn the selected code, to prevent it registering alternate codes. For both schemes of course it is important that codes are sufficiently hard to guess.

Civitas [CCM07], an implementation with extensions of [JCJ05], provides strong guarantees of integrity and coercion resistance, including resistance against a coercer who is physically present during voting, as long as that coercer leaves the voter unsupervised at least once. This is achieved by giving each voter one true voting credential, plus an algorithm for generating false credentials with which to fool the coercer. The security guarantees depend on trusting the voter's computer, which has to do cryptographic computations. Helios [Adi08] also provides very strong integrity guarantees, and uses a series of voter challenges [Ben06] to avoid having to trust the computer. However, this scheme is not receipt free. Our work achieves (almost) the best of both worlds, offering receipt freeness without having to trust the computers used for voting. The main shortcoming compared to Civitas is that we do not defend against against a coercer who intercepts the voter before or during voting, though token style mechanisms could possibly be incorporated to counter such threats. Our integrity guarantee is slightly weaker than that of Helios, being based on trusting a threshold set of election trustees. Furthermore, the Vote Codes must be kept secret to preserve both privacy and integrity. This is described in detail below.

2.1   Registration

Secure voter registration and coercion-resistant distribution of voting credentials are probably the most difficult open problems in Internet voting. Krivoruchko [Kri07] devised a distributed registration protocol, in which several registration servers each send a share of a credential to a voter's computer. Civitas uses a similar mechanism. However, both these schemes require significant computation at the voter's end, and we do not know how to extend their ideas to a scheme that avoids trusting the voter's computer. This leaves us with the traditional "secure" channel of the postal system, in which case the best we can say is that vote stealing is no easier than it is for paper-based postal votes (not a strong claim). Since our scheme is not coercion-resistant anyway, this level of security may be sufficient in some cases. An alternative is to insist that voters attend a registration centre in person to receive the code sheet. Registration centres could be opened weeks before the election, so this could still be much more convenient than requiring people to actually vote in person.

3   Security Properties of PGD

The enhancements to conventional code voting proposed here improve the security properties by providing an end-to-end auditable voting system. We should note that the degree of verifiability provided here is not as strong as that provided by some other voter-verifiable schemes, e.g. Prêt à Voter, [Rya07]. For Prêt à Voter, the guarantees of integrity are not conditional on the absence of collusion: any attempts to corrupt votes can be detected. For the present scheme, a sufficient collusion of trustees or the leakage of codes could lead to corruption of votes in a way that would not be detected.

Our scheme does provide a far higher degree of verifiability than conventional code voting. We summarise the key properties as follows:

Integrity

Cast as Intended. The received ack code allows the voter to verify that *some* ballot is included on her behalf on the Bulletin Board representing the batch of recorded votes. Assuming that no sufficiently large collusion of Trustees occurs and that code information is not leaked, the voter can be confident this encoded the candidate she intended. (She must also assume that the code sheets were properly audited, see Section 6.)

Counted as Cast and Tallied Correctly. These can be verified from the Bulletin Board using standard techniques, which do not require trusting any of the authorities.

Privacy

Receipt-Freeness. Receipt-freeness is ensured by the use of a single ack code for each code sheet. This means that voters cannot afterwards prove how they voted, even if the coercer has access to the Bulletin Board and the voter's private information and code sheet.

Coercion-Resistance. Our scheme does *not* as it stands provide protection against coercion initiated before voting, such as code sheet buying or direct observation of the voting process. For this purpose we would need extra mechanisms like stronger voter authentication or tokens in the style of Juels *et al* [JCJ05].

4   Code Voting

Code Voting provides a way to sidestep much of the inherent insecurity of the Internet: a code sheet is sent via a supposedly secure channel such as conventional mail, to each eligible voter. Each code sheet carries a unique ballot ID number and the list of candidates. For a typical implementation there is a random voting code and an acknowledgement code against each candidate. For each code sheet, the codes will be pairwise distinct and the codes vary (pseudo-)randomly from sheet to sheet. In effect, each voter is given their own personal code book to communicate with the voting system.

In order to place a vote, the voter logs onto the election's Vote Server and provides the ballot ID along with the code corresponding to their choice of candidate. The server verifies the validity of the ballot ID and vote code and responds with the appropriate ack code for the code sheet. The voter should check the server's response against the value shown on her code sheet. This will serve a dual purpose of confirming receipt of the vote code and providing a degree of authentication of the server to the voter.

A code sheet that includes vote and acknowledgement codes is shown in Figure 1.

After the election has closed, the submitted ID/codes will be translated back into the candidate choices. In a conventional code voting scheme, this latter step is typically not verifiable and requires significant trust to be vested in the tabulating authority.

Candidate	Vote Code	Ack code
Asterix	3772	8872
Idefix	4909	4044
Obelix	9521	1098
Panoramix	7387	4309
Ballot ID: 3884092844		

Fig. 1. Typical code sheet

5   Pretty Good Democracy

We now describe a simple enhancement to the basic code voting scheme described above that is designed to add an extra degree of assurance that votes are correctly tabulated. The key idea is to ensure that the Voting Server can only return the correct ack code to the voter with the cooperation of a threshold set of trustees who all participate in registering the vote on the Bulletin Board. Furthermore, rather than using a distinct ack code for each candidate, we use a single ack code per code sheet. This allows the posting of the ack codes on the Bulletin Board, allowing an extra level of verifiablity, while preserving receipt-freeness. Thus, if she wishes, a voter can additionally visit the Bulletin Board and confirm that her vote has indeed been registered. She cannot directly determine how her vote has been recorded. A typical code sheet for our scheme is shown in Figure 2.

Candidate	Vote Code
Asterix	3772
Idefix	4909
Obelix	9521
Panoramix	7387
Ack Code: 8243	
Ballot Id: 3884092844	

Fig. 2. Typical PGD code sheet for the enhanced scheme

5.1   Notation

Throughout this paper $\{x\}_k$ denotes the randomised encryption of x under the public key k. Public key is often abbreviated to PK.

Each code sheet will carry a unique serial number i. These serial numbers will be rather large, say twelve digits, so that, like credit card numbers, it will be hard to guess valid IDs. Let $VC_{i,j}$ denote the vote code for the i-th code sheet and a candidate indexed by j, with $j \in \{1, \ldots, c\}$. Similarly Ack_i denotes the acknowledgement code on the ballot with ID i. The vote and ack codes might typically be 4 digits.

5.2   The Election Roles

Here we outline the key roles of the scheme.

- A Voting Authority VA who generates the requisite number of vote codes and ack codes encrypted under the Trustees' PK.
- A set of Clerks, involved in the setup phase.
- A Registrar who decrypts the table provided by the Clerks and prints the code sheets.
- A Returning Officer who distributes the code sheets to the voters.
- A set of Trustees, who work with the Voting Server to register the votes on the Bulletin Board and reveal the ack codes. They have shares of the secret key corresponding to the threshold public key: PK_T.
- A Voting Server, who receives the votes, i.e. a serial number i and vote code $VC_{i,j}$, from each voter, then encrypts $VC_{i,j}$, and posts $(i, \{VC_{i,j}\})$ on the Bulletin Board.
- A set of Auditors responsible for performing various types of audit, on the initial set-up, on the information posted to the Bulletin Board, e.g. the zero knowledge proofs etc., and verifying the anonymising mixes.

5.3   Generating the Code Sheets

Firstly, the Trustees collaborate to generate a joint, threshold key PK_T with a distributed key generation protocol as originally described by Canetti et al. in [CGJ+99].

Suppose that we have v voters and c candidates. We need to generate sufficient code sheets, allowing for some random auditing, in such a way as to ensure that no single entity knows the codes associated with any ballot. The following construction achieves this in a simple and secure fashion. The Voting Authority generates $\lambda v(c+1)$ distinct codes of the appropriate form, say four to six digit codes[1], and then encrypts these under the Trustees' public key PK_T. This can be done in a fully open, auditable fashion on the Bulletin Board. The encryptions can be verified by simply revealing the randomisation factors (these will be re-randomised later). The initial encryptions could be performed with randomisations set equal to 1. The factor $\lambda > 1$ is just to allow for a sufficient proportion of the code sheets to be randomly audited and then discarded.

The Clerks are now responsible for putting the resulting batch of encrypted terms through a suitable number of re-encryption mixes. After this, the shuffled, re-encrypted terms are assembled into a table with $\lambda \cdot v$ rows and $c+1$ columns. Each row will now constitute the codes and ack for a code sheet, the last column being the encryption of the Ack Code. We will refer to this as the P table, in analogy with the similar construct in Scantegrity II.

---

[1] Obviously the codes must be long enough to allow $\lambda v(c+1)$ distinct values. The code length represents a tradeoff between usability and security, because short codes are easier for voters to type but also easier for attackers to guess. See Section 8 for a discussion of security threats related to guessing codes.

Note that all of these steps can be performed in the open on the Bulletin Board. The multiple secret shuffles ensure that nobody knows how the codes are grouped into code sheets. Note also that we need to ensure that each code sheet has distinct vote codes. This can be achieved by ensuring that the initial batch of codes are pairwise distinct. This may mean that the length of the codes needs to be increased, or if longer codes are regarded as undesirable, we could use several batches.

Notice that this construction ensures that all the terms have plaintext of the required form while at the same time ensuring that no single entity knows which codes are associated with which candidates or which codes appear on the same code sheet. This style of construction appears to be quite generic where it is required to generate a large number of encrypted terms all having plaintext of some constrained form. It will not be suitable for all contexts of course, for example, where the set of plaintexts generated at the outset from a strict subset all the possible valid plaintexts then the construction could reveal critical information. In the present case, this does not seem to be an issue.

Thus, each row of the table will correspond to a code sheet and has the from:

$$i, \{VC_{i,1}\}_{PK_T}, \{VC_{i,2}\}_{PK_T}, \ldots, \{VC_{i,c+1}\}_{PK_T}$$

Where $VC_{i,c+1}$ will serve as the Ack Code for the ith code sheet.

The entries in this table need to be decrypted and printed to the code sheets and distributed to the voters prior the start of the election. The decryption is performed by the Registrar by invoking the assistance of a threshold set of Trustees. The set of Trustees used here can be varied throughout the process, in particular, the Trustee who performs the final decryption step should be varied throughout in order to ensure that no single Trustee knows all the codes. Better yet, if we are using El Gamal, then each of a threshold number of Trustees can do a part of the decryption using their share, and the pieces can be assembled by the Registrar [CGS97]. That way, only the Registrar learns the decrypted values.

After decryption and (successful) auditing, the code sheets are distributed to the voters by the Returning Officer via the most secure feasible channel. (See the discussion in Section 2.1). It is assumed that exactly one code sheet is delivered to each eligible voter. We assume that the Returning Officer keeps no record of which sheets are distributed to which voters. We could for example require that the Registrar prints the code sheets in some secure fashion in privacy protected envelopes (using pressure printing?) or scratch strips. Another possibility is to distribute the job among several printers using the techniques of [ECHA09], which uses invisible ink to allow the printing of a secret without any single printer learning what has been printed. The batch would then be (physically) shuffled before being passed to the Returning Officer. (The ideal would be to use the printing process itself to combine the Trustees' shares so that nobody, including the Registrar, learnt any Vote Codes, but it is not clear how to do this.)

5.4   Setting Up the Bulletin Board

We now need to transform the P table into a form that can used in the tallying process. For this we need to permute the encrypted vote codes terms within each row and store the information defining the permutation in encrypted form (in a so-called *onion*) added to each row. The ack codes are left untouched. Furthermore, we want to do this in a distributed fashion such that no single entity knows the permutations. We adapt some techniques from the Prêt à Voter design suite and have a number of options that we outline below.

One option is to use a decryption mix based approach along the lines presented in Prêt à Voter 2005, [RS06b]. This has the advantage that we can straightforwardly deal with full permutations of the candidates but is less flexible and robust than the re-encryption based techniques outlined later. For decryption mixes, we define a *seed* space Ψ, say 64 bit strings, and an unbiased function Γ from Ψ to the set of permutations on the candidate set. Now, for the ith row of the P table, the first clerk chooses a seed $\rho_{i,1} \in \Psi$ at random and computes $\pi_{i,1} := \Gamma(\rho_i)$. The sequence of encrypted vote codes are re-encrypted and permuted according to $\pi_{i,1}$ and an initial onion is computed as $\{\rho_{i,1}\}_{PK_T}$. This is done independently for each row of the P table and results in a P_1 table which is posted to the Bulletin Board. This table has rows of the form:

$$i, \{VC_{i,\pi_{i,1}(1)}\}'_{PK_T}, \ldots, \{VC_{i,\pi_{i,1}(c)}\}'_{PK_T}, \{VC_{i,c+1}\}_{PK_T}, \Theta_{i,1},$$

where the prime denotes re-encryption and:

$$\Theta_{i,1} := \{\rho_{i,1}\}_{PK_T}$$

The second Clerk now repeats this process on the P_1, *i.e.* for each row generates a fresh seed, computes the permutation from this seed, re-encrypts the vote code terms and shuffles them according to the permutation. The new seed is added as a further layer to the onion. Thus the ith row of the resulting P_2 table has the form:

$$i, \{VC_{i,\pi_{i,2}\circ\pi_{i,1}(1)}\}_{PK_T}, \ldots, \{VC_{i,\pi_{i,2}\circ\pi_{i,1}(c)}\}_{PK_T}, \{VC_{i,c+1}\}_{PK_T}, \Theta_{i,2},$$

where

$$\Theta_{i,2} := \{\rho_{i,2}, \Theta_{i,1}\}_{PK_T}$$

And so on for as many Clerks as are deemed appropriate. Tabulation will proceed as in [CRS05]. We omit the details here.

Alternatively, if we use a randomizing encryption such as ElGamal or Pallier we can use re-encryption mixes to construct the Q table and to perform the tabulation. This is more flexible and robust but makes it harder to handle full permutations. A simple approach is to use just cyclic shifts of the vote codes, in the manner of [RS06a] [Rya08]. Thus each Clerk takes the table output by the previous clerk and, for each row, generates a fresh seed $\phi \in Z_n$, re-encrypts the vote code terms and cyclically shifts them $\phi \pmod{n}$ to the left. The new seed is folded into the onion exploiting the homomorphism of the encryption, which should be additive as in exponential ElGamal or Paillier. Thus, a row of the form:

$$i, \{VC_{i,j}\}_{PK_T}, \ldots, \{VC_{i,j}\}_{PK_T}, \{VC_{i,c+1}\}_{PK_T}, \Theta_{i,l},$$

is transformed to:

$$i, \{VC_{i,j+\phi \ (mod \ n)}\}'_{PK_T}, \ldots, \{VC_{i,j+\phi \ (mod \ n)}\}'_{PK_T}, \{VC_{i,c+1}\}_{PK_T}, \Theta_{i,2},$$

Where:

$$\Theta_{i,2} := \Theta_{i,1} \oplus \{\phi\}_{PK_T}$$

where $\oplus$ is the homomorphic operation on ciphertexts that adds the underlying plaintexts. The output of each step of the mix is posted to a Bulletin Board for subsequent audit.

Thus, the Θ_is are the usual Prêt à Voter style onions that encode the permutation π_i of the vote codes within the ith row of the Q table with respect to the P table. For c candidates the first c cells contain a vote code encrypted under the (ElGamal or Paillier) Trustees' public key PK_T, permuted within the row according to π_i. The encrypted ack codes remain in their previous position in the $c + 1$ column, followed by the Θ term.

Note that it is straightforward to introduce an extra onion that carries the definition of a full permutation in order to allow full permutation of the codes, in the manner of [Rya08]. In [Rya08], this resulted in the threat of "Italian" style attacks, in which an attacker could violate privacy by requiring the voter to record the candidate permutation and reveal it before the tabulation phase, so effectively identifying the ballot [RT09]. In our context however, given that the voter never sees these permutations, such attacks do not apply and hence it appears that this technique could be safely used.

5.5   Voting

In order to vote the voter logs in to the Voting Server, perhaps using some form of authentication. To cast a vote she simply enters the serial number of her code sheet and the vote code matching her candidate of choice. The information transmitted to the server consists of $i, VC_{i,j}$. The server knows no vote codes but might have a list of valid serial numbers. Votes with invalid serial numbers it will reject. For messages with valid serial numbers it computes $\{VC_{i,j}\}_{PK_T}$ and posts this to the i-th row of the Bulletin Board along with a zero knowledge proof (ZKP) of knowledge of the plaintext, [CP93] [JJ00]. The proof is in order to avoid the server simply taking one of the encrypted codes and re-encrypting it before posting.

Next the Trustees perform a check of this proof of knowledge of the plaintext, and, if valid, they perform a *Plaintext-Equivalence-Tests* (PET), of the $\{VC_{i,j}\}_{PK_T}$ term posted by the server against the entries in row i. (See [JJ00] and [TH08] for descriptions of PET tests on El Gamal and Paillier ciphertexts, respectively.) In essence, in order to find the required match within the permuted

Table 1. Protocol sequence

1. Voting Authority $\rightarrow$ Bulletin Board $\lambda v(c+1)$ encrypted codes
2. Clerks $\rightarrow$ Bulletin Board   shuffling of codes to produce
                                              the P table.
3. Trustees $\rightarrow$ Registrar   decrypted codes
4. Registrar $\rightarrow$ Returning officer printed code sheets
5. Returning Officer $\Rightarrow Voter_i$: i, $VC_{i,j}$ for $j = 1 \ldots c$, and Ack_i
7. $Voter_i$ $\rightarrow$ Voting Server: i, $VC_{i,j}$ for chosen candidate
8. Voting Server $\rightarrow$ $BulletinBoard$: i, $\{VC_{i,j}\}_{PK_T}$, proof
                                              of plaintext knowledge
9. $Trustees$ $\rightarrow$ $BulletinBoard$: flag Cell (i,j), jointly decrypt Ack_i
10. Voting Server $\rightarrow$ $Voter_i$: Ack_i

encryptions the following test is performed: Two encryptions (α, β) and (α', β') are equivalent (encrypt the same plaintext) if the decryption of $(\alpha/\alpha', \beta/\beta')^r$ outputs 1. r is a randomising factor that all the Trustees contribute to that serves to disguise the ratio of the underlying plaintexts, in the event that they are not equal. Where the Trustees find a match the relevant cell is thus flagged and they collectively decrypt the final Ack Code term. The Voting Server can now return the Ack code to the voter who can now check it against the value on their code sheet. The voter can of course later visit the Bulletin Board to confirm that their vote has been logged in the appropriate row. They cannot verify directly that their choice of candidate was correctly recorded due to the secret permutation of the positions of the codes posted on the Bulletin Board.

Note that the Server's proof of knowledge of the plaintext and the Trustees' proofs of plaintext equivalence are all posted alongside the appropriate row on the Bulletin Board. The Server's proof of plaintext knowledge counters ballot stuffing attacks in which a corrupt Voting Server simply posts a re-encryption of a randomly selected Vote Code from the appropriate row. (Though obviously it does not prevent a Voting Server who somehow learns valid Vote Codes from submitting them—see Section 8 for further discussion of this.) The Trustees' proofs of plaintext equivalence prove that the vote is being counted as it was cast, because it is being matched to the correct index on the ballot.

The full protocol sequence can be seen in Table 1.

The first five steps constitute the setup phase. In step five the Returning Officer distributes a code sheet to each voter via a supposedly secure channel such as conventional mail, denoted by $\Rightarrow$. Note that the only steps that involve the voter, aside from receiving the code sheet in step 5, are 7 and 10, and those both occur in the same session.

5.6 Tabulation

On the Bulletin Board, each row corresponding to a successfully cast ballot, there will be a flagged cell along with zero knowledge proofs and Plaintext Equivalence

Tests. The index of the column in which this cell has been flagged is noted. Thus, for each row that corresponds to a successfully cast ballot, an onion and and an index value are extracted giving the usual Prêt à Voter style (index, onion) pair. The onion defines the ordered list of candidates from which the index was selected. These pairs can be tabulated with mixnets in the usual fashion. For full details we refer the reader to [CRS05] [RS06a] [Rya08].

For completeness we outline the tabulation process for the cyclic shifts construction. Suppose that the cumulative cyclic shift applied to the ith row is s steps to the left. Suppose that the h cell is flagged. This means that the voter actually selected the $(s+h)$-th candidate in the base ordering. Thus, we transform the pair:

$$(h, \{s\}_{PK_T})$$

into:

$$\{h\}_{PK_T} \oplus \{s\}_{PK_T} = \{s+h\}_{PK_T}$$

The resulting cyphertext can now be put through a standard, robust, re-encryption mix and will decrypt to $h + s$, which taken $mod\ c$ gives the voter's original choice.

6 Auditing

In this section we outline the auditing procedures that serve to detect any malfunction or corruption during the setup and tabulation phases that could lead to an incorrect outcome.

6.1 Auditing the Election Setup

It is essential that the code sheets distributed to voters are consistent with the information posted to Q table on the Bulletin Board. More precisely, we need to check that the set of codes shown on any code sheet agrees with the codes buried in the encrypted terms on the corresponding row of the Q table posted to the Bulletin Board. Furthermore, the permutation of the codes on the Bulletin Board with respect to those on the code sheet should match the permutation encoded in the onion posted to that row. To address this we perform random checks on a suitable proportion of the code sheets. Prior to the election Auditors pick a random set of code sheets. For selected code sheets, a threshold set of Trustees are invoked to decrypt the vote code terms and the onion. The Trustees are required to provide proofs of these decryptions. With this information, the consistency of the selected code sheets and corresponding rows of the Q table can be verified.

If we randomly audit say half the code sheets and all of these pass the checks, then we can be confident that the remaining code sheets will also be consistent, assuming that there is no way to predict the audit selections. We must ensure that all audited code sheets be removed from the election. It must not be possible to cast a vote using an audited code sheet.

There are the usual chain of custody issues: we need to ensure that false code sheets cannot be substituted after auditing. Careful procedures can make this difficult. Also, we can randomly audit forms just prior to their being mailed out.

An alternative way to check consistency for a randomly selected set of code sheets is to require the Trustees to transform the code vote terms in each row according to the permutation in the onion on the Bulletin Board in a verifiable fashion and then decrypt the terms. These should agree with the sequence of vote codes on the code sheet.

6.2   Auditing the Tabulation

All the Zero Knowledge proofs posted to the Bulletin Board during the registering of votes should be publicly audited. This serves to counter attempts to corrupt votes by shifting the flagged terms. It also serves to counter ballot stuffing, *i.e.* simply flagging terms in rows corresponding to code sheets that were never used to cast a vote. An adversary attempting such ballot stuffing would have to construct corresponding zero knowledge proofs which could only be done with collusion with a threshold set of Trustees.

To detect any inaccuracy caused by the Talliers we employ standard mechanisms for auditing mixes and decryptions. The batch of index, onion pairs are put through anonymising mixes and then decrypted. All intermediate steps are posted to the Bulletin Board allowing verification, either via Random Partial Checking, [JJR02], or other techniques such as Neff's verifiable shuffles, [Nef01].

7   Error Recovery

7.1   Incorrect Ack Codes

So far we have described the unfolding of the protocol and outlined techniques to detect errors or corruption. Clearly we need to set up procedures for the case in which all does not go according to plan. In particular, we need to consider the situation in which the Ack_i returned by the server does not match with the ack code that appears on the voter's code sheet.

Certainly a number of voters who claim faulty ack codes raises doubts about the Vote Server. If the voting system relies on the availability of several servers (in fact, each Trustee could offer a voting service allowing the voters to choose) the discredited server is either defective or malicious and should be taken out of service. Additional information regarding recovery mechanisms for Prêt à Voter can be found in [BLRS06].

7.2   Multiple Voting

We need to clarify what happens when the Vote Server receives a second submission that purports to be from the same voter as one already received. One reasonable approach would be to run the PET tests privately (*i.e.* without posting them on the bulletin board) and tabulate only those submitted codes that matched a correct one, then count only one. Nevertheless, multiple valid Vote Code submissions for the same ID will still occur. This indicates malicious behaviour by someone who knows the codes, either an adversary to whom the information was leaked, or a voter trying to discredit the process. Perhaps the most reasonable approach is to publish on the Bulletin Board the first two valid submissions from each ID, but to include only the first one in the count. The Vote Server would be supposed to return the ack only to the first submitter. This does give an adversary a way of nullifying a person's vote, but only if she learns the Vote Codes beforehand, and it is detectable by the voter if either he looks at the Bulletin Board or he notices the absence of the return ack (which he might not if the adversary successfully sends it to him). It is unclear how to make this interact seamlessly with revoting techniques such as tokens.

8   A Threat Model

For the threat model we concentrate on malicious behaviour of the participating parties rather than outsiders, and on dangers that are distinct from other schemes. Principle dangers considered are undetected compromise of election integrity, compromise of ballot secrecy and denial of voting service.

8.1   Leaking of Codes

It appears that the most serious threat to the scheme is the possibility of information about vote codes leaking to the Vote Server. If the Vote Server gets to know alternative codes for a particular code sheet it can post an encryption of a code of its choice rather than the voter's choice to the Bulletin Board. The most likely scenario for such leakage is a malicious Registrar leaking codes to the Vote Server.

A number of counter-measures are possible, some of which we discuss in greater detail in section 9. One possibility is ensure that the Registrar does not know the association of the serial number with the set of codes. We might print a set of code sheets bearing only the candidate names and serial numbers and cover these with a scratch strip. Overprinted on the scratch strip would be another serial number that is related to the "real" serial number by a secret look-up table. Now, to print the codes, the Registrar would provide the overprinted code to a Custodian who would have access to the look-up table. The Custodian passes the "true" serial number to a threshold set of the Trustees who decrypt the codes on the appropriate row of the the P table and pass these back to the Registrar. Note that we can vary the set of Trustees used for each code and so ensure that no Trustee knows more than one code associated with a given serial number. To cast her vote, the voter needs to scratch of the strip and reveal the "true" serial number.

8.2   Vote Server

The Vote Server acting alone might try to cheat by trying to guess alternative, valid vote codes for a given vote represented by the identification value i.

If successful, this might threaten the integrity of the vote. The code length can be adjusted to make this is rather difficult and alerts can be raised if a Vote Server repeatedly posts invalid codes. This has to be balanced against the discrediting attacks that voters might try to launch, see below.

8.3   Trustees - Vote Server

A colluding threshold set of Trustees can undermine the accuracy by, for example, decrypting alternative codes and then constructing the zero knowledge proofs for this alternative code rather than a code submitted by the voter, then returning the correct ack code to the server. As long the Trustees are drawn from a pool of mutual distrustful entities, we can ensure that such a collusion is unlikely.

Furthermore, we can raise the collusion threshold: we arrange for the set of trustees used for tabulation is disjoint from the trustees used to register vote codes, and these have different public keys. Now the onions are encrypted under the public key of the tabulation trustees. This means that the registration trustees alone will not know the meaning of any particular code. Thus, even if the are in collusion, the best they can do is launch a randomizing attack. For pure cyclic shifts of the codes such an attack could be quite effective, as observed in [RT09]: ballots could be shifted from a popular candidate to a chosen candidate by an appropriate shift of the index value. In this case, using an additional onion to carry a full permutation, or the affine permutation techniques of [RT09] will counter this.

8.4   Voters Undermining the Credibility of the Vote Server

A rather different style of threat is that of a group of voters attempting to undermine the credibility of the system by deliberately submitting fake codes. This would result in the Vote Server posting incorrect codes and so being suspected of attempting to guess alternative codes. Clearly, since the security of our scheme rests on the Vote Server not knowing the contents of code sheets we cannot simply counter this be enabling the Vote Server to recognise codes that are not valid for any given code sheet. A possible counter-measure is to arrange for the entire space of codes to be rather sparse and give the Vote Server knowledge of the full set, but not of course any knowledge of how they are grouped into code sheets. This will allow the Vote Server to recognise attempts to submit fake codes. It does mean that the initial construction of the batch of codes and the P table cannot be done completely publicly on the Bulletin Board. This does not seem to matter however as the Q table will in any case be audited later. Alternatively, we publicly encrypt all possible codes of the appropriate format, shuffle them and then discard at random a suitable proportion.

8.5   Summary

We have discussed a number of threats against the scheme, the most serious of which is the leakage of information about the codes. This threatens not only the privacy but also the integrity of the election. The fact that the integrity guarantees depend on secrecy guarantees does mean that the level of assurance provided by such a scheme is significantly less than that provided by other verifiable schemes.

Balanced against this is the fact that vote casting and verification is significantly more convenient, both steps occurring during a single voting session. In effect the scheme is *vote, verify and go.*

9   Further Enhancements

The proposed mechanism for releasing the ack codes only if a threshold set of Trustees register a valid vote code gives a good level of assurance that, if the voter gets the correct ack code back then their vote will be correctly registered. Further mechanisms then ensure that correctly registered codes will be correctly decrypted and tabulated. Nonetheless the threat model has shown some weak points that require further discussion. In this section we discuss some possible enhancements that help counter this threat.

9.1   Encrypting Messages to the Vote Server

At the cost of requiring encryption at the client side, we can defend against a malicious Vote Server who learns the Vote Codes, preventing it from undetectably substituting codes other than those sent by voters. As before, voters cast a ballot by sending a Vote Code as well as a Ballot ID to the Vote Server, but now *both are encrypted under the Trustee key.* The server passes $\{i\}_{PK_T}$ and $\{VC_{i,j}\}_{PK_T}$ to the Trustees. After a threshold decryption of $\{i\}_{PK_T}$ the Trustees again use a *PET* to find the valid match for the received $\{VC_{i,j}\}_{PK_T}$ in row i of the Bulletin Board. Now, even if the Vote Server has somehow learnt which Vote Codes correspond to which IDs, it cannot identify which values to substitute in which messages.

We have to assume here that the malicious Vote Server can't link a voter's message to its ballot ID via some other channel, such as IP address. Otherwise it is straightforward to substitute any other valid Vote Code that the Vote Server knows for that ID.

9.2   Adding Salts to Codes

Another possible mechanism to counter the fact that the Registrar is a single point of failure for the secrecy of the codes is to use code sheets that require the voter to execute an easy arithmetic operation in order to get a hold of the true vote code. This would work best if the encryption scheme provided a corresponding homomorphic operation. For example, we could ask voters to add the salt to their Vote Code, then the trustees could add the encrypted salt to the encrypted Vote Codes on the bulletin board with an additive-homomorphic encryption scheme. It might be effective, yet simple enough, to let the voter calculate the sum of a received code and a digit of the birthdate, e.g. a two digit representation of the month. The voter could use their computer to check (or do) the addition for them (and the extent to which this constitutes "trusting the computer" would then depend on the voter). The salt is supposed to be somewhat-private data about the voter. The idea is to increase the difficulty for an attacker who learns a voter's Vote Codes. Such an attacker will now have to guess the salt in order to launch an attack. We add another authority, the Salt Authority, who knows some somewhat-private data about everyone on the electoral roll. For example, this could be whichever authority is trusted to maintain the electoral roll, and they could use birthdates or house numbers as the salt.

In this section we assume that it is *not* a secret which IDs went to which voters.

The Salt Authority learns from the Registration Authority which IDs were sent to which voters. It then posts to the bulletin board an encrypted salt $\{S_i\}_{PK_T}$ for each i. At voting time, the voter adds their chosen Vote Code to their salt (which they are supposed to know in advance) and sends the sum to the Voting Server. The trustees use the homomorphism to add $\{S_i\}_{PK_T}$ to the codes in row i before performing the PET.

We could even have several different Salt Authorities and allow voters to choose which salts they would like to add.

This scheme does not protect against a malicious Vote Server, or even an adversary who can intercept communications to the Vote Server, if that party knows the codes—such an adversary can perform a substitution attack very similar to the one described in Section 9.1. It does, however, make it harder for a third party who learns the codes to simply submit them to the Vote Server. For example, just stealing someone's code sheet from their mailbox does not allow an attacker to steal their vote.

9.3   Distinct Acknowledgement Codes Revisited

A further possibility is to re-introduce the the idea of distinct ack codes for each candidate, except that now we generate and distribute these codes independently from the vote codes. A simple way to achieve this is to construct a P table much as before except that now each entry is a pair of encryptions of codes: one vote code one ack code. Note that the table does not now need a $(c+1)$th column for the ack codes. We transform this into a Q table as before: for each row permuting the cells of the P table and storing the permutation in an onion, but keeping the vote/ack codes paired.

Now we have a Vote Code Registrar and an Ack Code Registrar. The former will decrypt the vote codes (with the cooperation of a threshold set of tellers) and print the vote code sheets. The latter similarly will decode the ack codes and print the ack code sheets. Matching vote and ack code sheets are mailed to each voter. This does mean that a record needs to be kept of which sheets go to which voter. Here again, we could use the idea of a pseudo-serial number overprinted on a scratch strip to counter threats to ballot privacy that might arise as a result of recording this information.

Now, when a vote is registered, *i.e.* the PET performed by the Trustees finds a match, the cell of the Q table is flagged as before. The Trustees decrypt the Ack code and pass this in secret to the Voter Server, who can then relay it to the Voter. The ack code is not posted to the Bulletin Board as this would violate receipt freeness.

This idea would work best if the vote codes and ack codes could be distributed independently, in such a way that no single entity knew both of them.

10   Conclusions

We have presented a simple enhancement to code voting that adds a degree of end-to-end verification with the voter needing only to confirm that the ack code returned by the Voting Server agrees with that on their code sheet. The scheme is receipt-free, in the sense that the voter cannot prove to a coercer how they voted. As it stands it is not resistant to direct coercion, where the coercer is present at or before the time of casting. To counter such direct coercion would require additional mechanisms such as the mentioned *re-voting* or the use of a form of *voting token*.

Arguably, the verification performed by the voters is simpler and more direct than with previous voter-verifiable schemes: all the voter needs to do is check that the ack code returned to them agrees with that shown on their code sheet.

The scheme sacrifices a little in terms of verifiability but gains significantly in terms of usability. Most other cryptographic schemes provide a stricter form of verifiability in that any corruption in the processing of votes will be detectable with an appropriate probability. Typically the probability of detection will grow, ideally exponentially, with the scale of the corruption. In PGD, leakage of information about vote codes could undermine the integrity in a way that would be undetectable. We have proposed a number of counter-measures to make such leakage unlikely, but the guarantees of integrity are still dependant on certain trust assumptions. The question then is whether the trade-off of the high degree of convenience of the scheme, the voter casts and verifies in a single session, against the sacrifice of unconditional guarantees of integrity is valid and in what contexts. We suggest that for certain types of elections, for example of officers of a professional organisation, that the trade-off would be valid. We would not propose the use of PGD for binding, political elections.

PGD requires a threshold number of Trustees to be online during the voting period to decrypt and return the ack codes. Although this does affect the system's reliability, it doesn't affect its integrity. Votes could still be posted on the Bulletin Board if fewer than the threshold were available, they just couldn't be decrypted or acknowledged until the necessary number of Trustees returned.

A topic for future research is how to distribute code sheet information on-line (or possibly in print, extending the techniques of [ECHA09]) so that only a large scale collusion could violate Vote Code secrecy. The goal is to ensure that the decrypted codes are only ever revealed to the intended voter. A further topic that requires further investigation is how to recover from erroneous or malicious behaviour by components of the system, including voters.

References

[Adi06]   Adida, B.: Advances in Cryptographic Voting Systems. PhD thesis. MIT Cambridge (July 2006)

[Adi08]   Adida, B.: Helios: Web-based Open-Audit Voting (2008)

[AdMPQ09]   Adida, B., de Marneffe, O., Pereira, O., Quisquater, J.J.: Electing a university president using open audit voting: Analysis of real world use of Helios. In: EVT 2009: Proceedings of the Electronic Voting Technology Workshop (2009)

[Ben06]   Benaloh, J.: Simple verifiable elections. In: Proc. 1st USENIX Accurate Electronic Voting Technology Workshop (2006)

[BLRS06]   Bryans, J.W., Littlewood, B., Ryan, P.Y.A., Strigini, L.: E-voting: Dependability Requirements and Design for Dependability. In: Proceedings of the First International Conference on Availability, Reliability and Security, ARES 2006 (2006)

[CCC+08]   Chaum, D., Carback, R., Clark, J., Essex, A., Popoveniuc, S., Rivest, R.L., Ryan, P.Y.A., Shen, E., Sherman, A.T.: Scantegrity II: end-to-end verifiability for optical scan election systems using invisible ink confirmation codes. In: EVT 2008: Proceedings of the Electronic Voting Technology Workshop, pp. 1–13. USENIX Association, Berkeley (2008)

[CCM07]   Clarkson, M., Chong, S., Myers, A.C.: Civitas: A secure remote voting system. Technical report, Cornell University Computing and Information Science Technology Report (May 2007)

[CGJ+99]   Canetti, R., Gennaro, R., Jarecki, S., Krawczyk, H., Rabin, T.: Adaptive Security for Threshold Cryptosystems. In: Wiener, M. (ed.) CRYPTO 1999. LNCS, vol. 1666, pp. 98–116. Springer, Heidelberg (1999)

[CGS97]   Cramer, R., Gennaro, R., Schoenmakers, B.: A Secure and Optimally Efficient Multi-authority Election Scheme. In: Fumy, W. (ed.) EUROCRYPT 1997. LNCS, vol. 1233, pp. 103–118. Springer, Heidelberg (1997)

[Cha01]   Chaum, D.: SureVote: Technical Overview. In: Proceedings of the Workshop on Trustworthy Elections, WOTE 2001 (2001)

[CP93]   Chaum, D., Pedersen, T.P.: Wallet Databases with Observers. In: Brickell, E.F. (ed.) CRYPTO 1992. LNCS, vol. 740, pp. 89–105. Springer, Heidelberg (1993)

[CRS05]   Chaum, D., Ryan, P.Y.A., Schneider, S.: A Practical Voter-Verifiable Election Scheme. In: De Capitani di Vimercati, S., Syverson, P.F., Gollmann, D. (eds.) ESORICS 2005. LNCS, vol. 3679, pp. 118–139. Springer, Heidelberg (2005)

[ECHA09]   Essex, A., Clark, J., Hengartner, U., Adams, C.: How to print a secret. In: Proc. 4th USENIX Workshop on Hot Topics in Security, HotSec 2009 (2009)

[HSS08]   Helbach, J., Schwenk, J., Schräge, S.: Code Voting with Linkable Group Signatures. In: Proceedings of Electronic Voting 2008 (2008)

[JCJ05]   Juels, A., Catalano, D., Jakobsson, M.: Coercion-resistant Electronic Elections. In: Proceedings of the 2005 ACM Workshop on Privacy in the Electronic Society, pp. 61–70 (November 2005)

[JJ00]   Jakobsson, M., Juels, A.: Mix and Match: Secure Function Evaluation via Ciphertexts (2000)

[JJR02]   Jakobsson, M., Juels, A., Rivest, R.: Making Mix Nets Robust for Electronic Voting by Randomized Partial Checking. In: USENIX Security Symposium, pp. 339–353 (2002)

[Kri07]   Krivoruchko, T.: Robust coercion-resistant registration for remote e-voting. In: Proc. IAVoSS Workshop on Trustworthy Elections, WOTE (2007)

[Nef01]   Neff, A.: A verifiable secret shuffle and its application to e-voting. In: Conference on Computer and Communications Security, pp. 116–125. ACM (2001)

[OSH08]   Oppliger, R., Schwenk, J., Helbach, J.: Protecting Code Voting Against Vote Selling. Lecture Notes in Informatics - Sicherheit, Schutz und Zuverlässigkeit (Sicherheit 2008) (2008)

[Pet05]   Peters, R.A.: A Secure Bulletin Booard. Master's thesis, Technische Universiteit Eindhoven (2005)

[RS06a]   Ryan, P.Y.A., Schneider, S.A.: Prêt à Voter with Re-encryption Mixes. In: Gollmann, D., Meier, J., Sabelfeld, A. (eds.) ESORICS 2006. LNCS, vol. 4189, pp. 313–326. Springer, Heidelberg (2006)

[RS06b]   Ryan, P.Y.A., Schneider, S.A.: Prêt à voter with re-encryption mixes. Technical Report CS-TR-956, University of Newcastle upon Tyne (2006)

[RT09]   Ryan, P.Y.A., Teague, V.: Ballot permutations in Prêt à Voter. In: USENIX/ACCURATE Workshop on Trustworthy Elections (2009), www.usenix.org/event/evtwote09/tech/full_papers/ryan.pdf

[Rya07]   Ryan, P.Y.A.: The computer ate my vote. Technical Report CS-TR-988, University of Newcastle upon Tyne (2007)

[Rya08]   Ryan, P.Y.A.: Prêt à Voter with Paillier encryption. Mathematical and Computer Modelling 48(9-10), 1646–1662 (2008)

[TH08]   Ting, P.-Y., Huang, X.-W.: Distributed Paillier plaintext equivalence test. International Journal of Network Security 6(3), 258–264 (2008), http://ijns.femto.com.tw/contents/ijns-v6-n3/ijns-v6-n3.html

[VG06]   Volkamer, M., Grimm, R.: Multiple Casts in Online Voting: Analyzing Chances. In: Proceedings of Electronic Voting 2006 (2006)

Pretty Good Democracy
(Transcript of Discussion)

Peter Y.A. Ryan

University of Luxembourg

Thanks for showing up first thing on the second day. This talk was going to be entitled Pretty Good Democracy, but out of courtesy to Phil Zimmerman I thought I should email him and ask him if he was happy with me using this title; and initially he seemed to be quite positive about it, but he's handed the rights of the name over to a company and they're not happy about me using the brand name, so strictly speaking the scheme won't henceforth be called Pretty Good Democracy, but for the purpose of the talk I'll refer to it as PGD.

So I'll talk a little bit about the challenge, but I don't think I need to stress that particularly as Matt[1] gave a nice talk about the challenges faced in trying to get secure voting to work properly. Then I'll talk very briefly about the key ideas of this PGD scheme. I should say immediately that I've been working on voting systems for a while, and particularly the Prêt à Voter system.

Prêt à Voter is a supervised polling station type scheme, PGD is a venture into the realm of Internet remote voting, a rather tentative and nervous venture into that area, but we'll come back to that later. I'll give you an outline of the scheme, then I'll talk about some of the threats that we're already aware of, and some of the ideas to try and counter those threats and improve the scheme. I should stress this is very much work in progress, and that it's joint work with Vanessa Teague in Melbourne.

The technical requirements for a voting scheme are that first and foremost we want it to be accurate, the outcome to be guaranteed, and not only accurate but seen to be accurate, and this is often usefully broken down into three phases: the requirement that votes are cast as intended by legitimate voters, are recorded as cast, and then counted as recorded. And of course we also want to ensure ballot secrecy at the same time, and this is what makes the whole problem so intriguing, that we've got these conflicting requirements of auditability and transparency on the one hand, and the secrecy and confidentiality on the other. A lot of these schemes provide notions of voter verifiability, and our scheme for example, does. This provides a kind of voter verifiability, but is subtly different because actually the voter doesn't get a receipt as such.

And of course throughout this we would like to try and reduce the assumptions we need to make (about the technology, the officials, and so on and so forth), to an absolute minimum, and there are discussions about whether it's possible to drive that down to zero, but we do our best to minimise it.

Another requirement that's important, is that, if we're talking about a general voting system, it really has to be extremely easy to use, hopefully just a

---

[1] Blaze, these proceedings

B. Christianson et al. (Eds.): Security Protocols 2009, LNCS 7028, pp. 131–142, 2013.

very simple linear sequence for the voters, and also easy for the voting officials to understand, and to understand recovery mechanisms, and so on and so forth. Because there are a lot of schemes out there which are very ingenious and involve rather fancy challenge response, cut and choose protocols run between the voter and the device, and these are technically beautiful things and give very high degrees of assurance, but in fact thereby become very vulnerable to social engineering attacks similar to the one that Matt mentioned yesterday where in effect the system deceives the voter as to what the proper sequence of the protocol is.

PGD is an enhancement of code voting, which is a very simple idea, and again I think it's due to David Chaum[2] originally, so it stems if you like from the observation that Internet voting and voter client devices are fundamentally insecure. So the idea is that you distribute by some supposedly secure channel like Snailmail, you distribute so-called code sheets to the voters, an individual code sheet to each voter, and the idea is very simple, in effect they are individual sort of code books for the voter to communicate with the voting system. There are random codes against each candidate, and of course they're distinct for each code sheet.

A typical code sheet then might have the list of candidates, a separate random vote code against each, and an acknowledgement code, a separate one against each, and typically a unique serial number for each code sheet. So the voting process is now very simple, the voter logs on to a vote server, possibly with some additional form of authentication, but maybe not, and simply provides the serial number of the code sheet, and then the code for their candidate of choice. And the vote server is supposed to respond with the correct ack code, it has a database, all the appropriate information, it sends that back, and so the ack code has a sort of dual role, first of all of reassuring the voter that the correct vote code reached the server, and also some degree of authentication I guess of the vote server that they're actually talking to the right device, and not some fake device.

So that's quite nice, you can see how it sidesteps a lot of the vulnerabilities of the Internet, leaving aside denial-of-service attacks. But of course crucially it doesn't provide any end-to-end verifiability. Again, this is a term some of you have come across, a lot of these schemes try to provide the so-called end-to-end verifiability, which is a guarantee that the vote gets traced all the way from being cast to ending up in the final tabulation. You can see from this there's no guarantee of what happens to the vote. There's a degree of guarantee that it's reached the voter server correctly, but after that, whether it actually fetches up in the final count, there's nothing here to guarantee that. So what PGD is attempting to do is enhance this a little bit and strengthen the end-to-end verifiability.

Let's plunge straight into two very simple ideas to enhance this. The first idea is that rather than just having the vote server having access to this database and all the ack codes in a straightforward way, we actually set it up in such a way that the knowledge of the ack codes is shared amongst a set of trustees in some sort of

---

[2] http://www.surevote.com/

threshold fashion, which I'll describe in more detail shortly. The effect of that is that the vote server can't simply return an ack code when it gets a voting code, it has to consult a threshold set of trustees to acquire knowledge of the ack code and thereby return it to the voter. And the idea is that in the process of having to consult the trustees, the trustees all cooperate in registering the vote code.

And the other trick is to actually do away with the separate ack codes against each candidate, we actually just use a single ack code per code sheet. Hopefully why we do that will become clearer in a moment. The point of that is to try and make the thing more receipt free than it would be otherwise.

If the voter gets the correct ack code back, that should provide them a greater degree of guarantee that their vote code will be accurately recorded on a web bulletin board. Again we have this notion of a secure web bulletin board which underlies a lot of these systems, which I don't really have time to go into, but hopefully you've come across before.

Frank Stajano: If the paper contains a series of numbers and some entity has printed it, how do we know that this entity doesn't know how I voted?

Reply: Well I come onto the issue of how these codes might get leaked, which is one of the threats to the scheme.

So if the voter gets the correct ack code back that should give them a fairly strong guarantee — I'll describe how strong a guarantee later — that their vote code has been correctly registered on the web bulletin board, and then basically we can sort of fit a Prêt à Voter backend to the tabulation, which I won't go into the details of, but hopefully you can see roughly, particularly if you're familiar with Prêt à Voter, you can see how the tabulation goes ahead in a verifiable fashion in the backend.

Our code sheets will look slightly different, we don't now have the ack code column, just a single ack code per code sheet, otherwise it looks rather similar.

Frank Stajano: So how does the voter know that the voting server had the code of the correct candidate? The acknowledgement code does not depend on for that.

Reply: No, it's independent of which candidate, but hopefully it will become clear as I get into some of the cryptographic details, why there is a certain guarantee of the correct code.

So the cryptographic set-up, just to give you the high level overview, the idea is, on the web bulletin board we set up a table, each row will correspond to a code sheet, and has in it the voting codes encrypted under the threshold public key of the trustees, and we'll see later that in each row they're in randomised order, and there's a sort of Prêt à Voter style onion in each row which describes how the codes have been permuted in each row.

I'll describe the construction of that in a bit more detail in a few slides, but let's just talk about the voting protocol itself first. It's very simple, again it's very similar to code voting. The voter provides the serial number of their ballot form and the appropriate vote code to the server, and then the server encrypts the vote code under the public key of the trustees along with some sort of zero-knowledge proof of knowledge of plaintext, so some kind of plaintext-aware encryption, Cramer-Shoup[3] or something (I'll say in a moment why that's important), and posts that to the appropriate row of the web bulletin board. OK, now the trustees step in. First of all they check the validity of the ZK proof, if that's OK then they go ahead and do a plaintext equivalence test of this encrypted term against the terms in the row, and if they find an equivalent they flag that, effectively it's flagged by the plaintext equivalence test. And if they find such a match, then they can do a threshold decryption of the acknowledgement code which is also in that row, and at that point it's revealed to the vote server and it can be sent back to the voiter

Ben Laurie: Does that mean the trustees know how he voted?

Reply: No it won't. The fact that there's this secret randomisation of the vote codes in the row means that the trustees don't know what that signifies in terms of the vote cast.

Michael Roe: What is zero-knowledge proving here, that they know the vote?

Reply: Well let me jump straight into the reason for that: the threat we were concerned about here is that the server might simply look at the web bulletin board, look at the encrypted terms in that row, just pick one at random and re-encrypt it, and submit that at this term.

Ben Laurie: So that may be re-encrypted in the encryption scheme?

Reply: Which we have to do, and you'll see that later.

Matt Blaze: That's a design decision, right?

Reply: Well, yes, we do it for a reason, it helps us with the distributed construction, which you'll see. So as I mentioned, the zero-knowledge proofs and PETs are posted, this is actually quite nice because it makes it harder to corrupt votes, or stuff ballots onto the web bulletin board.

So let me get into the distributed construction, which is what leads us to want to use randomising homomorphic algorithms. There is a question whether this is the right way to go, and we are considering other schemes which don't use that kind of primitive. But as it turns out actually that seems to be a very neat, simple construction which works rather well here. So let's suppose we've got N voters, we've got C candidates, so some voting authority entity generates a set of some multiple λ of $N \times C + 1$, where λ is 2 or 3 or something, depending how many you want to randomly audit subsequently, and they're all encrypted under the trustee public key. And then some further entities, voting clerks, put this whole batch through a set of re-encryption mixes, so they're repeatedly re-encrypted and shuffled. Once we've done this as many times as we want, we just assemble this into a table, λN rows and $C + 1$ columns. And just to remark in

---

[3] Ronald Cramer and Victor Shoup, "A practical public key cryptosystem provably secure against adaptive chosen ciphertext attack", Crypto 1998, LNCS 1462, pp 13–25.

general, this seems to be potentially quite a nice, generic construction, because quite often in voting schemes, and I guess other applications, when we want to produce encryptions of plaintext which are constrained in some way, and we want to prove that the plaintext satisfies some sort of constraint as in some interval or something, but without of course revealing exactly what the value is, and for that we typically have to come up with fairly fancy zero-knowledge proofs of that. Here we've actually managed to avoid this by doing a sort of batch processing which seems to be quite a sort of nice trick, which might be more generic, more generally usable.

So the result is we have a table which has rows of this form, each with $C + 1$ terms in it, for the first C terms will effectively serve as the voting codes for that code sheet, and the final column will be the acknowledgement code for that. I guess I'm assuming here that all the codes have the same form, five or six digit codes or something.

Now we come to the rather critical point, because at some point we've obviously got to print these code sheets and distribute them, and this is the pinch point in the whole scheme. There are various ways we could do this, but the most obvious way is to have a threshold set of trustees decrypt a row and print those values appropriately to the code sheet, and we might use some sort of fancy technology — pressure printing and things like this — to try and preserve the secrecy and so forth. This is the rather tricky stage in the scheme, and for that matter, in code voting. And then they're all handed over to some sort of registrar who distributes them to eligible voters, to their addresses. This is very much the weak underbelly of this scheme.

Jonathan Anderson: Is it very different from systems where you have a great big machine and some encrypted data goes in along with sheets of paper, and ballot papers just come out?

Reply: Well that's the kind of process that I have in mind, yes, how trustworthy that is really not to leak anything, you do need certain assumptions and so on in the process, which is a little bit worrying, but time permitting I'll come back to alternatives we might try to sidestep those issues. So that's given us what we call the P table from which we derived the code sheets. Now we want to produce what we refer to as the Q table (which is actually an analogy to the scantegrity scheme[4]), which is the table that we post to the web bulletin board. This differs from the P table in the sense that each of the rows has this permutation with respect to the P table that I mentioned earlier. So again, we can use a re-encryption shuffle mix to produce this: we can have a series of clerks, so the first clerk takes the P table, and on each row it does a re-encryption of the vote, the first C terms, and permutes them according to some randomly generated permutation, and it stores the information defining that permutation in an onion which it adds at the end of the row. And we can do this repeatedly, as many times as want. The net result is this table I'm calling the Q table, which has these vote codes, the vote codes have all been re-encrypted and

---

[4] http://www.scantegrity.org

multiply shuffled according to some secret shuffle, and the information defining that shuffle, that permutation, is fetched up in this onion at the end, and the ack code we just leave unchanged, and leave it in the same column. OK, so that's the table that we post to the web bulletin board, and is used for recording the votes and tabulating them subsequently. And you can see this has a flavour of Prêt à Voter if you've seen Prêt à Voter before.

Now we've basically set up all the mechanism we need to go ahead, but before we go any further we will want to do random audits of these things, so we pick out a random subset of the code sheets, and for those we require appropriate decryptions of the corresponding rows on the web bulletin board.

Matt Blaze: At this point the code sheets are not yet associated with a particular voter?

Reply: I guess at this point they wouldn't be associated, in fact in some sense ideally they won't be associated with voters at all.

Matt Blaze: At some point, they're going to put the mailing label on each vote.

Reply: Well you'll have to drop them in an envelope and send them off, but hopefully you can actually do that in a way which you don't even record the association.

James Malcolm: So this is down to a subset of the sheets before, and then the remaining ones are sent out?

Reply: Precisely, yes.

Joseph Bonneau: So if you don't know which code sheets go to which voter what's to stop somebody from breaking into the post office and stealing everybody in town's code sheet, and then voting for everybody in town, it won't be able to tell if that's happened?

Reply: Because the mail system is a secure channel, I mean, this kind of problem happens with absentee voting as well.

Joseph Bonneau: So in this scheme as soon as you have any code sheet that enables you to cast a vote?

Reply: Effectively it does, at least in the absence of other authentication mechanisms when you vote in, and that is an issue, and that means of course that vote selling and coercion is a problem. I'll come onto that as well, in a moment. So hopefully you get the gist of the construction and how we audit it.

I've already hinted at some of the threats, and I probably don't have time to go into much detail. I think it's clear that the really weak part of this scheme is the threat of leaking code information, and particularly if we have to at some point print them all to code sheets, that's clearly going to be very difficult to ensure that there isn't some leakage. This is really quite fundamental, because the leakage of the codes isn't just a confidentiality threat, in the scheme, perhaps I should have made it clearer, the key point is that the vote server shouldn't know information of alternate codes, and the point of that is to prevent it when it gets a vote coming in from trying to guess alternate codes for that code sheet, it doesn't really have an option other than to pass the correct code, the vote code, onto the trustees, OK, in the absence of knowledge of alternate codes for that code sheet, it would just have to guess, and hopefully we've got mechanisms to detect multiple guesses and so forth. Right, so that's the key point. But of course if codes start leaking then we undermine the integrity guarantees as well as the confidentiality, and that's the fundamental worry about this style of scheme, which might be enough to sink it. I hinted that one of the countermeasures is to use these plaintext-aware crypto, there are other possible countermeasures which I'll maybe come to.

Another thing we need to worry about is recovery mechanisms, I think this came out in discussion in Matt's talk. A lot of these schemes talk a lot about how you detect errors, corruption, and so on, but tend to talk very little about well what the recovery mechanisms are when you do start detecting. If you detect certain patterns, what do you do? Clearly we've got to think quite hard about this, one of the issues is if a voter gets an incorrect ack code back, or no ack code, what action should they take? So we have to have clearly defined procedures, and people that they report to, and probably alternative vote servers perhaps they can go to to try again, and so on. Some code voting schemes suggest the use of a finalisation code, a third column in the scheme, so only if the voter gets the correct ack code back do they actually submit the corresponding finalisation code. I'm personally not convinced this is a very effective mechanism, but some people seem to like it.

Jonathan Anderson: Well then the voter would want an ack to their finalisation, so you would need to send another of these?

Reply: Well exactly, this is why it doesn't really seem to buy you that much.

I think that it's the threat of confidentiality, of leakage of vote codes, which is the key weakness here. So we've been toying with various ideas to try and counter that, strengthen that. One obvious thing is perhaps to have dual channels of distribution, so not just send out these codes, print them and send them out over Snailmail.

There are various tricks.

One might be to go back to using visual crypto, there was a scheme long back by Naor and Pinkas[5] to do authentication using visual crypto, you'd send out a transparent sheet with a pattern of pixels on it, and then online you'd send another in effect sheet with pixels, and you'd overlay that on the screen and you'd see the password.

Paul Syverson: Are those schemes based on the one Adi Shamir came up with, and David Chaum's original design?

Reply: Well Adi Shamir did the original visual crypto, David Chaum came up with the use of it in a voting scheme, but there's another scheme which was to do online authentication, which is the one I was alluding to.

---

[5] Moni Naor and Benny Pinkas, Visual Authentication and Identification, Crypto '97, LNCS 1294, Springer-Verlag, pp 322–336.

Paul Syverson: Do you verify the screen and hold it up, I thought that was part of this?

Reply: No, in David's scheme you print two sheets, but you don't recombine it in the same way. So that might be one possible approach, but it strikes me that's going to be impractical, you know, getting things to the right size so they overlay is not going to be practical.

Another possibility is to have some sort of long term secret the voters hold which they can add to the codes, and then you can use this homomorphism to add them on a web bulletin in some sense, you have to be careful obviously that the algebra meshes. Another possibility, for which I haven't quite got the crypto to work, is to have some kind of scheme where you use a distributed construction and you send out these codes, keep them in their encrypted form, send them out online, but you arrange for voters to effectively get individual decryption keys for each of these codes, so the voter just provides to their device the appropriate decryption key, and so on. But if you can see how to make the crypto work, please let me know.

Ben Laurie: All of this sounds fantastically unusable to me, and the scheme itself sounds pretty unusable. Are you planning to test it?

Reply: Well it depends what you mean by test.

Ben Laurie: I observed the London elections, and if people can't even tick boxes correctly, the chance of them operating this kind of scheme is zero.

Reply: Well OK, when I said it seems simpler than other schemes, I was thinking of other cryptographic verifiable schemes.

Matt Blaze: I'm a little confused. Going back to some of your design constraints, you're assuming the postal system is usable as a secure channel *to* the voter. So why not simply use the postal system as the secure channel *from* the voters? If you have to mail something to someone and you assume the mail can't be tampered with, why not just have them mail their ballot back?

Reply: Well that would just be postal voting.

Matt Blaze: But this is still a postal system, so this seems to combine any trust issues you have with the postal system with any trust issues you have with the cryptography in this system. This means the system can be made strictly more secure by simply having them mail the ballot back without any actual usability issues, and their internet connection doesn't have to work.

Michael Roe: It's different from what a postal voting system is relying on, the difference is between saying that when you mail something through the post it goes to the person that the address is to, and the authentication that when you get the ballot coming in, you know who sent it.

Paul Syverson: Sure, you don't get that from a postal system.

Matt Blaze: But you will have a serial numbered ballot, on some piece of paper that I can tell is the one I sent you, and that's randomised in some way. What problem does what you are doing solve?

Reply: Well that's a good question, and one of the things we're hoping to get here is some degree of end-to-end verifiability, which I don't think postal voting gives.

Matt Blaze: Right, I think that's a good answer. Because you get the ack back, there's a two step protocol with standard absentee ballots, this is in fact a three step protocol, because of the acknowledgement code.

So you get a confirmation that it's been received, right.

Reply: Yes, and hopefully even slightly stronger than that: subject to certain assumptions there's a degree of end-to-end verification here. If you get the ack code that should imply that your vote gets accurately counted in the final tabulation. That's really what we're trying to achieve here. The starting premise was, well people have proposed code voting, it's not end-to-end, can we make it a bit more end-to-end, that was the starting intellectual challenge. Whether the final thing is really viable for anything practical is still I think open to question.

Virgil Gligor: Democracy is probably the most important multi-party computation. Now the part of that multi-party computation that security research is focusing on is integrity of the input. But in computation in general, input is probably not the most interesting part, and in all these stolen elections in recent years, very few of them have been stolen by people really cracking the crypto of submitting the vote. So there is the interaction between how we submit these inputs, and what is done in computation with these inputs, and whether people are turned away from inputting anything at all.

I'm wondering whether the techniques developed would justify maybe extending or zooming out from just input operations, and looking at broader security properties that one might require from democracy rather than just the integrity of the vote. So how the votes are counted, in a different kind of research about democracy they say, you give me who you want to win and you give me a set of preferences, and then I am going to design the counting system which will give you the desired winner. Is there any chance of interaction between these two threads of research?

Reply: Well I think it's starting to happen in the community, there is a bit of a community looking at the science of voting, in fact I think they're thinking of trying to start a journal precisely on that topic, which would go as far as looking at decision theory, and census theory, as well as things like securing the voting process and so on, so I think that is emerging.

Virgil Gligor: Can you say how you think cryptographic techniques and social choice techniques interleave?

Reply: Well to a large extent I think they're orthogonal. If you want to come up with one of these cryptographic schemes and you want something fancy, say single transferable vote, then you're going to have to make sure that you can carry the data items, the encoding of the right vector or something. One of the nice things about Prêt à Voter is that it seems to be rather good at doing that kind of thing in contrast to some of the other cryptographic schemes.

Matt Blaze: I think I can achieve what you're doing with a postal system. I think I can improve all your properties with a postal system simply by sending out a serial numbered ballot to everyone, they return the ballot, and then the ballots are available for inspection, all ballots are available for public inspection. So, if I want I can go after the count and I can confirm that my ballot was received, and I can count them myself if I want.

Reply: OK, but isn't that running into receipt-freeness type issues?

Matt Blaze: Well in any postal system we're not coercion free. If I'm mailing you something I'm still subject to coercion by somebody who supervises when I open the envelope and cast my vote, so we still have that problem.

Reply: I was going to come on to coercion.

Matt Blaze: If we're willing to sacrifice that property, which the PGD system seems to do, then I think we can achieve this without any crypto at all.

Reply: You're just posting anonymised ballots, and then you can go and look at the list of all the ballots and check that mine is there.

Matt Blaze: Oh yes, I can see that mine is there, and I can see that this other one who I don't know who's it was is also there.

Reply: Yes, and then you anonymise at the level of your voting precinct or whatever.

Matt Blaze: Right.

Reply: Well arguably yes, and subsequently I'm not making great claims for this scheme.

Matt Blaze: Oh no, I'm just trying to get at understanding what problems we're solving here, given that we're assuming the postal service is a secure channel[6]. If we're willing to do that it seems that we can achieve many properties.

---

[6] Editors' Note: The paradox here is similar to that which occurs with classical one-time pad. If a leak-proof channel, authenticated at both ends, exists to distribute the key from Alice to Bob, why not use that channel to send the message, which is of the same length? There are two obvious answers. The first is that Bob may be in a hurry at the point when he wishes to send the message, but ample time may be available beforehand for Alice to distribute the key. Quick voting outcome online may be a goal. The second, usually more important reason is that the slow key distribution channel need only be leak-evident, rather than leak-proof. Unsuccessful key distribution can be corrected. The final point to note is that if the message to be sent from Bob to Alice is short (relative to the key), then a uni-directional leak-evident channel going the "wrong" way between authenticated endpoints (i.e. conveying information only from Alice to Bob) suffices to provide confidentiality, authentication, and integrity for a message sent from Bob to Alice over an open, untrusted channel. A particular bit pattern can be reserved to mean "the key was compromised".

Reply: Well maybe, we should talk a bit more about this. I've wondered about how much you can do with pure voting and degrees of traceability subsequently in the tabulation process. We should come back to that.

George Danezis: I think the problem you describe, is a problem with your abstraction of elections. Effectively, as someone else said before, the process starts when people start submitting votes. You assume that there is already a secure registration process and a secured interaction process between the citizens and the State, to actually start. Getting a list of voters, let's say, already requires you to have some kind of secure channels and all that stuff, so probably integrating this phase into the voting scheme will help you solve this problem, rather than making the problem more complicated.

Reply: I take your point, it's certainly true of all these schemes, that it's all part of a much larger system which is the setting up of the electoral roll.

George Danezis: So far we've been shying away from looking at the registration processes which are key, because a lot of the fraud happens there. We fear they would make these systems more complicated, but I think they would actually simplify a lot of the things by making the assumptions concrete.

Reply: Yes, I think that's probably true, I agree.

Joseph Bonneau: Vote selling in this system is basically equivalent to mail absentee voting. Is that correct?

Reply: Well let's go with it for the moment.

Joseph Bonneau: It seems like vote selling is actually a lot worse now though because you can create a website and say, give me your vote code for Candidate A, and then the website will cast your vote and when it sees your ack code, and then it will send you a dollar on PayPal or whatever, and that seems much more likely to happen than somebody actually going and finding somebody to sell their absentee ballot in person.

Jonathan Anderson: But there's no way to confirm that it is the code for that candidate.

Bruce Christianson: You can give it any vote and still get your dollar, because the ack code is the same for all candidates.

Reply: Right. I'd better try and wind things up because we're overrunning. I was going to touch on coercion resistance and just say that as it stands it clearly isn't coercion resistant or resistant to vote buying. Potentially we could add extra mechanisms like the Juels Catalano Jakobsson typo tokens, although it's actually not so easy to see how to integrate it with this scheme because with the posting of material to the web bulletin board, if we're going to have to do a sort of re-voting process it's not quite clear how we overwrite or append further information to the web bulletin board, so that's kind of tricky.

So let me just wind up on the discussion. All I would say for this scheme is that it perhaps does buy you something in degrees of convenience. I claim it's slightly easier for the voter than some other schemes because for example with Prêt à Voter you cast your vote, you get some kind of receipt, and then subsequently you go to the web bulletin board and check that it's correctly posted there.

That's a bit more of a palaver, and there is some question whether people would bother to do that checking process. At least here everything happens in a single session, in theory you get your ack code back during the same session, you can check it immediately, so in that sense compared to some verifiable schemes it does seem to be a bit easier and simpler, more immediate for the voter.

I certainly wouldn't claim that a scheme like this is suitable for general political elections, but it maybe OK for student elections and things like this. The International Association of Cryptologic Research have been thinking recently about moving to Internet voting.

Matt Blaze: Perhaps not the most hotly contested elections in the world.

Paul Syverson: But one of the few where you will have people who will actually try to hack it themselves.

Reply: Yes, exactly.

There's been a long and rather fascinating debate about whether this is a good idea for all kinds of reasons you can imagine, not least that if it's successful, it might be seen as showing a precedent which politicians will then go along and say, if it's good enough for the International Association of Cryptologic Research, it's good for . . .

Design and Verification
of Anonymous Trust Protocols*

Michael Backes[1,2] and Matteo Maffei[1]

[1] Saarland University, Saarbrücken, Germany
[2] Max Planck Institute for Software Systems (MPI-SWS)

Abstract. Over the last years, the Web has evolved into the premium forum for freely and anonymously disseminating and collecting information and opinions. However, the ability to anonymously exchange information, and hence the inability of users to identify the information providers and to determine their credibility, raises serious concerns about the reliability of exchanged information.

In this paper we propose a methodology for designing security protocols that enforce fine-grained trust policies while still ensuring the anonymity of the users. The fundamental idea of this methodology is to incorporate non-interactive zero-knowledge proofs: the trust level of users are certified using digital signatures, and users assert their trust level by proving in zero-knowledge the possession of such certificates. Since the proofs are zero-knowledge, they provably do not reveal any information about the users except for their trust levels; in particular, the proofs hide their identities.

We additionally propose a technique for verifying the security properties of these protocols in a fully automated manner. We specify protocols in the applied pi-calculus, formalize trust policies as authorization policies, and define anonymity properties in terms of observational equivalence relations. The verification of these properties is then conducted using an extension of recently proposed static analysis techniques for reasoning about symbolic abstractions of zero-knowledge proofs.

1 Introduction

Over the last years, the Web has evolved into the premium forum for freely disseminating and collecting information and opinions. In particular, social networks and peer-to-peer (P2P) applications have proven to be particularly salient approaches for this task. However, not all information providers are willing to reveal their true identity; for instance, some may want to present their opinions anonymously to avoid associations with their race, ethnic background or other sensitive characteristics. Furthermore, people seeking sensitive information may want to remain anonymous to avoid being stigmatized or other negative repercussions.

---

* Work partially supported by the initiative for excellence of the German federal government, by DFG Emmy Noether program, and by MIUR project "SOFT".

B. Christianson et al. (Eds.): Security Protocols 2009, LNCS 7028, pp. 143–148, 2013.
© Springer-Verlag Berlin Heidelberg 2013

The ability to anonymously exchange information, and hence the inability of users to identify the information providers and to determine their credibility, raises serious concerns about the reliability of exchanged information. Trust management systems have become the most popular technique to determine which resources should be trusted, and to which extent. Except for some notable exceptions [1], trust management systems inherently rely on revealing the identities of the involved parties, and they hence do not live up to nowadays' anonymity demands. Indeed, devising security protocols that simultaneously satisfy conflicting security properties such as trust and anonymity requires significant extensions to the state-of-the-art. In particular, it is crucial to incorporate the most innovative modern cryptographic primitive in the design and the verification of security protocols: zero-knowledge proofs[1] [2]. This primitive goes beyond the traditional understanding of cryptography that only ensures secrecy and authenticity of a communication. The unique security features of zero-knowledge proofs, combined with the recent advent of efficient cryptographic implementations of this primitive for special classes of problems, have paved the way for their deployment in modern applications, such as anonymity protocols [3,1] and electronic voting protocols [4,5].

In this paper we propose a methodology based on zero-knowledge proofs for *designing* security protocols that enforce fine-grained trust policies while still ensuring the anonymity of the user. The fundamental idea of this methodology is to exploit digital signatures for certifying the trust level of users, and to let users prove the possession of such certificates in order to prove their trust level. Since the proof is zero-knowledge, it provably does not reveal any information about the users except for their trust levels; in particular, the proof hides their identities.

We additionally propose a technique for *verifying* the security properties of these protocols in a fully automated manner. We specify protocols in the applied pi-calculus [6], formalize trust policies as authorization policies, and define anonymity properties in terms of observational equivalence relations. The verification of these properties is then conducted using an extension of recently proposed static analysis techniques for reasoning about symbolic abstractions of zero-knowledge proofs [7,8].

2   Anonymous Proofs of Trust

We assume a public-key infrastructure and that users know each other's public key. Whenever user A wants to certify that she trusts user B, A signs B's verification key, thus obtaining the digital signature $\mathsf{sign}(\mathsf{vk}(k_B), k_A)$. Suppose now that B wants to send a message m to A in an authenticated manner, but

---

[1] A zero-knowledge proof combines two seemingly contradictory properties. First, it is a proof of a statement that cannot be forged, i.e., it is impossible, or at least computationally infeasible, to produce a zero-knowledge proof of a wrong statement. Second, a zero-knowledge proof does not reveal any information besides the bare fact that the statement is valid.

without revealing his identity, i.e., A should solely learn that this message was generated by a trusted user. This requirement clearly prevents B from simply sending a signature on m to A, since this would reveal his identity. In order to guarantee both trust (authentication) and anonymity, B instead runs a zero-knowledge proof showing that B knows a verification key signed by A as well as the corresponding (private) signing key, thus preventing impersonation attacks. Following [8], we represent this zero-knowledge proof as the following term:

$$
\mathsf{zk}_{\mathsf{ver}(\alpha_1,\alpha_2,\beta_1)\wedge\alpha_2=\mathsf{vk}(\alpha_3)}(\overbrace{\mathsf{sign}(\mathsf{vk}(k_B),k_A)}^{\alpha_1},\overbrace{\mathsf{vk}(k_B)}^{\alpha_2},\overbrace{k_B}^{\alpha_3};\overbrace{\mathsf{vk}(k_A)}^{\beta_1},m) \tag{1}
$$

We briefly describe the individual parts of this zero-knowledge proof:

- *Involved message components*: The messages $\mathsf{sign}(\mathsf{vk}(k_B),k_A)$, $\mathsf{vk}(k_B)$, and k_B constitute the *private component* of the proof; the semantics of [8] ensures that they are not revealed to the verifier. The messages $\mathsf{vk}(k_A)$ and m constitute the *public component*; they are revealed to the verifier. This proof hence does not reveal any information except for A's verification key and the message m to be authenticated; in particular, A does not learn the identity of B since B's verification key $\mathsf{vk}(k_B)$ is kept secret.
- *Proven Statement*: The statement to be proven is expressed as a Boolean formula $\mathsf{ver}(\alpha_1,\alpha_2,\beta_1)\wedge\alpha_2 = \mathsf{vk}(\alpha_3)$ over cryptographic operations. Here α_i and β_j constitute placeholders for the i-th element in the private component and the j-th element in the public component, respectively. We moreover write $\mathsf{ver}(\alpha_1,\alpha_2,\beta_1)$ as an abbreviation of $\exists k\colon (\alpha_1 = \mathsf{sign}(\alpha_2,k)\wedge\beta_1 = \mathsf{vk}(k))$, i.e., to denote that the A's signature on B's verification key is valid. In words, the statement hence says "B knows a signature α_1 of a message α_2 that can be checked using A's verification key $\mathsf{vk}(k_A)$, as well as the private key α_3 corresponding to the verification key α_2". Proving the knowledge of a certificate for B's verification key (without revealing the key and hence the identity of B) and the knowledge of the corresponding private signing key, however, ensures A that the message m in the public component comes from a trusted user[2].

Using zero-knowledge proofs in this manner constitutes a general approach for asserting trust, and it in particular allows us to implement fine-grained trust policies. For instance, B might be interested in proving that he is considered trusted by C_1 or C_2, without revealing which user C_i it is trusted by. Assume further that both C_1 and C_2 are trusted by A. Such disjunctive proofs aree viable tools for enhancing anonymity, e.g., to deal with the case that A asks C_1 and C_2 for a list of trusted users. This proof can be realized by the following zero-knowledge proof, assuming that A has been certified by C_1:

---

[2] Technically, we consider (an abstraction of) non-malleable zero-knowledge proofs, i.e., proofs that the adversary cannot modify without knowing the secret witnesses.

$$\mathsf{zk}_{\mathsf{ver}(\alpha_1,\alpha_2,\alpha_4)\wedge\alpha_2=\mathsf{vk}(\alpha_3)\wedge\alpha_4\in\{\beta_1,\beta_2\}}\left(\begin{array}{c}\overbrace{\mathsf{sign}(\mathsf{vk}(k_B),k_{C_1})}^{\alpha_1},\overbrace{\mathsf{vk}(k_B)}^{\alpha_2},\overbrace{k_B}^{\alpha_3},\overbrace{\mathsf{vk}(k_{C_1})}^{\alpha_4};\\\underbrace{\mathsf{vk}(k_{C_1})}_{\beta_1},\underbrace{\mathsf{vk}(k_{C_2})}_{\beta_2},\overbrace{m}^{\beta_3}\end{array}\right)$$

Another interesting case is when B wants to prove that he has been certified by both C_1 and C_2. Such conjunctive proofs are useful when trust policies take into account multiple trust certifications to upgrade the trust level of a user. This can be realized by the following zero-knowledge proof, which guarantees that the same (secret) verification key α_2 is used in the two (secret) certificates α_1 and α_4:

$$\mathsf{zk}_{\substack{\mathsf{ver}(\alpha_1,\alpha_2,\beta_1)\,\wedge\,\alpha_2=\mathsf{vk}(\alpha_3)\\\wedge\,\mathsf{ver}(\alpha_4,\alpha_2,\beta_2)}}\left(\begin{array}{c}\overbrace{\mathsf{sign}(\mathsf{vk}(k_B),k_{C_1})}^{\alpha_1},\overbrace{\mathsf{vk}(k_B)}^{\alpha_2},\overbrace{k_B}^{\alpha_3},\overbrace{\mathsf{sign}(\mathsf{vk}(k_B),k_{C_2})}^{\alpha_4};\\\underbrace{\mathsf{vk}(k_{C_1})}_{\beta_1},\underbrace{\mathsf{vk}(k_{C_2})}_{\beta_2},\overbrace{m}^{\beta_3}\end{array}\right)$$

3   Automated Verification of Proofs of Trust

Trust policies can be naturally formalized as authorization policies. For instance, consider the protocol described before, where A sends to B a certificate and B authenticates the message m with the zero-knowledge proof (1):

$$A \hspace{10cm} B$$

assume $\mathsf{Trust}(A, B)$

$$\xrightarrow{\hspace{3cm}\mathsf{sign}(\mathsf{vk}(k_B),k_A)\hspace{3cm}}$$

$$\text{assume } \mathsf{Send}(B, A, m)$$

$$\xleftarrow{\hspace{3cm}ZK\hspace{3cm}}$$

assert $\mathsf{Authenticate}(A, m)$

$$\text{where } ZK = \mathsf{zk}_{\mathsf{ver}(\alpha_1,\alpha_2,\beta_1)\wedge\alpha_2=\mathsf{vk}(\alpha_3)}\left(\begin{array}{c}\overbrace{\mathsf{sign}(\mathsf{vk}(k_B),k_A)}^{\alpha_1},\overbrace{\mathsf{vk}(k_B)}^{\alpha_2},\overbrace{k_B}^{\alpha_3};\\\underbrace{\mathsf{vk}(k_A)}_{\beta_1},m\end{array}\right)$$

We decorate security-related protocol events with *assumptions* and *assertions*. In the example, A assumes $\mathsf{Trust}(A, B)$ before certifying B. Moreover, B assumes $\mathsf{Send}(B, A, m)$ before sending the zero-knowledge proof to A. After verifying the zero-knowledge proof, A finally asserts $\mathsf{Authenticate}(A, m)$. We say that a protocol is safe if and only if in all protocol executions, even in the presence of an active attacker, every assertion is entailed by the previous assumptions and by the authorization policy. Formally, this is captured by the following authorization policy:

$$\forall A, B, m.\text{Trust}(A, B) \land \text{Send}(B, A, m) \Rightarrow \text{Authenticate}(A, m).$$

This policy asserts that A can authenticate message m (assertion Authenticate(A, m)) provided that this message has been sent by a user B (assumption Send(B, A, m)) that is trusted by A (assumption Trust(A, B)). We have specified this protocol as a process in the applied pi-calculus [9] and checked with our type system [7] that this protocol is safe with respect to the given authorization policy.

In order to define the anonymity property of the protocol, we consider a system with two users B_1 and B_2 trusted by A. Both of them receive a certificate from A and afterwards one of them authenticates a message with A. Intuitively, this protocol guarantees the anonymity of the sender if A cannot distinguish the process $S[B_1, B_2]$, in which the message is sent by B_1, from the process $S[B_2, B_1]$, in which the message is sent by B_2. This is formalized by requiring

$$S[B_1, B_2] \approx S[B_2, B_1],$$

where $\approx$ denotes the observational equivalence relation in the applied pi-calculus. We automatically checked this equivalence using ProVerif [10].

4   Open Challenges

In this short paper, we conclude by outlining a series of important challenges that have to be tackled for applying the proposed methodology to realistic scenarios.

First, the methodology for asserting trust using zero-knowledge proofs should be comprehensive enough to model popular trust models such as [11,12,13].

Second, currently used zero-knowledge protocols are still notoriously inefficient for many important classes of statements. However, recent results [14] show that it is possible to automatically devise efficient implementations of zero-knowledge proofs such as the one depicted in Equation (1). Enforcing anonymity in complex trust models, however, calls for efficient implementations of even wider ranges of zero-knowledge proofs.

Third, the advent of social network applications resulted in the demand for novel, more comprehensive requirements on both trust and anonymity. So far, many of these requirements lack a formalization and hence corresponding analysis techniques.

References

1. Lu, L., Han, J., Hu, L., Huai, J., Liu, Y., Ni, L.M.: Pseudo trust: Zero-knowledge based authentication in anonymous peer-to-peer protocols. In: Proc. 2007 IEEE International Parallel and Distributed Processing Symposium, p. 94. IEEE Computer Society Press (2007)

2. Goldreich, O., Micali, S., Wigderson, A.: Proofs that yield nothing but their validity or all languages in NP have zero-knowledge proof systems. Journal of the ACM 38(3), 690–728 (1991),
   http://www.wisdom.weizmann.ac.il/~oded/X/gmw1j.pdf
3. Brickell, E., Camenisch, J., Chen, L.: Direct anonymous attestation. In: Proc. 11th ACM Conference on Computer and Communications Security, pp. 132–145. ACM Press (2004)
4. Juels, A., Catalano, D., Jakobsson, M.: Coercion-resistant electronic elections. In: Proc. 4th ACM Workshop on Privacy in the Electronic Society, WPES, pp. 61–70. ACM Press (2005)
5. Clarkson, M.R., Chong, S., Myers, A.C.: Civitas: A secure voting system. In: Proc. 29th IEEE Symposium on Security and Privacy, pp. 354–368. IEEE Computer Society Press (2008)
6. Abadi, M., Blanchet, B.: Secrecy Types for Asymmetric Communication. In: Honsell, F., Miculan, M. (eds.) FOSSACS 2001. LNCS, vol. 2030, pp. 25–41. Springer, Heidelberg (2001)
7. Backes, M., Hriţcu, C., Maffei, M.: Type-checking zero-knowledge. In: 15th ACM Conference on Computer and Communications Security, CCS 2008, pp. 357–370. ACM Press (2008), Implementation available at
   http://www.infsec.cs.uni-sb.de/projects/zk-typechecker/
8. Backes, M., Maffei, M., Unruh, D.: Zero-knowledge in the applied pi-calculus and automated verification of the direct anonymous attestation protocol. In: Proc. 29th IEEE Symposium on Security and Privacy, pp. 202–215. IEEE Computer Society Press (2008)
9. Abadi, M., Fournet, C.: Mobile values, new names, and secure communication. In: Proc. 28th Symposium on Principles of Programming Languages, POPL, pp. 104–115. ACM Press (2001)
10. Abadi, M., Blanchet, B., Fournet, C.: Automated verification of selected equivalences for security protocols. In: Proc. 20th Annual IEEE Symposium on Logic in Computer Science, LICS, pp. 331–340. IEEE Computer Society Press (2005)
11. Jøsang, A.: An algebra for assessing trust in certification chains. In: Proceedings of the Network and Distributed Systems Security Symposium, NDSS 1999. The Internet Society (1999)
12. Xiong, L., Ling, L.: A reputation-based trust model for peer-to-peer ecommerce communities (extended abstract). In: Proceedings of the 4th ACM Conference on Electronic Commerce, EC 2003, pp. 228–229. ACM Press (2003)
13. Carbone, M., Nielsen, M., Sassone, V.: A formal model for trust in dynamic networks. In: International Conference on Software Engineering and Formal Methods, SEFM 2003, pp. 54–64 (2003)
14. Bangerter, E., Camenisch, J., Krenn, S., Sadeghi, A., Schneider, T.: Automatic generation of sound zero-knowledge protocols. IACR Cryptology ePrint Archive: Report 2008/471 (2008), http://eprint.iacr.org/

Design and Verification
of Anonymous Trust Protocols
(Transcript of Discussion)

Michael Backes

Saarland University

I should say up-front that our focus is more on design and verification, and on anonymity, and we take a pretty simplistic view on trust at the moment, but I really will appreciate your feedback on what else to model in the area of trust. This is joint work with Matteo.

What is anonymity? Let me make a general statement here, anonymity is a friend of the freedom of information, so if you are browsing the web it's actually convenient to anonymously collect data, and also to post data anonymously. However, anonymity is also the enemy of trust, because if you download things which have been posted anonymously, it's hard to say if they make sense, what the trust level is, what the level of integrity is, if you would trust a person that posted the stuff if you knew who the person was. So what you actually have are two conflicting requirements, anonymity on the one hand, trust on the other hand, so the question is, can we get both, stay anonymous but still be sufficiently convinced that whatever I'm getting from the internet from a certain protocol gives me a certain level of trust.

So these conflicting requirements are not really a novelty, for example, in e-voting we have just seen there is on one hand you have privacy properties, on the other hand you have stuff like verifiability, which to some extent seem to be conflicting[1]. Secondly, for example, I think you saw it yesterday[2], through the DAA protocol you have stuff like anonymity and remote attestation on the other hand, this is also conflicting to some extent.

Paul Syverson: Is it me that wants to be anonymous, and wants to trust what's coming from some place which may not be anonymous?

Reply: OK, there are several situations and scenarios you could conceive, but sometimes it's also nice to post something anonymously and get anonymous messages, and still you actually don't like to use all the confidence and trust that you could put into that. So if you're downloading anonymously posted information then it would be nice to know if the person behind that I would trust or not, at least this information, not who the guy is, but the level of trust. One solution which we have seen also yesterday is to use zero-knowledge proofs[3]. This is also what this talk is about, but I'll try to go one level deeper and really speak about how to model this symbolically, how to verify this very, very quickly,

---

[1] Ryan, these proceedings.

[2] Mukhamedov, these proceedings.

[3] Krenn, these proceedings.

B. Christianson et al. (Eds.): Security Protocols 2009, LNCS 7028, pp. 149–156, 2013.
© Springer-Verlag Berlin Heidelberg 2013

so not just say, we will use it and obviously it will work somehow, but really we can model it, we can analyse it, and then see how that works.

But how to use this for trust and anonymity? Let me give you, just for the sake of exposition, a simple view of how one could model trust, a very simplistic view on trust. So, for example, Alice could just say, I trust Bob, and you could model this if you don't care about anonymity at all, by just signing the verification key of Bob. It's a common way of saying, well, I trust you so I sign your stuff, give you a certificate if you wish on your verification key, and then Bob can convince other persons that he is trusted by Alice just by forwarding the signature, so forwarding the certificate, that's a common way of doing it. However, this of course does not give Bob any form of anonymity because you really have to output this stuff, and if you output the signature you output the actual verification key of yourself that reveals your identity. Yes, it's a nice way of discerning trust in this simplistic manner, but you are not anonymous.

Now the key idea, which is well intuitive, you don't need Bob's signature, but to prove using zero-knowledge that you know a signature. So you're not saying, hey I'm Bob, here's my verification key, here's my signature, please verify it. What you do is say, I know something, know a valid certificate from me that I am trusted by Alice, I'm not telling you who I am, you don't have to know, but I'm telling you I have something which could confirm to you if I showed it to you that I have a certain trust level. That's the overall idea, although this is probably appearing simplistic.

Let me just quickly say what zero-knowledge proofs actually are. So an example, you could show that you know a certain plaintext in a certain encryption. For example, you could imagine this person, he knows a certain public key, he knows the encryption of some message M under this public key, but this person does not know the message. So you could do a zero-knowledge proof which says that, I prove to you that this encryption is an encryption of a message with this public key, and I know this message.

Frank Stajano: Why do you encrypt the message with the public key?

Reply: Because you're encrypting not signing. I mean, the public key encryption scheme uses public key for encryption, right? So this is a nice way of showing knowledge of what's contained in something secret without opening it, that's the idea. The nice thing about zero-knowledge proofs if you look at them cryptographically, they really yield no information computationally except for the bare validity of the statement itself. I should say also, if one just briefly looks at this from a cryptographic perspective, these early zero-knowledges were terribly inefficient, essentially they were a conceptual framework for identifying what can be proven in zero-knowledge, and there were nice results like everything in NP and even slightly more, but go to the gate level, and this is so terribly inefficient you would never use it in practice. However, in recent years people have thought of coming up with efficient solutions for selected problems that you can prove in zero-knowledge, and these problems are getting broader, so this really paves the way for zero-knowledge proofs into modern applications, and that's nice, everybody uses this here.

So as I said, I will not only say we will use zero-knowledge and that's it, but also we can model this, we can analyse it. I will just give you some syntax here that you see how this works. We're interested in the following, zero-knowledge proof and trust. Imagine Alice sends a signature on the verification key of Bob to Bob, and now Bob would like to make a zero-knowledge proof saying, I know the signing key X corresponding to a verification key that is signed by Alice, or in other words, I have a certificate. But if you look at this formula, this is represented by the following symbolic string. It's a symbolic expression, it has a semantics underneath, but at the moment it is a symbol. It consists actually of three parts. One part is called the private part, this is everything that the zero-knowledge proof is supposed to not reveal. So for example, I know the signing key X, which is this thing, corresponding to a verification key, right, should not be revealed of course. That is signed by Alice's signature, yes. The second part describes those messages that can be or should be revealed by the zero-knowledge proof, for example, the message itself, and the verification key of Alice.

Ben Laurie: So the message itself is in three parts?

Reply: No, this is the actual signature itself.

Paul Syverson: The message is a message that Bob will want you to trust.

Reply: Right, typically you are saying, I'm posting a message and it's trusted. This is arbitrary, I mean, if you wish for the sake of exposition, drop it, right, fine with me. Some other communication goes into this stuff, but the only thing you would really like to reveal is the verification key of Alice, because there is no other chance to get this verified in reality.

The third part is the actual statement, and this is really just encoded in a formula, this means there exists a key for that, and then you are referring to this part, and all these private parts have placeholders α, so this key is called α_1, this verification key is α_2, and this thing is α_3, and then you can just encode this thing in this formula. I will not go through this, but then take the placeholders, write it in a propositional logical formula, and so existentially quantified here, and be done. The nice thing is, this is not only syntax, this has semantics underneath, general Dolev-Yao style manipulation semantics, but it's even nicer, you can give these people a cryptographic interpretation and it can prove itself to some extent, so this is great.

You can do lots of things with this and you can verify it, so let me first show you that you can do lots of nice things. For example, if you think about anonymity, you could make disjunctions on statements, for example, you could say, this guy gets the certificate Charlie trusts Bob, and then this guy says to Alice, hey, I'm either trusted by Charlie or David, but I'm not telling which one. And as you might expect, this is pretty good for anonymity, for example, Alice might ask Charlie for a list of trusted users, and then I must prove that there is a user in your trusted list that I am trusted by as well, but I'm not telling you which guy, I'm just telling you there exists some connection between us, and this is probably one of the strongest things you can hope to get. If you look at the formalization, this is actually pretty simple, it's pretty much the same thing, the only thing that happened here is, you later on have an additional disjunction where you say, this is user is either that one or that one. You can model arbitrary propositional formulas like this, conjunction and disjunction, and the nice thing, efficient zero-knowledge proofs are good for reasoning about conjunctions and disjunctions, this is because typically these things have some homomorphic properties, and something like conjunction forms into one operation, disjunction into something else, it doesn't always work, but this is something that is, these proof are actually pretty good in doing. Intuitively, if you go to the gate level then conjunction and disjunction are simple to model, take the respective gate, click it together, commit to the gate, be done.

Matteo Maffei: Do you think you could use something like this to build a web-of-trust type structure? Could you prove, I am in the trust structure, to some certain degree without actually showing which element you are?

Reply: As I said, we took a simplistic view on trust, modelling a web of trust is the natural next step. Is it possible, sure, it's definitely a property that's in NP, so we can prove it. Is it doable efficiently, I'm pretty sure it is, I have to check which scheme does it, but essentially being contained in the list of things was a proof of language membership, and this is typically doable efficiently, so I would conjecture that web of trust is a premium example for applying this stuff efficiently.

Paul Syverson: That's not quite clear because this is exactly the problem people who work on anonymous credentials have, not to just have one authority that gives the credentials, but actually having a hierarchy of authorities, and then just proving that you have a path from your credential to the root of this hierarchy, and I don't think they have efficient schemes for doing that yet. So if you actually solve that problem for the general web of trust model, probably you would also have a solution for this kind of hierarchy of credentials.

Reply: Sure, this is also why we do it simplistically on trust, the question is, how much on trust can you leverage into this kind of framework so that the sufficient solutions in crypto still exist. If I have limited connections, and I'm showing that I'm in a certain reachable set, then this is probably still doable. Really showing that there is a verifiably explicit path is harder, and it's not clear if it can be done. The question here is really, how far can you get whilst still being efficient. I mean, this is clearly doable, this is no problem, and proving that I'm in a set is efficient as well, no problem, but when you're doing this chain thing in the web, well let's see.

George Danezis: I think this is what Stefan Brands did.

Paul Syverson: Yes, and it comes back into fashion every two or three years.

Reply: With zero-knowledge schemes, and verifiable, even proved? As far as I know there was no formal verification of a zero-knowledge proof until ten months ago, so I would doubt that three years ago somebody did it formally.

Paul Syverson: It was not done in a formal language at all, he proved that he could come up with cryptographic results which showed you could have arbitrary stuff. He didn't prove that connection, that part was just clear and rigorous as opposed to proving it formally.

Reply: As I said, this talk is more concentrating on design and verification, and less on these things. The nice thing about zero-knowledge, they can be used for essentially everything, right, and if I'm not willing to go into the details I can essentially say, I'm proving in zero-knowledge that I am allowed to do this, and the schemes exist, but the question is, are they efficient? I would say, if you have lots of these things running in parallel, you will have lots of problems which you typically only find using formal verification, and not using informal proof.

Joseph Bonneau: In this scheme where the anonymous person in the middle would like to say either/or, basically anybody in the set of people you trust, somebody from that set signed my key?

Reply: That's one possibility.

Joseph Bonneau: But then do they have to know the entire set of people that the first group trust?

Reply: Sure, I mean, here in this simple example I've really just showed how to extend it to two persons, if you want to extend it to multiple ones, one possibility, a naïve one, would be, this person transmits the list of people that you trust and you're proving that you're on the list, or you can try to combine it with another zero-knowledge proof. For example, using commitments, I'm committing to a list, that commits to the people that I trust, and then I'm trying to do some zero-knowledge proof which in the end mingles it together, but this is way harder. So this is really just for showing how to get from one to more, but at the moment it doesn't solve or even track the problem, how does this person know that Charlie and David are a viable choice for proving this.

Joseph Bonneau: The property I'd like to see is that one person can prove to another that somebody who you trust trusts me, without finding out the whole set of people that you trust.

Reply: I see your point. One possibility is that you do some form of commitment to the people that you would like to have, and then you're making a zero-knowledge proof over the commitment. That's one possibility, but there might be more, but I think that's an orthogonal question.

Simon Foley: Your problem is similar to a database inference. If the people on the right-hand side start colluding with each other, in order to reduce the set, even though the guy in the middle is saying, well here's a range of people who may have signed my key, the people on the right-hand side are selectively choosing those sets to end up smaller.

Reply: OK, this contains two questions. One question is, can I be so mean to really pick this thing for later on, I have something like a tracker attack, that I can just mingle it down to some very specific choices. The answer is, this is possible in general of course, however, this is not an artefact of the zero-knowledge proof. The zero-knowledge proof, if done properly, composes universally, which merely means, if I'm proving lots of these things that I'm trusting A or B, and A or C, and A or D, they still cannot nail me down to A, this is not possible.

However, if they pick certain selected things here, but then my protocol has to ensure that I'm not so stupid as to answer all these things, that's a protocol property, not a zero-knowledge property. But of course, this is what you have to check. You could write policies later on, which I'll come to in a second, that try to check exactly that, so as to ensure I'm only outputting the stuff if I cannot be nailed down, because the second check locally from the stuff I've answered in the past. But let me come to this.

I wanted to speak actually about trust and anonymity. So far I've spoken about zero-knowledge. How to model trust? You can model this simplistically as trust policies, you would decorate your security protocols with so-called security rated events. With this decoration you assume certain things to happen, you assume somebody sent something, you assume some trust, and you make assertions, so for example if this happens you assert authenticate, because this is just symbolic decoration. You can make logical formulas over this, for example, if I trust you, and a Z operation happens, then authentication is OK. You can check all these things, if the formula is whole, under the assumption it can somehow reason about zero-knowledge, because this you have to do somehow. And the nice thing is, this works really works surprisingly efficiently. In Oakland last year for the first time, this was using our ProVerif, and this stuff here with trust was at CCS last year using type systems, and this is actually amazingly efficient, this terminates in the order of seconds for arbitrary protocol sessions run in parallel. And if it terminates and says, it's right, it really is a proof of being correct, so you err on the safe side: if it says, no, then you might have rejected a secure program, but if the thing says yes, then you can be sure. That's the opposite of model checking. If our system says, yes, then it's a sure proof that the stuff is correct, and it terminates extremely fast.

We are currently not only doing it abstractly in this applied pi-calculus, but really trying to do it in actual implementations written in ICF, and we have a type checker which seems to do what it should, but is still an ongoing work. One nice thing on a technicality, we had to extend existing work with so-called union intersection types, if you're familiar with type systems. Essentially it works like this, so you're getting a message from somewhere and you have to assign it a type, because then you can continue. The problem is in some cases you have no idea what the type is, you can just narrow it down to certain possibilities, but you don't know how to proceed, and union types essentially leave it open, so you say, it could be that or that, and let's go on, the same with intersection types. As I said, this is really efficient, it's also modular, it is quick, and it's compositional, as is the general property of doing stuff by type systems.

If you're interested in these tools they're just available under Apache Licence, download them, I think they're efficiently usable, they're fully automatic once you get some form of annotations, and they're fast.

OK, this was trust, maybe one slide on anonymity, how would you formalise anonymity? Anonymity is typically formalised as observational equivalence, so to prove anonymity you would consider the user here, and consider two scenarios: she is either interacting with this guy, or she's interacting with that guy. And if this is observationally equivalent, meaning that this person cannot tell the difference, then apparently you have the desired anonymity, because if you cannot tell apart, whether you communicated with this person or that person, the other person was clearly anonymous, that's the general way of modelling this. And the nice thing is, observational equivalence is well understood in the cryptographic community, so there are tools for doing this like ProVerif, and we included our stuff, so our stuff is accessible to ProVerif, actually off the shelf, we encoded it there, we used it for analysing different protocols, for example, we encoded the zero-knowledge proofs part of DAA, let it run, it terminated, it actually works.

George Danezis: You basically model zero-knowledge proofs as a black box, right?

Reply: Oh OK, this is a different question. So far all the modelling of zero-knowledge proofs are symbolic, so they are a black box, they are a symbol. But I should say last year at CSF we had a result on cryptographic foundations of zero-knowledge. It was slightly more restrictive than you might expect, but still doable for lots of cases, which means that if you analyse these things with a strong zero-knowledge proof — strong means, not the standard ones, but you need something like witness-indistinguishable, witness-extractable, and so on, so really sophisticated stuff, but for which schemes exist and are reasonably efficient I should say — then everything carries over to the crypto and the instantiation. I would say that this is an indication that we are on a good track, in the right direction.

Peter Ryan: You made a comment about observational equivalence versus algebra, as I understand it there's no consensus as to observational equivalence.

Reply: Concerning the notion I would say there is a pretty general agreement. The problem is they're still trying to find better ways for checking observational equivalence. The notion itself I think people agree, it's the standard notion in formal calculi. Of course there are variations, but I would say at the moment the core problem in the community is to not only use ProVerif, but people try to come up with other ways of checking observational equivalence, for example, there is some very nice work by Véronique Cortier[4] where they showed that, in some cases for some protocols, observational equivalence is essentially a trace property, so you can use much better stuff for checking it.

---

[4] Véronique Cortier and Stéphanie Delaune, "A Method for Proving Observational Equivalence", 22nd IEEE Computer Security Foundations Symposium, CSF2009, pp 266–276.

To conclude, our task here is to reason about anonymity in complex trust models. So far the trust models are not complex, I admit, but for example, web of trust would be a premium example, I would really highly appreciate any form of feedback on nice trust models that one would like to prove in zero-knowledge, and where we can check if this is doable. Our second major challenge, which is probably less important here, is to devise really efficient implementations of zero-knowledge schemes for desirable classes of proofs. Some people are working on this, this is still ongoing research in the crypto community, and this is kind of hard. The last one is in general, exploring the combination of anonymity on the one hand and a trust on the other hand, for example, in social networks.

Andy Gordon: I love this. You've got a theory about ProVerif, and are also using types. When you compare the results you can get using ProVerif versus the different type based approaches that you've tried — ProVerif can prove equivalences and it can also prove correspondences — can everything be done ProVerif, or is there a big advantage for types?

Reply: That's true. My experience is as follows: we started with ProVerif last year after proving DAA and anonymity properties. One thing was that ProVerif was not really robust to what we did, which means it very often did not terminate, and we made minor small changes which were semantically clearly equivalent, and then it terminated in let's say half an hour, and we tried often. So my impression was it was not robust. Moving to type systems had the advantage that once we got it done it's really a second question, and of course it gives you better scalability, compositionality, and so on. So at the moment I would say, if we ignore the scope of properties that we can analyse, type systems are superior for everything we are doing here.

Andy Gordon: I also have a practical question. That example you had where you were proving that you know one or another person had signed the key, is that implementable? You sort of implied it was.

Reply: This is implementable, there are efficient schemes that explicitly support the disjunction operator, just by the internal structure, essentially because in this model disjunction corresponds to a homomorphic step in the general construction.

Andy Gordon: OK, have you implemented it?

Reply: We are currently doing it, yes. There are some protocols that other people have implemented that do the job, meaning we're still trying to tailor it more towards our needs, but if you just would like to do it like this, you can take it off the shelf. Of course if you do more then you might need more, but this exists. And so if the question is, did we do this, the answer is, we are currently in the process of finishing it, but really meaning that, we have the implementation, we're plugging the pieces together, and we hope to be done in another three weeks, something like this. But at the moment it's really just plugging together what we already have implemented now.

Brief Encounters with a Random Key Graph

Virgil D. Gligor, Adrian Perrig, and Jun Zhao

ECE Department and CyLab
Carnegie Mellon University
Pittsburgh, Pennsylvania 15213
{gligor,perrig,junzhao}@cmu.edu

Abstract. Random key graphs, also called uniform random intersection graphs, have been used for modeling a variety of different applications since their introduction in wireless sensor networks. In this paper, we review some of their recent applications and suggest several new ones, under the full visibility assumption; i.e., under the assumption that all nodes are within communication range of each other. We also suggest further research in determining the connectivity properties of random key graphs when limited visibility is more realistic; e.g., graph nodes can communicate only with a subset of other nodes due to range restrictions or link failures.

The notion of the random key graph (a.k.a. "uniform random intersection graph" [1]) was introduced for probabilistic key pre-distribution in wireless sensor networks [2]. Recently, these graphs have been used for a variety of different applications, such as clustering analysis [3], recommender systems using collaborative filtering [4], and cryptanalysis of hash functions [5]. While random key graphs are not Erdös-Renyi random graphs (e.g., the probabilities that graph edges exist are not necessarily independent), they have similar connectivity properties under the assumption of "full visibility"; i.e., they obey a similar "zero-one" law as Erdös-Renyi graphs for some scaling of their parameters, whenever each node is within communication range of other nodes [6,7].

Recommender Systems Using Collaborative Filtering. Marbach [4] illustrates an application of random-key-graph connectivity for the modeling of recommender systems with collaborative filtering. In his model, there are N users and a pool of P_N objects. Each of the N users picks a set of K_N distinct objects uniformly and randomly from the pool, and ranks each object, where $K_N < P_N$. A recommender class C is defined as a set of users that gives the same ranking to any particular object that is ranked by at least one user of the set. This implies that (1) every subset of users in class C that rank a common object assigns the same ranking to that object, and (2) not every user in class C ranks all objects ranked by others in C; i.e., there exist users in class C that have not ranked objects ranked by others in class C.

A recommender system with collaborative filtering predicts the ranking a user would give an object that the user has not ranked, but that has been ranked by some other users in class C. However, to enable such predictions, the membership

B. Christianson et al. (Eds.): Security Protocols 2009, LNCS 7028, pp. 157–161, 2013.

of n users, $n \leq N$, in class C has to be identified. Hence, a question of interest is this: given P_N objects in the pool, how many objects need to be picked and ranked by each of the N users to identify the n members in recommender class C? That is, what is the lower bound of K_N?

To answer the above question, Marbach uses a graph, $G(K_N, P_N, N)$, and models recommender systems as follows. Let a user correspond to a node in graph $G(K_N, P_N, N)$. For any two users (nodes) of the graph, there is an edge between those users if and only if the following conditions hold: (1) there exists at least one object that is ranked by both users; (2) *any* object that is ranked by both users is given the same rank by those users. We note that both P_N and K_N are functions on n, and hence we denote them by P_n and K_n, respectively. Now let graph $G(K_n, P_n, n)$ be the sub-graph of $G(K_N, P_N, N)$, whose vertex set is class C and whose edge set is a subset of the $G(K_N, P_N, N)$ edges connecting vertices of class C. Marbach demonstrates that a necessary condition of identifying the membership of class C is that graph $G(K_n, P_n, n)$ be connected, and that $G(K_n, P_n, n)$ is almost surely connected if $\frac{K_n^2}{P_n} = \omega\left(\frac{\log n}{n}\right)$. Note that it is easy to show the probability that there exists an edge between two nodes of $G(K_n, P_n, n)$ is asymptotically equal to $\frac{K_n^2}{P_n}$ for certain values of n, K_n and P_n. In the context of secure wireless networks, Yağan and Makowski [6,7] show that when $P_n > 3K_n$ and $\frac{K_n^2}{P_n} \sim \frac{c \log n}{n}$, where $c > 0$ is a constant, the probability that $G(K_n, P_n, n)$ is connected goes to 0 as $n \to \infty$, for $c < 1$, and goes to 1 as $n \to \infty$, for $c > 1$. In other words, for certain values of n, K_n and P_n, the connectivity of graph $G(K_n, P_n, n)$ follows a zero-one law.

Trust Sub-Networks. Graph $G(K_n, P_n, n)$ can also be viewed as a trust sub-network for certificate evaluation in networks without a public-key infrastructure; e.g., ad-hoc networks [8]. In such networks, some certificates cannot be easily validated by clients (e.g., self-signed certificates), yet clients are expected to trust the validity of these certificates for use in security protocols. Let us assume that each of the n users of $G(K_n, P_n, n)$ is a certificate notary which serves a number of clients. These clients ask the notary to evaluate public-key or access control certificates that they receive from foreign sites and that they cannot validate. In a trust network, each notary evaluates K_n certificates it sees of the P_n being used among various sites of the Internet. If any of a notary u's clients asks for any of the K_n already evaluated certificates, u returns that certificate's evaluation (i.e., ranking). If u has not evaluated the certificate needed by one of its clients, u asks other notaries in trust network C for that evaluation. Notary u receives the certificate evaluation from any other notary with probability $\frac{K_n^2}{P_n}$, under the conditions established by the connectivity of graph $G(K_n, P_n, n)$. This evaluation is then sent by u to its client. Notary u returns an exception to its client if the certificate is not evaluated by any notary of the trust network C. We note that the robustness characterization of trust networks can benefit from the "redoubtable" and "unsplittable" properties of random key graphs [9].

An example of a practical system that resembles a trust sub-network is Perspectives [10]. The trusted notaries of the Perspective system can be viewed as the users of trust sub-network C. However, instead of returning a certificate evaluation, a trusted notary simply returns parameters of certificate use observed from its vantage point to its clients; e.g., use count observed.

Secure Connectivity to a Trusted Core of a Mobile Ad-hoc Network. Suppose that a subset of the nodes of a mobile ad-hoc network maintains full visibility; i.e., each node is within communication range of all other nodes [6,7]. We call this subset a "trusted core" since the secure connectivity of its nodes can be assured by probabilistic key pre-distribution similar to that for sensor networks. Since, by definition, ad-hoc networks do not have an infrastructure for secure communication, the secure key connectivity of a trusted core can provide the keying infrastructure for other mobile nodes that connect with each other via the trusted core. If we assume that the trusted core comprises nodes of the user class C defined above and its key connectivity is provided by graph $G(K_n, P_n, n)$ under the choice of parameters determined by Yağan and Makowski [6,7], then other mobile nodes can connect to each other either separately or via the trusted core. This is possible since the keying of the other mobile nodes can be viewed as the extension of the trusted core and can be performed in the same manner as the dynamic, ad-hoc, extension of a sensor network [2]. That is, each of the added mobile nodes can be pre-keyed with a set of K_n keys drawn from the same pool of size P_n of pre-distributed keys used for the trusted core. As long as the added mobile nodes remain in full visibility of the trusted core, their secure connectivity is assured with probability $\frac{K_{n'}^2}{P_{n'}}$, under the conditions established by the connectivity of the extended graph $G'(K_{n'}, P_{n'}, n')$, where $n' > n$ is the total number of nodes after the mobile nodes are added.

Analysis of Herding Attacks on Hash Functions[1]. Recently, Blackburn et al. [5] use the theory of uniform random intersection graphs (i.e., random key graphs) to analyze the complexity of the Kelsey and Kohno "herding attack" [11] on Damgård-Merkle hash-function constructions. In a herding attack, the adversary first commits to a hash value h and then is provided with a prefix p. The attacker needs to find a suffix s which "herds" to the previously committed hash value h. That is, given p, h, and a hash function $H()$, the adversary must find suffix s such that $H(p\|s) = h$. To launch a herding attack, Kelsey and Kohno build a 2^k-diamond structure by repeatedly utilizing a collision-finding attack against the hash function. Blackburn et al. find a flaw in the original analysis [11] and point out that the message complexity of building the 2^k-diamond structure is k times that suggested by Kelsey and Kohno. In analyzing the complexity of the herding attack, Blackburn et al. first derive the threshold of perfect matching in a random key graph and then apply the obtained result to the diamond structure. A perfect matching of a random key graph is a set of pairwise non-adjacent edges where every vertex of the graph lies on one edge of the set.

Further Research. The full visibility assumption, although interesting from a theoretical point of view, is often impractical in mobile ad-hoc (and sensor)

---

[1] This example replaces the analysis of a key-collision attack presented at the SPW 2009 workshop.

networks where communication range is constrained and sometimes unreliable. A set of interesting research questions arises when one considers the connectivity properties of random key graphs under the "limited visibility" constraint, already encountered in sensor networks [2]. Some robustness properties of random key graphs have already been considered; e.g., redoubtable and unsplittable graphs [9]. However, robustness properties of random-key-graph connectivity under the limited visibility assumption have not been considered to date. Of similar interest are questions of connectivity in random key graphs when some of the links of individual nodes fail.

Note: Since the presentation of this paper in April 2009, additional interesting properties of random key graphs have been investigated; e.g., k-connectivity [12], diameter size [13]. Random key graphs have also been shown to be good candidates for "small world" models [14].

Acknowledgement. This research was supported in part by CyLab at Carnegie Mellon under grants DAAD19-02-1-0389 and MURI W 911 NF 0710287 from the Army Research Office. The views and conclusions contained here are those of the authors and should not be interpreted as necessarily representing the official policies or endorsements, either express or implied, of ARO, CMU, or the U.S. Government or any of its agencies.

References

1. Blackburn, S., Gerke, S.: Connectivity of the Uniform Random Intersection Graph. Discrete Mathematics 309(16), 5130–5140 (2009)
2. Eschenauer, L., Gligor, V.D.: A Key-Management Scheme for Distributed Sensor Networks. In: 9th ACM Conference on Computer and Communications Security, Alexandria, VA (2002)
3. Goehardt, E., Jaworski, J., Rybarczyk, K.: Random Intersection Graphs and Classification. In: Lens, H.J., Decker, R. (eds.) Studies in Classification, Data Analysis, and Knowledge Organization, vol. 33, pp. 67–74. Springer, Berlin (2007)
4. Marbach, P.: A Lower Bound on the Number of Rankings Required in Recommender Systems Using Collaborative Filtering. In: IEEE Conference on Information Sciences and Systems, pp. 292–297. Princeton University, NJ (2008)
5. Blackburn, S.R., Stinson, D.R., Upadhyay, J.: On the Complexity of the Herding Attack and Some Related Attacks on Hash Functions. Report 2010/030 (2010), http://eprint.iacr.org/
6. Yağan, O., Makowski, A.: On the Random Graph Induced by a Random Key Predistribution Scheme under Full Visibility. In: IEEE International Symposium on Information Theory, Toronto, ON (2008)
7. Yağan, O., Makowski, A.: Zero-One Laws for Connectivity in Random Key Graphs. Technical Report, Institute for Systems Research, University of Maryland (February 2009)
8. Eschenauer, L., Gligor, V.D., Baras, J.: On Trust Establishment in Mobile *Ad-Hoc* Networks. In: Christianson, B., Crispo, B., Malcolm, J.A., Roe, M. (eds.) Security Protocols 2002. LNCS, vol. 2845, pp. 47–66. Springer, Heidelberg (2004)

9. Di Pietro, R., Mancini, L.V., Mei, A., Panconesi, A., Radhakrishnan, J.: Redoubtable Sensor Networks. ACM Transactions on Information and System Security (TISSEC) 11(3) (March 2008)
10. Wendlandt, D., Andersen, D., Perrig, A.: Perspectives: Improving SSH-style Host Authentication with Multi-Path Probing. In: USENIX Annual Technical Conference (June 2008)
11. Kelsey, J., Kohno, T.: Herding Hash Functions and the Nostradamus Attack. In: Vaudenay, S. (ed.) EUROCRYPT 2006. LNCS, vol. 4004, pp. 183–200. Springer, Heidelberg (2006)
12. Rybarczyk, K.: Sharp Threshold Functions for Random Intersection Graphs via a Coupling Method. The Electronic Journal of Combinatorics 18(1), 36–47 (2011)
13. Rybarczyk, K.: Diameter, Connectivity, and Phase Transition of the Uniform Random Intersection Graph. Submitted to Discrete Mathematics (July 2009)
14. Yağan, O., Makowski, A.: Random Key Graphs? - Can They Be Small Worlds? In: International Conference on Networks & Communications, pp. 313–318 (2009)

Brief Encounters with a Random Key Graph

(Transcript of Discussion)

Virgil D. Gligor

Carnegie Mellon University

The notion of the *random key graph*, which originally appeared in models of secure communication in wireless sensor networks, has been used in other applications, some of which are unrelated to cryptographic-key predistribution or sensor networks. In this presentation, I will outline some of these applications, which exploit the connectivity property of random key graphs and its similarity with that of random graphs. I'd like to start with the zero-one law for random-graph connectivity, then explain how (i.e., for what graph parameters) this law appears in random key graphs. Then, I will present three brief encounters with random-key-graph properties in new settings and perhaps speculate on other types of useful properties they might have.

Random graphs, denoted by $G(n,p)$, were defined by Paul Erdös and Alfred Rényi in 1959[1]. Informally, one can envision a set of nodes, n, and some probability, p, that an edge exists between any two nodes. This probability p depends on n and a scalar α, namely $p = \frac{\ln n + \alpha}{n}$, and the connectivity of $G(n,p)$ is provided by the much celebrated double exponential, $e^{-e^{-\alpha}}$, when $n \to +/-\infty$. Note that a *zero-one law of connectivity* emerges: $G(n,p)$ is almost surely connected if $\lim_{n\to+\infty} \alpha = +\infty$ (i.e., the one law) and almost surely disconnected if $\lim_{n\to+\infty} \alpha = -\infty$) (i.e., the zero law).

In 2002, Laurent Eschenauer and I defined a key predistribution scheme for large wireless sensor networks, which was intended to provide secure connectivity[2]. The scheme is very simple: before deployment, each sensor in a network of n nodes is independently equipped with K_n *distinct* keys selected uniformly at random from a pool of P_n. For example, the pool might have a hundred thousand keys, and for each sensor one draws independently and without replacement two hundred keys, and loads them in the sensor. The process is repeated for each of the n nodes. The main point is that K_n has to be much, much smaller than the $n(n-1)/2$ key copies one would need for pairwise connectivity of all n nodes, and yet it can assure key sharing between sensors with high probability. Eschenauer and I speculated that our simple scheme induces a graph – denoted by $G(K_n, P_n, n)$ here – that has a similar key-connectivity property as a random graph, based on simulations for a range of parameters we played with. But, of course, we didn't have a proof, and consequently we were called to task by

---

[1] Erdös P., and Rényi, A., "On random graphs," in *Publicationes Mathematicae* (Debrecen), 6:290297, 1959.

[2] Eschenauer, L., Gligor, V.D., "A Key-Management Scheme for Distributed Sensor Networks," In: 9th ACM Conference on Computer and Communications Security, Alexandria, VA (2002).

B. Christianson et al. (Eds.): Security Protocols 2009, LNCS 7028, pp. 162–170, 2013.

a number of people who pointed out that although we got some connectivity properties, they are not necessarily going to be those of random graphs.

Lo and behold in February 2009, Yağan and Makowski[3] of the University of Maryland demonstrated that if $K_n \geq 2$, $P_n > 3K_n$ and $p \sim \frac{K_n^2}{P_n} = \frac{\ln n + \alpha}{n}$, then the random key graph $G(n, K_n, P_n)$ is almost surely connected if $\lim_{n \to +\infty} \alpha = +\infty$ and almost surely disconnected if $\lim_{n \to +\infty} \alpha = -\infty$. In other words, one obtains exactly the same emergence of connectivity in a random key graph as that of an Erdös-Rényi random graph for an appropriate choice of parameters.

This is a nice result that made me wonder about what else we could do with this property of random key graphs. Recall that, in sensor networks, one can establish key connectivity between two nodes by a very simple procedure. Any node, which is pre-loaded with the sets of keys, can use a standard block cipher to encipher a constant with all the keys it has, and then broadcast the set of ciphertext blocks. Each recipient of the broadcast performs the encipherment of the same (public) constant and takes the intersection of the computed set and received set of ciphertexts, to establish common keys, if any. So ciphertext collisions are an indication of *key collisions* or sharing between nodes of the network and yield the random key graph in practice.

The fact that we have the zero-one law for connectivity of a random key graph, tells us the first interesting property that I'd like to illustrate, namely that we can have *location-independence* for network nodes. In other words, wherever a node is moved from one network location to another it has the same probability of being connected, namely $p \sim \frac{K_n^2}{P_n} = \frac{\ln n + \alpha}{n}$. So by changing node locations in a network one doesn't lose connectivity, provided that there is *global visibility* among the nodes of the network. That is, all nodes must be within direct communication range of each other. (As mentioned in the original paper, global visibility is not a property that typical sensor networks would have.)

So how else can we exploit random-key-graph connectivity when global visibility is assured? Well, the second thing we can do is to look at applications of *recommender systems with collaborative filtering*, which can also be modeled by random key graphs. Peter Marbach of the University of Toronto[4], pointed out that a number of companies, like Amazon and Netflix, use programs to figure out how to selectively serve ads to particular users. For example, say Matt [Blaze], Mike [Roe], Ben [Laurie], and I independently choose a bunch of books from some pool and rank them according to how much we liked reading them. Some of our book choices will be (e.g., pairwise) common and will have the same ranking. Then the provider of the pool, say Amazon, could serve ads in a selective way based on the random (key-like) graph induced by our independent choices; e.g., if I haven't chosen a book that Matt did, when I login at Amazon,

[3] Yağan, O., Makowski, A.: Zero-One Laws for Connectivity in Random Key Graphs. Technical Report, Institute for Systems Research, University of Maryland, February (2009).

[4] Marbach, P.: A Lower Bound on the Number of Rankings Required in Recommender Systems Using Collaborative Filtering. In: IEEE Conference on Information Sciences and Systems, pp 292-297, Princeton University, NJ (2008).

it could serve me an ad for a book that Matt picked, since its recommender system could compute the probability that I would rank that book the same way as Matt did. The idea is that Amazon would be selective in its advertising, which is supposedly a much better, namely more cost-effective way to serve ads than simply dumping random ads on its users.

Essentially what Marbach showed is that if one has a pool of P_N objects from which N users independently select and rank K_N objects, then whenever a user has a common ranking r with another user for the same independently selected object, one can construct a graph $G(K_N, P_N, N)$ among those users. That is, there is an edge between two users if and only if the following conditions hold: (1) there exists at least one object that is ranked by both users; (2) *any* object that is ranked by both users is given the same rank by those users. A recommender class C is defined as a set of users who independently give the same ranking to any particular object that is ranked by at least one user of the set. This implies that every subset of users in class C who rank a common object assign the same ranking to that object, and that not every user in class C ranks all objects ranked by others in C; i.e., there exist users in class C that have not ranked objects ranked by others in class C.

Marbach's observation was that instead of characterizing the minimum number of objects that need to be ranked by each advertising algorithm individually in collaborative filtering, one can provide a general property of all such algorithms. That is, one can find the minimum number of objects K_n of a pool of size P_n that n users need to rank so that advertisers can identify them as belonging to the same class C. The necessary condition for identifying class C is that a sub-graph $G(K_n, P_n, n)$ of $G(K_N, P_N, N)$ is connected. Graph $G(K_n, P_n, n)$ is almost surely connected if $\frac{K_n^2}{P_n} = \omega\left(\frac{\log n}{n}\right)$. In fact, the goal is to predict the ranking a user in class C would give an object he has not yet ranked, but which was already ranked by other users in C. So returning to my original example, if Matt, Mike, Ben and I independently rank some books and belong to the same class C, then I would receive an ad for a book that Mike and Ben ranked but which I did not. The probability that I would like that book as much as Mike and Ben is asymptotically equal to $\frac{K_n^2}{P_n}$ for certain values of n, K_n and P_n. That's really the idea here.

This was the first class of new applications for random key graphs. It turns out that one can use the connectivity properties of these graphs in *trust establishment* as well. For example, we can use roughly the same theory to evaluate (i.e., rank) self-signed certificates we receive from various sites of the Internet. In this context, one could evaluate the certificate ranking given by a class C of trusted nodes (i.e., users). The connected graph $G(K_n, P_n, n)$ allows one to predict the acceptance of new certificates by users of class C, which were already ranked by other users in C, with probability asymptotically equal to $\frac{K_n^2}{P_n}$. How users in class C independently reach their certificate-trust rankings is irrelevant here. Somehow they can decide to trust those certificates at some level (i.e., rank). The basic idea of predicting the acceptance of new certificates with some rank is the same as in predicting object (e.g., books) rankings.

Of course, one can envision other applications which are somewhat more far-fetched, but nevertheless interesting. Imagine that the pool of P_N objects is the set of known security flaws in system software, and that each flaw can lead to r attacks (a.k.a "exploits"). Imagine that adversaries independently pick flaws and their exploits. Over time, a defense agency observes a that a set of N adversaries launched at least K_N attacks each exploiting known security flaws. The agency can construct a graph $G(K_N, P_N, N)$ of adversary nodes with an edge between two nodes representing use of the same attack, namely the same flaw and exploit choices were independently made by the two adversaries. It turns out that, at least in the US, some government agencies have a pretty good idea who their adversaries are, and what attacks they have used, as they've seen lots of attacks exploiting lots of system flaws over time; e.g., there are thousands of attacks against US systems per day. A question of interest is: What *new attack*, namely known flaw-exploit pair, will one of these adversaries use next? The answer to this question can be predicted by using the recommender class C of adversaries, hence the connectivity properties of graph $G(K_n, P_n, n)$, and probability asymptotically equal to $\frac{K_n^2}{P_n}$.

Frank Stajano: Sorry, in what sense do you call it a *new* attack if it is known?

Reply: The exploit is known, but it is new to that particular adversary.

Frank Stajano: The attacker never used it before.

Reply: Yes, he's never used it before; right, that's what I intended to say.

The last example I'd like to present is a bit more involved but it also deals with discovery of *key collisions* based on ciphertext collisions in a similar manner as that used in discovery of key sharing in random key graphs. However, graph connectivity is not a relevant issue here.

Consider the standard notion of secure encryption modes, called *indistinguishability from random*[5], denoted by IND$. This notion is strictly stronger than "indistinguishability of ciphertexts," typically denoted by IND. What properties of IND$ do we know so far? We know that if an encryption mode has the IND$ property in an attack, say *chosen plaintext attack* (CPA), it also has the *key hiding property* defined by Marc Fischlin in 1999[6]. Informally, the key hiding property says that if one examines two ciphertexts produced by a key-hiding encryption scheme, one cannot tell whether the two ciphertexts were produced by encryption with the same key or with a different key. This is a very useful property for anonymity. For example, when one sees ciphertexts in a network one cannot link them to a particular key or to a particular transaction. It's easy to prove that IND$ implies key hiding (denoted by KH_2 here); e.g., when the adversary is allowed to launch a chosen-plaintext attack against two oracles

---

[5] P. Rogaway, "Nonce-Based Symmetric Encryption," In Proc. of Fast Software Encryption, 2004.

[6] Fischlin, M.,"Pseudorandom Function Tribe Ensembles Based on One-Way Permutations: Improvements and Applications," in Proc. of EUROCRYPT 1999, pp. 432-445.

implementing an IND\$ secure mode, the adversary cannot tell whether the two oracles use the same or different keys with more than negligible probability. It turns out that one can also prove, by reduction, that IND\$ security also implies key hiding with p oracles, where p is greater than 2, which we denote by KH_p. And it's also fairly easy (after you see the proof) to show that KH_p implies another property, which we call *existential key recovery* protection with p oracles, and denote by EKR_p. Informally, $EHR_p - CPA$ says that the adversary has access to p encryption oracles for a chosen plaintext attack and the adversary's goal is to recover at least one of the p keys used by the oracles for encryption in the IND\$-secure mode.

In general, we know[7] that IND\$ $\Rightarrow KH_p \Rightarrow EKR_p$ in several attacks, which include CPA, KPA (known plaintext attack) and PPA (predictable plaintext attack). The thing to notice is that these reductions are *non-tight*. Non-tightness of a reduction "Security Property B $\Rightarrow$ Security Property A" can be explained informally as follows. Let an adversary (i.e., a polynomially bounded program) A's advantage in breaking Security Property A in time t_A exceed ϵ_A. Then in a reduction, an adversary (i.e., polynomially bounded program) B can break Security Property B, by calling adversary A possibly multiple times, in time t_B with an advantage that exceeds ϵ_B. A reduction is said to be non-tight if ϵ_A is much greater than ϵ_B, or alternatively if the time t_A is much smaller than t_B. So how do we get non-tightness in the above reductions, say if Security Property B is IND\$ and A is EKR_p? In this case, the reduction leads to the relation $\epsilon_A \leq p \cdot \epsilon_B$, for a polynomially bounded variable p. In other words, the advantage of adversary A can become p times larger than that of B.

Note that in asymptotic proofs the rate of growth of the number of oracles, p, does not matter since ϵ_A and ϵ_B are negligible functions of a security parameter n. Hence, if in the expression $O(p) \cdot \epsilon_B(n)$ the number of oracles p available to an adversary grows, $\epsilon_B(n)$ decreases faster by increasing security parameter n, and thus the product will yield a very small upper bound ϵ_A for adversary A's advantage. Consequently, whether p is a small constant (i.e., the reduction is tight) or a very large value (i.e., the reduction becomes non-tight) makes absolutely no difference. However, when one instantiates an IND\$-secure encryption mode with a symmetric-key, block-cipher parameters and the magic of increasing security parameter n no longer works, since n does not exist in symmetric-key block ciphers. Hence, as conjectured by Koblitz and Menezes[8], non-tight reductions may lead to unforeseen successful attacks. In the balance of this presentation, I will illustrate key-collision attacks that invalidate the results of non-tight reductions obtained (by asymptotic proofs) above. To do this, I will use the easily proved fact that $EKR_p - CPA \Rightarrow EKR_p - KPA \Rightarrow EKR_p - PPA$.

Let's see how a key-collision attack can be launched in the Internet. The first question that I ask is: what's the probability that an adversary can launch a

---

[7] Virgil D. Gligor, Bryan Parno, and Ji Sun Shin, "Network Adversary Attacks against Secure Encryption Schemes," Technical Report CMU-CyLab-10-001, January, 2010.

[8] Koblitz, N., and Menezes, A., "Another Look at Provable Security II," R. Barua and T. Lange (eds.): INDOCRYPT 2006, LNCS 4329, pp. 148175, 2006.

successful $EKR_p - KPA$ attack and discover at least one key used in encrypting messages in an IND\$ secure mode? Such a mode certainly has the $EKR_p - KPA$ security property since $IND\$ - CPA \Rightarrow EKR_p - KPA$. To get a collision with a known key, I will use ciphertext collisions – obtained from plaintext block enciphering in a IND\$-secure encryption mode – much the same as those used to discover key sharing in the random key graph. If there is a key collision, then the adversary breaks the $EKR_p - KPA$ property with some advantage, and the advantage is exactly the probability of a collision.

How many KPA oracles p does the adversary have in the Internet? Assume that we have n hosts each of which has r connections encrypted in an IND\$-secure mode. The $p = n \cdot r$ oracles are available to a KPA adversary for free in the sense that Internet protocols may provide those cipherblocks of known plaintext blocks. For instance, an adversary can passively obtain encryption in $n \cdot r$ different keys of a known constant located at a fixed position in all messages. You may wonder, what would an Internet protocol encrypt constants at a fixed message location? Well, it turns out that some Internet protocols do, as I'll argue in a minute. Anyway, the larger point is that it's not just a single KPA adversary that can win, it's an entire network of adversaries that can win with a non-negligible probability of a key collision; i.e., *multiple adversaries* can launch key collision attacks. Hence, a provably secure IND\$ encryption scheme may become vulnerable to key collision attacks in the Internet. One such scheme that I will illustrate shortly is the standard nonce-based counter-mode. There is a variety of *stateful* countermode-based encryption schemes recommended by NIST and all are vulnerable to these attacks when implemented with standard block ciphers, including 2key-3DES and 128-AES.

But before I illustrate the key collision attack using a nonce-based counter-mode let me just say a few things about key-collision attacks, in general. The first attacks like this were actually done by Turing and his colleagues at Bletchley Park. We learned about them at a dinner with the late Harry Hinsley, a colleague of Turing's and former Master of St. John's College, Cambridge, at the 1995 *Security Protocols Workshop*. Hinsley also described these attacks in his 1993 book. In 1997, Steve Bellovin[9] published a paper illustrating how Internet protocols encrypt predictable plaintext; i.e., he found predictable plaintext in the TCP/IP headers, which get encrypted in IPsec.

Frank Stajano: Excuse me, what is the book?

Reply: The 1993 book is co-edited by Harry Hinsley and Alan Stripp and is entitled *Codebreakers: The inside story of Bletchley Park*, and I can give you the chapter and verse on those attacks.

By the way, Turing seems to be the first to use reduction arguments in cryptography. On page 159 of this book, Jack Goode, a statistician who was working

---

[9] Bellovin, S., "Probable Plaintext Cryptanalysis of the IP Security Protocols," In Proc. of 1997 Symposium on Network and Distributed Systems Security, ISOC, San Diego, February 1997.

with Turing, pointed out that by using reduction arguments, Turing decreased the effort to find the stecker positions of an Enigma machine by a factor of 26.

In 1996, Eli Biham published a technical report (which appeared later in *Information Processing Letters* in 2002[10]), where he also suggested key-collision attacks, but his were quite different. He used birthday collisions for keys, and of course none of those work for 128 bit keys and *probabilistic* encryption modes such as the ones I illustrate here. He looked for high-probability collisions when in fact one only needs a non-negligible probability to break these modes; e.g., the probability of a collision doesn't have to be 1; it can be 1 in a million; 1 in 2^{20} is huge compared to 1 in 2^{128}. Biham limited his attacks to *stateless deterministic* modes; e.g., he illustrated practical attacks only for the ECB mode, which of course is known to be broken in any case in other ways. Ross Anderson pointed out to him that probabilistic modes could also be broken. However these attacks were impractical with the modes illustrated, unless they use some version of DES-based encryption.

In the Spring of 1999, while at Cambridge University, I wrote a technical report called Symmetric Encryption with Random Counters, in which I gave examples of key-collision attacks for stateful encryption modes and I'll revisit those examples in this context now. Let us consider two standard modes of encryption published by NIST, namely *stateful countermode* (CTRC) and *stateful cipher-block chaining* (CBCC). The encryption of plaintext block x_i of any message in CTRC is given by the formula $y_i \oplus x_i = F_{Kj}(ctr_j + i)$, where y_i is the cipherblock obtained by using block cipher F with key K_j. The counter is initialized to a *nonce* per key as index j suggests. (Note that nonce-based CTRC is IND\$-CPA, not just IND-CPA, secure[11].) Now suppose that the nonce is known, as the standards allow; for example, it might be zero. So as long as the counter is correctly updated with every new message, this mode is secure. Also suppose that some block index i within a message format of a protocol (e.g., a header that is encrypted) contains a known plaintext x_i. Now note that for the first message encrypted in any key K_j the value of $ctr_j + i$ becomes a *known constant*. Hence an adversary can obtain the enciphering of constant $ctr_j + i$, namely $F_{Kj}(ctr_j + i) = y_i \oplus x_i$ in $n \cdot r$, in different keys K_j, where n is the number of Internet hosts each of which has r encrypted connections in countermode. If the adversary enciphers constant $ctr_j + i$ in T different keys offline, its probability of obtaining a key collision (i.e., its $EKR_p - KPA$ advantage) with one of the p cipher blocks obtained online becomes $\frac{n \cdot r \cdot T}{2^k}$, where k is the size of a key.

Key collision attacks are possible in other modes, such stateful CBC. For example, the NIST standards also tell us that in ordinary CBC one can compute the pseudo-random IV per message simply by encrypting a counter (surely with a separate key), which is not supposed to repeat, of course. The counter becomes the known constant enciphered in different keys, and its corresponding ciphertext

---

[10] Volume 84, issue 3, page 117.

[11] P. Rogaway, "Nonce-Based Symmetric Encryption," In Proc. of Fast Software Encryption, 2004.

is the pseudorandom IV, which is output since the IV must be sent to the recipient. This mode is also IND$-CPA secure.

What would the $EKR_p - KPA$ advantage of a *single adversary* be in practice? Let's assume that n is between 2^{24} and 2^{26}, representing between 2% and 7% of the current (2009) Internet hosts, which perform connection encryption in nonce-based CTRC and that they use a popular protocol, like SSL (which currently uses ordinary CBC). The number of hosts is similar to that of Facebook or MySpace users, or to the number of members of the Chinese Communist Party (which is currently about 70 million). So we are talking about reasonable orders of magnitude. So suppose that r is somewhere between 2^{28} and 2^{31}, which is also a reasonable number considering that connections to popular sites are up to 2^{38} nowadays, but let's not go that far, let's just say $r = 2^{28}$. Hence, for $(r = 2^{28}, n = 2^{24}, T = 2^{48})$ one obtains a lower bound and for $(r = 2^{31}, n = 2^{27}, T = 2^{50})$ one obtains an upper bound for the $EKR_p - KPA$ advantage. These $EKR_p - KPA$ advantage bounds are between 2^{-20} to 2^{-28} for 128AES, and 2^{-4} to 2^{-12} for 112 bit triple DES. These are very uncomfortable probabilities. Why? If one looks at the NIST key management guidelines one notices that 112 bit keys of 2key-3DES should last *until 2030*, but based on this attack you only have about 4 bits of security. And then 128 bit AES keys should last *beyond 2030*, but they actually only have about 20 bits of security.

How much might these attacks cost? The dominant cost is that of storage (and probably cooling costs) for $2^{48} \leq T \leq 2^{50}$ block encryptions. This would cost between \$.5M and \$2M, at \$65 per terabyte in early 2009, \$.3M and \$1.2M in late 2009, and \$ 62.5 K and \$250 K in late 2012 (at \$8 per terabyte).

Matt Blaze: That's disk storage, correct?

Reply: Yes, the predictions are that by the end of 2012 one will reach a conservative figure of about \$8 per terabyte. Storage prices still drop at 37% to 50% per year, it's slowed down a bit from halving a 50% drop every year, but it's still up there. The last costs mentioned are projections for three years from now.

Given these low costs of breaking standard encryption modes in $EKR_p - KPA$ attacks, one has to wonder about what can be done to fix the problem. We can do two things. One is to ask for the doubling of the key lengths. NIST is contemplating this option, although this not an easy matter. Changing the lengths of the keys is really very difficult particularly when these key lengths are hardwired in block ciphers. The second option is to change the guidelines and remove the mode options that are particularly vulnerable to $EKR_p - KPA$ attacks.

In summary, I showed that the Koblitz-Menezes 2006 conjecture that non-tight reduction proofs would lead to successful existential key recovery attacks is in fact valid at a relatively low cost. Paraphrasing a known maxim, "if an encryption mode is provably secure (in non-tight reduction proofs), it is probably insecure."

Dusko Pavlovic: The examples are convincing, but can you tell more about the proof that every non-tight reduction gives an attack? Is there an effective proof that you get a concrete attack, or do you just have the existence of attack?

Reply: The reductions of the chain IND\$ - CPA $\Rightarrow KH_p - CPA \Rightarrow EKR_p - CPA$ are non-tight, whereas $EKR_p - CPA \Rightarrow EKR_p - KPA$ is tight. The $EKR_p - KPA$ attack using an enciphered constant always works. In fact, even a weaker $EKR_p - PPA$ attack would also work in practice (i.e., with reasonable costs). Once an $EKR_p - KPA$ attack is successful, the entire chain of non-tight proofs fails.

Dusko Pavlovic: I don't doubt the examples, but just the proof itself; if I give you a non-tight proof, are you deriving from that a concrete attack on a protocol, or do you just have an existence proof?

Reply: In these examples, the non-tight reductions allow the direct derivation of concrete attacks. This is the case because the non-tightness factor p represents the number of oracles an EKR_p adversary has. There is no "magic" here. That is, there is no shortcut in these proofs that would change p from a polynomially bounded variable to a small constant factor. This means that one cannot convert them into tight proofs and hence the attacks could always be derived directly from the non-tightness factor. Thanks for asking this question, as I forgot to mention that these attacks are derived directly from the non-tightness factor p in these proofs.

I have to give credit to the Koblitz and Menezes paper[12], which also questions the value of non-tight reduction proofs that can be (magically) converted into tight reduction proofs (viz., Section 4.3, pages 8-9). Their paper, which contains several examples in which non-tight reduction proofs lead to invalid or impractical security results, left this open problem:

"Find an example of a natural and realistic protocol that has a plausible (non-tight) reductionist proof of security, and is also insecure when used with commonly accepted parameter sizes. (page 6)"

That is precisely what we found[13] and illustrated here, and one cannot get more commonly accepted (standard) parameter sizes[14].

---

[12] Another Look at Provable Security II, Indocrypt 2006, LNCS 4329, Springer Verlag.

[13] Virgil D. Gligor, Bryan Parno, and Ji Sun Shin, "Network Adversary Attacks against Secure Encryption Schemes," Technical Report CMU-CyLab-10-001, January, 2010.

[14] Note added in proof. Additional examples that also call in to question the value of non-tight reduction proofs are provided by Sanjit Chatterjee, Alfred Menezes, and Palash Sarkar in "Another look at Tightness," IACR Cryptology ePrint Archive 2011: 442 (2011)

Trust*: Using Local Guarantees
to Extend the Reach of Trust

Stephen Clarke, Bruce Christianson, and Hannan Xiao

School of Computer Science, University of Hertfordshire, UK
{s.w.1.clarke,b.christianson,h.xiao}@herts.ac.uk

Abstract. We propose a new concept called trust* as a way of avoiding the necessity to transitively trust others in a range of distributed environments. The trust* approach uses guarantees based upon already established trust relationships. These localised guarantees are then used to extend trust to a new relationship (which we call trust*) which can hold between principals which are unknown to and do not trust one another. Such chains of guarantees enable the risk involved to be shifted to another party (in a similar way to real world guarantees). If a guarantee is broken, some kind of 'forfeit' is imposed, either to compensate the client or to deter the server from doing it habitually. Due to trust (and hence also forfeits) being localised, the specific micro-payment and trust management mechanisms that are used to implement the protocol can be heterogeneous. This paper describes the concept of trust* and some possible applications within a domain where the service being provided is also electronic.

1 Building on Trust

Building trust on the Internet is a well researched area. Many solutions assume (often implicitly) that trust is transitive. Commonly used examples are reputation systems where each of its users has a reputation rating. These ratings can be viewed by other users and later increased or decreased depending on the outcome of a transaction. Such reputation systems are commonly used on the Internet for various purposes and generally work well. However, as mentioned, reputation systems have a vital flaw; they imply that trust is transitive [8,7]. Assume a user wants to determine the risk involved if they were to trust another (eg. to provide a described service) by looking at their reputation rating. This might contain comments and ratings left from previous transactions. It is unlikely that the user looking knows (or trusts) the other users who have left the comments. But even if they *do* know and trust the people who left the comments, they will still be transitively trusting the service provider in question.

The motivation behind this work is to find a new way of building on trust which avoids this need for transitivity. The ability to build trust in the real world is also a common necessity. In real world protocols, this ability is often facilitated by using a guarantor as a replacement for transitivity of trust. Guarantees work by shifting the risk to another party thus lowering the risk for the trusting party.

B. Christianson et al. (Eds.): Security Protocols 2009, LNCS 7028, pp. 171–178, 2013.

Trust* is based on the electronic equivalent of the real world guarantee solution. Say that Carol needs to trust Alice about something and doesn't personally know or trust Alice. However, Carol trusts Bob who in turn trusts Alice to do whatever it is Carol needs her to do. In order to change Carol's perception of the risk involved, Bob could guarantee to Carol that Alice will act as intended and offer Carol compensation if Alice doesn't. So, what's Bob's incentive to act as a broker between Alice and Carol? We'll come back to this later, but for now assume that Alice pays Bob a commission.

This concept of 'extending' trust in this way by using localised guarantees is what we call a trust* relationship. The trust*er (Carol) can then act *as if* they trust the trust*ee (Alice) directly. In order to shift the risk, forfeit payments are used. These will be discussed later, but assume for now that they are micro-payments. All forfeits are paid locally; if Alice defaults then Bob must pay Carol the agreed forfeit whether or not Alice pays Bob the forfeit she owes him (and the two forfeits may be of different amounts). Failure to provide a service - or to pay a forfeit - may result in an update to a *local* trust relationship.

Trust* can be composed to an arbitrary number of hops because all trust is now local and so are the forfeits. It is worth noting that trust isn't the same as trust* even in a one hop scenario. If Bob trust*s Alice to provide a service, it means that Bob trusts Alice to either provide the service or else pay the forfeit[1].

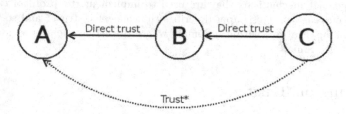

Fig. 1. A Trust* Relationship

2   Applications

There are several promising application areas to which trust* might be beneficially applied.

Spam-proof Email. Trust* could be used to implement an email system where messages can be forwarded with an accompanying guarantee claiming that the email is not 'spam'[2]. Spammers rely on sending millions of emails a day to

---

[1] It may be that Bob would rather have the money, and believes that Alice cannot provide the service, but will always pay the forfeit.

[2] The idea was inspired by a 1930's door bell system that was designed to stop unsolicited callers disturbing a household [13]. The door bell is activated by inserting a low value coin which upon answering is refunded if the caller is welcome, otherwise it is kept. This analogy has various flaws but the idea might be better suited to deterring spammers in the cyberworld. Although the coin value is low, to call at hundreds/thousands of houses would soon add up.

make any respectable profit so it would be unviable for them if even low-value guarantees were required. I'll happily read any email for 10p cash up-front. Now the spammers need to find a cheaper route based on this. This requires email users to filter out emails without guarantees, but existing spam filter applications can be used for this.

Grid Computing. How trust can be built in computational grids (which are likely to span organisational and domain boundaries) is a well researched problem [4,9,11]. Trust* could easily be applied as a solution and as most grids are used to share resource's across organisations, these resources could be used as the currency for forfeit and commission payments. Resources might include CPU cycles, storage or bandwidth. These typically vary in perceived value between the provider and receiver, so resources could also be brokered in this way, converting one resource into another.

Peer-to-peer Computing. When sharing files, most users feel more comfortable knowing that what they might download is licensed, or at least untampered with. Research into building trust in P2p environments has suggested ways of providing this comfort [10,14]. For example, the Turtle [12] P2p client allows a user to share data with 'friends' or those you already trust directly. In their paper, they suggest that Turtle can be enhanced with an economic model to encourage cooperation and sharing. Applying trust* would not only provide a mechanism to enable this but also allow new principals to join the sharing of files under guaranteed conditions. This application is similar to grid computing except the content itself is now the resource.

Volunteer Computing. Many volunteer computing projects require spare CPU cycles to be donated (during screensavers etc) by millions of users worldwide in order to solve a computationally difficult problem. Examples include SETI@Home, a SHA-1 collision search and many others. Multiple projects can be registered and administered using a client called BOINC [1]. There are many security issues [2] related to volunteer computing which could benefit from applying trust*. Volunteer computing differs from grid computing in that anyone can volunteer, whereas grids usually cross organisations which already have a reputation.

Second Life. Trust* could be extended to real world transactions such as e-commerce, but it's easier to keep a transaction purely electronic and use trust* in a virtual world. In Second Life, trust* could be used to facilitate the buying and selling of virtual objects. Second Life has its own currency (Linden Dollars) which could be used for making the required commission or forfeit payments. Also, Linden Labs have recently revamped their scripting language and cryptographic libraries within the virtual world which could make guarantee creation and verification possible.

Music Downloads. Many people now buy music online rather than buying a physical copy. Services such as iTunes offer single tracks for less than a pound. However, it is unknown to the downloader how much of this money is actually going to the artist or group who produced the music.

Trust* could be used to ensure that a music vendor (iTunes for example) will actually pass on the 30 pence (or whatever was agreed) to the artist. If they don't prove that they did, then the guarantor will pay the artist, prove that they did, and claim it back from the vendor later. This way the artist will always receive their royalties. A possible privacy issue is that proving the money was paid for a specific individual's purchase might divulge their identity to the recording company or artist. Various payment protocols address this, for example, anonymous payments which include a client challenge.

Charity Donations. Similarly, a website might include a sponsored link with a promise that 1p will go to charity for every click made. The individual clicking the link might want assurance that the intended charity will actually receive this donation. Here the forfeit would be to produce a receipt showing that the donation has been made, possibly by the guarantor.

3 Discussion

3.1 Networking Analogies

By now you will have noticed that many of the problems with deploying trust* are analogous to well known networking problems. Fortunately, the corresponding network protocol solutions also have trust* analogues. For example, finding the best route between two nodes on a network is analogous to finding an optimal route between two principals who wish to form a trust* relationship with one another. The six degrees of separation argument implies a trust* route can always be found but the best route could be the cheapest (according to commission or computational expense) or the most trusted[3]. It is assumed that any established network routing protocol will suffice for finding optimal chains of guarantors, although the choice of algorithm will have subtle consequences.

Another example is network back pressure. Analogously, if trust* is repeatedly broken between two principals, the guarantor is likely to either break the local trust completely (never provide guarantees again) with the principal being guaranteed (which corresponds to a link outage) or dramatically increase their commission or forfeit rates (which corresponds to a price increase, or a delay). If a particular link drops between two nodes, a route which previously utilised this link might become more expensive for surrounding nodes. This is likely to cause a bottleneck for other nodes following alternative routes and further increasing their cost. These issues can be addressed using network congestion control techniques, and so on.

One difference with conventional networking is that all our links are one way, because trust isn't generally symmetric, whereas most service contracts are bidirectional. This isn't a problem, because two trust* paths can be found in opposite directions via a different route of guarantors[4].

---

[3] Different levels of trust, forfeit and commission etc correspond to different network Quality of Services.

[4] The analogy is thus with a network of links which are uni-directional for data flow, although bi-directional for control flow.

3.2   Commission and Forfeits

The most obvious use of a forfeit is either to deter a principal from defaulting on what they have guaranteed or to provide a way of compensating the other party if they do. The commission payment was introduced in order to provide an incentive for a principal to act as a guarantor and can be seen as a spot price for a guarantee. A principal needing to be trust*ed could pay this commission to a guarantor who trusts them directly.

Forfeit and commission payments serve different purposes and don't need to be of the same type (or paid by the same means). Also, these payments and the actual service being provided need not be like-for-like.

The price of a guarantee or the forfeit that should be paid if it is broken are variable and could be set by a guarantor to reflect their perception of the risk involved in providing a guarantee. For example; as a risky guarantee is more likely to be broken, a higher forfeit might be required by the guarantor. A low risk guarantee is unlikely to be broken so the guarantor will get his incentive through the commission as a forfeit payment is less likely to happen. Another incentive to provide a guarantee is to make a profit from a forfeit. Assume that Alice is trust*ed by Carol with Bob providing the guarantee to Carol. If Alice defaults, the forfeit from Alice to Bob might be more than Bob has to pay Carol[5].

These considerations lead to some interesting effects regarding the commission and forfeit rates along a chain of guarantees. In this scenario, if Alice was to default the guarantee, only Alice will be out of pocket as the forfeit rate is higher at her end of the chain (and decreases towards the trust*ing end). Every guarantor will make a profit in this case but if we consider a longer chain where risk perceptions fluctuate, guarantors might lose out. For this reason, it is likely that guarantors will only provide guarantees where they believe the rates involved will make them better off in most cases. This flexibility of perception is vital in ensuring that guarantors get their incentive and principals who might default are sufficiently deterred.

3.3   Heterogeneity

In order to implement the trust* relationship mechanism, whether to initiate, provide, or receive a guarantee, a way of making decisions and payments is necessary. In our initial implementation, we used the Keynote trust management system [5] to act as the core decision maker and also to provide the syntax and semantics of the guarantee credentials and policies. To make payments, a micropayment system [6] (also implemented in Keynote) provided a way for principals to pay commission and forfeits to each other. However, one of the advantages

---

[5] Note that this gives Bob an incentive to hope that Alice defaults. Alternatively, Alice may pay Bob a commission instead of a forfeit, in which case Bob hopes that she doesn't default. The second case is like buying insurance. Commission c has the same expectation (but lower variance) for Bob as pqf, where p is Bob's estimate of the chance of Alice defaulting, and q is his assessment of the chance of Alice paying the forfeit f.

of our approach is that both the trust management and payment systems can be heterogeneous due to the fact that trust (and payments) are confined or localised. If a guarantee has been made from one principal to another, any trust management and micro-payment schemes could be used between them. At the same time, other pairs of principals might use completely different schemes. As long as an agreement has been made in advance on how the protocol will be followed between a specific truster and trustee, then it doesn't matter what is being used in other parts of the chain.

3.4 Anonymity

Do guarantees ever need to be verified outside of the localised trust relationship? In our protocols, each guarantee is verified by the principal receiving it locally. Once a chain of guarantors has been found (say between Alice and Carol via Bob), how does Alice prove to Carol that she is in fact guaranteed to use Carol's database? Some kind of access control credential could be used to encode the guarantee chain details which can be verified by Carol. However, Carol doesn't need to know who Alice is. All Carol needs to know is that she has received a guarantee from someone whom she trusts (Bob) and from whom she can claim a forfeit if Alice misuses the service provided. Carol doesn't care about any other local agreement in the chain, just the one between Bob and herself. Consequently, the trust* mechanism can be deployed in protocols where anonymity is required[6].

Trust* is intended to be deployed in environments where there is no universally trusted arbiter or referee. If Carol starts claiming that every email she receives is spam, Bob will either stop providing the guarantees, or will charge more for providing them. Alternatively, Alice may form a cycle of trust; Alice might trust Dave (who trusts Carol) to refund her forfeit if it is unfairly claimed.

3.5 Payment by Resource

Micro-payments are generally considered to be small electronic monetary transfers. Due to the heterogeneous nature of the localised trust between individual pairs of principals, the payment could be something of a more immediately valuable commodity to them (in comparison to using purely monetary payments). As mentioned, payment could be by a resource such as CPU time, database access or bandwidth.

If a guarantor is taking payments of one type (from a principal they trust) and making payments of another type (to a principal who trusts them), the guarantor is effectively acting as a resource broker between these principals. Also, trust* could be used alongside an existing trust infrastructure and use payments of an existing commodity such as reputation ratings or credit (maybe when a forfeit

---

[6] Indeed, the guarantee chain can be used to provide anonymity. Of course, the trust* mechanism could also be extended to situations where a guarantee chain needs to be identified (and verified) during audit. For example, an auditor might want to verify each guarantee which extends trust between Alice and Carol in order to prove a forfeit is payable (analogous to a bail bond agent or bounty hunter etc).

hasn't been paid). Indeed, existing trust or reputation could also be used as a commodity of payment. The point is that this flexibility should make it possible to use trust* to complement existing infrastructures rather than replace them.

4   Conclusion

The whole concept of extending trust to trust* makes use of already existing trust relationships rather than creating new ones. It uses guarantees to bridge the gap between unknown principals with a sequence of localised agreements which remove or reduce the perceived risk of the trust*ing principal and shift it towards the principal being trust*ed.

The next stage of this work will involve applying the idea of trust* to some of the various applications outlined in this paper. The chosen applications will be modelled using a discrete event simulator such as Repast [3] upon which trust* will be applied. This will be a means to defining the boundaries of the existing model. For example, problems might become evident when applying trust* to grid computing that weren't in the spam-proof application.

Trust* is flexible in that it can be used in many different applications, however because it builds upon already existing trust, it won't need to replace any existing trust infrastructures. It will integrate with them and can utilise existing commodities such as reputation.

A   The Anti-spam Protocol

This protocol shows how trust* might work in the spam-proof email application. It involves three principals with one path of delegation, as in Fig 1. Alice wants to email Carol; Carol trusts Bob and Bob trusts Alice. Note that the forfeit and commission payments, as well as the email itself, go in the opposite direction to the arrows of trust.

The tokens need to be crypto-protected but Alice, Bob and Carol can be identified by anonymous keys. We assume that the message; $A \longrightarrow C$: Please may Alice have a token for Carol, forfeit=0, commission=.10 will always work.

1. $A \longrightarrow B$: Please may Alice have a token for Carol, forfeit=f, commission=c
2. $B \longrightarrow C$: Please may Alice have a token for Carol, forfeit=f', commission=c'
3. $C \longrightarrow B$: Token for email from Alice to Carol, id=x, etc
4. $B \longrightarrow A$: Token for email from Alice to Carol, id=x, etc
5. $A \Longrightarrow C$: Email (token x in header)
6. $C \longrightarrow B$: Token x is OK/spam
7. $B \longrightarrow C$: Cheers/here is the forfeit
8. $B \longrightarrow A$: Token x is OK/spam
9. $A \longrightarrow B$: Cheers/here is the forfeit

References

1. BOINC, http://boinc.berkeley.edu/
2. BOINC, http://boinc.berkeley.edu/trac/wiki/SecurityIssues
3. Repast Agent Simulation Toolkit, http://repast.sourceforge.net/
4. Basney, J., Nejdl, W., Olmedilla, D., Welch, V., Winslett, M.: Negotiating Trust on the Grid. In: 2nd WWW Workshop on Semantics in P2P and Grid Computing (2004)
5. Blaze, M., Feigenbaum, J., Ioannidis, J., Keromytis, A.: The Keynote Trust-Management System (1998), http://www.crypto.com/papers/rfc2704.txt
6. Blaze, M., Ioannidis, J., Keromytis, A.D.: Offline Micropayments without Trusted Hardware. In: Syverson, P.F. (ed.) FC 2001. LNCS, vol. 2339, pp. 21–40. Springer, Heidelberg (2002)
7. Christianson, B., Harbison, W.S.: Why Isn't Trust Transitive? In: Lomas, M. (ed.) Security Protocols 1996. LNCS, vol. 1189, pp. 171–176. Springer, Heidelberg (1997)
8. Jøsang, A., Gray, E., Kinateder, M.: Analysing Topologies of Transitive Trust. In: Proceedings of the Workshop of Formal Aspects of Security and Trust, FAST, pp. 9–22 (2003)
9. Mezzetti, N.: Towards a Model for Trust Relationships in Virtual Enterprises. In: International Workshop on Database and Expert Systems Applications (2003)
10. Mondal, A., Kitsuregawa, M.: Privacy, Security and Trust in P2P environments: A Perspective. In: PDMST 2006: 3rd International Workshop on P2P Data Management, Security and Trust. DEXA Workshops, pp. 682–686. IEEE Computer Society (2006)
11. Olmedilla, D., Rana, O.F., Matthews, B., Nejdl, W.: Security and Trust Issues in Semantic Grids. In: Proceedings of the Dagsthul Seminar, Semantic Grid: The Convergence of Technologies (2005)
12. Popescu, B.C., Crispo, B., Tanenbaum, A.S.: Safe and Private Data Sharing with Turtle: Friends Team-Up and Beat the System. In: Christianson, B., Crispo, B., Malcolm, J.A., Roe, M. (eds.) Security Protocols 2004. LNCS, vol. 3957, pp. 213–220. Springer, Heidelberg (2006)
13. Popular Science. Dime put in slot rings doorbell (1933), http://blog.modernmechanix.com/2007/05/05/dime-put-in-slot-rings-doorbell/
14. Wallach, D.S.: A Survey of Peer-to-Peer Security Issues. In: Okada, M., Babu, C. S., Scedrov, A., Tokuda, H. (eds.) ISSS 2002. LNCS, vol. 2609, pp. 42–57. Springer, Heidelberg (2003)

Trust*: Using Local Guarantees to Extend the Reach of Trust

(Transcript of Discussion)

Bruce Christianson

University of Hertfordshire

This is work done with Stephen Clarke, who's just there lurking, and Hannan Xiao, who was here yesterday but can't be here today. The motivation is that we often want to do business, or conduct transactions, with strangers, people we haven't done business with before. Reputation systems don't really work, or at least reputation systems for giving reputations to strangers don't work. Now most people say that that's because you don't know the people giving the reputations, I want to make the slightly stronger claim that even if you did know all the people who gave all the reputations, and you trusted them all, that still wouldn't help. This is basically because trust isn't transitive. The fact that Alice trusts Bob, and that Bob trusts Carol, isn't enough to ensure that it's appropriate for Alice to trust Carol, because the fact that Carol gives Bob a good service doesn't mean that Carol is going to give Alice a good service. It might be that Bob is a regular customer, it might be that there's some other reason why Carol's giving Bob a good service. Perhaps she fancies him. The assumption that we're going to make, for the purpose of this talk, is that local trust management is a more tractable problem than the one that we started with here. If you have people that you do business with all the time, then there are various systems that more or less allow you to do get a particular service in such a way that it's either cheap or reliable depending on which has more utility in that circumstance.

So what we wanted was something that would allow us to reduce the "global trust management of strangers" problem to a "local trust management for people who regularly do business with each other" problem, that we thought might be a bit more tractable. But we didn't want to reduce it to a particular local trust management *mechanism*, we wanted something that would allow you to use whatever local trust management system you prefer.

In the real world there's quite a straightforward solution to this which is the use of third party guarantors. If you want to rent a flat from a landlord and he says, ah you're a student, you have to go and find someone willing to guarantee that you will pay the rent. The point is that that doesn't make the landlord trust the tenant any more than they did, OK, there's still no transitive trust, it's simply that if Alice doesn't pay the rent, Carol trusts Bob to make her whole. Bob then has the problem of whether he was right to trust Alice, and whether Alice is eventually going to repay him. Even when it all works, people's assessments of the probability of something going wrong, or the cost of something going wrong, are likely to be very different. It may simply be that Bob has more knowledge

B. Christianson et al. (Eds.): Security Protocols 2009, LNCS 7028, pp. 179–188, 2013.
© Springer-Verlag Berlin Heidelberg 2013

than Carol and consequently he's more willing, because he believes he's taking a much smaller risk than the risk that Carol believes she's taking, and perhaps he's willing to do it in exchange for some compensation. What's Bob's incentive? Maybe Alice pays him commission, maybe Carol pays him commission, possibly out of the rent that Alice pays when she pays. But the key point is, that all the trust relationships are now local trust relationships between people who know each other and do business with each other. Clearly each trust relationship can get updated independently. If Alice defaults, either Bob pays Carol or he doesn't, either Alice pays Bob or she doesn't, each trust relationship is being updated locally, independently, on the basis of a local transaction. And clearly you can extend this idea to multiple hops, and that's the relationship that we rather naughtily call Trust*.

So here you have the idea of David trusting Carol, Carol trusts Bob,

Bob trusts Alice, there's some notion of a forfeit; there's a notion of a guarantee with a forfeit being paid if the guarantee is broken. For the moment think of the forfeit being a micropayment, using whatever your favourite micro payment system is. We started off using keynote because we could do both the local trust management and the micro payment in keynote. But the micro payments are also all local, you never make a payment to somebody who is more than one hop away from you in the chain.

Now it's important to notice that even in just a one hop relationship, Trust* isn't quite the same as trust, because with Trust* what I am asking Bob to believe is that Alice will *either* provide the service *or* pay the forfeit; and Bob might believe that Alice is completely hopeless at providing the service and will never succeed in doing so, but also believe that she will give him a penny every time she doesn't, so he will just sit there clicking until Alice gets tired and stops paying, or withdraws the service.

Ben Laurie: I don't quite understand how this maps to the example you gave before, where Alice is the tenant and Bob is the guarantor, what service is Alice providing Bob when Alice is the tenant? And what forfeits does Alice pay? I'm not understanding how these two map onto each other.

Reply: In this example here Carol is the landlord, Alice is the tenant. Let's assume for the moment that Alice pays Bob a commission to guarantee her, Alice pays Bob a certain proportion of the rent to act as a guarantor, and that's the service that Bob is providing to Alice. The service that Bob is providing to Carol is that if Alice defaults Bob will then pay the rent.

Ben Laurie: Yes, and what's the forfeit for Alice?

Reply: That's between her and Bob. It may be that the forfeit that Alice has to pay Bob is bigger than the forfeit that Bob has to pay Carol, in which case Bob will be hoping that Alice fails. It may be that Alice pays Bob a flat commission, and in that case Bob is hoping that Alice doesn't default because he'll be out of pocket if she does. There are some interesting consequences to those trade-offs, which I'll talk a little bit more about later.

Paul Syverson: So in the first case that you stated, that is, if the forfeit Alice would have to pay would be greater than what Bob would have to pay, presumably he is in a position to guarantee this in a way that Carol wasn't, because otherwise why does Carol need Bob, right?

Reply: That's exactly so, yes, and it may also be that Carol has either ignorance or false belief about what Alice is likely to do.

Matt Blaze: So you are essentially describing credit performance loss/laws?

Reply: Yes indeed. I was just about to make the point that Trust* isn't quite transitive either, it's like connections in the network. If A is connected to B and B is connected to C, that doesn't meant that A actually is connected to C, it means that A could be connected to C if you were willing to tear down the connections that already exist and reuse the resources. So just as "connectability" is transitive, it's actually the predicate of "Trust*-ability" that is transitive, rather than Trust* itself, but that's good enough.

And there are various problems, which you've probably already spotted: for example, how does Alice choose a good route to Alice, there's lots of possible chains of guarantors, how does she pick the best? Obviously that depends on whether she would rather have certainty about paying a fixed commission or whether she's willing to risk a given chance of a forfeit, which in turn depends on whether she does this kind of transaction a couple of times a year, or whether she does it millions of times a day.

There's issues about exposure, this has already been mentioned, how does Bob ensure that he hasn't issued so many guarantees that if a bad thing happens he is going to be micro bankrupt, or whatever the phrase is. Bob could end up owing billions of milli cents.

So the interesting thing is that these problems all have analogies with fairly well known networking problems: how do I find the best route from A to B; how do I prevent flooding; how do I do congestion control; how do I prevent buffer exhaustion, committing to provide buffers for more traffic than I can supply; and so forth.

Paul Syverson: How do I provide guarantees against massive default on all the mortgages I guarantee?

Reply: That kind of thing, yes.

Jonathan Anderson: That's unnecessary.

Reply: That corresponds to withstanding a denial of service attack actually.

Michael Roe: From the financial analogy, if Bob has given guarantees on behalf of lots of different Alices, the failures of those different Alices may be correlated for reasons Bob doesn't know, because he doesn't know what they're depending on.

Reply: That's exactly true. Bob may believe that certain risks are uncorrelated, and in fact they're highly correlated. There's a famous story of an insurance company where they had insured a Stradivarius, and a very rare parrot, and owing to a series of events that you would never get away with in a novel, involving cancellations and re-routings, they came within an inch of travelling on the same transatlantic plane. The insurance company found out about this in the nick of time and paid a substantial amount to prevent them from being shipped on the same aeroplane. Bob can't do that, because on the internet nobody knows everything.

So we have analogies with routing problems, back pressure problems, pacing congestion control and so forth, the argument is that fortunately you can also take any well known solution to one of these well known networking problems, and translate the solution back into the Trust* context.

Sören Preibusch: Can you give some details now on the deployments you're envisioning?

Reply: Oh applications. Would it be helpful to look at applications now and then come back to the networking problems? [Shuffles slides.]

Sören Preibusch: Yes, so I can see when you use this.

Reply: Here's some sample applications. One possible application is grid computing, where you want to farm a problem out over a widespread grid, but you're not clear whether the computation is going to be done correctly, and there's a cost to you if it's not, it means you end up having to validate and do it somewhere else.

Sören Preibusch: So how do I know, can I even decide whether that's correct or not?

Reply: You can always get someone else to do it and check. The point about grid computing is that it's entirely possible to validate it. Bruno Crispo's student Bogdan Popescu wrote a good thesis about this very problem[1], that provided some of the motivation for this work.

Peer-to-peer is another example, some of you who were here a few years ago may remember Turtle[2], which is an example of a peer-to-peer system used to do filesharing where you want to have only local trust. The advantage of deploying something like Trust* is that it allows you to extend the Turtle protocols to a much wider range. In the case of grid computing you could imagine that instead of using micro payments you could actually use grid resources as the payment system, so the forfeit would be in terms of entitlement to bandwidth, CPU cycles, memory use, and so forth, within the grid. In the case of peer-to-peer computing the content itself is now a resource and so you might imagine using that as the payment medium for a commission.

Sören Preibusch: That seems kind of weird to me, in the grid computing example, the service you're providing, and the forfeit, are in the same . . .

Reply: In the same currency, yes.

---

[1] "Design and Implementation of a Secure Wide-Area Object Middleware" PhD Dissertation, Vrije Universiteit, Amsterdam.
[2] See LNCS 3957, pp 213–230.

Sören Preibusch: So if you failed to provide the service, why on earth would you pay the forfeit?

Reply: Well it's the same with the rent example, the rent is paid in money, the commission's paid in money, the forfeit's paid in money, but you've got this whole chain and different local transactions.

Jonathan Anderson: But MacDonald's did the same thing though, we'll make you your order in 30 seconds or else we'll give you a voucher for a free Big Mac.

Reply: Yes, exactly. But you might have to wait for it.

Michael Roe: Pizza delivery as well.

Reply: Snow Crash[3] starts with a pizza delivery that almost fails, yes. Those were motivating examples of the kind of problem that we walked in the door with. You want to do business with a stranger, within a context that you do business in a lot, but you don't actually know that particular endpoint. What can you do to allow you to do the business with some security that you'll be compensated. Or, indeed, either that you'll be compensated, or that nasty people will be deterred.

Another type of application is music downloads. For example, if I download this music how can I be sure that the artist will be paid? How can I be sure that the artist really will get their 20p for every time I download this mp3 file. You can use a Trust* chain to ensure that the artist is paid: eventually you're either going to get proof that the artist was paid in respect of your download, or the guarantor is going to have to pay the artist 20p and produce the receipt for that.

Click here, every time you click on this link we give a penny to your favourite charity, Free Kevin Mitnik, or whatever. The same principle applies, you can use a Trust* chain to guarantee that even though you're clicking on a website you've never used before, run by people you don't particularly trust, you know that your charity is going to get that penny one way or the other. Similarly in Second Life, you can imagine buying and selling virtual objects, the crypto that's available to user avatars in Second Life is getting steadily better, and could just about mount the protocols now. Does that help?

Sören Preibusch: Well, your initial grid was eBusiness, so then I think, OK, I'm not going to pay for this, it's all done.

Reply: You've never been ripped off on the internet?

Sören Preibusch: No.

Reply: OK, you don't have a problem.

Sören Preibusch: I mean, do people really need this?

Reply: Well I'm a computer scientist, I'm not concerned with giving people what they need [Laughter], that's the first answer, the argument for looking at this is it's an interesting idea which has applications that relate to the rest of

---

[3] Neal Stephenson, 1992.

computer science. But the motivation that I gave at the beginning though was perhaps a little misleading, because in eBay type environments you're hoping to get posted a real banjo through the post, or something like that, whereas the domain that I'm describing here is one that's entirely within the electronic world, both halves of the contract are in cyberspace. So I am not really advocating this as a mechanism for making eBay safer to buy things from strangers on, that's purely a motivating example.

Jonathan Anderson: But this is the same technique that eBay and PayPal use, they say, you will get your item or else we will pay and we will go after them.

Sören Preibusch: eBay is the middle man.

Reply: Yes, and if you trust eBay then you've effectively got a two hop Trust* chain that works.

Michael Roe: It's a similar kind of thing with spam, you sign up to get your email sending accounts and pay a certain amount of money, and your service provider guarantees that the messages you were sending were not spam or they cancel your account.

Reply: It's strange that you should mention spam, because that is the next application that I'm going to look at. But it might be worth going back and doing just a little bit more theory first, because spam as an application has a couple of features that are slightly more complex.

OK, so problems with Trust* correspond to network problems, and interestingly if you have customers with different views about the relative values of commissions (which they get upfront) and forfeits (which they might or might not get if you default), you can regard those as corresponding to different Qualities of Service. So when you're looking for a connection from Carol to Alice, you can specify the Quality of Service which you want, and then the routing algorithm is one that gives you the best route for that specified Quality of Service.

Ben Laurie: You say that as if we could actually do this for network Quality of Service?

Reply: All I'm undertaking to do is reduce these new problems to well-known networking problems that we already know that we can't solve [Laughter]. We can't solve networking problems perfectly, but in practice we can do it well enough. Similarly, if Bob gets completely fed up with paying forfeits for Alice, that corresponds to a link outage. If Bob gets a little bit fed up with paying forfeits for Alice and puts the price up, that corresponds to time delay increasing on a link which will cause traffic to be re-routed, which will in turn cause traffic congestion in the vicinity of the link, which in turns means intermediate nodes have to apply back pressure and use dynamic congestion control and so forth.

The only slight thing that you have to remember is that our links are one-way as far as data is concerned: trust isn't transitive, but it's not symmetric either. So our links are bi-directional for control flow, but the data only goes one way across it. It's not a problem, because by the six degrees of separation argument[4] there always is a route in the opposite direction, it probably just goes through a different chain of people. So you get these cycles of trust. That's not quite as daft as it seems, because electronic contracts usually involve something changing hands in each direction, there's some sort of guarantee you need in each direction, and a lot of other approaches to this simply assume that the path can go along the same route of nodes in both directions, whereas we want to avoid that assumption, which we regard as problematic.

Coming back to the issue of commissions or forfeits, there's two reasons why you might make charges. One, which we've already looked at, is where you are in some sense compensating the client for the fact that they didn't get the service, we will compensate you for the fact that your burger was nasty, by giving you another one, or whatever. The second possibility is that we're imposing the forfeit simply to deter the server from habitually failing to provide the service. In this case the amount that you'd have to fine a server to achieve this is much smaller than an amount that the client would accept as compensation, it's simply the certainty of being forced to pay up or else driven out of business, that provides the server with an inducement to perform the contract. Spam is an example, you can calculate how much you'd have to charge a spammer for each piece of email they sent to make them stop, and it's an amazingly low figure, it's much less than you would charge for reading an email.

Perception of risk differs, and Carol's assessment of whether Alice will default, or whether Bob will pay up, might be very different to David's assessment, or to Bob's own assessment. The final point is the value of certainty: there's a two-way market in uncertainty, people buy both lottery tickets and insurance policies, so people are willing to trade variance up or down, even though they know that both the lottery organisers and the insurance company will make a profit.

A point I've already mentioned is the influence on the desired outcome: if Alice's forfeit is bigger than Bob's, Bob has an incentive to want Alice to fail, if Alice pays commission up front, then Bob wants Alice to succeed, and in certain circumstances the choice of optimal route is not neutral with regard to the outcome of the contract.

Paul Syverson: Utility is not linear in dollars.

Reply: Exactly so, yes. Money now may have a higher value than the statistical expectation of the same amount of money later on. A lot of analyses make the naïve assumption that the probability p of receiving an amount f is worth pf, and this is precisely the assumption which breaks down.

Paul Syverson: It's not just the hyperbolic discount about future events though, it's also that an income of a dollar a week to me is virtually invisible, but the small possibility that I might at some point win a gazillion dollars . . .

Reply: Yes, or a gazillion dollar lawsuit instead of spending a pound a week on insurance. To a large extent the utility depends on who you are, and in particular

---

[4] "Chains" (1929) by Frigyes Karinthy.

on how many of these transactions you're doing in a typical day. Very often the variance is more important than the expectation. I remember doing some consultancy for some people who provided services to an insurance company, you're trying to estimate derivatives of these various dreadful marginal things they use, and I asked what sort of error is tolerable on the expected values, and they said, it doesn't really matter, if our expectation model is out by 3% we can just put our premiums up by 3% next year, on the other hand, if our calculation for the standard deviation is wrong by 3%, this is a disaster, because something that we thought was four sigmas away from the mean is actually less than 3.9 sigmas away, so our probability of going bankrupt has just doubled, which is the sort of thing that really does keep us awake at night. Conversely, if it's actually significantly bigger than you thought it was, you've got a lot of money sitting in a contingency fund on a short-term pull that you should have invested long-term and your shareholders are losing out. So it's known that standard deviations are often much more important than expectation, and yet we often don't model that.

So a very crude model is just to say, well the utility of a possible forfeit is the expected value of the forfeit minus some constant α (which depends on the user) times the standard deviation of the forfeit. The constant is user dependent, because high-volume users who do lots of transactions will probably tolerate a much lower α value. I am aware that this is a very crude model, but it turns out to be sufficient to illustrate the principle. So, for example, if our forfeit payment is essentially binomial[5], then the variance is $p(1 - p)$ per transaction, so you get this obvious series which you can expand. The key point is that if α is very small, if you've got someone like an insurance company who does squillions of these transactions a day and so is willing to operate with a very small value of α, then it does behave exactly like pf as you would expect. But if your assessment of the probability of collecting or paying one of these things is small relative to the value of α^2, where α is as small as you are comfortable with, then the utility behaves like $-\alpha\sqrt{pf}$, it's actually negative, and it varies like the square root of the probability of default, it's not linear. And there's an interesting crossover zone in the middle, and this is where the action is. This of course is going to affect the routing scheme, it puts a high added value on going indirectly via a broker, or via somebody who's effectively acting as a broker. The definition of a broker is somebody whose α value is at least an order of magnitude smaller than yours.

We've looked at a number of applications, but here's a *contravariant* application, which means that the arrows go the opposite way to what you have come to expect. This is a spam-proof email system. Carol trusts Bob, Bob trusts Alice, Alice wants to send Carol an email, Carol doesn't want to read spam. Well actually, Carol's position is that she's willing to skim-read any email in exchange for 10p in her pocket, that's about £200 an hour. Half an hour of reading spam before breakfast, have Sunday off, that's about £30K a year pocket money, but of course Alice wants to find a cheaper route. So here Alice is the service provider and Carol is the client, that's why it's contravariant application, it's not the way round you'd expect.

---

[5] I've never thought it was a coincidence that Professor Moriarty wrote a treatise on the Binomial Theorem.

Simon Foley: This is like examples of multi-lateral security where I'll give you 50p up front if you answer my telephone call.

Reply: Yes. There's a long tradition of similar incentive schemes, all the way back to a patented invention in the American Midwest, a doorbell that you had to put a dime in before it would ring. If you were someone who had been invited to dinner, then you'd get your dime back, but if you were an insurance salesman you wouldn't. The point is, a dime is nothing, but if your business is making cold calls, and you're making several hundred house calls a day (including empty houses), it starts to mount up. So you can think of this as an electronic analogy of exactly that idea.

I'm going to break with convention by putting up an actual security protocol here [Laughter] but as you see, Alice says to Bob, may I please have a token to send an email to Carol, Bob passes this along to Carol as a request from him (but with different forfeit and commission parameters), Carol says, OK, I trust Bob not to be responsible for me receiving spam, here's a token with a unique identity. Alice can then use this token to get past Carol's spam filter directly (the email doesn't go via Bob), and then Carol either says, that was OK, or, that was spam; Bob either says, fine here is 10p, or he doesn't, and Alice either repays Bob or she doesn't, and so on.

Frank Stajano: Why do we need Bob?

Reply: Because Carol doesn't trust Alice.

Frank Stajano: What, to pay her 10p?

Reply: To not send her spam.

Frank Stajano: Why does Carol need to trust anybody? Couldn't Alice just send Carol the 10p before sending the email?

Reply: That's fine for Carol, but that way Alice is 10p out of pocket.

Frank Stajano: So Alice doesn't trust Carol to return the 10p either?

Reply: That's exactly the next point, you're on my next slide.

Sören Preibusch: The thing is, maybe C does not know A?

Reply: Yes, C and A may be unknown to each other.

Sören Preibusch: So if C is the professor and gets a lot of student emails that are spam then he needs a secretary.

Reply: Yes, for example.

Sören Preibusch: And students are notoriously short of money at times.

Reply: Yes, and professors are short of time. So you'd be better to email me via one of my PhD students for instance. But to move onto the point that Frank introduced, what if Carol just starts claiming that everything is spam? Every message she gets she just says is spam. The naïve answer is to say, well Bob will either stop providing guarantees, or he'll put the price up, back pressure will work, and eventually Carol will stop getting emails that she wants to get and so she'll ease off or she'll be eased out.

But an alternative is to exploit the idea that we have a cycle of trust, you can imagine Alice simply completing the cycle by saying, well, Dave trusts Carol not to claim falsely that the contract wasn't performed, Edwina trusts Dave, Franz trusts Edwina, Alice trusts Franz, and now everything's OK. If Carol claims that it was a spam email when it clearly wasn't, Alice will get her 10p back.

Further extensions. Heterogeneity is free: all transactions are local, so it doesn't matter if you're using different payment mechanisms, different trust management mechanisms, and different everything you like. If you're in different domains, you're using different resources, it doesn't matter in the least.

Anonymity is almost free: the point was made that Alice and Carol don't necessarily know who each other are, well neither of them actually needs to know who the other is. There's a little bit of care needed with some of the cryptographic tokens, and some of the protocol mechanisms need reworking, but you can run this over a Tor-like network without many changes.

Commodity-broking is a benevolent side effect: if you've got people who are paying and receiving in different type of resources, they are effectively acting as commodity brokers, and you can tune the system so that they're brokering the commodities in exactly the way that you want.

And finally there is the nice possibility of using the elusive quantity of "global reputation" *as* the payment commodity for the services and goods that you want.

Ben Laurie: Doesn't Carol find out who Alice is then?

Reply: She doesn't need to.

Ben Laurie: By being in a longer chain?

Reply: Yes. Bob has to trust Alice, Carol has to trust Bob, Dave has to trust Carol, everybody has to know who their neighbours are, you're back in a similar situation to Turtle. It does mean that the secret police have to go through every node one by one.

Michael Roe: So the Washington Post knows who their journalists are, and the journalists know who their sources are?

Reply: And their source knows who the criminal is, you the reader know who the Washington Post is, and yes it's lunchtime.

Paul Syverson: There's a paper that appeared in the Journal of Philosophical Logic in 1987 by Fagan and Hopper, entitled I'm OK If You're OK on the Notion of Trust and Communication, in which they set out formally the requirements for trust to be transitive[6].

Reply: Now that's a very good point. Those of you with long memories will remember a talk I gave at the 4th Security Protocols Workshop[7] entitled Why Isn't Trust Transitive, that was in part a response to that paper.

---

[6] Ronald Fagin & Joseph Y. Halpern, 1988, I'm OK If You're OK: On the Notion of Trusting Communication, Journal of Philosophical Logic, 17(4), 329–354.

[7] See LNCS 1189, pp 171–176.

Alice and Bob in Love

Cryptographic Communication Using Shared Experiences

Joseph Bonneau

University of Cambridge Computer Laboratory
jcb82@cl.cam.ac.uk

Abstract. We propose a protocol for secure communication between two parties who know each other well using only pre-existing shared knowledge from their shared life experience. This could enable, for example, lovers or close friends to communicate over a one-way channel without prior key exchange. Our system uses a flexible secret-sharing mechanism to accommodate pieces of personal knowledge of variable guessing resistance and memorability, with reasonable overhead in terms of computation and storage.

1 Introduction

Traditional cryptographic communication relies on artificially-created high entropy random strings as secret keys. In some cases, two parties who know each other well may already share enough secret knowledge, in the form of experiences and emotions, to enable secure communication. For example, a husband and wife will both remember many details of their courtship that no other parties know, while a group of siblings can recall minutia of their childhood which are unknown outside of the family.

In this work, we explore cryptographic communication using this naturally-shared secret knowledge in situations where it is otherwise not possible to share a cryptographic key. Our goal is to design a secure protocol for encryption over a one-way communication channel. Abstractly, Alice wishes to send Bob a message, and she can only use her shared experiences with Bob to ensure confidentiality and integrity of the message. This will be achieved with a secure protocol for converting answers to personal questions into a high-entropy key suitable for conventional encryption.

We assume that Alice must send her message urgently without actually meeting Bob to exchange key material. This may be because the message is being sent for future decryption by Bob. For example, Alice may be writing a will that she can keep hidden in her lifetime, but she encrypts it using personal secrets shared with Bob, so that only he can read it after her death. Another example is encryption of backup key material intended for oneself in the future, in the case of accidentally losing a stored key or forgetting a password. This is the example which has motivated previous research [1,2], though we consider this example as a special case of a more general concept.

B. Christianson et al. (Eds.): Security Protocols 2009, LNCS 7028, pp. 189–198, 2013.

2   Related Work

2.1   Personal Knowledge Questions

Most experience in designing personal-knowledge questions (PKQs) has been as a backup authentication method for websites in the case of forgotten passwords. The classic example is a bank which requires a user to enter his or her mother's maiden name to reset a password or PIN code. Just wrote a survey of PKQs in the context of web re-authentication which enumerated the many different design parameters from a usability standpoint [3].

Our application is much more demanding than online authentication, where it is possible to limit the number of guess an adversary can make. Still, it will be critical to have some understanding of the entropy and memorability of PKQs, since they are our primary means of turning shared entropy into cryptographic keys. The few formal studies conducted have found that questions typically used in practice have very poor security characteristics. Rabkin surveyed PKQ systems used in real banking websites, and reported that a large number of questions suffered from either poor usability or vulnerability to mining data available on the web [4]. For example, an earlier study by Griffith and Jakobsson discovered exactly the mother's maiden name of over 15% of Texas residents using publicly available data [5]. Concurrent research in the field of social network security has found that simply knowing a victim's list of friends can enable inference of private information such as gender or political beliefs [6,7], making the secure choice of PKQs difficult.

Jakobsson et al proposed "preference-based authentication" to decrease the reliance on publicly available information by using questions such as "do you like country music?" [8]. They later refined their system and conducted extensive user studies [9] and found that preferences are much more difficult to mine from the Internet, while still being highly memorable.

2.2   Password Backup Systems

We are inspired by two previously proposed schemes for cryptographically secure password backup. Ellison et al. proposed a scheme in 1999 for encryption using "Personal Entropy" [1]. This system involved hashing a set of answers to stored PKQs into a set of shares of a secret, and using an (n, t)-threshold secret-sharing scheme to recover a master key.

Frykholm and Juels proposed another scheme in 2001 [2], based on fuzzy commitment, which relied on mapping a user's set of answer to PKQs to the message space of an error-correcting code, then decoding to recover the master key, which was chosen at random from the space of valid codewords. This scheme is provably secure under certain assumptions about the coding system, in that an attacker's probability of successfully guessing the correct master key is bounded by the min-entropy of the set of possible answers.

3   Desired Properties

Either of the password backup schemes describe in Section 2.2 could be adapted for our desired scenario of communication between two different parties. However, we would like to add several new features.

3.1   Accommodation of Variable Entropy in PKQs

Previous schemes haven't been designed to combine PKQs of different strength levels. It is feasible that we may wish to encrypt based on the answers to several questions whose answer is a name (*e.g.* "What was our neighbour's oldest son's name growing up?") in addition to many true-false or multiple-choice questions, which are easier to create but also easier to guess. Previous schemes map all questions into equally sized blocks to make design simpler. We will design for questions whose answer-spaces have different entropy, considering this a desired property for a secure and usable system.

3.2   Accommodation of Variable Recall Probabilities

Another inflexibility in the previous schemes is the assumption that all answers have an equally likely chance of being forgotten or not known at the time of decryption. This is reflected in that errors in the response to any question are treated equally by the error correction scheme. We wish to efficiently accommodate questions whose recall probabilities vary. For example, a sender may be close to 100% certain that the recipient can answer a certain question, and thus not provide any error tolerance for this question and force an adversary to guess it correctly. Similarly, some questions may be known to be likely to be forgotten, and will require extra error tolerance to ensure the system is usable.

3.3   Key Strengthening

Since we are limited by the ability of our user interface to extract memorable and unpredictable answers, we can use key strengthening [10] to increase the difficulty of brute-force guessing of possible answers. This is simple in our application since our system already consists of converting answers to PKQs into a master key. We will add the extra step of hashing our pre-master key 2^s times before it is used to decrypt message content. This effectively adds s bits of work for an attacker attempting to guess the correct answers. For $s \sim 10 - 20$, it will add only a small amount of slowdown to decryption using a desktop computer, which is acceptable since our system is expected to be used only in rare circumstances.

3.4   Sacrificed Properties

In order to achieve the above properties, we are willing to sacrifice several performance properties, considering our system to be a rarely-used emergency protocol. In particular, we are willing to add considerable storage overhead to an encrypted message, and slowdown in encrypting and decrypting. We will examine a sample requirement of storage and slowdown in Section 4.5.

4 Proposed System

4.1 Protocol Description

Encryption under our system will consist of choosing a set Q of questions $\{q_0, \ldots, q_m\}$, and providing a corresponding set of answers $A = \{a_0, \ldots, a_m\}$. We then randomly pick a pre-master key K_P, and compute the master encryption key according to our desired level of key-strengthening:

$$K_M = \mathbf{H}^{2^s}(K_P) \tag{1}$$

The critical step in our protocol which is different from previous systems is that encryption will require enumerating subsets of A which allow for recovery of K_M. We will not limit the system to subsets of a specific size, but allow for total flexibility. To achieve this, encryption will require explicitly listing subsets $A_i \in A$ along with decryption information. We denote the set of sets of acceptable answers as

$$A^* = \{A_i \in A : \text{knowledge of } A_i \text{ shall enable decryption}\} \tag{2}$$

We will use a trivial secret-sharing scheme to accomplish this, namely, using exclusive-or to combine hashes of answers to derive a subset key for each $A_i \in A^*$:

$$K_i = \bigoplus_{a_j \in A_i} \mathbf{H}(a_j \| j) \tag{3}$$

We include the question number j in each hash to force the adversary to search over all answers to all questions.

We then generate a master key K_M uniformly at random. For each subset key K_i we then compute the offset O_i which allows us to recompute the master key after our desired level of key strengthening:

$$O_i = K_M \oplus \mathbf{H}^{2^s}(K_i) \tag{4}$$

To send a message M, Alice transmits:

$$\mathbf{AE}_{K_M}(M\|A),\ Q,\ O \tag{5}$$

We use standard a symmetric-key authenticated encryption function $\mathbf{AE}$, such as AES-GCM, to ensure confidentiality and integrity. We note that Alice must transmit the offset O_i for every answer set $A_i \in A^*$. We will examine the storage requirements in a sample deployment in Section 4.5. We also note that Alice appends the correct answers to her questions to the plaintext before encrypting, this will be discussed in Section 6.1.

Given correct receipt of the information from Equation 5, Bob will examine the questions Q and provide his own answers $\tilde{A}$, which may of course differ from the correct answers. The decryption software will then search through subsets $\tilde{A}_i \in \tilde{A}^*$, for each subset computing:

$$\tilde{K} = \mathbf{H}^{2^s}\left(O_i \oplus \bigoplus_{a_j \in \tilde{A}_i} \mathbf{H}(a_j \| j)\right) \tag{6}$$

If Bob's subset of answers is correct, that is, $\tilde{A}_i = A_i$, then this decryption will successfully invert the decryption of Equations 4 and 3, and Bob will have recovered K_M. Any incorrect answer within $\tilde{A}_i$ will produce a pseudo-random $\tilde{K} \neq K_M$.

Superficially, the encryption software must perform a search over all sets in $\tilde{A}^*$, as no information is provided about which answer was specified incorrectly. We hope that, in practice, there will be a manageable number of such subsets. A very helpful interface feature, however, is to provide a "don't know" answer for Bob, so that the decryption software can avoid searching over subsets known to contain a wrong answer.

4.2   Difficulty of an Attack

The attacker receives the set of questions Q and must go about trying to guess enough of the answers to reconstruct the key. We assume that for each question, the sender can estimate a reasonable lower bound on the difficulty of an adversary guessing the correct answer. Specifically, we estimate the *min-entropy* H_∞ of each question, which is equal to $- \lg(p_{max})$, where p_{max} is an attacker's estimated probability of the most likely answer[1]. We denote H_∞^i for the min-entropy of question q_i.

Given our use of secret-sharing subsets, the attacker doesn't need to guess all answers successfully, only the answers in one subset $A' \in A^*$. There are many such subsets which will work, but the attacker can be assumed to target the weakest subset, that is, the subset A_{attack} which minimises:

$$H_{attack} = \sum_{a_i \in A_{attack}} H_\infty^i \qquad (7)$$

The metric H_{attack} can be thought of as modelling an imaginary attacker who has an infinite supply of different messages sent from Alice to Bob, and will only guess the most likely answers to the weakest sufficient subset of answers to each message before discarding it and attacking the next message. This is the strongest possible attacker; an attacker which proceeds to guess less likely answers or larger subsets will only have lower guessing efficiency. The imaginary attacker with an infinite supply of messages will only succeed with probability $2^{-H_{attack}}$ with one guess each, thus H_{attack} is an effective lower bound on the workload of an attacker.

Due to our key-strengthening, the attacker must actually perform an 2^s invocations of $\mathbf{H}$ to check each guess. Thus, the effective attacker workload is $H_{attack} + s$ bits.

4.3   Probability of Successful Decryption

We also consider the probability that Bob will be able to successfully decrypt the message. We assume that for each answer a_i, Bob has an associated probability of

---

[1] Despite its common use for the purpose, Shannon entropy is not a sound measure of guessing difficulty. Min-entropy is an effective lower-bound on the difficulty of guessing a sample drawn from a known probability distribution.

correctly recalling it, denoted as r_i. Although there are some known techniques to increase r_i, such as normalisation of answers to prevent mistakes due to spelling or punctuation [2,3], there is little recourse if Bob has legitimately forgotten too many answers. We assume that Bob will only supply answers once, he will not perform his own meta-search through likely possible answers, as this is unlikely to be feasible from a usability standpoint.

Similar to the case for the attacker, Bob needs to remember some subset of answers $A' \in A^*$. The probability of doing so is the somewhat unwieldy expression:

$$p_{\text{success}} = \sum_{A' \in A^*} [\prod_{a_j \in A_i} r_j \cdot \prod_{a_k \notin A_i} (1 - r_k)] \tag{8}$$

4.4   Optimisation of Parameters

The encryption software is free to choose the subsets A^* which allow for successful decryption given the user's choices for Q, and estimates of the min-entropy H_∞^i recall probability r_i for each question. It can optimise either for maximum decryption probability given a required security parameter $H_{\min}$, or for maximum security given a required minimum decryption probability $p_{\min}$. In either case, we initialise our state as:

$$A^* = \{A\}; \ H_{\text{attack}} = \sum_{a_i \in A} H_i; \ p_{\text{success}} = \prod_{a_j \in A} r_j \tag{9}$$

This corresponds to requiring that every answer is provided correctly, and gives maximal entropy and minimal decryption probability. We then add the subset $A' \notin A^*$ for which the entropy H_{attack}, as defined in Equation 7, is maximal, which becomes the new estimated strength of the entire encryption. After we add A', we update:

$$H_{\text{attack}} := \sum_{a_i \in A'} H_\infty^i; \ p_{\text{success}} \mathrel{+}= \prod_{a_j \in A'} r_j \cdot \prod_{a_k \notin A'} (1 - r_k) \tag{10}$$

Note that, as we add to A^*, H_{attack} is monotonically decreasing while p_{success} is monotonically increasing, building up to their correct values as defined in Equations 7 and 8. The stopping conditions are obvious, either we continue until the next subset A' to add would result in $H_{\text{attack}} < H_{\min}$, if we have a minimum security requirement, or we continue until $p_{\text{success}} \geq p_{\min}$, if we have a minimum decryption probability requirement.

4.5   Example Values

We consider an example scenario in which Alice provides 20 questions, each of which has a min-entropy H_∞ of 4 bits and a recall probability $r = 0.9$. Of course, our system is designed to support different values for each question, but we consider a simple example to calculate the resulting message size and security.

A reasonable choice is to enable decryption if at least 16 answers are guessed correctly:

$$A^* = \{A' \in A : |A'| \geq 16\} \tag{11}$$

The total number of correctly decrypting sets is then:

$$|A^*| = \binom{20}{20} + \binom{20}{19} + \binom{20}{18} + \binom{20}{17} + \binom{20}{16} = 6,196 \tag{12}$$

The probability of successful decryption, as defined in Equation 8, is:

$$p_{\text{success}} = \sum_{A' \in A^*} [\prod_{a_j \in A_i} r_j \cdot \prod_{a_k \notin A_i} (1 - r_k)] = \sum_{16 \leq i \leq 20} 0.9^i \cdot 0.1^{20-i} = 0.957 \tag{13}$$

The attacker's workload, defined in Equation 7, is that of any set of 16 answers, which is:

$$H_{\text{attack}} = \sum_{a_i \in A_{\text{attack}}} H_\infty^i = 16 \cdot 4 = 64 \tag{14}$$

Assuming we desire 80 bits of security, we require each offset O_i to be 80 bits. Each offset represents a subset of at least 16 of the 20 answers, which we can efficiently encode by listing the excluded items in a maximum of 20 bits (5 bits each for up to 4 excluded answers). Thus, we need to send a maximum of $6,196 \cdot 100 = 619,600$ bits to represent O, which is ≈ 75 kB.

Our attacker will have a maximal success probability of 2^{-64}, so we can use $s = 16$ to make her total workload equivalent to 2^{80} invocations of the hash function $\mathbf{H}$.

Finally, even if our recipient must search every subset in A^*, this will require a total of $6,196 \cdot 2^{16} \leq 2^{29}$ invocations of $\mathbf{H}$.

5   Sample Experiment

The author conducted a small experiment to test the feasibility of the proposed protocol. Questions were written for eight different people whom the author has known for an extended period of time. One hour was spent writing questions and estimating their strength and probabilities for each recipient[2]. The resulting number of questions and message sizes are listed in Table 1.

Each recipient received 12–16 questions, and needed to answer between 5 and 12 of them in order to successfully decrypt. This variation was due to the varying estimates of guessability between different recipients, for some it was easier to craft difficult-to-guess questions and for others it was necessary to rely on a larger number of relatively weak questions. This also led to a large variation in message size, between 1 kB and nearly 400 kB, depending mostly on the number of sufficient subsets for decryption which required sending additional offsets.

---

[2] The one-hour time limit seemed to be a lower limit, it is surprisingly difficult to remember and write good questions for use in this system.

Table 1. Number of questions sent and total message overhead for each of the 8 study participants, requiring a minimum estimated security of $H_{attack} = 64$ in each case

recipient	$|Q|$	H_{max}	$p_{success}$	$|A^*|$	$\min(|A_i|)$	storage (kb)
ex-sig. other	15	76	0.724	189	12	1
sister	13	87	0.878	707	8	6
mother	12	88	0.937	1013	7	9
brother	16	98	0.979	10345	8	151
former roommate	13	93	0.974	11153	5	159
sig. other	16	89	0.977	14471	8	200
father	14	95	0.959	16498	6	225
childhood friend	16	101	0.989	27260	8	390

Each recipient attempted to answer their own questions only once. Every participant answered enough questions correctly to successfully decrypt, though every recipient was incorrect on multiple questions. The totals are listed in Table 2. Overall, 82 of 114 questions, or 72%, were answered correctly. By the author's estimates during the experiment, close to 85% of questions were expected to be answered correctly. Breaking down the causes of incorrect answers, 6% were due to spelling disagreement, and a further 7% were due to synonym replacement[3] and 16% of questions were legitimately forgotten or not known, close the original estimate of success. This suggests a bias towards ignoring the possibility of input mistakes when estimating the probability of a correct answer.

Each recipient also was encouraged to attempt to guess the answers to every other recipients' questions as many times as they were willing to. Many of the recipients, being family members and long-term friends, knew each other well. Thus there were a number of successful guesses, also listed in Table 2. A total of 13 questions, over 10%, were successfully guessed by another participant in the study. Nearly all of these were either one of the author's siblings guessing a question intended for the other sibling, or one of the author's parents guessing a question intended for the other parent, demonstrating the difficulty of separating these pairs of people. None of the recipients had enough questions guessed to successfully decrypt, although in several cases enough questions were asked to push H_{attack} below 40 bits (prior to key-strengthening).

Overall, the experiment suggested that such a protocol is possible with reasonable real-world parameters (one hour of time to create questions and less than 1 MB of storage overhead). All messages were successfully decrypted with only very rudimentary software making no effort to correct typos or spelling mistakes. However, the experiment also demonstrated that accurately estimating the probability of recalling answers is very difficult, and that acquaintance attacks by people who know the sender or recipient can be a significant problem.

---

[3] For example, one recipient answered "Pt. Reyes" instead of "Drake's Bay" which is an equivalent name for the same physical place.

Table 2. Number of questions successfully answered by intended recipients, as well as guessed correctly by any other recipient.

recipient	$|Q|$	$|A^*|$	successful answers	guessed answers
ex-sig. other	15	12	12	0
sister	13	8	10	2
mother	12	7	8	3
brother	16	8	13	4
former roommate	13	5	10	1
sig. other	16	8	14	0
father	14	6	7	3
childhood friend	16	8	10	0

6   Open Questions

6.1   Sender Authentication

So far we have only considered the question of confidentiality of the message being sent to Alice, and this was all that was needed in prior systems which only considered encryption to oneself. In our scenario, we may ask if there is any secure way for Bob to ensure that a message he receives encrypted in our scheme really came from Alice, as claimed. We conjecture that this problem is far more difficult to completely solve. There does exist a degree of implicit authentication in that Bob knows the sender is somebody who knew a significant amount of personal information. In our proposal, we have included a MAC of all correct answers in our system as a weak indication to the recipient that the sender did in fact know all of the correct answers. We could consider adding some additional personal information to the encryption which was not already used.

We feel that this provides little security against a malicious attempt to forge a message from Alice. Presumably, such an attack could be constructed by, for example, breaking into Alice's email address and reading old correspondence, burgling Alice's home, or dumpster diving to collect discarded material. This sort of attack is far easier to pull off than a compromise of the confidentiality of the system, because the attacker must only find enough information that seems "personal enough" for Bob to assume it was Alice herself which sent the message. To decrypt an intercepted message, the attacker must find specifically the information chosen by Alice to encrypt, which is far more difficult.

6.2   Fuzzy Matching

Another desirable trait is fuzzy matching of answers. That is, instead of requiring that Bob answer some subset of questions *exactly*, we can allow him to answer fewer questions exactly and be close on some questions. For example, if the question is, "When is cousin Jeff's birthday?", Bob may guess April 12 when the correct date is April 14. Intuitively, Bob has demonstrated some knowledge of the correct answer while still being wrong. An ideal system would enable the recipient to learn a varying amount of the pre-key based on closeness to a correct answer. This may be useful in textual questions as well, if a name is misspelled but still largely correct.

In our current system, this functionality is missing. The closest we can do is normalise answers, say, by removing spaces and capitalisation, or more aggressively by applying the Soundex algorithm to mask spelling errors. In the case of numbers or dates, they can be rounded. Neither of these methods are ideal, as they assist with guessing attacks, and may not be helpful in that two close answers may still be rounded to different values. An open question is how to design a system that will allow for fuzzy matching of answers.

References

1. Ellison, C., Hall, C., Milbert, R., Schneier, B.: Protecting secret keys with personal entropy. Future Gener. Comput. Syst. 16(4), 311–318 (2000)
2. Frykholm, N., Juels, A.: Error-tolerant password recovery. In: CCS 2001: Proceedings of the 8th ACM Conference on Computer and Communications Security, pp. 1–9. ACM, New York (2001)
3. Just, M.: Designing and evaluating challenge-question systems. IEEE Security & Privacy (2004)
4. Rabkin, A.: Personal knowledge questions for fallback authentication: Security questions in the era of facebook. In: SOUPS: Symposium on Usable Privacy and Security (2006)
5. Griffith, V., Jakobsson, M.: Messin' with Texas Deriving Mother's Maiden Names Using Public Records. In: Ioannidis, J., Keromytis, A.D., Yung, M. (eds.) ACNS 2005. LNCS, vol. 3531, pp. 91–103. Springer, Heidelberg (2005)
6. Xu, W., Zhou, X., Li, L.: Inferring privacy information via social relations. In: International Conference on Data Engineering (2008)
7. Lindamood, J., Kantarcioglu, M.: Inferring private information using social network data. Technical Report UTDCS-21-08, University of Texas at Dallas Computer Science Department (2008)
8. Jakobsson, M., Stolterman, E., Wetzel, S., Yang, L.: Love and authentication. In: CHI 2008: Proceeding of the Twenty-Sixth Annual SIGCHI Conference on Human Factors in Computing Systems, pp. 197–200. ACM, New York (2008)
9. Jakobsson, M., Yang, L., Wetzel, S.: Quantifying the security of preference-based authentication. In: DIM 2008: Proceedings of the 4th ACM Workshop on Digital Identity Management, pp. 61–70. ACM, New York (2008)
10. Kelsey, J., Schneier, B., Hall, C., Wagner, D.: Secure Applications of Low-Entropy Keys. In: Okamoto, E. (ed.) ISW 1997. LNCS, vol. 1396, pp. 121–134. Springer, Heidelberg (1998)

Alice and Bob in Love

(Transcript of Discussion)

Joseph Bonneau

University of Cambridge

I'm Joseph Bonneau for those of you who don't know me. I'll talk about this natural entropy concept that I want to use to do encryption, I'll propose a pretty short and simple crypto protocol. I actually did this experimentally since writing the pre-proceedings paper, so I'll talk about how that went, it was kind of interesting. Hopefully I'll have a lot of time left over for discussion, because there's a lot here that is pretty hard.

I guess cryptographers are in the habit of saying that human memory is bad. It's actually really good for a lot of things, it's just not good for things that are very high entropy, like crypto keys, but my theory is that people remember things that have actually happened and experiences of other people quite well. So my guiding idea here is that there's all these people in the world who you actually share a lot of entropy with naturally without having to put it explicitly in a form of a crypto key. So these are people like people you've dated, people in your family, the really close friends in your life. So my question is, can we use this huge amount of shared experience that you have with these people to do cryptography.

Humans can do challenge-response pretty well with other humans. If you are a fan of American cinema there is a movie that came out a couple of years ago called, There Will be Blood, and it contains a really dramatic scene where the main character has the other guy claiming to be his long lost brother from when they were both five, and he asks him this really dramatic question, and bam, the guy didn't get it right so he knew he wasn't his brother. That's not the end of the movie if you haven't seen it yet, a lot more stuff happens. And then this one I pulled off the web, I thought it was really interesting: this is a chat, conversation between some guy named Evan, and Kelvin's chat account, this actually happened on Facebook I believe. What really happened here is that Kelvin's account got compromised by some guy in Nigeria, and "Kelvin" sends this story to Evan saying, I'm lost in London, I need money to get home, send me $900 on Western Union. Unfortunately this kind of scam happens all the time, but Evan is on top of it so he asks Kelvin, what was the name of our High School mascot, and "Kelvin" typed in the name of their High School, which was not very good by Evan because I Googled this and I found the mascot out in about five seconds, so he probably could have done a lot better, this wasn't the best question for Evan to ask.

Michael Roe: It might be the first question he might have asked him, but if he got the right answer back, he should have asked another one.

B. Christianson et al. (Eds.): Security Protocols 2009, LNCS 7028, pp. 199–212, 2013.

Reply: Yes, my theory is that, when you can go back and forth and ask another question based on the person's answer, I think humans can do a reasonable job of authenticating other people that they know well. So here's the stick figure diagram to represent that, with Alice and Bob, note the hearts, because they have some intimate relationship going on. I think that in a pretty secure way Bob can repeatedly ask questions and establish that he actually is talking to Alice.

Matt Blaze: Terminator 2, really?

Reply: OK, somebody's paying attention, that's good.

Paul Syverson: Because this thing, what day of the month was our first date, is the sort of thing that a wife asks of a husband, and then he has no clue, right.

Bruce Christianson: If he gets the wedding anniversary right you know it's a ringer.

Reply: Right, we'll get to this later in the talk, I actually used this question with my ex-girlfriend when I was doing my experiment, I asked, what day of the month was our first date, and she wrote Friday.

Virgil Gligor: And that's why she's ex?

Reply: Exactly. I mean, I think this process can fail for a lot of reasons, a lot of the questions might not be answered correctly, but if the husband says, I don't remember the day of our first date, the wife might say, shame on you, but then ask a few more questions and say, yes, it's probably him and he forgot. Humans can do this sort of thing naturally with no training, and no crypto. What I want to do in this talk is say, can we do this in a one-way fashion where Bob is actually sending an encrypted message to Alice, and it's encrypted based on all these questions. We're using the same concept but we're doing something more here, we're actually trying to get confidentiality, and we're trying to do it over a one-way channel. So we want to design some scheme where Bob sends a whole bunch of questions and an encrypted message along with maybe some decryption software, Alice can try and answer these questions, and if she does it right she'll get the message, and hopefully nobody else can impersonate Alice here.

Applications, this is probably my weakest slide. Hopefully there are some applications for this. I was thinking maybe there's some emergency distress scenario where you really have to get a key out and you haven't pre-shared any keys. The drafting a will story I thought was interesting, which is a case where maybe you draft this will which of designed for your wife to read after you pass away, and you don't want her to know that you're actually drafting it, so you don't want to share keys, so you would use this scheme. And then actually you could be doing the scheme with yourself, writing down a bunch of questions that you think only you know the answer to, you could also do that if you want to back up passwords or other secret stuff, and this is the only context where this has really been studied before, writing down a bunch of questions that only you know the answer to.

So my goal in doing this, is to try and get something that at least looks like cryptographic security.

Alastair Beresford: Could you also have something where, to recover your login credentials for a social networking site, you have a set of questions that you have to answer to a set of different friends, so you can prove to a social networking site that you are that person. You can go back in if you can prove you are this person to some friends that you have already configured as friends.

Reply: That's a really good idea. It might be hard in that you have to get all the friends to participate and do this securely, and they might not have the incentives, but that could potentially be really good. OK, so I'm going to try and get some semblance of cryptographic security, at least have a formula that says I have 64 bits of security. It's going to be very hand waving, but I want this to be really easy for the recipient to use, and to try and maximise this pool of entropy that we do have available to us. Things that I will throw out the window right away, the performance of this is not going to be great, there's going to be a huge overhead for each message, and it's going to take some time to actually do the encryption, which in practice I think isn't a problem, because it takes so long to think up these questions that that's the dominant step anyway. And it's not going to be simple for the sender to do this, so my thinking here is that the sender is going to have to be fairly sophisticated and understand things like estimating how much entropy there is in the answer to a question. I couldn't find a good way to get around that.

My inspiration for building this protocol, there have been two papers written about this in the password backup scenario. Both of these did a simple thing where you have a list of questions and you do secret sharing between those questions. I'm basically going to do the same thing, the crypto is not the interesting part of this. People have studied the general question of how well people remember these questions about personal knowledge, it's been studied mostly in the concept of re-authentication, which is what happens after you lose your password, and most of the studies have found that it's pretty hard to find questions that you can't find the answer to on Google, and that people remember well. So I'm going to add something, I can potentially adapt the password backup schemes more directly to this, but I'm going to try and build a scheme that's more flexible, so that you can designate for each question how much entropy you think there is in the answer, and you can specify how likely you think the receiver is to remember the answer.

The encryption process is fairly straightforward. The sender writes out this list of questions, they have to write the answers too, and then for each question they estimate how much entropy they think there is in the answer, and the probability that the recipients can remember the thing. In my implementation, it's really straightforward, you just write an XML file with questions, and this is one that I sent in my experiments. You can probably see right away that the entropy is probably close to three here, maybe a few answers are a little bit more likely than others, but the fact that I'm saying I think the person that I'm sending this message to has a 95% chance of remembering this, that number inherently has to come out of thin air. Like we were talking about yesterday, even big companies can't really manage uncertainty, and certainly when you're designing this the probabilities are going to be very inaccurate, but hopefully if we are conservative enough we'll still have security and reliability.

Dusko Pavlovic: Is this question still going to that ex-girlfriend?

Reply: This question? I don't remember who this went to. Probably my current girlfriend. But what's the relevance of that question?

Bruce Christianson: He's trying to check that you're really Joseph.

Reply: You failed! The encryption protocol, I tweaked one thing from how I wrote it up in the paper, so keep that in mind. The software is basically going to designate every subset of answers that we think has shown enough knowledge to enable decryption, I'll talk about how we do that in a second. This is nothing fancy, this is just doing secret sharing by brute force, so every subset of answers that you think is OK will have a share for that subset. This is adding a lot of storage because we have to add data for all of these subsets, in practice this wasn't a big problem, and it ended up being like 50K. For each one of these subsets of answers that you think is sufficient for decryption, we just hash all of the answers together, we do a key strengthening step where we hash that a bunch of times, and then we are going to store an offset to get this master key that we're later going to use for the message. Again, I don't think anything really fancy is going on here. The critical thing to note is that as this set of subsets gets bigger, our storage is increasing, and the amount of work to actually encrypt is increasing.

Paul Syverson: So in this scheme the person who's doing the recovery, not only has to know these subsets, but they have to know whether or not they know. Because if you think that you're answering 12 questions, and maybe two or three of them you're getting wrong, but you're not even really sure which two or three.

Reply: The person doesn't have to know, the software can do the search for you.

Paul Syverson: Oh, so you're just going to put them all together and then as long as any subset works, that will do?

Reply: Yes, the software will try every subset until it fails or decrypts the thing.

George Danezis: In a generic way, I think this looks rather like a paper I read a while ago about extracting cryptographic keys from noisy readings like biometrics, have you looked at this paper? You're about to present a scheme like that in your next line.

Reply: I think that's the way that the Juels password recovery scheme worked, because he cited those papers. The reason I did the less sophisticated thing, I remembered those schemes didn't seem to work well if you're combining sources of entropy that are different.

George Danezis: They are based on coding theory, effectively your key is in space, and your apply some coding scheme so you can correct some errors by finding the closest form to whatever reading you have. So it's basically about making a good coding scheme, that takes into account the error profile that you have.

Reply: I'm not going to say I'm doing a better job, there's a good chance I'm doing a worse job, but I looked into it and the reason that I decided to do this simpler fairly brute force type thing is that, the papers I read on it make the assumption that they have a constant amount of entropy in each one of the shares.

Bruce Christianson: They assume all bits are equal.

Reply: Yes.

Michael Backes: You mentioned a key strengthening step. If K_i is a low entropy secret, then applying a known function a gazillion times will give the same entropy. So how did this strengthen the keys?

Reply: It's not increasing the amount of entropy, it's just making the brute force for an attacker more painful. This basically adds work for the attacker, because every time they want to try some guess for the answers then they have to compute this hash function 2 to the S times, so it's just a slowdown, but that's standard key strengthening.

Matt Blaze: I apologise for asking this a little late, but I wanted to make sure that I said the right thing, so are you familiar with Markus Jakobsson's Preference Space[1]? Because it seems that in particular he's got some numbers on how much entropy there is in very similar kinds of questions to the ones you're looking at.

Reply: Yes I have a slide on that later. Basically the preference thing doesn't work from one person to another person very well; there is almost no preference that you know about another person that nobody else knows. The questions have to be very, very specific.

Matt Blaze: Sure, but the paper that I'm thinking of as being perhaps relevant, is his work on estimating the amount of entropy in each preference, which seems similar to what you're using.

Reply: I have a slide later on that too. I think that also doesn't quite work in this scenario.

OK, so anyway, that's my secret sharing scheme, and then once we have that, next bit is trivial, this is just an encrypted MAC, and you have to send along the

---

[1] "Quantifying the security of preference-based authentication" by M.Jakobsson, L.Yang and S.Wetzel (2008).

questions and these offsets. I have the answers to the questions, and the offsets all being encrypted and authenticated, and I'll talk later about whether or not that really provides authenticity, I think that's in a way the best we can do. And then the software is going to pick this subset given all the questions and answers that the user writes out, this ends up being a really straightforward search, and it's easy to do. It may seem like you have to do brute force over the power set of A, but there's a trivial recursive algorithm to do this.

OK, so I think the crypto is easy. It got interesting when I tried to actually do this, I coded this scheme up, and I designed the most sophisticated experiment I could do, which was me sending messages to people I actually know. My working theory is that this scheme, for a given sender there's maybe ten recipients in the world who you can really do this with, because it is really, really hard to sit down and think up questions that you're convinced that exactly you and one other person know the answer to. So I did it with four members of my family, my parents and two siblings, girlfriend and ex-girlfriend, which was interesting, and then two male friends of mine, my roommate from college and another friend. When I did this I limited myself to spend 60 minutes coming up with questions for each person. I tried to be pretty strict about it, so I came up with the questions without looking at photos; I thought it would be really easy if I could look at my email history with these people, but I limited myself to just a blank piece of paper, and 60 minutes. I set my security parameter to be 64 bits of estimated entropy, and based on my estimates of entropy and recall, I was able to come up with a set of questions for every person that my software told me would have a really high chance of being decrypted. In terms of estimating entropy, for the simple stuff I tried to be pretty conservative, these are some examples of some of the things I used. I think in the abstract a first name has maybe 8 bits of entropy, within 1 or 2 bits I think that's probably right. I'll talk about this a little bit more later, but I think as long as you're fairly conservative this scheme should work.

So I sent out these eight messages to people, I told them they had 24 hours, everybody said it was really fast, it took them 10 minutes to write the answers, they sort of instantly either knew or didn't know. The other thing I did was to try and simulate how hard it would be for an attacker who had some real inside knowledge, I sent everybody's messages to everybody else. So obviously within my family it's a group of people who all know each other well, so it was interesting to see what questions they were able to guess from the others.

Bruce Christianson: So they're now spending an extra hour?

Reply: Yes, so after the first pass of answering their own questions they looked at other people's questions and tried to guess them.

Paul Syverson: Didn't you have to then also think about your questions like, oh I can't ask my brother about this because I don't want my parents to know?

Reply: Yes, particularly with the girlfriend and the ex-girlfriend.

Frank Stajano: As a reverse game you could do it, you give them the questions and say, who do you think I asked these questions of.

Reply: I actually did that and they were able to figure that out pretty well. I'm glad I did this because it forced me to really focus on things that I didn't think other people would know even given the identities of the other people in the survey. So here's how the parameters worked out, it was usually about 13, 14, 15 questions that I got out in an hour. The entropy I estimated was usually about 90 bits, of which I was requiring the receiver to show that they knew 64 bits of that entropy in order to decrypt, and the success probability was based on my own estimates of how likely I thought people were to remember things. It turned out to be wildly optimistic as we'll see.

This number of subsets was low enough that I didn't think it's a performance killer. Six people were actually able to decrypt successfully, which is not what I was hoping for. I predicted, the average would be 95% for the likelihood that people would remember, and I actually got 75%, so I was pretty far off there. But looking at what actually happened, my two parents were the ones who couldn't decrypt, in particular my father was a disaster, he only got half of his questions right. But if you look, at the errors, a lot of the errors are in this input column, which means they actually remembered the thing, and they showed me enough, looking at it as a person that I'd say, yes, they actually remembered the thing, but they didn't input it in the right way and so it got hashed to different things. This is the column of what was actually guessed, so you see, fortunately girlfriends it turns out are the easiest people to do this scheme with, I was able to come up with tons of stuff, nothing was forgotten, and nothing was guessed, which was good. You can see that within my family things were being guessed, most of the guessing that was successful was people in my family guessing answers to questions that I sent to other people in my family. And then curiously my two friends were able to guess one question about each other.

So that was my experiment. The really key takeaway from this is that the thing that really hurts is that it's really hard to get people to input the answer in the way that you are thinking of it. Spelling problems, some are fairly simple, and you could do a scheme where you remove all the vowels from answers that would take care of things, like the name Rachael can be spelt different ways, along with a bunch of others. Some of the spelling errors are a little bit more complicated and hard to deal with. And then you get these weird phrasing things where I tried to have hints and say, only use one word, or phrase it in the past tense, which people seemed to ignore. Like in this bike example, I said, phrase in the past tense, and my mother wrote riding. Stuff like that is just pretty hard to deal with. And in terms of this, how often do people know that they don't know, a third of the wrong answers were the person writing, don't know, which is what I instructed them to do if they didn't know. And there was one example of a question where the answer was wrong because I actually wrote the wrong answer down as the sender, as in completely wrote the wrong answer down, didn't actually remember the thing, which was strange. In terms of the actual forgetfulness errors, in every case when I debriefed people afterward and said, how could you not remember it was this, and they always said, oh I totally remember now, I just blanked when I saw the thing. So here's the distribution of the errors.

In some sense I was disappointed in human memory, that it didn't do as well as I thought it would, but I think that if we could deal well with the input problem this scheme would be a lot better. The number of times people actually remember is 85% in my really small sample, and I think that's enough for this scheme to work.

Matt Blaze: I noticed you didn't have a category of, remember an incorrect thing, so what movie did we go to, and where you disagree about what movie it is.

Reply: Oh yes, for the actual forgetfulness, one third said, don't know, the other two thirds remembered the wrong thing. I did do a normalisation path, I was expecting people to enter things wrong, so I coded some pretty simple stuff like converting the lower case, throwing out punctuation, getting rid of words like "the" and "and", which actually saved me in a few cases. But my thinking is that to get this scheme to be even moderately practical you'd have to have really very aggressive normalisation of answers.

Michael Roe: Some things like colours or movie titles, or breakfast cereal, you can normalise by having a big lookup table in the system , so if any question's answer is a colour, then you can have a table of the colours and choose which one is the nearest.

Peter Ryan: Yes, but they'll say turquoise when it was actually teal.

Reply: I did multiple choice where it was reasonable to do so, the problem is that like if it's, what was the name of so and so, particularly with last names, the table needs to be really gigantic.

Michael Roe: But you could do a match on say the phonebook, so you've got a list of big names, and then you do a Google-type search, did you really mean to type X.

Reply: I don't think the phone book thing works because if this woman's name was Rachael with ae in it, and the recipient typed Rachel with just an e, they've actually typed a valid name, it's just the wrong valid name, so the phone book wouldn't fix that.

Michael Roe: So you've got to create the tables so that everything is far enough apart in the stated areas.

Bruce Christianson: Yes, that's it. And for multi-choice you only need to have enough distracters to give you the entropy you want, so a limited range of breakfast cereals would do.

George Danezis: I was thinking you could give about 100 yes/no questions, basically binary choice questions, and with the error rate you have, that should actually give you the right entropy. People effectively do it all the time on Facebook, people actually love doing this stuff.

Reply: Mathematically that's really good, the reason that it doesn't work (you can try and do it as a thought exercise) is think about somebody you really know well, your mother perhaps, and try and think of something that exactly you and she know, and nobody else. It's a really small set of things, and coming up with 100 yes/no questions I think would be almost impossible.

Bruce Christianson: You're saying that a small number of richly structured high entropy questions is better.

Reply: Yes. A lot of the time the questions that I actually had with my college friends were like, we were travelling in Mexico one time and we met this really crazy bus driver, what was the guy's name, and then you get maybe eight bits out of that, but it really only gives you one bit as a yes/no question.

Simon Foley: Although George's scheme could be really good for a threshold encryption kind of problem, like for the last will and testament thing.

Reply: Yes, I guess if you were going to divide it between a lot of people, yes/no is nice, it gets rid of a lot of these problems.

Frank Stajano: I really like this scheme, maybe the objection from the crypto viewpoint Ben had is that you then attack this individual, you can say, OK, I'm going to spend £50 on a private investigator to figure out these 8 bits, you can do that independently of the rest. So it's not really 64 bits, where you have brute force everything at once to get the key. Here the pieces can be validated independently from each other.

Reply: Right, I tried as a sender to make that hard, I had a few rules I followed like a no Facebook rule, I didn't ask any questions that I could find on the web. The question is, how do you pick questions that private investigators have no hope of finding out, which is what I tried to do, I tried to be like, we were on a bus one day with this guy, and nobody else was there. That's the stuff you hope a private investigator can't find out. I think the security of this on paper looks sort of reasonable, but there's so many assumptions being made.

Frank Stajano: The point that I'm making is more structural, it's that you can find out, independently of the other questions, a group of bits at a time. So if you had an interception of your message on the way to the destination, then a private investigator could go and ask the questions sneakily of the real target, they could do it to some of the answers.

Bruce Christianson: And then there would be much less to brute force. The danger is that some of the bits of entropy are not actually independent, in the sense that somebody either knows all of them or none of them. Therefore the risks are higher than you think, it's this variance versus expectation thing.

Simon Foley: Also another interesting question is how many new questions can you come up with as timely clues, because at some point you want to re-key, or in Frank's case somebody's discovered the answers to your existing questions.

Reply: Well, I don't know that you really need to re-key. Can you send the same questions over and over again? If you believe they were secure the first time they should be secure the second time.

Ross Anderson: During the Serbian war I recall TV news reports about the rescue of a pilot of a downed Black Hawk, and the US Airforce protocol was to get one of his buddies from flight training school over there in the rescue plane, and as the rescue team were approaching the guy was asked half a dozen questions on the radio to verify that he was who he said was, and that he wasn't acting under duress. Now this prompts a protocol whereby you set up a secret at the other end and you then interrogate each other, so you and your father will then interrogate each other, you and your ex-girlfriend, etc. In theory that should work better, in practice it would be fascinating to see what the usability issues were especially with non-computer science folks. How good could people be at identifying another person by challenge response conducted by means of a keyboard rather than by means of voice[2].

Paul Syverson: I'm worried about the social engineering attack, because once you've used these questions once, if I want to attack, now I'm going to go to the recipient in a completely innocuous context and try to bring out the answers in conversation, and I imagine you could do a fair amount of that.

Matt Blaze: But similar protocols are used by American Express, and maybe some other credit card companies, to confirm your identity when you are calling from a new phone. I remember one instance, I got a call, they wanted to confirm my charge, and you know, I said, well I'm not in the habit of revealing financial information to people who call me, how do I know you're American Express, and they said, call the number on the back of your card, and I called the number on the back of my card and then they asked, well how do we know you're Matt Blaze. And the way they established this is, they said, OK, two weeks ago you had dinner at a restaurant in Philadelphia, what was it, and asked me a couple of questions about charges on my account.

Reply: And that was actually from the human, not machine generated.

Matt Blaze: Right. But you know, they weren't with me at dinner, where I got billed, so the credit card company were using my account information, and a lot of the questions I couldn't answer, but I could answer enough to satisfy them. So I suspect they may have some data on entropy, because at least they're willing to use this. I mean, it might be snake oil or it might be...

Reply: There's a slight difference there though. The reason in this scenario that I was really heavily constrained, is that if it's a question that you're convinced that nobody else will know the answer to, or be able to hire a private investigator to

---

[2] This amounts to a new twist on the original Turing test.

find out, that's a really, very limited set of events, that aren't on your credit card receipt, and aren't written about anywhere. So yes, the credit card people have an easier scenario, but it's also a more practical one. That's why I'm interested in this kind of thing, not because I think this is a pressing need, but because I'd like to push forward our general understanding of authenticating humans.

Paul Syverson: I once got a call from a bank or credit card company, and they wanted me to give them my social security number, and I said, nuts, and then I said, well you tell me, and they said, nuts, and I hung up. My wife immediately said, why didn't you just give them the first digit and they could give you the second digit, and then you could give them the third digit, which is a very nice, simple two-way protocol.

Reply: Yes, so could we turn this into a two-way protocol, that's a good question.

Paul Syverson: I was thinking about the movie example you had, and whether you could do a two-way protocol there. I didn't see the movie, but I could imagine somebody saying like, oh the younger brother who lived there, he had a bad leg, and then you would know, well he really is telling the truth even though he can't remember the question exactly.

Reply: Well one question is probably not enough if it's only an 80% recall rate, it's probably not a good idea to shoot the guy.

Paul Syverson: It depends on your threat model, you know.

Simon Foley: Well if it's two-way and if the questions are contextual then presumably the entropy is greater than the entropy of the individual. Because the question I ask you is based on the question you gave me, and the answer I might give you, and the context of the question that you asked me.

Paul Syverson: I also suspect that a mentalist, one of those people who pretends to be a mind reader, could totally break through that, most people are very susceptible.

Alastair Beresford: Addressing Frank's question earlier about all the questions being separate, could you have one question whose answer you then use as the start of the next question, so the answer to the first one is, for example, what drawer in the house do you use to store your keys, and then the next question is

Reply: I actually did that a couple of times in the questions that I sent out, again because they were normally honed on specific incidents I could remember with the person. There was one example where it was three questions long, I said, remember this baseball game we went to a long time ago, and this crazy fan yelled this, who was he yelling at, and then at that same game, who was the starting pitcher for the other team, and my friend actually remembered it too, so it was beautiful. That works really well when you can do it, but there were a lot of things where there was really only one thing to ask about the memory, so I couldn't really figure out how to do it.

Sören Preibusch: And some people remember things better than others, especially computer scientists are believed to be a bit autistic and not remember things about other people.

Reply: Well my father couldn't remember anything.

Alastair Beresford: That's a fact about fathers I think.

Reply: Yes, and age too. Maybe the fact that my parents had more difficulty than anybody else is because they're also 30 years older than everybody else who I tried it with.

Simon Foley: So it's the key material that expires.

Michael Roe: Seriously, to work out probabilities you ought to try this with a more widely selected group of people, I mean, not your friends, but somebody else and their friends.

Reply: I had a whole bunch more slides that I won't worry about, but I had one question: the experiment I did, obviously from a scientific standpoint has a lot of problems, it's a tiny sample, and the experimenter is the one doing the research, and all these other things, but I think it's very hard to design these experiments in a more general way because you have to actually get people do it with their friends and how do you do that in a lab environment? It takes a long time, so it's an open question, how to do this experiment in a more valid way.

Michael Roe: Could you make it into a Facebook application?

Alastair Beresford: You could use George's idea where it's like a quiz about how well do you know your friends, but you try and build the whole thing so you can then also look at prejudice and size, so make it a sort of covert channel.

Reply: Yes, I had that thought actually, and I think it's a good idea. The issue then is, to get people to really do this protocol from the sender side. They have to be tagging entropy and doing other things that most people probably won't want to do on Facebook just for free.

Michael Roe: Maybe restricting yourself to multiple choice is the way to get people to do it.

Simon Foley: But these are like those faces, where you were presented a plane of pictures of people's faces, and the faces that you choose is effectively your password.

Reply: How is that like this?

Simon Foley: Well, in the sense that it's multiple choice, but they're having to remember the particular faces that they choose, and so you might decide well I'm just going to remember maybe people I think are the prettiest in these pictures.

Reply: Yes, although we're drifting away from the question of basing it on things that you aren't remembering just for the sake of authentication, but things that are in your head anyway. But yes, it's a whole world of what people can remember.

George Danezis: You can avoid having people setting the questions by just judging how well someone knows someone else's character, so asking them effectively a thousand questions, and just relying on the advantage that someone that knows you is likely to have when they actually answer them.

Reply: So where are you going to get these thousand questions?

Ross Anderson: Markus Kuhn has a similar system where he asks you a large number of questions about your preferences and that's in the profile which you might be interrogated on later.

George Danezis: And then if you ask the others what do you think?

Bruce Christianson: The answer would be to these questions.

Reply: Yes, that could be a good way to do that.

Matt Blaze: Wait a minute, when I asked about that it was a bad way.

Bruce Christianson: Obviously the correct answer would depend on who was asking [laughter].

Reply: Actually my answer is that I think that that's a good thing to try, but I don't think it will work. I think the preferences that you know about other people are the same preferences that other people know.

James Malcolm: Yes, it wouldn't be an individual thing.

Bruce Christianson: It wouldn't distinguish you from somebody else who you just know well.

Reply: The core hardness, which I think made my recall probabilities low, is that I was asking my brother things that I knew my sister didn't know, because my sister was in the survey too, and in terms of my brother's preferences, he likes surfing but my sister knows that too. So if you really want to encrypt for one specific member of your family I think the preferences idea fails, so I'm back to saying it's a bad idea. It would be interesting to see if you could do it, but I think it won't work.

James Malcolm: I was wondering about getting a bunch of our students to do this, and I thought, oh dear, I don't think they're going to come up with questions that work. Just coming up with the questions I think is quite hard.

Reply: Yes, that was the main thing I found, because I sat myself down with a 60 minute timer, and I was usually struggling in the last ten minutes to write a few more questions. It's really hard to come up with the questions.

Matt Blaze: Is it actually necessary in a motivating example to come up with questions that distinguish between people that you know.

Reply: It might not be.

Matt Blaze: A motivating example, I'm a friend of yours from High School, you know, we went to High School together, well if you can establish that you are any one of the people in that class then I'm confident that you are.

Reply And you're probably not doing a scam.

Matt Blaze: And if you're trying to claim that you're a different friend that I went to High School with, I don't really care that much.

Reply: Yes, so you're doing what you said not to do in your talk yesterday[3], you're relaxing the assumptions.

Matt Blaze: I said I shouldn't do that.

Reply: Yes, that might be a much more tractable problem. You could argue that the difficulty is getting my brother and not my sister, maybe that doesn't really matter because I also trust my sister. The problem is what happens when you have a falling out with your sister and she still knows all this stuff, and she's walking around.

Paul Syverson: You could also look at the amount of separation because you have fifteen questions, four of which you're pretty sure both your brother and sister know, but the rest they don't, first you narrow down to that set, and then you can split.

Reply: And that's essentially what I got, because even though I tried to not have this happen, my brother and sister each got like three or four of each other's questions, but I guess that's still bought some security.

Paul Syverson: They're still not going to get each others keys, out of that overlap?

Reply: They have a shorter brute force, but they're maybe not the ones doing brute force.

Michael Roe: As the experimenter you might be particularly good at choosing questions with high entropy, so the experiment you want to do is to get somebody else who's more typical to choose the questions, and then see how badly they work.

Reply: Yes, I'm afraid to do that experiment, but yes, how well the scheme would do if it's released into the wild, I'm not making any claims.

---

[3] Blaze, these proceedings.

Why I'm Not an Entropist

Paul Syverson*

Naval Research Laboratory
syverson@itd.nrl.navy.mil

Abstract. What does it mean to be anonymous in network communications? Our central thesis is that both the theoretical literature and the deployed systems have gotten the answer essentially wrong. The answers have been wrong because they apply the wrong metric to the wrong adversary model. I indicate problems in the established adversary models and metrics for anonymity as well as implications for the design and analysis of anonymous communication systems.

1 Introduction

Anonymous communication is the quintessence of brief encounter. For anyone to whom it is anonymous, such communication cannot be linked to an individual, for example to its source or destination. But it also cannot be linked to any other instances of communication. If it could, it would be part of a communication profile, hence pseudonymous communication rather than anonymous. Anonymity thus guarantees that an encounter is brief rather than leaving this to chance.

Anonymity is also an area of security that is much younger than, for example, confidentiality. Mechanisms and networks for anonymous communication have been designed for only about thirty years [6] and deployed for not quite half that time [21,35,19]. We do not have nearly as much experience with deployed systems on which to build theory, definitions, and models as many other areas of security, for example confidentiality or authentication. Though the field has developed and adapted, the basic conception of what it means to be anonymous has persisted throughout its history.

That conception is of anonymity as about indistinguishability within a set. The idea is thus that there is a set of possible senders, and the adversary cannot adequately distinguish amongst the members of that set. (For brevity and convenience I focus discussion on sender anonymity of a message.) I call this *the entropist conception* of anonymous communication. I am motivated in choice of terminology here by general Rényi entropy rather than Shannon entropy specifically (H_2 in the ordering of Rényi entropies). Thus I am including everything from simple cardinality of the set of possible senders (the log of which is Hartley entropy, H_0) to the other extreme of min entropy (H_∞). However, I am more

---

* A version of this paper was originally presented to the 17*th* Security Protocols Workshop, Cambridge UK, April 2009, which had as its theme "brief encounters". This is a substantially revised and expanded version of the originally presented paper.

B. Christianson et al. (Eds.): Security Protocols 2009, LNCS 7028, pp. 213–230, 2013.

focused on the conception of anonymity as indistinguishability within a set (possibly according to some probability distribution) than on any particular mathematical characterization of it. I will argue that this basic conception—a conception that underlies virtually all extent work on anonymous communication—is not appropriate for the fundamental role it has been given.

Before getting into details, I set out some general principles for security metrics and system design that I believe should be uncontroversial. It is on the basis of these principles that I will make my case.

- To be useful, security metrics should reflect the difficulty an adversary has in overcoming them. (So, for example, a metric for a security property should not depend on variables whose values do no significantly impact whether the adversary succeeds in attacks on that property.)
- To be meaningful, security metrics should not depend on the values of variables for which we cannot make adequate relevant determinations or predictions. (It might be sufficient to determine or predict bounds, distributions, etc. for those values rather than the exact values themselves, provided they are relevant. For example, to observe that a value will always be finite will usually not reflect a bound that is relevant to a practical security metric.)
- Though security through obscurity is rarely a good system design strategy, if your design provides your adversary with an explicit target that he has available resources to overcome, you are doomed to fail.

It is crucial to understand that our fundamental complaint against entropism is *not* that entropy fails to ever properly say anything about the uncertainty we may have about senders or receivers of messages. The problem is that entropism fails to tell us much about the adversary's amount of knowledge (or lack of knowledge) that is useful in saying how secure our practical anonymity systems are, or how secure a given use of one of them is. Starting from an entropist conception of anonymity has led to a focus on system properties that are not the most important to system security, has led to system assumptions that are not reasonable in practice, has led to adversary models that are not reasonable in practice, and has led to both theory and system design for anonymous communication that fail in significant ways. The remainder of the paper investigates these points in light of the above principles. We concentrate herein on problems with the existing approach, but we will at least briefly consider potential alternatives to replace it with.

2   Wait. I Thought You Said You're *Not* an Entropist.

There are many circumstances where the entropist conception of anonymity makes perfect sense, for example, in an election where there are registered voters casting ballots. An entropist approach can protect the anonymity of voters by confounding of associating voters with ballots and provides a good metric for that protection. (This assumes that appropriate other protections ensure that each registration represents exactly one voter, that each voter casts at most one ballot per election, and assumes that enough eligible voters vote, that enough voters cast ballots for each of the options—if that is of concern, etc.)

As a more exotic example, in the 1970s the United States and the Soviet Union sought to limit the number of nuclear missiles they both had through cooperation and inspection while maintaining security guarantees. A large part of one of the major initiatives involved shuttling Minuteman missiles about in a field of silos to preclude successful first-strike attacks directly on all available missiles. The plan also included techniques for communicating to the adversary an authenticated, integrity-protected report from each silo. The report indicated whether a missile was in the silo or not, but without the adversary being able to determine which silo the report was from (except by silo-unique but random identifier). In a field of 1000 missile silos, the adversary could be sure that exactly 100 would be occupied but would not know which ones were occupied. Note that this anonymity system used "dummy packets" in the form of huge "transportainer" trucks continually shuttling either actual missiles or dummy loads between silos. Talk about system overhead! See [40] for more details about the plan.

As a less exotic example, suppose an intimidating colleague or perhaps the boss is repeatedly but obliviously doing something that is inappropriate and bothers several coworkers: leaving the food area or bathroom a mess, telling jokes or making comments that some find offensive, etc. Nobody wants to be the one to complain to the offender. Also they don't want to embarrass or perhaps encourage ire by giving the impression that this was a topic of full group discussion and decision making, whether or not that is true. They just want it to stop. Thus they wouldn't want to use a collaborative anonymity mechanism to send this message unless it was also being used to send others. Put differently, they want the recipient to know that one of them sent the message, rather than that all of them sent it, even though only one copy was delivered.

Finally, a similar example that comes closer to our intended topic below. Suppose it is important to release some information to the press or the public without attribution. The information is posted to a public site. It is known that only a relatively small number of people had prior access to the information, so it was one of them, but we don't know which one. (Let us assume and ignore that the relevant set of people is known, and that there is no doubt that they are the only ones who had the information. Also assume that the authenticity of the information is evident or confirmed once revealed.) It could be government information (good or bad) of important public interest where overt indication of which knowledgeable person released the information would be a distraction from the public good of the release. Alternatively, perhaps the release is intentional and important but cannot be overtly approved for some reason, and if the "leaker" were known, s/he would be punished, officially or otherwise.

Entropism is about using entropy as the meaning, the criterion for anonymity or how anonymous something is. That has drawbacks because, as an average, it necessarily does not capture everything important. To the extent that entropy is the measure of anonymity it drives system design to maximize entropy, which may not be the same thing as maximizing anonymity in ways that matter. It is just one number, or a few numbers, such as the Shannon entropy and the min entropy. Any of these might be fine as a measure of anonymity in an appropriate context. None is fine as *the* measure of anonymity. As *the* measure it effectively becomes the definition for a relatively complex concept which is no better served by limiting to any single definition than is the overall field security by limiting to a single definition of 'security'.

In all of the just given cases, there is a set of possible sources (or locations) and the relevant security issue is the uncertainty within that set. For some of the cases, the exact set may not be known, but reasonable bounds can be given for both set size and uncertainty. Uncertainty on a known or approximately known set is clearly the significant concern in these cases, but what are examples where entropy is not appropriate? We will argue that entropism is the wrong approach to design and evaluation of the most well known and widely used systems for protecting the anonymity of communication.

3   Protecting Anonymity

Tor is a very widely used and deployed onion-routing network, which means that it gets its protection from creating cryptographic circuits along routes that an adversary is unlikely to observe or control. As in previous onion-routing systems, in the currently deployed Tor design this is achieved by choosing unpredictable routes through the network. This could, however, also derive in part from the inherent difficulty an adversary has attacking a particular part of the network [25,26] or from other sources. We will return to this below. Also like other onion-routing systems, Tor passes traffic bidirectionally along those circuits with minimal latency [44]. It is common in the literature to characterize the anonymity protection Tor provides in entropist terms. For example, "[t]he anonymity provided by Tor relies on the size of the anonymity set. Currently, there are around 1500 ORs, and an estimated quarter million Tor users." [43].

Assume I am a user of the network who picks his entry node the same way the vast majority of users do and then visits a hostile website. On the entropist conception, my anonymity is the same as any other user of the network. With about a quarter million active users that gives me a (Shannon) entropy of about 18 with respect to being identified as going to this website. But the number of users is only an estimate, and the system is designed so that nobody should be able to actually see connections coming from all of them. Further, talking about the number of users ignores how attacks actually happen.

An adversary observing an entry node and an exit node of the Tor network through which I am, e.g., browsing the web can trivially link the two ends of the connection and correlate source to destination. This has been an acknowledged feature of the design since its inception [14]. By the same timing correlation, an adversary that controls or observes a destination website and the entry node will be able to identify the source address of the user accessing the website. Against these attacks the number of other users is all but irrelevant.

In this case, entropy fails our second criterion for a security metric. We cannot determine the number of users on the network in general or the number using circuits with the same entry and exit nodes at the time of the attack. We can estimate these numbers based on network measurements such as given above. That would, however, only tell us the average number of users during various periods in the past. What should matter for my (entropist) anonymity with respect to the adversary is my distinguishability from other users during the attack. If we cannot know when the attack occurs, could we give at least a lower bound on the anonymity set size during any reasonable candidate attack period? The answer is no. This means that we cannot use set size or indistinguishability within a set as a metric of my security when using the system. Could it be because nobody knows the anonymity set size so that my protection is absolute?

No. Entropy also fails our first criterion for a useful security metric: it should reflect the difficulty an adversary has in overcoming security and should not depend on variables whose values do not significantly impact the adversary's success. We could imagine rare cases where two Tor circuits through the same entry and exit nodes might be hard to distinguish by at least a completely passive adversary, but it is well known and accepted that whether you are the only user of those nodes during the attack or there are a hundred others, linking your source and destination is trivial. So the anonymity set size cannot be determined, and the difficulty of the most salient attacks are not affected by what it might be.

Perhaps we are discussing uncertainty on the wrong set. Perhaps the number of users has only an indirect effect on the security of Tor traffic. We have repeatedly observed that the primary threat we are discussing is the end-to-end timing correlation. The relevant set is thus the number of locations at which traffic might enter and exit the network.

In the scenario in which I go to a hostile website, what will matter is the nodes through which I can enter the system. If I make that choice the same way as everybody else, then I currently have on the order of three hundred choices.[1] So an entropy of a little over eight. But that assumes that the probability of entry node choice is uniform. This is not actually true. It is weighted by node bandwidth and other factors that we will not go into. We could still calculate the entropy of a typical connection entering the network. But even if we ignore that and assume the choice of entry nodes was uniform we must ignore something else as well—how likely a node is to be compromised. Suppose that, instead of choosing uniformly (or possibly weighted to help maintain performance), I always choose my entry nodes to be just one of a handful of nodes. If the nodes in that handful are all run by highly trusted and technically competent friends who would never betray me, my anonymity is clearly better than picking uniformly from the much larger set: the hostile website will never identify me through the

---

[1] For those who know about entry guards, we are describing the choice of entry guards not the subsequent choice of route once guards are chosen. For those who do not know about entry guards, please do not be distracted by this footnote.

cooperation of a hostile entry node.[2] My anonymity protection has far more to do with the security of that first node I choose in my path than with the number of other users or even other possible first nodes. Again, this is a variable that does not affect the difficulty of attacking my anonymity.

Using entropy as a security metric for anonymity conflates the adversary's uncertainty with the effort needed to reduce that uncertainty. This conflation is fine as long as the effort needed to reduce uncertainty is more or less uniform in the degree of uncertainty (as would be the case for, e.g., key length for a well designed block cipher). When it is not, failing to focus on anonymity protection distorts both security analysis and secure system design.[3]

Even within the entropist conception something akin to the distinction between entropistic anonymity and anonymity protection is recognized. In [37], Pfitzmann and Hansen distinguish between anonymity and strength of anonymity: "Robustness of anonymity characterizes how stable the quantity of anonymity is against changes in the particular setting, e.g., a stronger attacker or different probability distributions. We might use quality of anonymity as a term comprising both quantity and robustness of anonymity. To keep this text as simple as possible, we will mainly discuss the quantity of anonymity in the following, using the wording 'strength of anonymity'." But they still make entropy the primary measure of how well anonymity is protected. "All other things being equal, global anonymity is the stronger, the larger the respective anonymity set is and the more evenly distributed the sending or receiving, respectively, of the subjects within that set is." They do note how individuals may have weak anonymity regardless of the average uncertainty across the anonymity set. "Even if global anonymity is strong, one (or a few) individual subjects might be quite likely, so their anonymity is weak. W.r.t. these 'likely suspects', nothing is changed if the anonymity set is made larger and sending and receiving of the other subjects are, e.g., distributed evenly. That way, arbitrarily strong global anonymity can be achieved without doing anything for the 'likely suspects' [7]." This distinction in [7], however, is intended to cope with the influence of statistical outliers on average uncertainty within a set versus uncertainty concerning an individual and thus to suggest using quantiles as a metric for those cases. It does not at all question the basic idea that anonymity is based on a level of uncertainty from within a known set.

To reiterate, the problem with the entropist conception is not that entropy entirely fails to reflect uncertainty (once the situation is properly described). The problem is that focusing on the size of a known set of users and their distinguishability within it skews system design as well as what gets analyzed in a way that obscures rather than enhances our understanding of the anonymity

---

[2] Whether or not these nodes are known to be affiliated with me now becomes relevant, which depends on the probability that the second node in my path is compromised (and ignoring links as possible places of compromise) [34]. We will touch briefly on such issues below.

[3] For a cryptographic analogue see the discussion of locally unpredictable delaying functions in [20] wherein most of the bits of a function might be easy to compute, but a few of them require much more effort.

protection provided by our systems. Wanting to communicate anonymously and so making entropy the focus of your anonymity design is like wanting to be married and so making expected-number-of-spouses the focus of your matrimony design. If that is indeed you primary focus, you are likely to end up with a strategy of, e.g., proposing indiscriminately to as many people as possible.[4]

If probability of node compromise could be assumed to be roughly uniform (and ignoring links), then network size would be a primary determiner of anonymity protection. Similarly, if we could produce bigger, more uniform looking (to the adversary) sets of senders and recipients, that might actually be useful. But that is not a realistic view of how large, widely used anonymity networks work. They are comprised of fairly dynamic and diverse collections of users communicating over nodes that are diversely trusted by diverse parties and that are diversely configured versions of diverse platforms. And these nodes are connected over diversely trusted links (based on ASes, ISPs, geography, etc.). Unlike designing a closed secure system, there is no point in even discussing trying to make the degree of security of all of the different parts of the network roughly comparable. We will touch on more centrally operated systems below. We will also see that the number of nodes in an open system does play a role in the protection a system offers, but only in combination with the resistance those various nodes have against adversaries.

In security analysis, most adversaries are worst-case, possibly subject to some constraints on ability. But they can attack any message anywhere. 'Attack' might just mean observe, but the adversary can be in the worst possible place. If there is a subset of nodes, or messages that he is able to attack, it is assumed that these can be the optimally most effective nodes or messages. We will next consider what an adversary can do and where.

4   What Is an Adversary?

"Keep your friends close, and your enemies closer."

Sun-tzu — Chinese general and military strategist (c. 400 BCE)

Computer security, including anonymity, is fundamentally tied up with the idea of an adversary. Indeed the primary difference between security and other types of computer assurance is the assumption in security that there is a potential for intentional misuse of some sort as opposed to simply accidental errors or defects. An old security maxim puts it this way: a system without an adversary model cannot be insecure, just surprising.

Research into design and analysis of anonymous communication began in the cryptologic community where vetting and deploying cryptosystems and protocols takes a long time and where a practical break in a deployed system can have serious and widespread consequences. A nice example of this is the evolution from initially discovered weaknesses to practical attacks on MD5. Some vulnerabilities are only of theoretical importance, however. Though they may

---

[4] Thanks to Nick Mathewson for this analogy.

motivate further research, they will never themselves be implemented in a significant practical attack even if systems are never modified in response to them. They will never be the lowest hanging fruit. Contrast this with the Dolev-Yao adversary model [17], an attack against which typically implies dangerous real-world attacks against any implementation of a protocol that is vulnerable to it. Anonymous communications research started with the crypto approach of looking at how hard it is to break the design of an isolated component that might be crucial. The community has still not fully recognized the very limited usefulness such an approach would have for designing and analyzing practical widescale systems for anonymous communication.

Mix networks get their security from the mixing done by their component mixes, and may or may not use route unpredictability to enhance security. Onion routing networks primarily get their security from choosing routes that are difficult for the adversary to observe, which for designs deployed to date has meant choosing unpredictable routes through a network. And onion routers typically employ no mixing at all. This gets at the essence of the two even if it is a bit too quick on both sides.[5] Mixes are also usually intended to resist an adversary that can observe all traffic everywhere and, in some threat models, to actively change traffic. Onion routing assumes that an adversary who observes both ends of a communication path will completely break the anonymity of its traffic. Thus, onion routing networks are designed to resist a local adversary, one that can only see a subset of the network and the traffic on it.

Given the fundamental differences in the mechanisms they employ, the adversaries they are intended to resist, and their basic designs (not to mention typical applications) it might seem impossible or at least astonishing that anyone who works in this area would ever confuse the two. Yet for years it has been common for publications by even top researchers in anonymous communication to refer to onion routing networks as mixnets or vice versa. All deployed onion routing networks do use some form of layered encryption on traffic they carry, encryption that is gradually removed as it passes through the network. And this is also true of decryption mixnets (re-encryption mixes work differently). Thus there is a clear similarity between the two in at least this respect. Still, given the differences, it would be surprising if this were enough to confuse an expert. But, if you start from an entropist conception of anonymity the confusion becomes less surprising: if you start from an entropist conception of anonymity, all anonymity designs are trying to make a given set of users (or user communications) less distinguishable. If one motivates design by starting with such a set and seeing how well the system obscures identification of its elements, the security contributions of an onion routing approach are harder to see. Any distinction between onion

---

[5] Other typical and highly salient distinctions include that all existing onion routing network designs are for carrying bidirectional low-latency traffic over cryptographic circuits while public mixnets are designed for carrying unidirectional high-latency traffic in connectionless messages. (An exception is the Web MIXes design [3] as deployed in JonDonym [27], which creates bidirectional circuits through a mix cascade to carry public web traffic.)

routing networks and mixnets, if recognized at all, is then likely to be couched only in terms of differences in intended application or engineering tradeoffs of security (in the entropist model) versus performance. Even we designers of onion routing systems have been occasionally guilty of falling into this idiom.

But does using the entropist conception reveal potential low-hanging fruit for current or future real systems? To answer this we should consider adversaries that can conduct practical attacks. For brevity's sake, I describe only the one that matters most in examining if entropism is the best approach for widely-used systems like Tor [44], Mixmaster [30], and the Anonymizer [2], viz: **The Man**.[6]

The Man owns big chunks of the anonymity infrastructure, either because he simply set them up himself, or because they are not hardened against takeover. He can also get access to ISPs, backbones, and websites, will know ancillary things, and, if targeting you, will have you specifically under physical surveillance. Think organized crime, state level actors (intelligence, secret police), etc. The Man subsumes the other adversaries we might consider.

In the literature, a standard anonymity adversary is the global-passive adversary (GPA), who controls no nodes in the anonymity network but can observe all traffic on all links to and from that network as well as between nodes of the network. This adversary can observe all sending and receiving behavior by all principals interacting with the network. It thus fits nicely in the entropist model of anonymity and facilitates formal analysis therein. While nice for producing both positive and negative provable results, the GPA is too strong to be realistic because it can observe absolutely every link everywhere regardless of network size. Good security counsels a conservative view, assuming an attacker that is stronger than anything one would encounter in practice. The GPA might thus be considered an overstatement of The Man—except that the GPA is also much too weak; it cannot even briefly delay a packet passing over a single link under its observation. As has long been recognized, the GPA is both too strong and too weak for low-latency distributed systems like onion routing [38,42,14].

All low-latency systems as currently designed and deployed are essentially broken against The Man, but often much weaker adversaries are adequate. Single proxies are vulnerable to timing attacks by much weaker adversaries, for example, a single well-placed network observer, and of course communication is vulnerable to the proxy itself if it is corrupt or compromised. Realtime web cascades, such as JonDonym [27] are generally to be comprised of nodes run by recognized but not mutually trusting authorities and thus to distribute trust possibly without the complications of a large, diversely trusted network. A single observer, as would threaten a single proxy, will not be effective. Two such well-placed observers or corrupt insiders, however, would be. If one could enforce uniform sending and receiving behavior of a persistent set of users, a stronger adversary might

---

[6] We ignore herein any attacks other than by compromising or observing network elements, and by altering and observing the timing and/or volumes of traffic sent over network elements and connecting links. For example, any attacks by injecting identifying information into an anonymity circuit or anonymous message are beyond our scope.

be needed. But there is to date no accepted scheme for practically doing this against even a passive adversary. And, if there were, that would not defeat an adversary that selectively blocks or manipulates traffic at sources or destinations. Versions of onion routing that do not use entry guards [34] are statistically broken against a small number of well-placed attackers for longterm repeated connections between the same sources and destinations.

As has already been noted, an adversary observing an entry node and an exit node of the existing Tor network can trivially link the two ends of the connection and correlate source to destination regardless of the number of users of these or any other nodes. Anonymity is broken if the endpoints are owned and not if they are not. There are also potential attacks such as website fingerprinting [22,28] or network latency [23] that require only the entry node to be observed by the adversary. But, in contrast to the entropist view, this again is not significantly affected by the number of other simultaneous circuits initiating at that node and not affected at all by the numbers of circuits elsewhere in the network.

The problem Mixmaster faces against The Man is not the strength of its component protection mechanisms per se but its usability and the implications thereof. (Similarly for Mixminion [9]). With enough compromised nodes it becomes more likely that messages will traverse an entirely compromised path, but many paths might be at most partially compromised. And in mix systems, unlike onion-routing systems, it is not trivial to recognize the same traffic when it is observed in two places. Thus, the number of messages entering and leaving uncompromised mixes does affect uncertainty, and that is indeed the focus of much analysis of mix systems. But there are important factors that largely obviate the protection this might afford.

User configurability and interface play a role [41,13,15] in the amount of use an anonymity system gets, but just as important is the latency inherent in the design: the less the latency the more the system becomes vulnerable to correlation attacks. But, keeping the latency high as in remailer mix networks means that only the users with the most sensitive requirements will use the system [1]. And the most common interactive bidirectional applications such as web browsing, chat, or remote login will not work at all, which is probably an even larger factor limiting adoption. Tor has an estimated quarter million or more concurrent users routing over thousands of network nodes. Though Mixmaster has been around longer, it has had perhaps a few hundred users on any given day, and the network has never been more than a few dozen nodes. Mixmaster's numbers have not grown significantly for years, and the incentive issues we have been discussing imply this to be an inherent limitation. If your goal is to have legal deniability for activity this may be adequate, at least initially before The Man has decided to focus on you. But if your adversary *is* The Man, then avoiding suspicion at all is likely an important goal. As such a few hundred initially possible sources or destinations hidden by a few dozen nodes is just inadequate. Simple externalities such as geographic locations associated with IP addresses, previously known associations, etc. are likely to narrow the initial set even further very quickly [12]. And The Man can own many of the nodes in the network if he so desires so that the already small number of initially unexposed source-destination pairs shrinks commensurately.

The important thing is that the number of possible targets and number of initially needed network observation/compromise points is small enough to be within the capabilities of The Man to bring other resources to bear irrespective of the ability of the anonymization network to render its users indistinguishable. The issue is not simply a question of uncertainty in identifying a large set of senders and/or recipients, it is an issue of available resources and their expected effectiveness. Yes, The Man strives to reduce his uncertainty about linking senders and recipients, but the measure of his ability to succeed is not the size of those sets or probability distributions on them. Rather it is the resources it will take him to place himself in a position to learn those linking relations. And uncertainty about which elements to attack to improve his position may also play a role, but its role is not as important as the expected cost and benefit of attacking each of them, especially if he has the capability to effectively attack all of them—as is the case for the deployed Mixmaster network.

It is true that entropist approaches might help narrow the initial set of a few hundred senders of a given message. For example, if communication pairs are maintained over hundreds of communication rounds, then statistical disclosure [10,29] may be useful. And The Man should be able to further reduce anonymity within network traffic by DoS attacks on uncompromised nodes [16,4]. If that would be too easily detected, The Man can combine DoS with bridging those nodes via trickling and flooding from his own clients [39] and owned nodes or links. Note that while these active attacks can be analyzed in the entropist model for effectiveness, no entropist view is necessary to simply deploy them in order to slightly improve the efficiency of an already effective compromise. They are just not the attack threats that matter most when going against The Man.

In sum, all current low-latency anonymity systems are broken against The Man. Onion-routing systems by nature of their potential for wide distribution are relatively resistant to other kinds of adversaries. Mix networks, such as Mixmaster and Mixminion, do have measures against The Man. But they are overkill against other expected attackers. This, coupled with the overhead of trying to use them, limits the numbers of both users and infrastructure providers to a point that they are vulnerable to direct inspection and attacks by The Man for which the anonymizing network becomes irrelevant. While entropist techniques can play some role here, they are not the central issue.

5   So What Is Anonymous Communication?

What the entropist conception gets right is that, like other security properties, anonymity protection is determined by the amount of work an adversary needs to do to overcome it. What it gets wrong is the kinds of work the adversary needs to do. We have observed so far that an anonymity breaking adversary generally does not do best by focusing directly on reducing an initially known set of senders (receivers, etc.) to the point that the sender is uniquely determined or has low enough entropy to be considered busted. The entropist approach will yield theoretically interesting analyses. It will yield system designs that might be useful in controlled settings like elections, where we can control or predict the number and nonidentity of participants and where anonymity within expected-size sets is useful. But the entropist approach is not appropriate for general communication on large diversely shared networks like the internet. I do not set out here a definitive answer of what to replace it with: this is a breaking paper not a design paper. I do, however, offer some hints and suggestions.

As we have noted, putatively more secure designs, such as DC-nets or mix networks, are actually not secure against the intended adversary unless there is a significant increase in both network size and persistent users. And usability and incentive issues make that unlikely. A network might scale up to a point that, even if The Man were able to compromise much communication passing through the network, any individual communication would not be likely to be de-anonymized. P2P anonymity designs have this potential, although they require further scrutiny because they are complex, and attacks on, e.g., network discovery or versions of sybil attacks seem hard to eradicate. Decentralized designs with semicentralized management of network information, such as Tor's, also have this potential. But in either case one is forced to make some assumptions about the likelihood that a given percentage of nodes is under hostile control, and this can be impossible to gauge. Any design that assumes a roughly uniform distribution of resistance to attack across all nodes is likely doomed if The Man can own botnets within the network (and why shouldn't he?). A useful metric should therefore evaluate rather than assume how hard it is for the adversary to own a portion of the network. This much is true of mix networks as well as onion-routing networks and true of peer-to-peer as well as more centralized versions of either of these.

How can we gauge an adversary's difficulty in owning chunks of the network and the traffic flowing over them? We need not analyze how hard it is to contribute hostile servers, break into nodes, steal administrative passwords, control or observe inputs and outputs to nodes etc. For our metrics we just need a representation of the possible outcomes of that analysis. Our observations suggest that it will be useful if those outcomes are not considered uniform across all nodes. So it is not just a question of implementing the strongest component design and deploying it widely. We will also need to consider how much the adversary learns from the nonuniformity itself. We should also consider initial awareness of the network, whether the adversary knows the same network elements and structure as do the communicants he is attacking. Such considerations are a focus of our current ongoing research.

6   Rotor and Other Immodest Proposals

In this paper we have argued that entropist metrics for anonymity are not appropriate to widely shared and deployed anonymity networks. We have observed that they rely on variables for which it is unrealistic to attach values and that would not significantly affect how well anonymity is protected if they could be determined. For less widely deployed networks, whether centralized or distributed, they provide the most relevant adversary with a set of communicating pairs that he has the resources to deanonymize.

We end with some implications for anonymity research and system design. In the mid nineties (before decent SSL encryption was available in every browser) encrypted traffic was relatively rare on the internet; the mere fact that a message was encrypted made it interesting. Thus, we used to say that if you encrypt your traffic at all, you should make sure you encrypt it well because it is likely to be scrutinized. The same point applies to anonymizing your communication. Unlike choosing good algorithms and increasing keylength for encryption, however, usability and incentive limitations make it unlikely that users and nodes for mix networks will ever increase adequately to exceed the resources of The Man. And even if they did, there is no way to have any meaningful assurance about the distribution of noncollaborating users. More importantly, there is no way to have meaningful assurance about the distribution of noncollaborating network nodes. Our first modest suggestion is thus that existing mix networks for general internet use should simply be abandoned for other than research purposes. They should continue to be studied for there inherent interest. And, they should be used for applications where it is possible to manage and measure the sets of distinct users and anonymity providers and the probability distributions on their behaviors, voting being the clearest example. But for general internet use, they are overkill against almost every adversary except unrealistic ones like the GPA or incredibly strong ones like The Man. And, because of usability and incentive limitations, in practice they do not scale enough to protect against The Man anyway. On the other hand a widely distributed network like Tor may already offer better, though still inadequate, protection. If we modify the design of onion-routing networks like Tor so that trust is incorporated into routing (as we discuss briefly below), then it should be harder for The Man to attack where he must to be effective.

Also, we should not worry (too much) about partitioning attacks. In distributing network directories, Tor has conservatively opted for distributing awareness of the entire directory to clients. This has presented scaling challenges, but the ability to differentiate users by partitioning what they know and don't know is not fully understood. And there have been published epistemic attacks on both mix and onion-routing network designs [8,11]. But unless the adversary is approaching The Man in both capability and intent, this is not a significant concern. And if the adversary is on the order of The Man, then this is not effective. A caveat is that the design should not allow simple actions on the part of a small player, one that can affect at most a small part of the infrastructure, to partition to a point that it can effectively isolate a small number of clients with little effort. Entropy is not useless for characterizing anonymity, it is just not the primary measure of a practical anonymity network's security and as such should not be the primary driver of design.

If the primary measure of anonymity is how hard it is for an adversary to observe or own parts of the network that allow him to conduct attacks, then we can represent the amount of trust we have that a node will not be compromised and then route accordingly. In addition to anonymity system nodes, the same basic trust notion can be applied to links and destinations. We are currently researching such modeling and analysis of trust and have several initial results for optimal route selections assuming simply that network nodes are trusted at different levels [25]. Our results are based on a partial adversary that can attempt to compromise a fixed fraction of network nodes and succeeds for any given node n_i with probability p_{c_i}. This is a variant of the roving adversary introduced by Ostrovsky and Yung [33] and applied to anonymous routing in [42]. What we add is the idea of trust in a node n_i, represented as $1 - p_{c_i}$ and applied as just described.

We expect the adversary model that we ultimately develop fully will add mobility to the above, much as Ostrovsky and Yung's original work did. This will allow for an iterative attack in which an adversary can discover parts of the network, trust relationships, communication patterns, etc. and then apply what is learned at each stage to conduct further attacks. Anonymity then becomes a question of what an adversary can uncover given a budget of resources expended over an attack of a given duration.

Once better understood, one could imagine a trust-based onion routing network: roTor. This would be a variant of Tor built to counter such an adversary that gets its protection through trust; hence the name.[7]

A rotor network may have a place for mixing too. Routing based on trust could mean that the expected chance that a given communication is compromised is quite low. But, for very sensitive communications it still may pay to have some defense in depth so that observing in a few opportune spots will not yield easy timing correlations. The goal is likely to be hiding of particular linkings rather than avoiding suspicion that the communicants talk at all. But that is likely to yield rather different designs from existing mixes and mix networks, for example, embedding messages to be mixed by an intermediate node inside of web traffic on a low-latency circuit.

This last section has been fairly speculative so as to attempt to give at least one vision of what definitions and system designs might replace entropism. Whether or not these ultimately prevail, however, is not the central point of

---

[7] Tor began as *the* onion routing, designed as one of the original NRL onion routing projects, in contrast to the many other onion routing designs that followed the NRL original. It is also a recursive acronym for *Tor's onion routing*. ('Tor' has never been an acronym for *The Onion Router*—as generally misstated in the press, nor has it ever been proper to write it 'TOR'.) Though that is perhaps enough of a hint to make the following implicitly obvious to the reader, we note that 'rotor' is a sesquipalendromic sesquirecursive acronym for *rotor onion T^3or's onion rotor*, which itself expands into *rotor onion [Tor's trusted through] onion rotor*. As also implied by the name, the T-words rotate so that it also expands to *rotor onion [trusted through Tor's] onion rotor* and to *rotor onion [through Tor's trusted] onion rotor*, all three of which should be viewed as in the same equivalence class. Defining the algebraic structure for the equivalence relation is left as an exercise for the reader. Note also that the nodes of a rotor network are the network rotors; thus a rotor network *in sensu composito* is also a rotor network *in sensu diviso*.

this paper. The central point is that the model on which all existing work on anonymity, the entropist model, is broken for open or widely shared communications. That result remains, even if we do not know definitively what to put in its place.

None of the usability, incentive, or usage observations made herein are particularly novel. However, engendered by its fundamental entropism, the community still operates on a premise that mix networks are more secure. Those of us who have made such observations have even sometimes moderated our assumptions so that mix networks are described as more secure in principle if not in current deployment. But taking the next steps implied by these observations has not even been overtly broached. All of us have still clung to an entropist view of anonymity and thus to the systems and analysis it engenders. Hopefully, this paper will give us the push we need to let go.

Wait, what about interference attacks that allow remote observation without compromising or directly observing nodes and links [32,31,18]? Sorry. We've got an answer, but there's no room in the margins. See the next paper.

Acknowledgments. I thank Claudia Diaz, George Danezis, Roger Dingledine, Aaron Johnson, and Nick Mathewson for helpful discussions that led to better articulations of the ideas in this paper. (Nonetheless any remaining incoherence is my own.) This work supported by ONR.

References

1. Acquisti, A., Dingledine, R., Syverson, P.: On the Economics of Anonymity. In: Wright, R.N. (ed.) FC 2003. LNCS, vol. 2742, pp. 84–102. Springer, Heidelberg (2003)
2. The Anonymizer (2009), http://www.anonymizer.com/; Homepage of the company that offers the Anonymizer Proxy Service. Original Anonymizer first described in [5]
3. Berthold, O., Federrath, H., Köpsell, S.: Web MIXes: A System for Anonymous and Unobservable Internet Access. In: Federrath, H. (ed.) Anonymity 2000. LNCS, vol. 2009, pp. 115–129. Springer, Heidelberg (2001)
4. Borisov, N., Danezis, G., Mittal, P., Tabriz, P.: Denial of service or denial of security? How attacks on reliability can compromise anonymity. In: De Capitani di Vimercati, S., Syverson, P., Evans, D. (eds.) CCS 2007: Proceedings of the 14th ACM Conference on Computer and Communications Security, pp. 92–102. ACM Press (2007)
5. Chaum, D.: Untraceable electronic mail, return addresses, and digital pseudonyms. Communications of the ACM 4(2), 84–88 (1981)
6. Chaum, D.: Untraceable electronic mail, return addresses, and digital pseudonyms. Communications of the ACM 4(2), 84–88 (1981)
7. Clauß, S., Schiffner, S.: Structuring anonymity networks. In: Goto, A. (ed.) DIM 2006: Proceedings of the 2006 ACM Workshop on Digital Identity Management, Alexandria, VA, USA, pp. 55–62. ACM Press (2006)
8. Danezis, G., Clayton, R.: Route fingerprinting in anonymous communications. In: Sixth IEEE International Conference on Peer-to-Peer Computing, P2P 2006, pp. 69–72. IEEE Computer Society Press (2006)

9. Danezis, G., Dingledine, R., Mathewson, N.: Mixminion: Design of a type III anonymous remailer protocol. In: Proceedings of the 2003 IEEE Symposium on Security and Privacy, Berkeley, CA, pp. 2–15. IEEE Computer Society (May 2003)

10. Danezis, G., Serjantov, A.: Statistical Disclosure or Intersection Attacks on Anonymity Systems. In: Fridrich, J. (ed.) IH 2004. LNCS, vol. 3200, pp. 293–308. Springer, Heidelberg (2004)

11. Danezis, G., Syverson, P.: Bridging and Fingerprinting: Epistemic Attacks on Route Selection. In: Borisov, N., Goldberg, I. (eds.) PETS 2008. LNCS, vol. 5134, pp. 151–166. Springer, Heidelberg (2008)

12. Danezis, G., Wittneben, B.: The economics of mass surveillance and the questionable value of anonymous communications. In: Anderson, R. (ed.) Fifth Workshop on the Economics of Information Security, WEIS 2006 (June 2006)

13. Dingledine, R., Mathewson, N.: Anonymity loves company: Usability and the network effect. In: Anderson, R. (ed.) Fifth Workshop on the Economics of Information Security, WEIS 2006 (June 2006)

14. Dingledine, R., Mathewson, N., Syverson, P.: Tor: The second-generation onion router. In: Proceedings of the 13th USENIX Security Symposium, pp. 303–319. USENIX Association (August 2004)

15. Dingledine, R., Mathewson, N., Syverson, P.: Deploying low-latency anonymity: Design challenges and social factors. IEEE Security & Privacy 5(5), 83–87 (2007)

16. Dingledine, R., Syverson, P.: Synchronous Batching: From Cascades to Free Routes. In: Martin, D., Serjantov, A. (eds.) PET 2004. LNCS, vol. 3424, pp. 186–206. Springer, Heidelberg (2005)

17. Dolev, D., Yao, A.C.: On the security of public-key protocols. IEEE Transactions on Information Theory 2(29), 198–208 (1983)

18. Evans, N.S., Dingledine, R., Grothoff, C.: A practical congestion attack on Tor using long paths. In: Proceedings of the 18th USENIX Security Symposium, Montreal, Canada, pp. 33–50. USENIX Association (August 2009)

19. Goldschlag, D.M., Reed, M.G., Syverson, P.F.: Hiding Routing Information. In: Anderson, R. (ed.) IH 1996. LNCS, vol. 1174, pp. 137–150. Springer, Heidelberg (1996)

20. Goldschlag, D.M., Stubblebine, S.G., Syverson, P.F.: Temporarily hidden bit commitment and lottery applications. International Journal of Information Security 9(1), 33–50 (2010)

21. Helmers, S.: A brief history of anon.penet.fi - the legendary anonymous remailer. CMC Magazine (September 1997)

22. Hintz, A.: Fingerprinting Websites Using Traffic Analysis. In: Dingledine, R., Syverson, P. (eds.) PET 2002. LNCS, vol. 2482, pp. 171–178. Springer, Heidelberg (2003)

23. Hopper, N., Vasserman, E.Y., Chan-Tin, E.: How much anonymity does network latency leak? In: De Capitani di Vimercati, S., Syverson, P., Evans, D. (eds.) CCS 2007: Proceedings of the 14th ACM Conference on Computer and Communications Security, pp. 82–91. ACM Press (2007); Expanded and revised version in [24]

24. Johnson, A., Syverson, P., Dingledine, R., Mathewson, N.: Trustbased anonymous communication: Adversary models and routing algorithms. In: CCS 2011: Proceedings of the 18th ACM Conference on Computer and Communications Security, ACM Press (October 2011)

25. Johnson, A., Syverson, P.: More anonymous onion routing through trust. In: 22nd IEEE Computer Security Foundations Symposium, CSF 2009, Port Jefferson, New York, USA, pp. 3–12. IEEE Computer Society (July 2009)

26. Johnson, A., Syverson, P., Dingledine, R., Mathewson, N.: Trust-based anonymous communication: Adversary models and routing algorithms. In: CCS 2011: Proceedings of the 18th ACM Conference on Computer and Communications Security. ACM Press (October 2011)
27. JonDonym – the internet anonymisation service (2008), https://www.jondos.de/en/; Commercial version of the qJava Anon Proxy (JAP). Initially published description in [3]
28. Liberatore, M., Levine, B.N.: Inferring the source of encrypted HTTP connections. In: Wright, R.N., De Capitani di Vimercati, S., Shmatikov, V. (eds.) CCS 2006: Proceedings of the 13th ACM Conference on Computer and Communications Security, pp. 255–263. ACM Press (2006)
29. Mathewson, N., Dingledine, R.: Practical Traffic Analysis: Extending and Resisting Statistical Disclosure. In: Martin, D., Serjantov, A. (eds.) PET 2004. LNCS, vol. 3424, pp. 17–34. Springer, Heidelberg (2005)
30. Möller, U., Cottrell, L., Palfrader, P., Sassaman, L.: Mixmaster protocol - version 3. IETF Internet Draft (2003)
31. Murdoch, S.J.: Hot or not: Revealing hidden services by their clock skew. In: Wright, R.N., De Capitani di Vimercati, S., Shmatikov, V. (eds.) CCS 2006: Proceedings of the 13th ACM Conference on Computer and Communications Security, pp. 27–36. ACM Press (2006)
32. Murdoch, S.J., Danezis, G.: Low-cost traffic analysis of Tor. In: Proceedings of the 2005 IEEE Symposium on Security and Privacy, IEEE S&P 2005, pp. 183–195. IEEE CS (May 2005)
33. Ostrovsky, R., Yung, M.: How to withstand mobile virus attacks. In: Proceedings of the Tenth ACM Symposium on Principles of Distributed Computing, PODC 1991, pp. 51–59. ACM Press (1991)
34. Øverlier, L., Syverson, P.: Locating hidden servers. In: Proceedings of the 2006 IEEE Symposium on Security and Privacy, S&P 2006, pp. 100–114. IEEE CS (May 2006)
35. Parekh, S.: Prospects for remailers: where is anonymity heading on the internet? First Monday 1(2) (August 5, 1996), http://www.firstmonday.dk/issues/issue2/remailers/
36. Serjantov, A., Dingledine, R., Syverson, P.: From a Trickle to a Flood: Active Attacks on Several Mix Types. In: Petitcolas, F.A.P. (ed.) IH 2002. LNCS, vol. 2578, pp. 36–52. Springer, Heidelberg (2003)
37. Pfitzmann, A., Köhntopp, M.: A terminology for talking about privacy by data minimization: Anonymity, unlinkability, undetectability, unobservability, pseudonymity, and identity management, version v0.32 (December 2009), http://dud.inf.tu-dresden.de/Anon_Terminology.shtml, Regularly revised and updated version of [36]
38. Reed, M.G., Syverson, P.F., Goldschlag, D.M.: Anonymous connections and onion routing. IEEE Journal on Selected Areas in Communications 16(4), 482–494 (1998)
39. Serjantov, A., Dingledine, R., Syverson, P.: From a Trickle to a Flood: Active Attacks on Several Mix Types. In: Petitcolas, F.A.P. (ed.) IH 2002. LNCS, vol. 2578, pp. 36–52. Springer, Heidelberg (2003)
40. Simmons, G.J.: The history of subliminal channels. IEEE Journal on Selected Areas in Communications 16(4), 452–462 (1998)
41. Syverson, P., Reed, M., Goldschlag, D.: Onion Routing access configurations. In: Proceedings DARPA Information Survivability Conference & Exposition, DISCEX 2000, vol. 1, pp. 34–40. IEEE CS Press (1999)

42. Syverson, P., Tsudik, G., Reed, M., Landwehr, C.: Towards an Analysis of Onion Routing Security. In: Federrath, H. (ed.) Anonymity 2000. LNCS, vol. 2009, pp. 96–114. Springer, Heidelberg (2001)
43. Tang, C., Goldberg, I.: An improved algorithm for Tor circuit scheduling. Technical Report CACR 2010-06, University of Waterloo, Center for Applied Cryptography Research (2010),
http://www.cacr.math.uwaterloo.ca/techreports/2010/cacr2010-06.pdf
44. The Tor Project (2009), https://www.torproject.org/; Homepage of the non-profit organization that maintains and develops the Tor network. Original Tor design first published in [14]

Why I'm Not an Entropist
(Transcript of Discussion)

Paul Syverson

Naval Research Laboratory

The previous talk[1] was about trying to get entropy, and I'm going to talk about ignoring entropy. It's natural to talk about anonymity in a workshop about brief encounters and security protocols, I would say anonymity is the quintessence of brief encounter, you only have a brief encounter if in fact you are anonymous, so you need to be anonymous to guarantee that it is brief, otherwise it is at best pseudonymous, because you're preserving state from one instance of communication to another.

Now this is the standard definition of anonymity that's been around for a long time, anonymity is when you've got a bunch of Alices in some set and the attacker can't figure out, can't distinguish, which of them is talking to Bob. Now can't distinguish might mean that you have a set of some size and that's the measure of indistinguishability, or you might have some kind of probability distribution. This is what I call the entropist conception. I don't want to get too hung up on the term entropy, I thought it was reasonable because it ties up with a lot of different notions. There's lots of different notions of entropy: basic anonymity set sizes, Hartley entropy, everybody uses Shannon entropy, some people feel that min entropy is more appropriate for some things.

I don't really care too much about the specific mathematical characterisations, and I think there are lots of places where entropy is quite useful. What I want to question, is the notion of entropy where you just have some set — and typically we pick on the senders as the quintessential example, but it could be any number of things, Pfitzmann and Hanson[2] called it items of interest — and that you have some kind of uncertainty in that set, on the part of the adversary. The reason this is important is because this is the notion of anonymity that underlies virtually all system design, all theory, all research. Everything in anonymity basically has this as its starting point, and the reason I want to talk about it is because I think we've just been doing it wrong for thirty years.

Now, I should qualify what I mean by that. I think there are plenty of places where this is a very useful and right notion. We were talking about voting earlier this morning, I think that's a perfectly reasonable place to look at entropy as a measure of anonymity. But my focus is in looking at large-scale internet type communications: web browsing, or sending email to people who may not know anything about your anonymity system but you still have to communicate with

---

[1] Bonneau, these proceedings.

[2] "Anonymity, Unobservability, and Pseudonymity – A Proposal for Terminology" by Andreas Pfitzmann and Marit Köhntopp in LNCS 2009: Designing Privacy Enhancing Technologies.

B. Christianson et al. (Eds.): Security Protocols 2009, LNCS 7028, pp. 231–239, 2013.

them, these are standard uses for which the paranoid cyberpunk sort of people think, oh, I've got to have this kind of thing, and I think that's wrong, this is not how to do it.

For one, it may not be meaningful to even stipulate some unique set, there may not be a set on which you can attach any measure in any reasonable way. I would say that what you want to ask is, how hard is it for some attacker to break the anonymity of the system, and that's going to be your anonymity metric. I'll come back later to talking about the steps, where the details are, how do you decide what hard means. But the important thing is that I will argue (this is mostly a breaking not a constructing paper), is that the entropy approach, the entropist's approach, does not provide a good measure of anonymity for these sorts of systems. So just in case I was being too gentle, my goal is to fundamentally remake our understanding of anonymity for widely used Internet communication systems.

These are not all the anonymity systems out there for communication, there's tons of them, but these are some that have had the most wide use in the last many years. They're either centralised or distributed, I'm going to ignore the centralised ones, they have single points of failure and other issues, and I'm going to focus on the distributed ones. You basically have two broad types, most of these are some flavour of onion routing, and then the other alternative, for high-latency systems, is essentially some kind of mix network. Onion routers are not mixes at all, people always think they're based on it, it's a popular misconception, but I can tell you since I came up with it, that onion routing was not at all based on mixes. Anyway, the reason that we make this distinction between low and high-latency is, the low-latency systems are totally vulnerable to correlation attacks: because it has to be low-latency you can just look at the pattern of packets and messages as they go through the system, and you can just watch the pattern and you can break it. If you've got more latency, as you do in a mix system, then you can start mucking around with the order and the timing, and you can make it much harder to do this. This has been confirmed over and over again in experimentation, and in analysis that basically there's nothing that beats this against any kind of reasonable attacker, usually anything that's proposed is hugely expensive, and it doesn't work anyway, so this is just something you have to live with.

So the prevailing wisdom is that the high-latency systems are more secure, because you don't have this correlation attack, and it also complicates some other kind of attacks as well. The trade-off is they can't be used for interactive things, low-latency things, you can't do web browsing over them, you can't do remote login, you can't do a lot of things that people like to do. So my question is, if this is supposed to be the more secure system, what is it more secure against?

In order to think about that you have to say, well what is your adversary, so the question then is, what is a reasonable adversary when you're talking about a practical anonymous internet communication system. There's lots of different possible things you might be worried about, but I think they're pretty much subsumed by one adversary that you can focus on, and that's The Man.

The Man owns huge chunks of the anonymity infrastructure because he's either compromised them, or he's providing it, you know Tor is volunteer networking, he can just volunteer; so is Mixmaster. He certainly is going to have access to ISPs, backbones, what have you servers. About individuals he's going to know answers, maybe not to all the questions we were just hearing about, but to the things that you can find on Facebook, he's going to know that, and maybe some other stuff as well, and if he cares about you he is going to tap your phone, he's going to follow you around.

So you should be thinking of The Man as on the level of, state level actors, intelligence organisations, secret police; it could be organised crime, maybe a large corporation if they're going up against their adversary or something. This is the adversary that your basic cyberpunk is convinced is after them. So the question is, how well do you actually do against The Man.

Now it's important to keep in mind he's really big, he's really powerful, but he's not global, and he's not omnipotent.

Matt Blaze: But that's just what you want us to think, because you're part of The Man.

Reply: I'm not at liberty to discuss that on the record, but if you want to take that offline I know a pub where we can, yes.

Ben Laurie: The Man has just asked me to point out that Google is global and omnipotent.

Reply: I would contend not, but thank you for pointing out that I was right to bring corporations into that. If you're not worried about The Man then certainly doing mixing is just overkill, right, because if you're not worried about somebody who's watching all these things everywhere then you don't need this level of protection. But the flipside is that if you are worried about The Man, if you're worried about him suspecting you and keeping an eye on you because he thinks you're doing bad things, mix networks aren't going to help you either.

That's because they don't scale, and I'll come back to that point, but I would like to dismiss one property that I think mix networks do provide reasonably well, and that's plausible deniability[3]. Even the mix nets that are in wide use on the internet today, have maybe a couple of hundred users at most on any given day using them, that's probably generous, and there's maybe a dozen or two dozen nodes in the network at peak, but I would contend that the deniability you get in this setting is basically irrelevant. This is because you're playing a shell game, and The Man just isn't going to care because, 50 or 100 people is basically nothing, he doesn't care where the pea is, he's just going to watch all of you. Maybe he doesn't know that you sent this particular message, but if your goal is to hide the fact that you associate with somebody, once he's got a set of maybe 50 or 100 people, right, that's enough, that's just a tiny set, you just watch all 50 or 100 and game over.

---

[3] See "Cryptography and evidence", Michael Roe, University of Cambridge PhD dissertation, available as http://www.cl.cam.ac.uk/techreports/UCAM-CL-TR-780.pdf.

Now you might get out of this if you could just build a big mix network, because as I said, he's not global and he's not omnipotent, and they could scale in principle, but they can't, they haven't, and they won't. This has to do with usability and incentives, because most people are quite correctly not at all worried about The Man. There's very few people who would be right to worry about The Man, and most of the people who do worry about The Man are not those people. People are worried about identity thieves, or abusive ex spouses or whatnot, and for these purposes a distributed low-latency system is going to be more than adequate. Mixmaster, you've got maybe 200 users a day protected by a few dozen mixes, so your entropy is maybe 7, maybe 8 bits, and that's your original entropy, assuming that The Man isn't applying any exogenous information, which he probably is. If you're something like Al Qaeda, he's probably got a pretty good idea who's in Al Qaeda and who isn't, even though he doesn't have it exactly. But if you're going to be hiding, of course he can own several of the mixes, plus he's going to be able to see all the communication certainly on all the links, but even within some of these mixes they're not going to be doing anything. So the bottom line is, with like 200 people maybe initially, you can expect that he's not going to really have to watch those 200 people, he's going to have to watch maybe 20.

Now for Tor circuits it gets a little more complicated. I'm assuming I don't have to explain what a mix is, or what Tor is.

Bruce Christianson: You're amongst friends here Paul.

Reply: It's a mix, you get a bunch of stuff, you throw it in, you shake it up, and then when it comes out you can't tell which thing that came out, was what thing came in there, that's a mix. So for Tor, I would say that this point is even more clear, that it's hard to say what the set is because who's using it from one day to the next is going to vary, so the set you saw yesterday may have nothing to do with the set you saw today, whereas if you watch the mix network for a day you're going to know everybody who sent into it and out of it, for a day you'll know everybody who sent that day. George is saying, no, how could you not know?

George Danezis: Because a lot of messages will have actually originated from the previous day, and will be in queues, and a lot of messages that came in on that day will go out the next. It is actually a distribution along a huge set.

Reply: But the expected time that a message sits in a mix now is not all that long, and again, it's this trade-off, I mean, the longer it sits the smaller the user set.

George Danezis: But anonymity sets are defined on basically infinite populations because there is a possibility your message comes up in a million days. This is at the core of your argument, I think.

Reply: This is back to the plausible deniability thing, you watch it for a month, the probability that a message that was sent in was from before that month is very small, you're still only looking at 200 people.

Bruce Christianson: Paul's argument is that the odds favour The Man.

Joseph Bonneau: Well if the question is what holds up in court, I think that evidence ...

Reply: No actually, I'm ignoring that, that was my point about the shell game. This is more like your favourite Schwarznegger movie, you know, where you have the über bad guy who has some vague Eastern European accent, right, and you have the two like naïve stick figures from xkcd standing there passing something behind their back, and they're like, ha ha, you don't know which of us has the object you want, and he just shoots them both. The Man doesn't care. Now there are people that some people would call The Man, and he does care, he's going to follow due process and stuff, but I'm just contending that the size of the number of people amongst whom you're hiding is so small that The Man is just going to watch all of you. If you want to hide the fact that I sent the message with this content, yes, it will work, and that's OK, but most of the people are not using it for that purpose, they don't want The Man to know that I might be the guy who's sending to this other guy, and there's just so few people that you're looking at, it doesn't work.

Now, with Tor, I think you're actually in some sense better off against The Man in that, because it's so big and distributed, you have some statistical chance of not getting watched. But I did a paper with Lasse Overlier back in 2006[4] in which we found that if you could find only a single Tor node, you could find a hidden server in the Tor network in minutes. This was a surprise. We knew in principle you could do it, we didn't know you could do it that quick and easy, that network is a little smaller, etc, etc, but this was one of the things that made us change the way we decided to handle connecting up to the network. Instead of saying, well I'll just connect up a completely random route, the point was, statistically you get owned fast. Many people don't realise, because onion routers are not mixers and because of the end-to-end correlation attack, if you owned both ends of the communication, then you know who's talking to whom, it doesn't matter what happened in the middle. Basically we don't try to solve that problem, we just live with it, but if statistically, if you're going to open up a bunch of connections you're going to be found pretty fast, so just accept that and pick one or a small number of starting points, hope you picked right the first time, and that they're not compromised, if they're compromised all of your traffic is compromised, but you were pretty badly off anyway, this way if none of them are compromised then you will never be owned, so that's nice. But of course never isn't never, because sooner or later things go down and stuff, and you have to rotate, then get new Guard Nodes and so on, and because of that, eventually you get caught by The Man, so Tor's not going to help you either.

So what can you do? The main point of my talk was that you're screwed, but I'm not going to end on that pessimistic note, I'll have another one later. What I think the entropist gets right is that anonymity, just like any other security

---

[4] "Locating Hidden Servers", in: Proceedings of the 2006 IEEE Symposium on Security and Privacy.

property, is about how hard is it for the adversary to break what you have, and what the entropist conception gets wrong is that the measure of the work is not how hard it is to narrow down a set. Even though if you are breaking anonymity you can find a set and you can show that, when you're done breaking it, there's a smaller set than you started with. One issue is that it's not necessarily a subset, that's one way in which entropism breaks, but more importantly, I just don't think that's how what's going on is happening, that's just like an epiphenomenon that you notice afterwards.

So here's some suggestions, and I don't claim that I've got it right now. One thing you could do for the metric is just consider how hard is it to gain access to all the things that The Man needs to own. I'm not really sure how you want to measure this, one thing you might just say is, give The Man a budget in dollars, and for example, to own a node, ask what's the cheapest way? It might be to bribe a janitor, it might be to get a server in the same facility and then if you can somehow have access to that, maybe you actually have to do some crypto breaking things, so how many FPGAs do you have to get, and how much does it cost to program it. And then your metric for anonymity is just going to be the expected value of dollars and time to do the break.

George Danezis: I'm worried that you're going to finish on a happy note.

Reply: Oh no, I've got a couple of more slides.

George Danezis: In order to get a figure in dollars with the expected cost of actually getting someone, OK, that effectively assumes that you have a probability model that takes the adversary model, the adversary capabilities and can actually cost them as well, and also the system, the observation and all that stuff that are the result of the adversary's capabilities, and then effectively do an analysis that tells you, what is the probability of getting the right people, and then find out how much they need to invest until they nab someone.

Now my argument is that this is actually a more general process than the process of taking effectively a probabilistic model assuming a particular adversary model, and then concluding probability distribution then entropy. So effectively what you're saying is we need to do more in order to have a more complete picture of how good the anonymity we get is in practice, and for realistic adversaries. But my argument is that in order to do the costing, the risk management, the risk analysis, and all the costing you'd have to do, you will do exactly the same process mathematically as calculating the entropies. You will have to have a probabilistic model of the observations.

Reply: You know what asset you think you're protecting, so you can say, I know what I'm hiding behind, and this is the usual difference between vulnerability and threat, I know what I've got and how it's protected, and then I can then consider, it's a separate thing whether or not the adversary knows, for example, that this piece is behind that piece. Now, you know, he might just jump past some of the pieces, but I can still effectively think about it iteratively, and I can say, look, once the adversary breaks this, then he's going to learn more, he's going to figure out, oh now I can try to do these other things, but at no point does he have some sort of single set that he's trying to somehow narrow down, he's just gaining more information. I'm not claiming that I actually, know what we should have, this is the part where I think I'm weakest, but I'm just saying that what we did have is pie in the sky.

Ross Anderson: There's a very interesting distinction here between capital cost and marginal cost for The Man. The Man here in Britain at present pays an ISP £500 to get some traffic data off somebody, and presumably a similar fee to put a black box on a LAN, and if you're a small ISP you have got the black box already. There is a measure to centralise all traffic data in a big database in Cheltenham, and having spent £15 billion on that, The Man's marginal costs for future enquiries is zero. Now given the way that economics works with big capital costs and low marginal costs, there are things we can say about this, they're subtle and they're non-linear.

Reply: Yes, but I would say that The Man has not compromised your anonymity unless you're going to and from locations in Britain entirely in your communication, and he's willing to analyse all that data to look for the correlations of the timing and such.

Ross Anderson: But if The Man has got a black box in every ISP in Britain, and assume that The Man can download applets into the black boxes, then there are various distributed correlation algorithms that it might be quite fun for an engineer to design.

Reply: Right, but already right upfront he's only going to win on the things he can see, so if you don't happen to be seen, then he wins on one end of the communication but he doesn't necessarily win on the other in that case, it's a jurisdictional arbitrage point.

George Danezis: Paul, I think you're overly worried about the fact that the adversary does not see part of the stuff that is going on in a big population of users, let's say like in Tor. But as Donald Rumsfeld said, there are known knowns, known unknowns, and unknown unknowns, and to some extent this is a known unknown, in that I know as an adversary that I can intercept 10% of the communications, and therefore I know that roughly 90% of the users I cannot see. That does not mean that I cannot have a good probabilistic model of what is my probability out of the people I see, is it someone communicating with someone else, or is it just that I don't see it at all. And actually you need to have an estimate of this figure in order to even cost how expensive this is.

Reply: But you're assuming something that I reject, which is that the goal of The Man is to see as much as he can.

George Danezis: The goal of The Man is to detect someone.

Reply: To detect something particular, he's not trying to just hoover things up.

Sandy Clark: Paul, I disagree because of the incident in San Francisco where they slipped the fibre into a box-type trunk, they were just collecting masses of data to see what they could find for a one time expense.

Reply: Yes, right, OK. That's perfectly compatible with what I'm saying, that would go into your evaluation of what it costs. The point is, any communication going through that part is going to be whatever it costs them to set that up, that's it. But I think that largely you are screwed against The Man, the only way forward, to the extent that there's something to go forward on, is going to be once you bring trust into ...

George Danezis: How do you measure how screwed you are against The Man here? I think that's what we're nitpicking about, what is your measure of how bad things are?

Reply: Well tell me who The Man is first of all, because I don't think there is just one, The Man, there's going to be different ones. If you're British Intelligence I think you're probably not as worried about The Man that Ross just told us about, as you are about certain Other Men, right. I think that what you need to do, a priority that you might have, is if you can bring some sort of notion of trust into this. I have a forthcoming paperwhere we look at, suppose you do actually have paths.

This is a preliminary result, just looking at the nodes in the network itself. Right now there's no reason not to think that some large intelligence organisations own 10%, 20% of the nodes in the Tor network. I don't know that they do, but I don't know that they don't, so if you're using the Tor network and if your adversary is for the moment limited to the nodes themselves, that's still a big problem. But if you have some sort of trust metric you can put on the nodes, you don't want to reduce yourself to the initial problem we were trying to solve when we set up onion routing, which was, we can't make this a Navy only system, because anything that pops out of it will be known to come from the Navy, you still have to share the thing, but you still want to have a trusted subset, so how do you do smart routing so you're not revealing that but you're still picking things that are more trusted in an effective way. And we have some optimal route selection results that are forthcoming on that, that's the theory side.

I assume a lot of you know that Tor stands for Tor's onion routing, that's where the name comes from. A lot of people write the onion router, that's completely wrong, that's something somebody in the press messed up, but oh well. Anyway, as I tried to argue, I think for The Man it's already more secure than Mixmaster because at any given point The Man is going to see all the communication going into and out of Mixmaster, going back for some time, and he won't for Tor, so there's at least some sense in which you're better off. But you're still not safe against The Man, and I think you need some sort of notion of trust built in. I think that once you add trust to something like Tor, you have something that I call RoTor, this stands for Rotor onion Tor is trusted to onion router, which I think is the world's first sesqui-palindromic sesqui-recursive acronym, because of course Tor is also an acronym, and it's palandromic both in the acronym and in the wording, but of course, if this is an equivalence class that you can rotate, it's a rotor right, so you rotate through, so it's all the same.

Matt Blaze: It is currently recursive?

Reply: Yes. If you add trust in then I think you have at least a chance to beat The Man. So in conclusion, the entropist approach doesn't tell you anything really useful and interesting about how good you are against the adversary that prompted the designs in the first place. I think we need to fundamentally rethink the theory underlying this. And in particular the mix networks, which were really designed against The Man; you should stop fooling yourself.

Deriving Ephemeral Authentication
Using Channel Axioms

Dusko Pavlovic[1,*] and Catherine Meadows[2]

[1] University of Oxford, Department of Computer Science, and
Universiteit Twente, EWI/DIES
dusko@cs.ox.ac.uk
[2] Naval Research Laboratory, Code 5543, Washington, DC 20375
catherine.meadows@nrl.navy.mil

Abstract. As computing and computer networks become more and more inter-twined with our daily lives, the need to develop flexible and on-the-fly methods for authenticating people and their devices to each other has become increasingly pressing. Traditional methods for providing authentication have relied on very weak assumptions about communication channels, and very strong assumptions about secrecy and the availability of trusted authorities. The resulting protocols rely on infrastructures such as shared secrets and public key hierarchies that are too rigid to support the type of flexible ad-hoc communication we are growing accustomed to and beginning to rely upon.

Recently, different families of protocols allow us to weaken assumptions about trusted infrastructure by strengthening the assumptions about communication channels. Examples include proximity verification protocols, that rely, for example, on the round trip time of a challenge and response; and bootstrapping protocols that rely upon human-verifiable channels, that is, low-bandwidth communication between humans. The problem now becomes: *How do we ensure that the protocols are achieve their security goals?* A vast amount of literature exists on the formal analysis of cryptographic protocols, and mathematical foundations of protocol correctness, but almost all of it relies upon the standard assumptions about the channels in end-to-end, and so its usefulness for nonstandard channels in pervasive networks is limited. In this paper, we present some initial results of an effort towards a formalizing the reasoning about the security of protocols over nonstandard channels.

1 Introduction

Pervasive computing has become a reality. We have long been used to the idea that computers are everywhere, and that we interact with multiple devices that can interact with each other and with the Internet. But there is another important aspect of pervasive computing. Not only has the concept of a computer and a computer network changed, but the notion of a communication channel is changing as well. Wireless channels, of course, have been a common part of computer networks for some time. Quantum channels are appearing on the horizon. But what is really interesting is the way the nature

---

* Supported by ONR. Current address: University of London, Royal Holloway, Department of Mathematics/ISG.

B. Christianson et al. (Eds.): Security Protocols 2009, LNCS 7028, pp. 240–261, 2013.

of the information sent along these channels is changing. Information is no longer restricted to input typed in by users, but includes environmental information gathered by the network itself, including location, biometric information, and weather and motion data picked up by sensors.

These new concepts of channels have also resulted in new methods for authentication. The old mantra of "who you are, what you know, and what you have," has been extended to include concepts such as "where you are" (verification of location and/or proximity), "what you are" (use of techniques such as CAPTCHAs to verify that the entity on the other end is a human being [2]) and "what you see" (use of human-verifiable channels to boot strap secure communication, as in [20,29]).

An important thing to note is that these new methods of authentication do not exist on their own. They are typically integrated with more traditional authentication and key exchange protocols that use more conventional channels. This is partly because the new channels may have particular properties that make them less practical to use than conventional channels except when absolutely necessary. Human-verifiable channels are limited in bandwidth. Channels used to implement proximity verification and CAPTCHAs rely on strict timing properties. And even when the new channels do not have these limitations, it will be necessary to integrate them with standard channels so they can be used to interface with traditional systems.

When integrating specialized channels with traditional channels for authentication, one is usually faced with a number of choices. One needs to choose when to use the specialized channel, what information to send on the specialized channel, and what information to send on the conventional channel. Different choices can have different effects on the security, applicability, and efficiency of an authentication protocol.

In this paper we introduce a system for reasoning about authentication using multiple types of channels with different types of properties. The system consists consists of two parts. The first is a graphical language for displaying cryptographic protocols that use different types of channels. This is based closely on the usual graphical methods for representing secure protocols. The second is a logic for reasoning about the security of authentication protocols that use different types of channels. This logic is an extension of the Protocol Derivation logic described in [6,22]. Both language and logic are intended to be used to reason about, not only individual protocols, but families of protocols, in order to help us identify and reason about tradeoffs.

Outline of the Paper. In Section 2 we discuss the problem of modeling pervasive security protocols. In Section 3 we describe the introduction of channel axioms into the Protocol Derivation Logic. In Section 4 we introduce the problem of distance and proximity bounding, provide axioms for channels, and discuss how it they can be reasoned about in PDL. In Section 5 we provide a similar discussion of human-verifiable authentication via social channels. In Section 6 we conclude the paper and discuss plans for future work.

2   Modeling Pervasive Security Protocols

A protocol is a distributed computational process, given with a set of desired runs, or the properties that the desired runs should satisfy. To prove security of a protocol we usually demonstrate that only the desired runs are possible, or that the undesired runs can be detected through participants' local observations.

Security protocols are thus naturally modeled formally within a process calculus, as in [22]. In order to model security protocols in pervasive networks, we extend the process model from [22], used for analyzing security protocols in cyber networks. The main complication is that in this previous work, as in most work in the analysis of security protocols, the network itself was kept implicit in the process model, because every two nodes can be assumed to be linked, without loss of generality. The network infrastructure provides for that. More precisely, the network infrastructure provides the service of routing and relaying the messages, and hides the actual routes and relays (unless they change the messages, in which case they are considered to be attackers). From user's point of view, it looks like the messages are delivered directly from the sender to the receiver, and the network infrastructure is abstracted away.

In a pervasive network, the assumption that there is a link between every two nodes is not justified: some devices have a range, some have access to one type of channels, some to other type of channels, and they may not have any direct, or even indirect links to connect them. To express this, we must make the network explicit.

Moreover, the toolkit of security primitives and security tokens, available to establish secure communication, is essentially richer in pervasive networks.

2.1   Principals and Security Tokens

Principals are the computational agents that control one or more network nodes, where they can send and receive messages. A principal can only observe (and use in his reasoning) the events that happen at his own network nodes.[1]

Security tokens are the data used by the principals to realize secure communication. Informally, security tokens are usually divided in three groups:

- something you know: digital keys, passwords, and other secrets[2]
- something you have: physical keys and locks, smart cards, tamper-resistant devices, or
- something you are: biometric properties, e.g. fingerprints, or written signatures, assumed to be unforgeable

The difference between these three types of security tokens lies in the extent to which they can be shared with others:

- what you know can be copied and sent to others,
- what you have cannot be copied in general, but can be given away, whereas
- who you are cannot be copied, or given away.

Standard end-to-end security is in principle realized entirely by means of cryptographic software, and the principals only use the various kinds of secrets. This means that *a*

---

[1] We shall model his observations of the actions of others as messages of special kind, i.e. received over the *social channels*.

[2] i.e., data distributed to some principals and not to the others; data known to all are not very useful as security tokens.

principal can be identified with the list of secrets that she knows. If Alice and Bob share all their secrets, then there is no way to distinguish them by the challenges that can be issued on a standard network[3]. For all purposes, they must be considered as the same principal.

In pervasive networks, on the other hand, security is also supported by cryptographic hardware: besides the secrets, a principal is also supplied with some *security devices.* They are represented as some of the network nodes, given to the principals to control. A dishonest principal (or an honest certificate authority) can relinquish control of a security device, and give it to another principal.

To capture the third and the strongest kind of security tokens, and distinguish the principals by who they are, we need some *biometric devices.* They are represented as network nodes. Principals' biometric properties, on the other hand, are represented as some of the network nodes as well, available to respond to the challenges from the biometric devices. The only difference of a biometric property p from the other network nodes given to a principal A to control is that p always remains under A's control, and cannot be given away to another principal. We call the networks equipped with biometric devices and biometric properties — biometric networks.

2.2   Modeling Networks

In modeling security, principals can be identified with their security tokens, since security tokens are the material that security is built from. Summarizing the preceding section, we can say that

- in end-to-end networks (or cyber-networks), the only security tokens are the secrets, and the principals are reduced to *what they know*;
- in pervasive networks, the security tokens also include some security devices, and the principals are identified not just by what they know, but also by *what they have*;
- in biometric networks, the security tokens furthermore include some biometric properties, and the corresponding biometric devices, needed to test them; the principals are identified not just by what they know, or what they have, but now we take into account *who they are.*

Communication Networks. A *communication network* consists of

network graph $\mathcal{N}$, consisting of a set of nodes N, a set of links L, and a source-target assignment $\langle \delta, \rho \rangle : L \longrightarrow N \times N$, inducing the matrix representation $\mathcal{N} = (\mathcal{N}_{mn})_{N \times N}$ with the entries $\mathcal{N}_{mn} = \langle \delta, \rho \rangle^{-1}(m,n)$ for $m, n \in N$,
channel types C, and the type assignment $\theta : L \longrightarrow C$,
set of principals (or agents) $\mathcal{A}$, partially ordered by the subprincipal relation $\leqslant$,[4].

---

[3] We assume that they share the secrets dynamically: if a new one is sent to one, it will immediately be shared with the other. This implies that they also observe the events on the same set of network nodes.

[4] Briefly, A is a *subprincipal* of B is A "speaks for" B in the sense of [1,14] or "acts for" B in the sense of [19]

control $\copyright : \mathcal{A} \longrightarrow \wp N$, such that (1), and often also (2) is satisfied:

$$A \leqslant B \Longrightarrow \copyright A \subseteq \copyright B \qquad (1)$$
$$A \nleqslant B \wedge A \ngeqslant B \Longrightarrow \copyright A \cap \copyright B = \emptyset \qquad (2)$$

Remark. In a cyber network, the end-to-end assumption, that all security is done at the "ends" and any route "in-between" is as good as any other route implies that the network service can be reduced to an assumption that there is a single link between every two nodes, i.e. $\mathcal{N}_{mn} = 1$ for all m and n. Moreover, $C = 1$, i.e. all channels are of the same type, insecure. So the only nontrivial part of the structure is $\copyright : \mathcal{A} \longrightarrow \wp N$. But controlling one network node or controlling another one makes no difference, because a message can always be sent from everywhere to everywhere. So the only part of the above definition visible in the process model needed for cyber security is the poset $\mathcal{A}$.

Cyber Networks: Principals Are What They Know. The fact that the principals can be identified with the lists of secrets that they know is represented by an inclusion $\Gamma : \mathcal{A} \hookrightarrow T^*$, which we call *environment*. However, since a principal may learn new secrets when a process is run (or during a protocol execution), her environment may grow: at each state σ, she may have a different environment $\Gamma_\sigma A$ such that for every transition $\sigma_1 \longrightarrow \sigma_2$ holds $\Gamma_{\sigma_1} A \subseteq \Gamma_{\sigma_2} A$. During a protocol execution, different principals may thus become indistinguishable if they learn each other's secrets, since $\Gamma A = \Gamma B \Rightarrow A = B$. This means that the set of principals $\mathcal{A}$ may also vary from state to state in the execution: there is a family $\mathcal{A}_\sigma$, with the surjections $\mathcal{A}_{\sigma_1} \longrightarrow \mathcal{A}_{\sigma_2}$ for every transition $\sigma_1 \longrightarrow \sigma_2$, induced by identifying the principals that become indistinguishable.

In the cyber network model, a principal may have a number of internal actions involving creating nonces, incrementing counters, etc. But the principal has only three types of external actions: send, receive, and match. In the last, the principal matches received data with what he or she is expecting. In some models, receive and match are identified.

Pervasive Networks: Principals Are What They Have. A *pervasive network* is obtained by distinguishing, within a cyber network as defined above, a set of mobile nodes (i.e. security devices) $\widetilde{N}$, from the fixed nodes $\overline{N}$, so that $N = \widetilde{N} + \overline{N}$.

Besides the send, receive, and match actions, the process calculus now has two new kinds of actions, which allow each principal to:

- move a mobile node under his control, and reconnect it elsewhere in the network;
- pass control of a mobile node to another principal.

This means that the network connections and controls of the mobile nodes can dynamically change during a process run.

Biometric Networks: Principals Are What They Are. A *biometric network* is obtained by distinguishing, among the nodes of a pervasive network as defined above, two more sets

- $B_r \subseteq \tilde{N}$ of *biometric properties*, and
- $B_c \subseteq N$ of *biometric verifiers*.

The intended interpretation of these two sets of nodes is implemented by ther requirement that:

- control of the elements of B_r cannot be passed to another principal,
- the elements of B_c are related with the elements of B_r, so that the former can issue biometric challenges to the latter.

2.3 Message Delivery Modes

The main source of the new security phenomena in pervasive network is the fact that different types of channels have different message delivery modes.

In cyber networks, a message is usually in the form A to $B : m$, where A is the claimed sender, B the purported receiver, and m the message payload. As explained before, the network service is implicit in this model, so that A and B refer both to the principals and to the network nodes that they control. All three message fields can be read, intercepted, and substituted by the attacker. The point of the end-to-end security is that the receiver can still extract some assurances, even from a spoofable message, because the various cryptographic forms of m limit attacker's capabilities. Moreover, this message form is an abstract presentation of the fact that the message delivery service provided by the network and the transportation layers, say of the Internet.

In pervasive networks, different channel types provide different message delivery services. In general, there is no universal name or address space, listing all nodes. Annotating all messages by sender's and receiver's identities thus makes no sense, and the principal's identities are added to the payload when that information is needed.

There may be no link between two nodes, and no way to send a message from one to the other. On the other hand, a message can be delivered directly, e.g. when a smart card is inserted into a reader, without either of the principals controlling the card and the reader knowing each other.

The different message delivery modes determine the different security guarantees of the various channel types.

3 Templates and Logics

3.1 Templates

In this section we give an introduction to the use of templates and logics.

A *template* is a graphical specification of the desired behavior of a protocol that can be filled in with a number of actual protocol specifications. A template begins by describing the different types of channels available between principals. This is done simply by drawing a line indicating a channel between two principals that share the channel. Different types of lines indicate different types of channels. Messages passed between principals along a channel are indicated by arrows between principals corresponding to the channel type. Internal transitions are indicated by arrows from a principal to itself.

For example, the following template gives a common situation in which Alice generates a nonce (vx), and sends a cryptographic challenge $c^{AB}x$ containing x to Bob, after which Bob sends a response $r^{AB}x$ to Alice. Note at this point we give no details about the operations c^{AB} and r^{AB}.

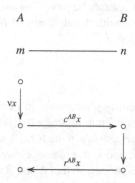

Fig. 1. Challenge-Response Template

What we would like to say, of course, is if that Alice creates x and sends $c^{AB}x$ to Bob, and subsequently receives $r^{AB}x$, she knows that Bob sent $r^{AB}x$ after receiving $c^{AB}x$. The Protocol Derivation Logic we describe below will give us a way of stating and proving this requirement.

3.2 Protocol Derivation Logic (PDL)

PDL Syntax. PDL is a descendant of an early version of the Compositional Protocol Logic (CPL) [9] and has certain of its axioms in common with it. Like CPL, it is intended to be used to prove security of protocols without explicitly specifying the behavior of the attacker. Unlike CPL, it is a logic about authentication only, although it can be interfaced with a companion secrecy logic [22] when it is necessary to reason about secrecy. In PDL principals are partially ordered sets where $A \subset B$ (A is a *subprincipal* of B) if A "speaks for" B in the sense of [1,14] or "acts for" B in the sense of [19]. The logic makes use of cryptographic functions that only certain principals can compute; thus keys do not need to appear explicitly unless we are reasoning about key distribution.

In PDL principals exchange messages constructed using a term algebra consisting of constants, variables, and function symbols. The term algebra may obey an equational theory E, or it may be a free algebra. The constants and variables used in the term algebra may or may not obey a type system which is specified by the protocol writer.

We consider a protocol as a partially ordered set of actions, as in Lamport [13], in which $a < b$ means that action a occurs before action b. We let $(t)_A$ denote t being received by A, $\langle t \rangle_A$ denote a message being received by A. We let $\langle t \rangle_{A<}$ where $t = f(x_1, \cdots, x_n)$ denote A creating t by applying the function f to the arguments $x_1, \cdots, x_n$ and then sending it ; thus this is the first time A sends t. We let $x \prec y$ denote the statement "if an action of the form y occurs, then an action of the form x must have occurred previously." We let $\vee.\ n$ denote the generation of a fresh, unpredictable nonce, n, and $(\mu.\ n)_A$ denote the generation of some arbitrary term n that A has never generated before. We think of $\vee$ and μ as acting a binders and write them as such. Finally, we let $A : S$ denote A knows S, and HA to denote that fact that A is an honest principal following the rules of the protocol.

We let $\langle\langle s \rangle\rangle_A$ denote A sending a message that was computed using s. We let $((s))_A$ denote A receiving a message that was computed using s. Finally, we let $\langle\langle s \rangle\rangle_{A_l}$ denote A's computing s for the first time (that is, the first time for A) and sending it in a message.

We use certain syntatic subterm conventions to determine if a term was used to compute a message. Suppose that $\langle m \rangle_A$ or $(m)_A$ is an event. We use the convention that if s occurs as a subterm of m then s could have been used to compute m. We conclude that s *must* have been used to compute m is for all legal substitutions σ to the variables in m, and for all $y =_E \sigma m$, s appears as a subterm of y. [5]

We define a legal substitution as follows:

Definition 3.1. *Let $\mathcal{P}$ be a protocol specification, together with a type system T. Let R be an description of a run in $\mathcal{P}$ where R is a set of PDL events partially ordered by the $<$ relation. We say that a substitution σ to the free variables in R is legal if*

1. *If a type system has been specified, then for any variable v in R, σR is well-typed, and the type of σv is a subtype of the type of v, and;*
2. *The run σR does not disobey any PDL axioms when s a subterm of event $(x)_V$ or $\langle x \rangle_V$ occurring in R is interpreted as $((s))_V$ or $\langle\langle s \rangle\rangle_V$, respectively.*

To give an example, consider the run

$$(\vee x)_B.(z)_A < \langle x \rangle_{B_<}$$

The substitution $\sigma z = x$ is not legal, since it would violate the PDL axiom (which we will present later) that says that a fresh variable can't be sent or received until if is sent for the first time by its creator.

In the case in which the term algebra is a free algebra, we conclude that, for any message m sent or received, s is a subterm of m means that s must have been used to compute m. For other term algebras obeying some equational theory, this may not be the case. Consider the following:

$$\langle x \rangle_A < (x \oplus y)_A$$

where $\oplus$ stands for exclusive-or with the usual cancellation properties $x \oplus x = 0$, $x \oplus 0 = x$. It is easy to see that if $\sigma y = x \oplus z$ we get

$$\langle x \rangle_A < (z)_A$$

---

[5] Note that the convention used here is a little different from that used in [16] in which the interpretation in terms of legal substitutions was only used for received messages.

so that x was not necessarily used to compute the message that A received.

In [16], we develop a syntactical means of checking, for the basic PDL axioms, whether or not a message was created was created using a term x, where the term algebra in question is the free algebra augmented by exclusive-or.

PDL Axioms. PDL axioms are of three types. The first type describe basic properties of the communication medium. These are standard axioms that do not change; the main innovation of the work we describe in this paper is that we will be introducing new channel axioms for different types of channels. The second type describes the properties of the cryptosystems used by the protocols; these need to be augmented whenever a new type of cryptosystem is used. The third type describes the actions of honest principals in a protocol run. These, of course, are different for each protocol.

The basic channel axioms are as follows:

The receive axiom says that everything that is received must have been originated by someone:

$$A : ((m))_A \Rightarrow \exists X. \langle\langle m \rangle\rangle_X < < ((m))_A \tag{rcv}$$

The new axiom describes the behavior of the v operator.

$$(vn)_B \wedge (a_A = ((n))_A \vee \langle\langle n \rangle\rangle_A) \Rightarrow (vn)_B < a_A \tag{new}$$
$$\wedge\ (A \neq B \Rightarrow (vn)_B < \langle\langle n \rangle\rangle_B < ((n))_A \leq a_A))$$

where $FV(a)$ denotes the free variables of a. Thus, any event a involving a fresh term must occur after the term is generated, and if the principal A engaging in the event is not the originator of the term B, then a send event by B involving n and a receive event by A involving n must have occurred between the create and a events.

An example of an axiom describing the properties of a cryptographic function, is the following, describing the behavior of pubic key signature.

$$\langle\langle S_A(t) \rangle\rangle_X < \implies X = A \tag{sig}$$

This simply says that, if a principal X signs a term t with A's digital signature and sends it in a message, then X must be A.

An example of a protocol specification is A's role in the challenge-response protocol:

$$\mathsf{H}A \implies (vx)_A.\langle\langle c^{AB}x \rangle\rangle_A$$

In other words, if A is honest she creates a fresh value x and sends it in a challenge.

We are now able to express the Challenge-Response requirements template that we expressed in graphical form in Section 3.1 in PDL as follows:

$$A : (vx)_A.\ \langle\langle c^{AB}x \rangle\rangle_A \qquad\qquad < \qquad\qquad ((r^{AB}x))_A$$
$$\implies \langle\langle c^{AB}x \rangle\rangle_A < ((c^{AB}x))_B < \langle\langle r^{AB}x \rangle\rangle_B < < ((r^{AB}x))_A \tag{cr}$$

We consider it a proof obligation that will be discharged in PDL.

Suppose that we instantiate c^{AB} with the identity and r^{AB} with SIG_B. Then we can prove the challenge-response axiom in the following way.

1. We start out with what A observes: $A : (vx)_A.\ \langle x \rangle_A < < (S_B(x))_A$

2. Applying the rcv axiom, we obtain $A : \exists Q. \langle\langle S_B(x) \rangle\rangle_Q < (S_B(x))_A$
3. Applying the new axiom, we obtain $A : ((\nu x))_A. \exists Q. \langle x \rangle_{A<} < ((x))_Q < \langle\langle S_B(x)\rangle\rangle_{Q_(} < (S_B(x))_A$.
4. Applying the sig axiom, we obtain $q = B$, and we are done.

For the purposes of analyzing protocols that use different types of channels, we will need a means of specifying which channels we are using. Thus we extend PDL with a channel notation. We denote send actions taken along a channel κ as $\langle a : \kappa \rangle$ and receive actions taken along κ as $(a : \kappa)$. When no channel is specified we assume that standard cyber channel that obeys only the rcv and new axioms is being used.

4 Timed Channel Protocols

4.1 Proximity Authentication

Our assumptions about cyber channels are very basic: 1) if a message is received it must have been sent by somebody, and 2) a few simple assumptions about the ordering of actions involving nonces. However, there are many cases where that is not enough. We consider for example the authentication problem in Section 3.1 as it might arise in a pervasive setting. In a pervasive network, Alice is, say, a gate keeper that controls a smart card reader m, which is a network node. Bob arrives at the gate with his smart card n, and creates a network link between m and n. Alice may not know Bob, but she is ready to authenticate any principal X who arrives at the gate, and links his smart card x to the reader m. She will allow access to anyone whose credentials are on her authorization list. Authentication with a fresh nonce bound to the secret credentials is necessary to prevent replay. This *Gate Keeper* Challenge-Response template extends Fig. 1 by one prior step, where Bob identifies himself to Alice by sending his name. The point of discussing this very simple scenario is to emphasize the *role of the network link* in the authentication. The goal of the authentication is to assure that

- (a) Bob is authorized to enter, and
- (p) he is at the gate.

While the authorization requirement (a) is emphasized, the proximity requirement (p) must not be ignored. If it is not satisfied, then an intruder Ivan may impersonate Bob. Ivan needs to control a smart card reader m' at another gate, where real Bob wants to enter; and he needs to establish a radio link between the card reader m' and a smart card n', with which he himself arrives at Alice's gate.

In a cyber network (assuming that the radio link between m' and n' is realized as an ordinary network link), this would be a correct protocol run: Ivan is only relaying the messages. Indeed, Bob's and Alice's records of the conversation coincide, and the matching conversation definition of authenticity is satisfied.

In a pervasive network gate keeper model, the above protocol run is considered as a Man-in-the-Middle attack: although unchanged, the messages are relayed through the nodes under control of a non-participant Ivan. This would allow Ivan to impersonate

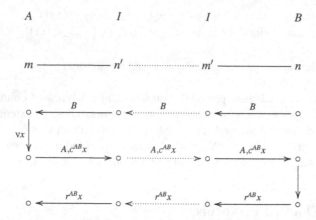

Fig. 2. Attack on Gate Keeper Protocol

Bob and enter Alice's facility unauthorized. These attacks, by the way, are not hypothetical; for example they have been demonstrated by Tippenhauer et al. in [27], in which location spoofing attacks on iPods and iPhones are implemented.

This example shows why pervasive networks require stronger authentication requirements than those routinely used in cyber security. The strengthening requires verifying not just that the principal Bob has sent the response, but also that he has sent it directly from a neighboring network node. This is the *proximity* requirement. It arises from *taking the network into account*, as an explicit security concern.

One way to verify whether a proximity requirement is satisfied is to use timed channels in distance bounding protocols. That is, if we can measure the time between the sending of a challenge and the receipt of the response, and we know the speed at which the signal travels, we can use this information to estimate the distance between two devices. The trick is to do this in a secure way.

4.2 Proximity Verification by Timing

Timed Channels. We model a timed channel simply as a channel that allows the sender to time the message it sends and receives. More precisely, the difference between the timed channel and the standard channel is that

- the send and receive times can be measured only on the timed channel,
- the purported sender and receiver are a part of every message only on the standard channel.

Timed Challenge-Response. The main assumption about the timed channels is that the messages travel at a constant speed c, and that the length of network links is approximately d, say at most $d + \varepsilon$. By measuring the time t that it takes to a message x to arrive from a node m to a node n, one can verify whether x has travelled through a direct link by making sure that $ct \leq d + \varepsilon$. If Victor is the owner of the node m and Peggy owns the node n, then Peggy can prove to Victor that she is in the neighborhood

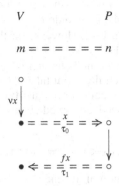

Fig. 3. Timed Challenge-Response Template

by very quickly responding to x, say by fx. If Victor sends x at time τ_0 and receives fx at time τ_1, then he needs to verify that $c(\tau_1 - \tau_0) \leq 2(d + \varepsilon) + \theta$, where θ is the time that Peggy may need to generate and send fx.

The *timed challenge-response* template, capturing this idea, looks like this: where the principals are now V (Victor the Verifier) and P (Peggy the Prover).

An action along a timed channel is called *timed* if the principal performing it notes the time (on its local clock) at which it was performed, *untimed* if the principal does not. A timed action a performed by a principal N is denoted by $\tau_i a$, where a is an action and τ_i denotes the time at which N performed the action. The taking of the time measurement in the diagram is noted by a bullet • under the name of the principal performing the action. Intuitively, this template says that after sending a fresh value x at time τ_0 and receiving fx at time τ_1, Victor knows that there is someone within the range of at most $\frac{c}{2}(\tau_1 - \tau_0)$. This template can be interpreted as a specification of the security property of the function f.

We make a comment here about implementation of timed challenge and response. For example, consider the case where f is the identity. Peggy can start responding to Victor as soon as she receives the first bit of x. Depending on the degree of accuracy needed, this can give Peggy a considerable advantage. Thus, unless Peggy is a trusted principal who will wait until she receives the entire nonce, it is advisable to use a bit-by-bit challenge and response, where the chance of Peggy guessing the correct bit response is bounded above by a constant. We can then choose x large enough so that the chance of Peggy cheating without being detected is negligible. A more thorough discussion of bit-by-bit challenge and response and the security issues involved in implementing it are found in [7]. In this paper we abstract away from these issues and make the notation $<$ stand for both the conventional and bit-by-bit notions of precedes.

Specifying Timed Channels in PDL. PDL has already been used to analyze distance bounding protocols in [16], for which we defined a timestamp function and some axioms governing it. However, this had the disadvantage that we could not specify in a natural way the actions for which timestamps were or were not defined. Moreover, specifying axioms in terms of which channels they apply to allows us to structure our specifications in a more modular way, in keeping with the spirit in which PDL was developed. In this section we describe how to do this, using a timestamp function similar in construction to the one used in [16]. However, in this case the function is used to describe properties of the channel.

An event a taking place along a timed channel is denoted by $\tau_i a$, where τ_i is a real number denoting the time at which the event takes place. Since recording of time can only take place on timed channels, and axioms involving timed channels involve time-recorded events only, we do not need any timed channel identifier. We have one axiom, saying that local times increase:

$$\tau_0 a_A < \tau_1 b_A \implies \tau_0 < \tau_1 \qquad \text{(inc)}$$

We also use the following definition of distance:

Definition 4.1. *Let A and B be two principals. We define the* distance *between A and B, or $d(A,B)$ to the minimum τ of all possible $(\tau_0 - \tau_2)/2$ such that the following occurs:*

$$(\nu n)_A . \ (\nu m)_B . \ \tau_0 \langle\langle n \rangle\rangle_{A} < \ ((n))_B < \langle\langle m \rangle\rangle_{B} < \ < \tau_1 \ ((m)) \ _A$$

The inc axiom guarantees that this is well-defined.

Security Goals of Proximity Authentication. The task is now to design and analyze protocols that validate the *proximity challenge-response template*, which is the timed challenge-response template augmented with a conclusion about time and distance. It is expressed in PDL as follows:

$$V: \ (\nu x)_V . \ 0 \langle x \rangle_V \qquad < \qquad \delta(f^{VP}x)_V$$
$$\implies 0 \langle x \rangle_V < \quad (x)_P < \langle f^{VP}x \rangle\rangle_{P} < \ < (f^{VP}x))_P < \delta(f^{VP}x)_V \ \wedge \ d(V,P) \le \delta \quad \text{(crp)}$$

The (crp) template says that, if V creates a nonce, and sends it along the timed channel at time 0, and then receives a response at time δ, then P must have received the challenge after V sent it and then sent the response before V received it. Moreover, the distance between V and P is less than or equal to δ.

4.3   Distance Bounding Protocols

The simplest way to achieve our goal is to combine the cryptographic challenge-response from Fig. 1 with the timed challenge-response from Fig. 3. The authentication reasoning will then follow from the templates (cr) and (crp), taking $c^{VP}x = x$ in the former, sending both challenges together. The only part of the cryptographic challenge sent on the standard channel that is not sent on the timed channel are the purported sender and receiver. So they need to exchange some messages on the standard channel, to tell each other who they are.

Cryptographic response to a challenge usually takes time to compute. This means that it either (1) needs to be sent separately from the timed response, or (2) that it must be very quickly computable, as a function of the challenge. These two possible design choices subdivide distance bounding protocol in two families: those with two responses, and those with one response.

The easiest approach, from a design point of view, is to use two responses, since this allows one to avoid the challenging task of developing a function that both provides the necessary security and is fast to compute. However, in order to accomplish this the two responses must be linked together securely.

The approach of using two responses is that followed by the original distance bounding protocol of Brands and Chaum [3]. There, the response sent on the timed channel is the exclusive-or of the prover's nonce with the verifier's, sent as a sequence of one-bit challenge-response pairs. The response sent on the conventional channel is the digital signature on the two nonces. The binding message is a commitment (e.g. a one-way hash function) that the prover computes over its nonce, and sends to the verifier before the responder . In Čapkun-Hubaux [5] the binding function is the same, the timed challenge and response is a single exchange of nonces, and the response sent on the conventional channel is a hash taken over the nonces. In Meadows et al. [16] the response sent over the timed channel is a one-way hash function taken over the prover's name and nonce, exclusive-ored with the verifier's nonces. This combination of commitment with timed response reduces the message complexity of the protocol.

Hancke and Kuhn [16], who developed their protocol independently of Brands and Chaum, take the approach of using just one response. They do that by using a function $\boxplus$ which is quick to compute, but for which it not possible for a principal who has seen $x \boxplus y$ for only one value of x to compute y. This is obviously impractical to use if y is a secret key shared between verifier and prover, so instead prover and verifier use a keyed hash computed over a fresh values and a counter exchanged earlier in the protocol.

A detailed formal analysis of Hancke and Kuhn's distance bounding protocol has been presented in [24]. A sketch of a PDL analysis of the Brands-Chaum protocol is given in [23] [6].

5   Social Channel Protocols

Social channels arise from the fact that many pervasive devices, such as cellular phones, PDAs, and laptop computers, use their humans not only to promulgate in space, but also to exchange information. For instance, a great part of the initial address books on many devices is usually received through this channel: a human manually enters some addresses of other devices. The devices often use their humans to exchange short messages.

5.1   A Timed Social Protocol That We All Use

Often, an address received through a human channel is authenticated using a timed channel: one device sends a message to the other one through a network channel, assumed to have some minimal speed, and then it observes through the human channel whether the message is received by the other device within a reasonable amount of time.

---

[6] The details of these analyses were written after the workshop version of the present paper was completed.

This protocol can be interpreted as *binding a challenge sent on a timed channel with a response on a human channel*. This binding is assured by the human observing the caller's number on the receiver's device. The run is thus in the form

$$A \qquad\qquad B$$
$$\bullet = = = \overset{m}{\underset{\tau_0}{=}} = \Rightarrow \circ$$
$$\downarrow$$
$$\odot \overset{}{\underset{\tau_1}{\longleftarrow\!\sim\!\sim\!\sim}} (m)$$

where the notation $b \underset{\tau}{\rightsquiggly} \odot$ means that the $\odot$-side *sees* the other side perform the action b at time τ. In this case A sees B perform $b = (m)$, i.e. he receives m. This message may be just A's own identifier. Although m thus may not be fresh, if the waiting time $\tau_1 - \tau_0$ is sufficiently small, the chance that the message that B receives is not the same message that A has sent is assumed to be negligible.

5.2 Formalizing Social Channels

The non-local observations through social channels have deep repercussions on the problems of authentication. As pointed out in the beginning, the source of the problem of authentication in computer networks arises from the fact that all observations are local: a computer Alice can only observe her own actions (among which are the actions of sending and receiving messages). However, a mobile phone Alice can ascertain that another mobile phone Bob has received her message, if their humans are standing next to each other, observing both devices. The other way around, the mobile phone Bob can ascertain that Alice has sent that message, because Bob's human has seen the message on Alice's screen, and Alice's human pushing the send button. Moreover, besides observing each other's actions, Alice and Bob can also send and receive brief messages through their humans, which are considered authentic because the humans observe each other.

Formally, we consider social actions in the form

$$<B \text{ to } A : \vartheta>$$

which intuitively mean that Bob displays a term or an action ϑ for Alice to see. We attempt to capture this intended meaning by the following axioms

$$<B \text{ to } A : \beta> \implies A : \beta_B \tag{sc1}$$
$$<B \text{ to } A : \beta> \triangleright <C \text{ to } A : \gamma> \implies A : \beta_B \triangleright \gamma_C \tag{sc2}$$
$$<B \text{ to } A : \beta(t)> \vee <B \text{ to } A : t> \implies \sigma t \in \Gamma_A \tag{sc3}$$
$$\forall T \in \Theta \forall t \in T \exists u \in T . \, u \neq t \wedge \sigma u = \sigma t \tag{sc4}$$

which should be read as follows:

- (sc1) If A observes the action β_B, then she knows that β_B really occurred.
- (sc2) If A observes the action β_B before γ_C, then she knows that β_B occurred before γ_C.
- (sc3) If A observes an action with a term t, or is shown the term t itself, then A knows the digest σt.
- (sc4) For every sufficiently large set of terms T, and every $t \in T$ it is feasible to find a different term $u \in T$ with the same digests $\sigma t = \sigma u$.

Intuitively, the prefix σ can be construed as a short hash function, leading to many collisions. Still more concretely, in the above scenario with mobile devices, this corresponds to the fact that Alice's human sees Bob's human receive a message, but if the message is long, he can only see a part that fits on Bob's screen; if the message is numeric, he can only discern a couple of digits. Therefore, many messages look the same, and the message that Bob has received may not be the one that Alice had sent after all.

The task is to design protocols to bootstrap authentication using these low bandwidth fully authentic social channels.

Graphic notation. In protocol diagrams, we use the following graphic elements:

- $\beta_B \rightsquigarrow \odot_A$ represent $<B$ to $A : \beta>$
- $\beta_B \overset{\sigma t}{\rightsquigarrow} \odot_A$ represents $<B$ to $A : \beta(t)>$
- $\circ_B \overset{\sigma t}{\rightsquigarrow} \odot_A$ represents $<B$ to $A : t>$

The annotations by σ can be omitted, since they are redundant. Yet it is may be useful, at least in the initial derivations, to keep a reminder that all social communication is low bandwidth, and should be viewed as digested through a short hash function σ.

5.3 Socially Authenticated Key Establishment

We begin from one of the simplest protocol tasks: Bob announces his public key e (or an arbitrary message) on the standard channel, and his human displays a digest on the social channel to authenticate it. The two announcements can be made in either order:

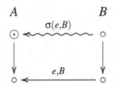
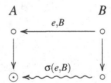

Both cases are open to a Man-in-the-Middle (MitM) attack. The problem is that, by axiom (sc4), the Intruder can easily find a public/private key pair $(\breve{e}, \breve{d})$ such that $\sigma(\breve{e}, B) = \sigma(e, B)$. As always, the Intruder is also assumed to be in control of the standard channel. So in the first case, he can find $(\breve{e}, \breve{d})$ such that $\sigma(\breve{e}, B) = \sigma(e, B)$, and replace Bob's announcement of e, B by $\breve{e}, B$. In the second case, the Intruder needs to intercept and hold Bob's announcement of e, B, compute $\sigma(e, B)$, find $(\breve{e}, \breve{d})$ as above, announce $\breve{e}, B$

in Bob's name, and wait for Bob's human to announce the digest $\sigma(e,B) = \sigma(\breve{e},B)$. In both cases, the Intruder ends up with the key $\breve{d}$ to read the messages sent to Bob, and Bob cannot read them.

Social Commitment. The MitM attack on the social channel authentication can be prevented in the same way as in the case of timed channel authentication: by binding the communications on the two channel types. For this purpose, Bob generates a fresh nonce, to be included in the social digest. The value of this nonce is publicly announced only after of the key, so that the Intruder, at the time when the key is announced, cannot know what the value of the digest will be, and cannot look for the collisions. On the other hand, in order to bind this nonce to the key (and to the protocol session, in order to prevent confusion), the nonce needs to be *committed* from the beginning, and, of course, decommitted in time to verify this binding. The two abstract templates above thus refine to:

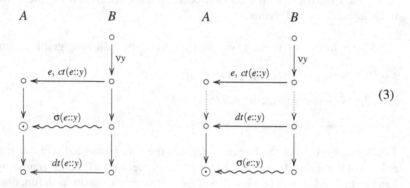

$$(3)$$

Authentication before Decommitment. A particularly simple instance of the template on the left has been discussed by Hoepman [11]. The nonce y is also used as the private key, corresponding to the public key $e = g^y$. He takes the simple commitment schema where $ctx = Hx$ is just a sufficiently strong hash function, whereas the decommitment is simply $dtx = x$. The protocol boils down to

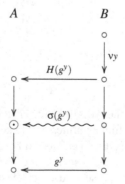

Of course, the main point of the Diffie-Helman exchange it to get a shared key g^{xy} by composing the above protocol with its mirror image, where Alice generates x and announces g^x. Hoepman also considers a final key validation phase. There are interesting possibilities to employ social channel here as well.

Authentication after Decommitment. The problem with the template on the right hand side in (3) the is that the Intruder can simply hold the commitment message until the decommitment is sent, and then proceed with the MitM attack as before. To prevent this, we need to introduce a message from Alice at the dotted lines, confirming that the commitment is received. Note that this message needs to be authenticated as well: if the Intruder can fake it, he can get the decommitment from Bob, and again launch his MitM attack. But the only way to authenticate Alice's message, in absence of all other infrastructure, is the social channel again. So Alice needs to generate and send a fresh value as her acknowledgement, and this value also needs to be included in the social digest. Hence the following template

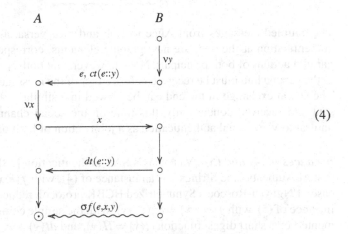

$$(4)$$

Remark. Authentication on the social channel does not follow the challenge-response template of authentication. There is no reason why it should: the challenge-response template implements *indirect* authentication, based on demonstrating a capability (to invert cryptographic functions, or to quickly respond on a timed channel), whereas the social channel implements a *direct* authentication, based on observing other principals' actions.

Mutual authentication. The analogous use of the nonces x and y in (4) is quite convenient when both Alice and Bob want to announce their keys. Alice's nonce x, used in (4) just to acknowledge receipt of Bob's commitment can now also be used to bind Alice's announcement to its social digest, whereas Bob's nonce y, which was used for this purpose in (4) can now also be used to acknowledge receipt of Alice's commitment. Composing (4) with its mirror-image version, where Alice and Bob exchange the roles, thus leads to a remarkably symmetric protocol.

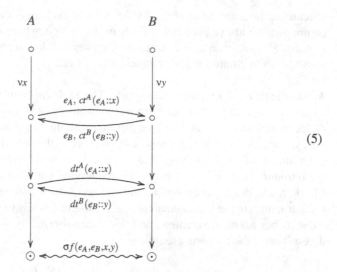

$$(5)$$

The coupled messages from Alice to Bob and vice versa, as well the mutual social authentication at the end, are new graphic elements, corresponding to concurrent, or parallel actions of both principals. Note, however, that both concurrently sent messages in the second line must be received before either of the messages in the third line is sent. The social exchange in the end can be viewed in a similar way, as a pair of messages sent and received concurrently, this time on the social channel; but it may be more natural to view social authentication as a joint action of both principals.

Instances of (4) and (5). Vaudenay's SAS-authentication [28] (where SAS stands for "Short Authenticated Strings") is an instance of (4), with $f(e, x, y) = x \oplus y$. The special case of Nguyen-Roscoe's Symmetrized HCBK protocol, reduced to two principals is an instance of (5), with $f(e, x, y) = e :: (x \oplus y)$, with the simple commitment schema[7] implemented by a short digest function $ct(y) = H(y)$, and $dt(y) = y$. Security of this protocol essentially depends on the special properties of this function, discussed in detail in [21].

HCBK protocol: matching conversations socially. The paradigm of *"matching conversations"* is, in a sense, the ultimate goal of authentication: if Alice's and Bob's views of all their conversation coincide, then they surely see their actions correctly, since Alice sees her own actions correctly, and Bob his. In order to match their views, each of them must derive the actions of the other from their own.

Nguyen and Roscoe's HCBK protocol [21] directly attacks the problem of *simultaneous mutual authentication of whole groups* of principals. The strategy is to use social channels for *direct simultaneous matching of the conversations*: all principals announce on their social channels the digests of their views (records) of the conversation conversations, and their humans check that the digests match. This is a remarkably direct approach to authentication.

---

[7] They include Bob's identity explicitly in the commitment. We keep principal's identity implicit in every commitment.

The point is that template (5) readily lifts from 2 to n principals: instead of just Alice and Bob sending their commitments in parallel, and then waiting for each other, all n principals can do that in parallel. The process expressions above remain quite similar to the two party case above. The technical proviso for this extension is that a suitable format for n-way matching on the social channel needs to be agreed upon. In particular, the principals must agree about

- (1) a method for each of them to arrive to the same ordering of the announcements that each of them has recorded, and needs to hash,
- (2) a social protocol to compare the values of all digests.

Both problems require "breaking the symmetry" in a coordinated way. The first one can be deferred to the social channel, by adding an initial social message, announcing a linear ordering of all principals' names. The second problem, minimizing the number of comparisons between the digests, requires imposing a tree structure on the group. Both problems have been major concerns in the Bluetooth design [12].

6 Conclusion

We have described some of the different types of channels that arise in pervasive networks, and the challenges and opportunities they give for authentication. We also give a formal description of several types of channels that arise in pervasive computing, and demonstrate a graphical template language for describing the behavior of protocols that make use of these different channels. We also describe some of the axioms that describe the behavior of some of these channels.

We are currently extending our work to develop logic for reasoning about the security of authentication protocols that make use of these different channels. We have found earlier that this approach, combined with the use of graphical templates that can describe both abstract and concrete specifications of protocols can be useful, not only in describing and organizing protocols that already exist, but generating new protocols that satisfy different types of requirements. We expect this to be the case here as well.

We do not intend to limit ourselves to proximity and social authentication. We expect this approach to work for other types of channels as well. In particular, we intend to investigate applications of our approach to quantum cryptography. Any quantum protocol, in order to be practical, will need to be harnessed together with conventional protocols as well. Although there as been a substantial amount of work on formal methods for quantum computation and quantum cryptography, very little of it addresses this aspect of the problem. We expect our methods to provide a natural way of doing this.

References

1. Abadi, M., Burrows, M., Lampson, B., Plotkin, G.: A calculus for access control in distributed systems. ACM Transactions on Programming Languages and Systems 21(4), 706–734 (1993)
2. von Ahn, L., Blum, M., Hopper, N.J., Langford, J.: CAPTCHA: Using Hard AI Problems for Security. In: Biham, E. (ed.) EUROCRYPT 2003. LNCS, vol. 2656, pp. 294–311. Springer, Heidelberg (2003)

3. Brands, S., Chaum, D.: Distance Bounding Protocols. In: Helleseth, T. (ed.) EUROCRYPT 1993. LNCS, vol. 765, pp. 344–359. Springer, Heidelberg (1994)
4. Burrows, M., Abadi, M., Needham, R.: A Logic of Authentication. ACM Transactions in Computer Systems 8(1), 18–36 (1990)
5. Čapkun, S., Hubaux, J.P.: Secure positioning in wireless networks. IEEE Journal on Selected Areas in Communication 24(2) (February 2006)
6. Cervesato, I., Meadows, C., Pavlovic, D.: An encapsulated authentication logic for reasoning about key distribution protocols. In: Guttman, J. (ed.) Proceedings of CSFW 2005, pp. 48–61. IEEE (2005)
7. Clulow, J., Hancke, G.P., Kuhn, M.G., Moore, T.: So Near and Yet So Far: Distance-Bounding Attacks in Wireless Networks. In: Buttyán, L., Gligor, V.D., Westhoff, D. (eds.) ESAS 2006. LNCS, vol. 4357, pp. 83–97. Springer, Heidelberg (2006)
8. Creese, S., Goldsmith, M., Roscoe, A.W., Zakiuddin, I.: The attacker in ubiquitous computing environments: Formalizing the threat model. In: Proc. FAST 2003, pp. 83–97 (2003)
9. Datta, A., Derek, A., Mitchell, J., Pavlovic, D.: A derivation system and compositional logic for security protocols. J. of Comp. Security 13, 423–482 (2005)
10. Desmedt, Y.: Major security problems with the 'unforgeable' Feige-Shamir proofs of identity and how to overcome them. In: Proc. Securicom 1988 (1988)
11. Hoepman, J.-H.: Ephemeral Pairing on Anonymous Networks. In: Hutter, D., Ullmann, M. (eds.) SPC 2005. LNCS, vol. 3450, pp. 101–116. Springer, Heidelberg (2005)
12. Jakobsson, M., Wetzel, S.: Security Weaknesses in Bluetooth. In: Naccache, D. (ed.) CT-RSA 2001. LNCS, vol. 2020, pp. 176–191. Springer, Heidelberg (2001)
13. Lamport, L.: Time, clocks, and the ordering of events in a distributed system. Commun. ACM 21(7), 558–565 (1978)
14. Lampson, B., Abadi, M., Burrows, M., Wobber, E.: Authentication in distributed systems: theory and practice. ACM Trans. on Comput. Syst. 10(4), 265–310 (1992)
15. Meadows, C., Pavlovic, D.: Deriving, Attacking and Defending the GDOI Protocol. In: Samarati, P., Ryan, P., Gollmann, D., Molva, R. (eds.) ESORICS 2004. LNCS, vol. 3193, pp. 53–72. Springer, Heidelberg (2004)
16. Meadows, C., Poovendran, R., Pavlovic, D., Syverson, P., Chang, L.: Distance bounding protocols: Authentication logic and collusion attacks. In: Poovendran, R., Wang, C., Roy, S. (eds.) Secure Localization and Time Synchronization in Wireless Ad Hoc and Sensor Networks, pp. 279–298. Springer (2007)
17. Meadows, C., Syverson, P., Chang, L.: Towards more efficient distance bounding protocols. In: SecureComm 2006 (August 2006)
18. Mink, A., Ma, L., Nakassis, T., Xue, H., Slatter, O., Hershman, B., Tang, X.: A quantum network manager that supports a one-time pad stream. In: Pro. 2nd International Conference on Quantum, Nano, and Micro Technology (February 2008)
19. Myers, A.C., Liskov, B.: Protecting privacy using the decentralized label model. ACM Transactions on Software Engineering and Methodology 9(4), 410–442 (2000)
20. Nguyen, L.H.: Authentication protocols based on low-bandwidth unspoofable channels: a survey (2008), http://web.comlab.ox.ac.uk/people/Long.Nguyen/
21. Nguyen, L.H., Roscoe, A.W.: Authenticating ad hoc networks by comparison of short digests. Inf. Comput. 206(2-4), 250–271 (2008)
22. Pavlovic, D., Meadows, C.: Deriving Secrecy in Key Establishment Protocols. In: Gollmann, D., Meier, J., Sabelfeld, A. (eds.) ESORICS 2006. LNCS, vol. 4189, pp. 384–403. Springer, Heidelberg (2006)
23. Pavlovic, D., Meadows, C.: Deriving authentication for pervasive security. In: McLean, J. (ed.) Proceedings of ISTPS 2008. ACM (2008)
24. Pavlovic, D., Meadows, C.: Bayesian authentication: Quantifying security of the Hancke-Kuhn protocol. E. Notes Theor. Comp. Sci. 265, 97–122 (2010)

25. Schaller, P., Schmidt, B., Basin, D., Čapkun, S.: Modeling and verifying physical properties of security protocols for wireless networks (April 2008)
26. Singleé, D., Preneel, B.: Location verification using secure distance bounding protocols. In: International Workshop on Wireless and Sensor Network Security. IEEE Computer Society Press (2005)
27. Tippenhauer, N., Rasmussen, K., Popper, C., Čapkun, S.: iPhone and iPod location spoofing attacks (2008), http://www.syssec.ch/press/location-spoofing-attacks-on-the-iphone-and-ipod
28. Vaudenay, S.: Secure Communications over Insecure Channels Based on Short Authenticated Strings. In: Shoup, V. (ed.) CRYPTO 2005. LNCS, vol. 3621, pp. 309–326. Springer, Heidelberg (2005)
29. Wong, F.L., Stajano, R.: Multichannel security protocols. IEEE Pervasive Computing 6(4) (December 2007)

Deriving Ephemeral Authentication
Using Channel Axioms

(Transcript of Discussion)

Catherine Meadows

Naval Research Laboratory

This is joint work with Dusko Pavlovic and it is our take on what we can contribute to brief encounters. So what's involved in having some sort of authenticated brief encounter? You're taking part in some sort of transaction or whatever that's based upon properties that are fleeting, and so these may be things such as proximity, you want to exchange key material with somebody who's near you, or do something else based on the fact that that principal is near you: direct human to human communication, direct physical contact, all these things can be involved, and they're either things that you're trying to verify, or that you're actually using as evidence to create your picture.

The trouble is, these sorts of properties are things you really can't use crypto alone to verify. But you may be able to use some other techniques to verify, for example, that say a signal is coming from a certain direction, or that you're in direct physical contact with something, and for these you're going to have to use different types of communication channels, and these communication channels are going to have different properties, which you can use to verify the conclusions, to provide evidence for the conclusions you want to make. But the thing is these are going to be *different* channels, and you want to put all these channels together and make a conclusion, and you can't do that unless you have some way of securely binding these channels to each other. So, for example, you may need to know that information coming to you on one channel is coming from the same principal as the information that's coming to you from another channel, and so you need to securely bind all these channels to each other, and to any other conventional channels that may be used in crypto as well. And that's basically what I'm going to talk about.

So here's an example, proximity authentication. OK, so this is a very basic problem. Here's a gatekeeper, that's Alice with the stop sign, over in the background there, that's legitimate principal Bob, and in the middle we've got Mr Mafia the attacker. Mr Mafia wants to get inside the gate, and so when Alice sends a cryptographic challenge to Mr Mafia, he doesn't answer, he just sends that challenge over to Bob, who may be talking to another gatekeeper, or thinks he's talking to another gatekeeper, and Bob sends the response, Mr Mafia gets it and forwards it to Alice. And now what's interesting here, this is an attack, Alice thinks she's letting Bob in, but she's actually letting in somebody else, but in terms of conventional networks, Mr Mafia is perfectly legitimate, he's a router, he's routing Alice's challenge to the correct person and then routing the

B. Christianson et al. (Eds.): Security Protocols 2009, LNCS 7028, pp. 262–268, 2013.

response back to Alice, that's what he's supposed to be doing, but that's not what he's supposed to be doing here.

So you need to build more into this, you need to build in more properties of the channel. Here we're using a wireless channel, so one obvious thing you can do is compute the time of the round trip. So Alice sends a wireless challenge, a timed challenge to Mr Mafia, and if Mr Mafia does the diversion thing to Bob, it's going to take too long, and Alice will know he's cheating. But she'll also need to do the crypto to verify who it is, and crypto itself introduces a delay which adds noise, so you typically do this over two channels. But you don't want to do it this way: here's Alice, she sends a timed challenge, and Mr Mafia sends a timed response, and then she sends a crypto challenge, and Mr Mafia just forwards that one over to Bob. So there's a lot of work that you have to do to make sure that these two channels — the crypto verification, you get on one channel, and the timing verification you get on another — are both talking about the same thing, and that's what's non-trivial. This is just one type of example, this same type of problem shows up a lot, anything where you're using different types of channels to try and put together some secure picture of what's going on.

Now I'm going to give a little more technical example, which is the Brands-Chaum distance bounding protocol. Again, you're doing proximity verification, Alice and Bob have switched genders, V is Victor for verifier, P is Peggy the prover, and the idea is that the prover wants to prove that she is close to Victor, and Victor wants to know that the prover is close, and that she's not pretending to be close. The prover first creates a nonce and then commits to the nonce, and sends the commitment to Victor. Victor creates his own nonce, and then he sends it to the prover, to Peggy, along a timed channel. Peggy gets this, and then she responds right away with the exclusive-or of the two nonces. Actually, what really happens in Brands-Chaum is this is a bit by bit challenge and response, so Victor sends the first bit of the challenge, and Peggy sends the first bit of the response, and they just keep on iterating. And then at the very end, after all this, Victor still doesn't know for certain who Peggy is, so Peggy opens her commitment and also includes Victor's nonce, and then signs the whole thing and sends it to Victor. This was something that was originally proposed for smartcards, back in the 90s, but with interest in wireless proximity verification it's also been considered as a solution to that type of problem too.

I gave a talk about this distance bounding at Microsoft Research about three years ago, and Tuomas Aura was in the audience and he said, well there's an obvious attack on this. And here's the obvious attack: an honest prover talks to an honest verifier and they go through the entire protocol, but here's an intruder out at the end here, and the intruder is able to cause Peggy's message not to reach Victor, somehow he manages to destroy it, he creates some sort of denial of service attack on the network, or whatever, and then he responds, he just takes Peggy's message and applies his own signature, and once he's done that the intruder has convinced Victor that he's the one who's close, not Peggy. It's a simple attack, and there's also a very simple defence, all you have to do is have

Peggy take commitment over her identity as well as her nonce, and then when Victor tries to verify the commitment at the end of the protocol he would see that something is wrong.

After this was pointed out to me I looked at Brands and Chaum's paper again. They don't have an explicit threat model, but they did think very carefully about different types of threats, and they just didn't seem to think that this type of threat was a problem, they didn't say it wasn't a problem, they just didn't mention it. So I said, well what is the scenario they're using? They weren't thinking of a wireless network, they weren't thinking of networks at all, they were thinking of smartcards and readers, so you have a smartcard, you put it in a reader, and in their scenario, as far as I can tell, if you have an honest smartcard and an honest reader, so here is our honest smartcard and here's our honest reader, then nobody should be able to get in the way between you two, you have a secure connection, so that type of attack should not be a problem. And that's the only thing I could think of, you might be able to come up with other explanations, but that seems like a plausible one, considering that they had thought very carefully about all the other types of threats, it seemed somewhat odd that they would have just missed this one, unless they really didn't consider it a threat.

But this actually points out two things. One is that you do have to be very careful to think about how to bind your channels together securely, it's not trivial. And the other thing is, you have to be very careful to think about what sort of channels you're using, and to remember that the properties of your channels can change. So if you're trying to port something from one application to another you have to revisit all your assumptions, and you may, if you're trying to do some sort of verification of security, which you should, you're going to have to take into account those assumptions. And that's the sort of thing we've been doing.

Now I'll go into a bird's eye view of the approach we've been taking, which is our protocol derivation logic, or PDL for short. It uses the basic ideas, the basic approach of Burrows, Abadi and Needham logic, which describes what honest principals can derive from participating in a protocol. So it doesn't have an explicit model of an intruder in the logic, you know, there's no axioms about intruders. I mean, we have an intruder model, it's just not at the level of logic. And our level of abstraction is also at a much lower level than Burrows, Abadi and Needham's, which eliminates a source of ambiguity.

And we basically have three types of axioms. One is the properties of the communication channel, and originally we were reasoning about traditional computer networks, those channel axioms were fixed, and there's actually very few of them, there's just two. Next, axioms about cryptographic algorithms, every time you introduce a cryptographic algorithm you have to come up with a new axiom, but you also need to justify that axiom. And finally protocol axioms, which just describe, what honest principals do in a protocol, so every time you create a new protocol you would create a new set of protocol axioms. There's not too many types of events, there is sending messages, receiving messages, you can generate random nonces, you can generate counters which are not random, they're just new because you haven't generated them before, and you can compute functions. And these are partially ordered according to time. Actually, I shouldn't really say time, they're in a precedence order, so there's no clock running, you just know that one thing happened before another thing. And so all our reasoning is of the form, if you know that a certain set of events happened in a certain order, generally because you're a participant in the protocol, and you either perform those events, and you perform those events, you know, you send some things and you receive some things, then you know a certain other set of events happened and also in a certain order. So that's the idea in a nutshell.

We use templates too, we have high level templates and then we fill in the details, so we start, and we create a set of proof obligations until we finally get down to the level where we can use our axioms to give us the proof. So here, is the basic template, that shows up in all sorts of cryptographic protocols, and it's basically, I create a nonce, and I send it out into the ether, and then I get the nonce back transformed somehow. So here's Alice, she creates her nonce, she sends a challenge, and the important thing about this challenge is it has to be the first time she's sent anything involving that nonce, and then later on she gets a response. And what she wants to conclude is, well she sent her challenge, some V received the challenge, and then that V computed a response, and then Alice received the response, and from that she can conclude the usual sort of things you usually want to conclude in cryptographic protocols. But you need to actually find out, what sort of channels are they using, what sort of cryptographic functions are they using.

We're actually going to add a little more detail to this template. The particular problem I introduced was the timed challenge response, so we need a timed channel, and a timed challenge response template. Now Victor sends his challenge at a certain time, and the time is not global time, it's just Victor's local clock, and then he gets back a response at a time delta. He wants to conclude the same thing he wanted to conclude from the other template, except we also get a relationship between delta and the distance between Victor and Peggy here, and this comes from because the delta gives you the round trip time of this message, and so delta has to be greater than or equal to the distance between V and P. So those are our templates, so these are the things we are trying to prove, and usually what happens is that a protocol is not simply one of these templates, to use these templates you may actually glue several of them together, you may put some more stuff around the template, but these templates are like your basic building blocks.

I want to talk a little bit about some of the channel axioms we used. These are the traditional Dolev-Yao axioms, so there's not very many of them. One is described as the received axiom which says, if Alice gets something then she knows somebody had to have sent it, messages do not arise out of thin air, somebody has to send them. The other one is the new axiom which describes the behaviour of nonces, and that says, if V creates a nonce, any action involving the nonce must have occurred after V created it, and so specifically if the other action involves a principal A who isn't V, then we have: V created the nonce, he must have sent it, A must have received it, and then the action occurred. And you can get from these two, if you want to prove one of these templates you start with, I sent a message, I sent a challenge and I got back this response, well somebody must have sent that response, and then this tells you in what order all the events happened, well they must have actually received my nonce, whoever it is, and then they must have responded, and that gives you timeliness. And then if the way you implement the challenge and response involves some cryptographic algorithms, you can use those to get who this principal actually is there responding. So the basic idea is pretty straightforward.

So we're using other channels, and in particular, we have a timed channel because Victor is now timing when he sends his challenge, and when he gets his response. And we don't really need too many more axioms for that other than, time is always increasing, that's so the idea of distance is well defined, we can define distance as a lower bound on the deltas. We also need to reason about Brands-Chaum, when you put a smartcard in an ATM machine, and our idea is that while that smartcard is in that ATM machine, nothing is going to come between them. And so if you believe that then you can express it as an integrity channel, basically each integrity channel has a different identifier I, and for each integrity channel I , there exists an X and a Y, such that if some Q sends a message along the channel I , then either $Q = X$ or $Q = Y$. So the idea is, if you're sitting at one end of this integrity channel and you get a message from somebody, you get two messages along that integrity channel, you can check whether or not you sent them, and then if you didn't send them then you can conclude that both those messages were sent by the same principal, which is a very handy thing when you want to securely combine two messages. We need another axiom actually to prove Brands-Chaum that says, honest principals don't forward messages along integrity channels, because otherwise you could get a principal who innocently plays the role of Mr Mafia, so we rule that out.

If you look at Brands-Chaum again, at just the two outside messages, that's just the un-timed challenge response template. If we look at the two inside messages together with the commitment and the opening of the commitment, that gives you the timeliness, OK, and that gives you the fact that Peggy could have responded early, because she committed to her Y before she sent this message. If she hadn't committed to something, then because of the properties of exclusive-or she could have just sent any random delta. And then we use the integrity channel axioms, and we also need to use an additional assumption that no dishonest principal is within the proximity range. That's because there's a conspiracy on all these types of protocols where you have one attacker who's close and one is far away, and the close guy does the time part and the far away guy does the authentication part. If you assume all the attackers are outside the range then that attack doesn't work. And we put this in so we can prove that the security properties the protocol has and not pay attention to the properties it doesn't have, and not try to prove the properties it doesn't have.

So that's a very high level sketch of the approach we take, but basically the idea is, you have these very high level ideas, templates of what you're trying to prove, and you work your way down, all the way to rather simple axioms, and the idea which can be a lot of work, is coming up with some way to justify these axioms.

We've been doing a lot of analyses of, not only of Brands-Chaum, but other distance bounding and different types of range justification protocols. A range justification protocol (to put it in a nutshell) is one where Peggy is trusted. And in particular we've been working on one, the Hancke-Kuhn[1] distance bounding protocol, which turns out to be a fascinating protocol from a cryptographic point of view. As far as I can tell, nobody's tried to do any sort of formal proof or cryptographic proof of the security of this protocol, but it all hangs together and works beautifully, and it relies on this function, it's a one-time one-way function, you can use it once, and it has the property of a one-way function, but if you use it twice it falls apart, and so the protocol has a lot of safeguards in it to keep you from using it twice. What we've been doing is developing the cryptographic theory to reason about this, and it basically involves keeping track of the information that is leaked as you participate in this protocol.

Another thing that we've been looking at is analysis of bootstrapping protocols using human verifiable channels. A human verifiable channel is, say I look at something on a computer, and I can read it off, and I know it's on the computer because I'm looking at the computer (or a radio, or a device, or whatever). These are also of course low bandwidth, because I can't read and remember a very long number. And there's been a lot of protocols, Frank has done some really groundbreaking work in this area, and there's been a lot of work on different types of protocols using human verifiable channels to perform different types of authentication. But I think this kind of approach, breaking down the channels and coming up with a simple set of axioms, could be very useful here.

Another thing we've been thinking about, although we haven't done this yet, there's a whole class of protocols involving computers and humans, some of them we don't even think about as protocols explicitly, such as airport security protocols. You go into an airport, you basically have a series of protocols that involve different channels. First of all you get your boarding pass, that involves a channel with a machine over the Internet, then you go through security, and that involves interacting with a human being and also with the machine that screens your luggage, and the other human being who interacts with that machine. Then once you're through there you board the aeroplane, and there again you go through another protocol that has two channels, one with the gate agent and one with the gate agent's machine. And somehow you're supposed to put this all together to get some sort of argument that terrorists are not going to get on that plane. And what's interesting is that Bruce Schneier has published some stuff on a few of these protocols where he finds out where you can get around them by exploiting the fact that the channels are not really securely bound together, and when he shows you how you can break them it looks very obvious because

---

[1] "An RFID distance bounding protocol" Securecomm '05, pp 67–73.

once you see the gaps between the channels, once it's pointed out to you, it is quite easy to see.

Jonathan Anderson: In this analysis, were the assumptions that you make about the channels and things explicit? Because when you were talking about things like smartcards, where you assume that you have an anonymous card and anonymous reader, that there's nothing in-between.

Reply: Yes, and it may not necessarily be the case, but I've heard about attacks on ATM machines, where they put something that spies on you as you as type in your PIN, and I don't know that you actually need to corrupt the ATM machine to do that. So it's conceivable that that channel axiom I have is wrong, but that seemed to be the assumption that Brands and Chaum are making.

Frank Stajano: I'm interested in how you model the properties of a channel, is it the case that you need to see someone's invention, and then you figure out a way of mathematically describing it, or is there a general model you have about describing properties in the channels?

Reply: I don't think we have a general model yet, I think it's too early to say we have a general model. We've started thinking about things, but we haven't been thinking at this level of generality for that long. We started out by thinking about traditional channels, and then it occurred to us to start applying the logic to distance bounding protocols, and Dusko pointed out, why not think about this as properties of the timed channel, and then we had timed channels. Then it occurred to us, well we don't have to stop there, but we haven't really gotten far enough along yet where we say we have a general approach to reasoning about channels, or describing the properties of channels.

Frank Stajano: We have been doing lots of work on protocols that use multiple channels, and the work that I and Bruce Christianson did with our students[2] is about how to use multiple channels to do this without giving times. We have this new work we are doing[3,4], that there may be a channel whose property is that you cannot relay it, and if you use that then you don't need to bound the time.

Reply: Yes, that's actually a trust assumption we needed in the analysis of Brands-Chaum.

Frank Stajano: It could be a physical property of the channel.

---

[2] See LNCS 4631 pp 112–132 and LNCS 5964 pp 133–146.

[3] Frank Stajano, Ford-Long Wong and Bruce Christianson, "Multichannel Protocols to Prevent Relay Attacks", Financial Cryptography 2010: LNCS 6052 pp 4–19.

[4] Bruce Christianson, Alex Shafarenko, Frank Stajano and Ford-Long Wong, "Relay-proof channels using UWB lasers", LNCS 7061.

A Novel Stateless Authentication Protocol

Chris J. Mitchell

Information Security Group
Royal Holloway, University of London
http://www.chrismitchell.net
me@chrismitchell.net

Abstract. The value of authentication protocols which minimise (or even eliminate) the need for stored state in addressing DoS attacks is well-established — the seminal paper of Aura and Nikander [1] is of particular importance in this context. However, although there is now a substantial literature on this topic, it would seem that many aspects of stateless security protocols remain to be explored. In this paper we consider the design of a novel stateless authentication protocol which has certain implementation advantages. Specifically, neither party needs to maintain significant stored state. The protocol is developed as a series of refinements, at each step eliminating certain undesirable properties arising in previous steps.

1 Introduction

It has long been recognised that a requirement for stored state is an undesirable feature in almost any protocol (although the absence of statefulness can also cause practical problems, as has been the case with HTTP). This is particularly significant for security protocols, in which a requirement for stored state can be used as a means of launching denial of service (DoS) attacks (see, for example, section 1.6.6 of Boyd and Mathuria [2]). During the 1990s considerable efforts were made to devise authentication and key establishment protocols which minimise the requirements for stored state at the server in client-server protocols; one major objective of this work was to minimise the threat of DoS attacks.

Whilst preventing exhaustion of table space was the original motivation for state elimination, there are other good reasons to minimise requirements for stored state. For example, state minimisation can greatly simplify network protocols by reducing the complexity of the associated state machines. The cost is typically slightly longer messages (since messages become the new repository of state). Of course, this observation is not new at all — indeed, HTTP cookies are hardly a revolutionary new idea!

In 1997, Aura and Nikander published a key paper on this topic [1]. They describe how protocols can be made stateless by 'passing the state information between the protocol principals along[side] the messages'. Such state information (forming a cookie — as in HTTP) can be protected using a MAC computed using a secret key known only to the server.

B. Christianson et al. (Eds.): Security Protocols 2009, LNCS 7028, pp. 269–274, 2013.

Oakley, a protocol proposed for use in the Internet, and which also can be configured to avoid the need for server state, was proposed at around the same time by Orman [3]. Photuris, another session key management protocol that can be regarded as a development of Oakley, due to Karn and Simpson, is defined in RFC 2522 [4]. A much broader discussion of some of the anti-DoS measures incorporated in these and other similar protocols is provided by Oppliger [5].

The emphasis of past state-minimisation work has primarily focussed on eliminating stored state at the server. However, in the new world of transient relationships and peer/peer communications (which are not restricted to the client/server paradigm), it is necessary to try to protect both parties engaging in a protocol. This provides the motivation for the work described in this paper, i.e. to design an authentication protocol which minimises (ideally eliminates) stored state for *both* parties in a secure interaction.

2   A Simple Scheme

One simple possibility would be to use a time-stamp based protocol. A simple example of such a protocol is the following one-pass protocol, in which entity B is authenticated by entity A:

$$B \rightarrow A : t_B || f_{K_{AB}}(t_B || i_A)$$

In the above description, $||$ denotes concatenation[1], t_B is a timestamp generated by B, f is a MAC function, K_{AB} is a secret key shared by A and B, and i_A is an identifier for A. Such protocols are widely known and have been carefully analysed. The protocol specified is actually standardised in ISO/IEC 9798-4 [8] and similar protocols have been discussed in the literature (see, for example, Protocol 3.4 of Boyd and Mathuria [2]). This protocol can be used twice to achieve mutual authentication.

This approach requires securely synchronised clocks. This may cause serious problems in practice; in particular, this does not seem like a good solution for a transient relationship scenario. In the absence of an existing security management infrastructure, it is unclear who would define how clocks should be synchronised. In any case, this protocol, like any timestamp-based protocol, does not prevent replays within a short time window of the original transmission (see, for example, section 10.4.1 of [9]).

One way of avoiding the use of timestamps (and the associated problems) is to use a key idea from the Aura-Nikander paper [1]. Whilst the emphasis in this paper was on eliminating server state, the ideas presented there work just as well in eliminating client state. The key idea is to pass 'the state information between the protocol principals along[side] the messages'. This motivates the work we describe next.

---

[1] As discussed in [6,7], this concatenation must be done in such a way that the resulting data string can be uniquely resolved into its constituent data strings, i.e. so that there is no possibility of ambiguity in interpretation.

3 Working towards a Solution

We use shared secret-based unilateral authentication protocols throughout as simple examples. It seems reasonable to suppose that these protocols can be extended and modified to use asymmetric cryptography and/or to provide mutual authentication.

3.1 Putting a Nonce into a Cookie

We first consider the following two-pass (stateless) nonce-based unilateral authentication protocol:

$$A \to B : n_A \| f_{K_A}(i_B \| n_A)$$
$$B \to A : n_A \| f_{K_A}(i_B \| n_A) \| f_{K_{AB}}(n_A \| i_A)$$

where n_A is a nonce chosen by A, K_A is a key known only by A (and used only for generating and verifying cookies), and other notation is as before. The string '$n_A \| f_{K_A}(i_B \| n_A)$' functions as a cookie for the nonce n_A, which is sent with the nonce to avoid A having to remember it (cf. Photuris [4] and/or page 27 of Boyd and Mathuria [2]). This protocol is based on a 2-pass protocol standardised in ISO/IEC 9798-4 [8], where the modification essentially transfers A's stored state into the message. When A receives the response from B, A can first process the cookie to recover its stored state prior to verifying the response from B.

One advantage of this protocol is that A now only has to remember a single secret K_A, which can be the same for all interactions with other parties. The main remaining problem is that A cannot verify that the cookie $[n_A \| f_{K_A}(i_B \| n_A)]$ is fresh. That is, B can use the cookie to send a series of responses, all of which will be accepted. Even worse, a third party could intercept and replay B's original response, which will also be accepted.

Of course, as is stated on page 27 of [2], the cookie could be bound to the connection. However, if A allocates a new number for each authentication protocol instance, makes the cookie a function of this number, and keeps a log of current protocol instances, then this simply makes the protocol stateful again!

3.2 Using a Timestamp

One solution to this problem would be to use a timestamp instead of a nonce in a two-pass protocol. One exchange of this type is as follows:

$$A \to B : t_A$$
$$B \to A : t_A \| f_{K_{AB}}(t_A \| i_A)$$

where t_A is a timestamp chosen by A, and other notation is as before. It is important to note that, just because the scheme uses a timestamp, does not mean that synchronised clocks are needed. Only A checks the timestamp that it generates itself.

Unfortunately, this scheme allows Gong-style preplay attacks (cf. pages 22/23 of [2]), as follows. Suppose C wishes to impersonate B to A at some future time. C (pretending to be A) engages in the protocol with B, using a future value of A's clock. C can now replay this message to A at the future specified time, and successfully impersonate B.

4   The Main Proposal

The scheme we now propose combines the ideas introduced in the previous subsection, i.e. to use cookies and a timestamp-based nonce. That is, we use the same scheme as just described except that A also computes and sends a cookie with the nonce/timestamp (which must also be sent back by B). B responds with a MAC on the concatenation of the nonce/timestamp, the cookie, and the name of A, and also sends copies of the nonce/timestamp and the cookie. A can verify the cookie, verify the MAC, and finally verify the freshness of the timestamp.

An example protocol of this type is as follows:

$$A \rightarrow B : t_A || f_{K_A}(i_B || t_A)$$
$$B \rightarrow A : t_A || f_{K_A}(i_B || t_A) || f_{K_{AB}}(t_A || i_A || f_{K_A}(i_B || t_A))$$

where the notation is as before. As previously, this scheme does not require A's clock to be synchronised with anyone. In fact, the timestamp could simply be generated using a continuously clocked counter. Use of the cookie prevents preplay attacks involving a third party.

The inclusion of a session identifier in the cookie would enable A to match the response from B to a higher-layer protocol communications request (e.g. from an application).

However, replays within a time window are still possible. There are two obvious ways of fixing this. The first (and the widely discussed solution to this problem) would be to keep a log of recently accepted messages. In our context this solution is not so elegant, since it re-introduces state, albeit of a bounded size. The second solution would be to keep track of the timestamp/counter for the most recently received (accepted) message and to only accept 'newer' messages. This also involves the maintenance of state, but in this case of fixed size, regardless of the number of concurrent communications partners.

The latter approach could be generalised to the maintenance of a list of information regarding accepted messages for recent timestamps ('recent' is a well-defined concept as long as the counter increases at a roughly steady rate). Again, although this is stored state, this should not be such a big problem since it will only contain information about valid messages received, which can be removed as soon as the timestamp 'expires'.

5   Concluding Remarks

We have proposed an authentication protocol which minimises state for both parties in an authentication exchange. In particular, the client only needs to maintain a small list of values which does not grow as the number of parallel communications sessions grows. This is at the cost of slightly longer messages. The scheme builds on ideas of Aura and Nikander, [1].

Although we have proposed a stateless authentication protocol, there are many unresolved issues, including the following.

- The scheme we have proposed provides only unilateral authentication (of B to A). It would be interesting to devise a mutual authentication scheme. Of course, this could be achieved by simply using two instances of the scheme we have proposed, although it would be interesting to see if efficiencies could be achieved by devising a more integrated protocol.
- In this paper we have almost exclusively considered schemes based on the use of MACs. Whilst MACs are simple to compute and are widely used, a wide range of other cryptographic primitives can be used to achieve entity authentication. It would therefore be interesting to see if similar protocols could be devised using, for example, digital signatures.
- The presentation given here has been completely informal, and no attempt has been made to establish the security of the proposed schemes. Whilst this is reasonable when looking at what might be achieved, if schemes of this type are to be used in practice then it would be highly desirable to prove them secure in an appropriate model (first addressing any identified issues, where necessary).
- Finally, it would also be interesting to see how protocols of this type could be integrated into practical protocols.

More generally, it would be interesting to consider the applicability of stateless (cookie-based) protocols to a variety of communications models. For example, if all the interactions in the application are request-response, then stored state may be completely unnecessary from the application perspective. Even where a connection is set up, only a party wishing to initiate message transmissions, rather than responding to a request, needs to maintain state. A security protocol that avoids state would be particularly apposite in such applications.

Acknowledgements. The ideas described here evolved out of helpful discussions with Colin Boyd and Andreas Pashalidis, although any errors and omissions are entirely my fault.

References

1. Aura, T., Nikander, P.: Stateless Connections. In: Han, Y., Okamoto, T., Quing, S. (eds.) ICICS 1997. LNCS, vol. 1334, pp. 87–97. Springer, Heidelberg (1997)
2. Boyd, C.A., Mathuria, A.: Protocols for key establishment and authentication. Springer (2003)
3. Orman, H.: RFC 2412, The OAKLEY key determination protocol. Internet Engineering Task Force (1998)
4. Karn, P., Simpson, W.: RFC 2522, Photuris: Session-key management protocol. Internet Engineering Task Force (1999)

5. Oppliger, R.: Protecting key exchange and management protocols against resource clogging attacks. In: Preneel, B. (ed.) Secure Information Networks: Communications and Multimedia Security, IFIP TC6/TC11 Joint Working Conference on Communications and Multimedia Security, CMS 1999, Leuven, Belgium, September 20-21. IFIP Conference Proceedings, vol. 152, pp. 163–175. Kluwer (1999)
6. Chen, L., Mitchell, C.J.: Parsing ambiguities in authentication and key establishment protocols. Journal of Electronic Security and Digital Forensics 3, 82–94 (2010)
7. International Organization for Standardization Genève, Switzerland: ISO/IEC 9798-4: 1999/Cor 1:2009, Technical Corrigendum 1 (2009)
8. International Organization for Standardization Genève, Switzerland: ISO/IEC 9798-4: 1999, Information technology — Security techniques — Entity authentication — Part 4: Mechanisms using a cryptographic check function, 2nd edn. (1999)
9. Dent, A.W., Mitchell, C.J.: User's Guide to Cryptography and Standards. Artech House, Boston (2005)

A Novel Stateless Authentication Protocol

(Transcript of Discussion)

Chris J. Mitchell

Royal Holloway, University of London

I appreciate I'm the last talk of the day before the dinner, so the good news is, I haven't got very many transparencies.

I want to talk about state. I think it's fair to say that stored state is generally regarded as a bad thing. The more we can get rid of stored state the better we would be. I'm sure there are exceptions to this rule, but it's a nice rule of thumb at least. And through the 1990s there was a lot of effort made to devise protocols which minimise requirements for stored state, particularly in the server in client server protocols. One major goal of this effort was to try and get rid of obvious denial of service attacks where you just exhaust the server's state table. Now I would suggest, given the theme of this workshop, that there are other good reasons for getting rid of state, not just denial of service, but perhaps you can make network protocols simpler, and perhaps more reliable, make implementations easier to prove correct, and so on, by getting rid of state and therefore simplifying the state machine for the protocol. What's the cost? Well typically you would make the messages slightly longer because you can't really get rid of state all together, you have to put it somewhere, and you put it in the messages, and so the cost is going to be slightly longer messages. This isn't a new idea for goodness sake, after all in http we've been using cookies for a long time, well at least those of us who enable cookies on our machine have.

Matt Blaze: So when you say a protocol, you're not speaking exclusively a security protocol?

Reply: Well that's the main theme of this talk.

Matt Blaze: State-elimination pre-dates security protocols, I mean, stateless file system protocols have been around a long time.

Reply: I wouldn't claim to be a network expert, but hopefully this doesn't conflict too seriously with established wisdom.

Virgil Gligor: Yes, this is generally OK, except that it optimises in the wrong direction. The cheap resource is now storage and the expensive resource is communication.

Ben Laurie: No, that's not true. The reason you don't want state is actually because it's really expensive to maintain global state consistently.

Virgil Gligor: But we don't make messages longer to keep it in messages.

Ben Laurie: Sure you do. When you keep your preferences in a cookie for example, that's state.

B. Christianson et al. (Eds.): Security Protocols 2009, LNCS 7028, pp. 275–281, 2013.

Sören Preibusch: HTML input fields are also state.

Reply: And of course there's this paper by Aura and Nikander from ICICS 97 called Stateless Connections, and this is very security specific. They describe how protocols can be made stateless, and they mean security protocols, by passing the state information between the protocol principals alongside the messages. We can protect the state information using a MAC, using a secret key belonging to the server. This is if we're trying to get rid of server state. So when the server sees it again they can check the MAC and say, oh yes, this is my bit of state, and I can process it accordingly, and when I've finished I generate a new cookie and put a new MAC on. And there's plenty of examples, Oakley, Photuris, IKE version 2; all nice schemes designed to get rid of server state, as security protocols that is.

OK, so the emphasis in the past has been primarily about getting rid of state from the server, but perhaps we need to rethink this in our new world where we have lots of transient relationships (I have to mention the theme of the workshop at some point) and we have lots of peer-to-peer communications as well as client server, and so maybe we want to worry about both parties in a protocol, not just the server.

So how can we get rid of state in security protocols? Well if we use timestamps, OK, time is a kind of state, but it's just one piece of state and it's the same for all protocol instances, so we can live with that. So you can have a nice simple unilateral authentication protocol where A sends to B a timestamp, and then a MAC protected version of the timestamp, perhaps concatenated with the identity of the recipient so that you can't do obvious reflections and so on. And here's a little bit of notation, little t subscripts will be timestamps, F will be MAC functions, K is a secret key, and I_B is an identifier. We can use a simple little protocol like that, they're widely known, well analysed, hundreds of papers have been written about such protocols. I should just add a little warning that this double bar denotes concatenation, but we have to be careful about this because there are some, at least theoretical, dangers about ambiguity, about moving the borderlines of where this concatenation sits. So for the purposes of this paper, whenever I use concatenation I mean some method of gluing these fields together that gives a unique decoding. It might be ASN.1, it might be anything you like, but as long as you get unique decoding them I'm happy.

Well this is nice, and it's kind of stateless, but it requires securely synchronised clocks, and perhaps that's not such a good idea for our transient relation scenario. Who is this local authority that says what the time is? Well OK, we do have some global authorities, but typically they're not sending out secure time signals. We can fix that, but this seems like an unnecessary and an inconvenient requirement. And going back to Needham and Schroeder, it's nice to get rid of timestamps. And we also have this problem about replays, but I don't want to talk about this too much because my solution also has this problem, so I should have put this in very, very small print.

If we want to avoid timestamps we need to go back to the Aura-Nikander paper. The ideas in that paper, are presented in a very general way, so we just have to read that paper carefully and plug in the ideas. So actually what I have to say, there's nothing really new, just go back and read this stuff that somebody thought out very carefully 12 years ago, and we have the answers we need. Of course that's usually the case, all the good ideas have already been had many times. The key idea is something I've said already, pass the state information between the protocol principals alongside the message, so basically use cookies.

Paul Syverson: Really this makes your presentation no longer stateless.

Reply: OK, sorry about that, well there's not too much state in this presentation. I'm going to start by presenting a couple of ideas that almost work, but don't quite work properly, and I'm going to work with shared secrets, and I'm going to do unilateral authentication, because that's easy. My belief (or hope) is that we can extend it to cover all the other interesting cases, but I haven't done the work, so that's why I've put (hope) in brackets. And I'm hoping the deadline for writing the paper is not too soon, and there will be time to fix this up.

The first idea is, take the simple two-pass nonce based unilateral authentication, basically I send you a nonce and you send me something back that's a function of the nonce, and we'll try and make that stateless, so that I don't have to remember the nonce. So as well as sending the nonce, which is this little n_A, I send a MAC. Actually the nonce and the MAC constitute the cookie, the MAC is computed using a key that only I know, so I have this little secret key that I just use for computing cookies, and I include the name of the recipient and the identifier of the nonce, I ship this off. B can't check this, but this is just cookie stuff, and B just knows that the rules say he has to send it back. So Bob sends back the cookie, and also a MAC computed on the nonce and the identifier of the originator, which is a standard authentication protocol, but with this extra stuff in there. So this string of the nonce and a MAC on the nonce functions as the cookie, and we've moved all of A's stored state into the message.

Ben Laurie: Is this a kind of `http` digest?

Reply: Oh OK, maybe everything here is already known. A now only has to remember a single secret, that's great, so A's got rid of her state. But the problem is that Alice can't verify whether this cookie is fresh or not because there's no time in this cookie, this cookie could have been generated anytime during the lifetime of this cookie key. One way of solving this is generating a new cookie key regularly, but I don't really want to get into that. During the lifetime of this key B can use the cookie to keep sending responses and they'll be accepted as fresh, and even worse, a third party could intercept any response and keep replaying it.

So let's think about a different solution, we could use the nonce based protocol, but instead of a nonce we'll use a timestamp. So this is a conventional nonce-based protocol, but instead of the nonce I put in a timestamp, little t, but it's a timestamp chosen by A. The thing is that B doesn't check the timestamp so we don't need synchronised clocks because only A checks the timestamp, so as long as A has got a clock that does most of the things you expect a clock to do, like only move in one direction, then we're alright, and as long as A can kind of work out whether things are recent or not. So it's a hybrid timestamp-cum-nonce protocol.

Sören Preibusch: But we need key K_{AB} now?

Reply: Yes, we have all along. There's always been a key K_{AB}. In fact I did confess to this, that I'm going to use shared-secret based authentication.

Virgil Gligor: Which of course is state. Either you are pregnant or you are not.

Reply: It's a different kind of state, I would argue, in the sense that I only have one key with one person, whereas I can have many sessions.

Joseph Bonneau: Why don't you just store the most recent session, and then you only need a low number of bits.

Ben Laurie: The point is it's not changeable state, I mean, you could burn it in your ROM and you would be fine, you can have a zillion copies.

Sören Preibusch: But then how many people can you talk to, if you bring in symmetric keys, then you bring in how many people and so on.

Ben Laurie: Yes, I forgot to ask about the number of users, I'm worried about that.

Reply: I suspect I haven't got the chapter and verse that I can just do Diffie-Hellman key agreement stuck on the front of this, if I have public key certificates for example. OK, I need some keys otherwise I can't do crypto. I'm using shared key crypto as an example, but I hope this can be extended to public key. And I realise that in real transient relationships we haven't necessarily got keys and certificates, but that's somebody else's problem in the great spirit of research, after all I'm not expecting people to actually use this stuff, for goodness sake. Sorry. You don't have to put that into the transcript do you?[1]

Simon Foley: But Chris, on this protocol surely couldn't Eve the attacker just send Bob some times for tomorrow, so Bob can't take any freshness. Like a free computation?

Reply: You're my pet student actually, because on the next slide, we have the classic what I call *preplay* attack. I think Li Gong was the first to point this out in print. You choose a future value of the clock and you get the right response, which will work at some future time. So this is a problem. So that's my second broken idea, the solution is to combine these two ideas, and hopefully you get something that can't be broken, well actually I couldn't break it when I was writing the blurb for this talk, but that's not to say that it's secure, but we'll come onto that in a moment. So this actually looks rather similar to the first idea, but instead of nonces, we have cookies again, but these are timestamps, so you can check their freshness.

---

[1] No, we didnt *have* to.

Virgil Gligor: If I understand, you say that it would be counter state? Well, you have to remember that the previous value to figure out that it's not repeated.

Reply: Yes, that's my next transparency. So the claim here is we don't need synchronised clocks, we can use counters, that only A checks the timestamp. We could include a session-identifiable cookie, so you could match the response to some higher layer protocol communications request, because why are we inaugurating this protocol? Maybe you want to set up a session, maybe you want to exchange secure messages, and that will be as a response to some high layer request, and maybe our goal is to try and make our network protocol, or the security layer, stateless, but obviously what's going on above, you're not setting up a secure channel or doing security stuff for no reason, there has to be some reason for this, so maybe a session identifier would be useful. We still have this problem of replays within the time window, which is I think is what you were saying, and the normal response to this is to keep a log of recently accepted messages, so we might be able to bound the size of this piece of state.

Virgil Gligor: Just like Kerberos 5 does, to cache?

Reply: Yes, or we could be a bit more brutal and just say we'll just keep the most recently received timestamp value. If messages get out of order, too bad, we just throw them away. Or we could just keep the last 20 values and tick boxes whether or not we've received that reply. So there are things that keep the state pretty small, and there's a trade-off between how brutal we are about how much messages get out of order.

James Malcolm: Would that state be per session or just per server?

Reply: This is per server.

James Malcolm: So it's not very much?

Reply: No.

Sören Preibusch: Well the good thing is the burden is put on the client, so it means the client won't run denial of service attacks on the scheme because it would run out of its own state.

Reply: Yes, OK, I guess I'm thinking of everybody as being clients in a sense.

Bruce Christianson: If it's a one-per-server counter, then any other clients can run a denial of service attack.

Sören Preibusch: Does it tend to be a global counter then?

Reply: Well each entity has a single counter which they use for talking to all other parties, and they maybe have to keep some way of working out which recent counter values have been used and which haven't in terms of replies.

Ben Laurie: That sounds like lots of state to me.

Reply: Well, you can be very brutal and just keep the most recent one you've received that's valid, and that's just one value.

Sören Preibusch: You mean like a sequence value?

Reply Yes.

Ben Laurie: Then you'd have a very inefficient protocol, because most of the time you're rejecting and re-sending.

Reply: Yes, OK, when then maybe I'll just keep a list of the 20 most recent values, and a one or zero depending whether I've received a valid reply or not.

Simon Foley: Or if you did something like a SIM cache, then it makes it harder for somebody to send a denial of service attack, because then they have to target the particular bucket that you're going to put your hash into.

Reply: Yes.

Michael Roe: If your counter is with a single peer, and you're running over some protocol like TCP, then you know messages won't get reordered because of the transport protocol. The attacker can read all the messages, but in the absence of an active attack, you could be sure that the messages will be single-file, so you only need to keep the last number on that session. But if you're trying to do it across several peers, like your server talking to hundreds of clients, it's quite likely you send out a message to Alice and a message to Bob, and you see Bob's reply before you see Alice's, so it doesn't seem to make sense to have one single counter across all clients in that sense.

Reply: OK, so we can't do the very brutal approach, but maybe we could do this other approach in a reasonably economical way.

Bruce Christianson: The other thing you can do is hash the shared key every time you use it, and the other side does the same[2]. That hashed value becomes the new key, and no additional state is needed.

Reply: Up to the keys, OK, that's a different solution, yes. Yes, I appreciate this is the obvious weakness.

Paul Syverson: You could avoid all these problems if you just keep some state around [laughter].

Jonathan Anderson: Maybe the interesting question here is figuring out exactly how little state you can get away with, if you want this, that, or some other property, what's the bare minimum that you need? I mean, we could say, well if we just did it like this, oh great, there's no state, oh but there's a problem so we've got to do it a lot better, and just turn it back into a really complicated thing.

Bruce Christianson: What you hope is that you can get the state down to just the shared key.

Virgil Gligor: I think the good thing about keeping this ephemeral state in the server, it changes as time goes on, right, because a window advances?

---

[2] LNCS 2133, 182–193.

Reply: Yes.

Virgil Gligor: The good thing is that if the system crashes you don't have to remember the boundary, right, so in some sense this is ephemeral state and it's cheap, you don't have to worry about recovery, and so you are alright. Basically with ephemeral state at the receiver, the server doesn't have to keep anything, so long as it's well clock synchronised within plus or minus five minutes, basically that is what Kerberos does, and so it minimises state in that sense.

Ross Anderson: But if you're only worried about ephemeral associations, I'm not sure there's many applications you'd have to worry about anymore. You just do the one where you can be stateless, you just redesign the system so that's true.

Sören Preibusch: I'm not sure of any deployments now where you actually want to use this protocol.

Cathy Meadows: There are various reasons you might not want to keep state around, such as using resources, what happens if you lose the information, and so forth. So there seems to be different parameters and different types of state you need to worry about, so maybe you could categorise the different types of state, and say, well we could minimise one maybe at the cost of losing another?

Virgil Gligor: So long as you don't have to worry about recovery, which you don't, having this sliding window may be the right thing to do.

Reply: Thinking about general protocols without specific use cases is hard because you say, well how many simultaneous sessions are you likely to want to manage, and I don't know, particularly in some future ubiquitous scenario, conceivably you could want to manage large numbers of sessions. I don't know how many people you might be going to be talking to in a short space of time.

Where do we go from here, well I would happily confess there are lots of unresolved issues, this is all about unilateral authentication, we probably want mutual authentication, we probably want to use public key crypto, I was just using shared key as a simple example. Of course we need to prove these things secure, and it may be that my example is not secure, I didn't find any obvious flaws, but we may need to fix some things in order to get the proof to go through, and maybe think about possible application scenarios. And think about when we want state, which I guess this goes towards what's already been said, think about the different kinds of state we need and the kinds of context when you might need state. My suspicion is, this has already been thought through very carefully by networks people not particularly worrying about security, my hope would be that we could also make security stuff manageable using cookies and so on, just like all the other information we might want to manage for protocols. OK, thank you very much.

The Trust Economy of Brief Encounters

Ross Anderson

University of Cambridge Computer Laboratory
Ross.Anderson@cl.cam.ac.uk

The security of ad-hoc networks has been a subject of academic study for about fifteen years. In the process it's thrown up all sorts of provocative ideas, from Berkeley's Smart Dust to our suicide bombing protocol [1,2]. Now that a number of ad-hoc network technologies are being deployed, it turns out that reality is even stranger. After giving an overview of the history, I'll look at what some real systems teach us.

Peer-to-peer systems were our first contact with this world; the ambitiously-named Eternity Service may be no more, but it inspired a host of other peer-to-peer systems that brought creative mayhem to the music industry and helped teach us the importance of incentives; people are more likely to defend things they care about than the more abstract free speech of remote users on unfamiliar topics [3,4]. More broadly, a literature grew up on reputation systems: the key idea here was that the initial establishment of a secure association was much less important than mechanisms to deal with its evolution afterwards. No-one can remember when they first decided to trust their mother, and many of us can't remember when we first met many of our friends [5]. Trust is organic; it grows and can also die.

The Resurrecting Duckling was our second contact [6]. Here the idea was to bootstrap trust using physical contact, as a means of introducing practical authentication into embedded systems for which the overhead of PKIs and crypto protocols was unacceptable. It found application, for example, in digital tachographs: the tachograph sensor acts as the mother duck and the vehicle unit, on initialisation, imprints on it by accepting a key offered by the sensor [7]. That this key is sent in the clear is immaterial. The threat model is that the truck driver, perhaps months after the official calibration of the device, attempts to tamper with the communication between the sensor and the vehicle unit. Wire-tapping of the key set-up is excluded by the environmental assumptions.

A third development was the HomePlug protocol [8]. This is used to support power-line communications between consumer electronic devices, and comes with two modes of operation: "simple connect" mode, which works like a tachograph by sending the key in the clear, and "secure mode" in which the user types a key provided on the device label into a network management station. An academic cryptographer might have hoped to see a protocol such as Diffie-Hellman here. We decided against this because users would still have to either verify a key checksum or copy a key in order to prevent middleperson attacks, and from the viewpoint of security usability, copying is much preferable to checking. It's also cheaper and more robust to do things simply.

B. Christianson et al. (Eds.): Security Protocols 2009, LNCS 7028, pp. 282–284, 2013.

A fourth development has been recent work on social networks, which taught us about the importance of topology, and gave us new insights into such matters as traffic analysis and anonymity. Again, the big issue isn't the key setup per se, but how you manage the evolution of the peer relationships afterwards. Node compromise is a big deal in some of these systems, while in others it's group compromise – the detection by authority of a covert community [9].

The latest development comes from industrial control systems, where some vendors are selling what they call "lick'em and stick'em" sensors that can be deployed rapidly in an industrial plant. For example, a process engineer can add an extra temperature sensor to a reactor vessel by just slapping it on the outside and letting it establish its own network to the control centre. At first sight, that can save a lot of money on cabling. But configuration management now becomes the bugbear: Homer takes the sensor destined for the tank of methyl isocyanate and slaps it in the sewage tank instead. And that isn't all. Ad-hoc deployments into private networks open up backdoors to the Internet that bypass the plant firewall, and there's always the small matter of battery replacement. An initially appealing solution can rapidly teach some hard lessons about lifecycle costs.

In short, the things that caused problems mostly weren't the things we'd expected to. The protocols community's traditional insistence on immaculate key establishment turned out to be overblown or even irrelevant in most of these applications; what mattered was what happens afterwards. It's about putting the effort into the right part of the security lifecycle. But that effort is still substantial, and if anything it's much greater than the cost of initial authentication.

So what does this teach us about brief encounters? I will use our now traditional definition of trust as the ability to do harm – a trusted system or component is one that can break your security policy. From this I believe a difficult conclusion follows. If you are going to trust a principal with whom you have only one brief encounter, then the mechanisms commonly associated with "ad-hoc networks" – namely the optimistic establishment of an association, followed by its continued assessment on the basis of subsequent behaviour – are inappropriate. They really work only where the encounters are repeated or prolonged; only then do tit-for-tat and various institutional and social sanction mechanisms kick in effectively.

Where the encounter is brief, the trust will usually have to be provided by some third party, most likely using one of the many conventional protocols discussed at these workshops in the past. A merchant won't give goods to a customer without either trousering her cash or executing an EMV protocol run with her chip card. Whether you trust the Bank of England to issue the notes or the Bank of Scotland to issue your chip card, you're still trusting a bank.

Of course this is widely misunderstood. Websites tiresomely demand passwords from one-off customers when all that really matters is the card transaction. Transactions are often asymmetric because of a power imbalance; the difficulty that bank customers have in telling fake PIN entry devices from real ones is just one example of many. Nonetheless a more mobile and fluid society, with more transient encounters, will on aggregate require more security protocol runs.

Perhaps they'd be designed better if we were more explicit about two things: how long the resulting security associations are intended to last, and who's guaranteeing what to whom. Knowing someone's name isn't the same as knowing their reputation, and being able to tarnish their reputation is usually little recompense afterwards (ask any of Mr Madoff's erstwhile customers). Clarity about these questions might hopefully shift the emphasis in many applications from "identity", whatever that is, to something more appropriate.

References

1. Kahn, J., Katz, R., Pister, K.: Emerging Challenges: Mobile Networking for Smart Dust. Journal of Communications and Networks 2(3), 188–196 (2000)
2. Moore, T., Clulow, J., Nagaraja, S., Anderson, R.: New Strategies for Revocation in Ad-Hoc Networks. In: Stajano, F., Meadows, C., Capkun, S., Moore, T. (eds.) ESAS 2007. LNCS, vol. 4572, pp. 232–246. Springer, Heidelberg (2007)
3. Anderson, R.: The Eternity Service. In: Proceedings of Pragocrypt 1996, pp. 242–252 (1996)
4. Danezis, G., Anderson, R.: The Economics of Censorship Resistance. WEIS 2004 and in IEEE Security & Privacy, vol. 3(1), pp. 45–50 (2004)
5. Anderson, R.: The Initial Costs and Maintenance Costs of Protocols. In: Christianson, B., Crispo, B., Malcolm, J.A., Roe, M. (eds.) Security Protocols 2005. LNCS, vol. 4631, pp. 336–343. Springer, Heidelberg (2007)
6. Stajano, F., Anderson, R.: The Resurrecting Duckling: Security Issues for Ad-hoc Wireless Networks. In: Malcolm, J.A., Christianson, B., Crispo, B., Roe, M. (eds.) Security Protocols 1999. LNCS, vol. 1796, pp. 172–182. Springer, Heidelberg (2000), http://www.cl.cam.ac.uk/~rja14/duckling.html
7. Anderson, R.: On the Security of Digital Tachographs. In: Quisquater, J.-J., Deswarte, Y., Meadows, C., Gollmann, D. (eds.) ESORICS 1998. LNCS, vol. 1485, pp. 111–125. Springer, Heidelberg (1998)
8. Newman, R., Gavette, S., Yonge, L., Anderson, R.: HomePlug AV Security Mechanisms. In: ISPLC 2007, pp. 366–371 (2007)
9. Anderson, R., Nagaraja, S.: The Topology of Covert Conflict. WEIS 2006; University of Cambridge Computer Laboratory technical report CL-637 (2005)

The Trust Economy of Brief Encounters
(Transcript of Discussion)

Ross Anderson

University of Cambridge

I sat down and scratched my head a bit, and wondered what I might possibly say about brief encounters, and I suppose it relates to what we were talking about last time, namely ad hoc networks, and the kind of trust relationships that get set up on the fly, or get set up informally. And so I have scraped together a few of the examples that we've worked with, and having dashed through these I will then try and draw a few conclusions.

The first encounter that we had with ad hoc stuff was the Protocols Workshop in 1996. The Penet Remailer operated by Julf Helsingius in Finland was used by all sorts of people who had some reason to want privacy, people dealing with abuse or whatever. Three times in '95 and '96 the scientologists went after them, flew some lawyers into Helsinki with a briefcase full of cash, got a court to give an order saying that the identity of a particular remailer user should be disclosed, and then Julf shut down Penet. This got us to ask for the first time, what's the scope of legal threats to the information society?

In fact, this incident was a repeat of some local history. Wycliffe translated the Bible into English in 1382, and that was easily enough fixed. When King's College was founded here, all the fellows had to take an oath that they would not promulgate the wicked and heretical teachings of Wycliffe, who was after all an Oxford man. But when a Cambridge man translated the Bible, William Tyndale in the 16th Century, he took a proper engineering approach, got one of these new fangled printing presses, and managed to distribute 55,000 copies of the Bible before they caught him and burned him at the stake. And that of course had serious social consequences, much more than the Oxford translation of the Bible had had, because technology had changed in such a way that the rich and powerful could no longer un-publish books that they didn't want to have had published simply by collecting the few handwritten copies, and getting people to swear oaths and stuff. So what's going to happen to society if books can once again be un-published? We've since seen it become normal, for example, that newspaper archives will edit out things that High Court judges were persuaded that they didn't like.

So we came up with the idea of the Eternity Service at the Protocols Workshop[1], a peer-to-peer file store. The idea was that you would donate say 100 Megabytes of your own storage on your disk, and you would get a number of tokens, mojos as they were later called, which you could then go and spend to

---

[1] "The Eternity Service" was later published in Pragocrypt, 1996, but see Ross J. Anderson, Václav Matyáš, Jr., Fabien A. P. Petitcolas, Iain E. Buchan, and Rudolf Hanka, "Secure Books: Protecting the Distribution of Knowledge", Security Protocols 5 (1997), LNCS 1361, 1–11

B. Christianson et al. (Eds.): Security Protocols 2009, LNCS 7028, pp. 285–297, 2013.
© Springer-Verlag Berlin Heidelberg 2013

get say 10 megabytes worth of storage distributed on the whole system. You protect the documents by encryption, fragmentation, redundancy and scattering, so that no individual user of the system knows whether the stuff that he's storing is scientology documents, or spanking pornography, or whatever, and so you've got complete deniability if the police come knocking, and selective service denial isn't possible. At least that was the idea.

The ideas that we had in that design were not only used in one or two very temporary anti-censorship systems that then vanished, like Publius, but more importantly in Freenet and Gnutella, once Napster was closed down. And so we now know what sort of attacks you have on systems like that. You spam them with poison content, you identify uploaders and sue them, in other words you do attacks on high order nodes in the network. The lesson that we draw from that is that in a network that anyone can join, it's not the initial authentication that matters so much as subsequent conduct: reputation, in other words. We even saw, four or five years ago, there was actually a workshop started on reputation systems and economics of reputation. It has not persisted as a subject because I think there's not enough to do and say on it, but of course you have got firms like eBay who use reputation systems as an important part of their mechanism.

The next thing was the stuff that Frank and I did ten years ago. We asked the question, what does it mean for a medical sensor to be secure? The model that we talked about there was that the doctor on a ward picks up a thermometer from a rack of thermometers at the central nursing station, and wants to mate that with her PDA, and also place it on or in a patient. So the doctors know the medical aspects of bonding with sticky tape or whatever, how do we do the digital aspects of the bonding? The first requirement we figured out was that the virgin thermometer should bond to the first device it sees, that is the first PDA that comes along and says, oi, I'm a doctor, I need your services, click. The thermometer then becomes a slave of that PDA. The second requirement is that the master should be able to break the bond, and Frank came up with this wonderful analogy of the ducking on hatching from the egg bonding to the first thing that it sees which moves and quacks, and so hence we got the idea of the Resurrecting Duckling[2] for this. So you've got a trust relationship established by physical contact, or something that's logically equivalent to that. It's something that you bootstrap essentially once, although you may have an ability to recycle the device, and this ended up being used in real stuff.

This is a picture of a tachograph, the device that gets put in Europe in trucks and buses in order to record speed and drivers' working hours. This is a sensor that goes in the gearbox and it sends back a bleep whenever the prop shaft turns. And this wicked thing here says it's a voltage regulator made in Japan, but actually it's made in Italy, and it interferes with the pulse train under the command of this device here. So this is Alice, this is Bob, this is Charlie, and this is David the Dongle. It lives on a key fob. If you press it once it throws away 10% of the pulses so that instead of being speed limited to 62 mph you can do 68 mph, drive down the M11 any day and you can see that these devices

---

[2] LNCS 1796, 172–194.

are in widespread use. Press it a second time and it throws away 20% of the pulses, you press it a third time and it throws away all the pulses, you can now have your one hour mandatory rest break while you're going down the M11 at 90 mph in your articulated lorry. And you press it a fourth time as the blue lights appear on the horizon, and it goes back to normal operation. And then if the police haul you up before the magistrates, then the magistrates say, 90 mph, was the vehicle fitted with a tachograph, yes Your Worship, was it in working order and duly calibrated, it appears to be so Your Worship, and did it record an over speed, no Your Worship, case dismissed. So there are some interesting electronic warfare aspects around this which we discussed elsewhere[3].

The interesting thing from our point of view was that when the European Union mandated encryption between this device and that device in order to try and mitigate this attack, how do you set up the keys? We got involved in this project just in time to stop them putting the same DES key into all three hundred thousand of these gearbox sensors that are manufactured every year. And this is in fact another example of Duckling, but contrary to one's physical intuition, the gearbox is the mother duck and the tachograph is the baby duck, so whenever the gearbox sensor sees a new tachograph it says, aha, you are my duckling, you will obey me, and you then check this by means of an audit facility in the device itself. So there's an example of how you go about setting up keys without the benefit of a PKI, by simply using the fact of first physical contact, first electrical contact, between a sensor and a meter. And that works, that's deployed.

The third thing that I'll talk about briefly is HomePlug. HomePlug AV is a 2006 standard, that I was one of the authors of, for power line communications at 150 Megabits per second. You find this deployed at the moment in the kind of products that enable you to plug a number of wifi hubs into the mains power in your house, your DSL modem then feeds the signal into the mains, and the wifi hubs can repeat it. It is hoped that from this Christmas you will see this in more and more devices, such as personal video recorders, hifis and so on, so you will be able in effect to have high performance networking around your home. And the majority of the engineering effort that goes in here is the error correction. The transmission properties of domestic power networks are truly appalling, and you need multiple layers of error correction and automatic repeat request, and so on, to make it work. But that's been done.

The problem is how you go about setting up keys between say your hifi and the new pair of speakers that you have just bought at the market this afternoon. The interesting problem that we faced designing this, perhaps similar to the problem facing the Bluetooth designers, is that you've got an enormous variety of devices from server grade PCs at one end to $5 speaker at the other end. Some have got no decent input, some have got no decent output, some don't have very much of either, and you've got all sorts of CPUs from Peanuts up to Pentium. So how does one go about designing this? Well the first thing to do is

---

[3] On the security of digital tachographs, Ross Anderson, In Computer Security — ESORICS 98, LNCS 1485, pp 111–125.

to understand your requirements, and 99% of users of something like HomePlug are not interested in security, just dependability.

The typical thing that goes wrong with HomePlug, because there were previous versions of it that used lower bandwidths and that we could learn from, is that somebody comes back from the market with their new electronics purchase, and if you've ever been in a Far Eastern city, Tokyo, Seoul, wherever, you see lots of people live in big apartment blocks, so you might have 20 stories of four apartments all off the same mains feed, so you've got 80 families, you plug in your new loudspeakers, you turn them on, and they go and mate with the hifi three stories up. So that's the principal engineering problem that you've got to stop. The other engineering problem that you have to stop is that your networks become too large, with large numbers of nodes relaying to other nodes, with many of the nodes being out of direct communication with your network controller, and this brings your virtual network to a stop because the complexity and manageability of it go downhill.

So usability is critical, network manageability is critical, and what kills you from the market point of view is too many returned devices, because if something doesn't work that you bought for $5 you take it back to the shop. So the big question was, do we use public key crypto? The thing that persuaded us not to use public key crypto is, suppose you have got one of the cases where you actually want security, not just dependability. Suppose you're a patent attorney and you're working on a billion dollar drug patent at home, and Markus comes along in his grey van and parks outside your house, he observes that you have got a Phillips set-top box, so he has brought with him a Phillips set-top box that has been trojaned, that has the probes attached to the bus, and he gets ready to attach that to your mains. He then gets his microwave set and beams high energy at your set-top box causing it to malfunction. The patent attorney who is sitting there watching football on the TV says, oh bother, goes to the PC that he uses as his network management station, and he sees it says, found Phillips set-top box with certificate ID blah, admit/deny, guess what he's going to do.

The relevant result here from security usability is that you don't want people to agree with a comparison of a certificate, you want them to copy it, that's the only thing that works in this kind of scenario. So you need to get the attorney to go and look at the label on the back of his set-top box and copy the certificate ID into his network management station. Without that you can't have a secure system. But if he has to do that then why are you messing around with public key gubbins? So in the end we decided to just print the AES key on the back of the device, on the device label, which enormously simplifies everything, and that's why HomePlug is now deployed as only two mode, secure and simple connect. Simple connect just sends a clear key on power-up, and the protocol's moderately hard for people to make an unauthorised implementation of, so for most practical purposes a bootstrap key in the protocol isn't a big deal. For secure mode you copy the AES key from the device. Is this not optimal, is this not a good example of where the protocol design process logically comes to a stop, with a simple robust way of doing things?

So there's three examples of key setup or equivalent in peer-to-peer or ad hoc networking systems where we're trying not to be involved with all the gubbins of PKI and so on.

I thought I'd mention in passing a paper that George and I wrote in 2005[4] where we started looking at the various peer-to-peer systems that had been deployed, and we came to the conclusion that basically peer-to-peer systems that had been designed by academic type people, like Eternity, Mojo Nation and Ocean Store and so on, didn't work — in the sense that they weren't widely deployed — because everybody shared everything, whereas the systems that prevailed in the market place had people sharing only their own stuff, Gnutella, Kazaa, and so on. So we did a model of this which said basically that people care about their own stuff, they fight hard to defend what they care about, if you have somebody who is campaigning against scientology, you won't fight very hard for the rights of people in Tennessee to view spanking videos. So past a certain level of attack you expect that the world will fragment into domains, and we can model that.

James Malcolm: Aren't these popular systems targeted onto a particular kind of media as well, so they tend to be, for example, only entertainment media?

Reply: There are all sorts of ways in which markets get fragmented, yes. That's worth bearing in mind as we come to the economic argument in a slide or so's time. The final thing by way of an example is industrial control systems, which Shailendra Fuloria and I have been looking at recently. This is one of the places in which ad hoc radio networks are being deployed. A number of firms sell what they call, lick-em/stick-em, sensors, and the idea is that if you've got an oil refinery and you decide that you would like to measure the temperature in a particular reactor vessel, you can buy one of their sensors, and you just stick it on the tank, and these sensors will then set up their own ad hoc network and relay stuff back to your control centre, so you don't have to mess around digging the ground up and putting cables in, and so on. The interesting thing is that although this cuts your initial deployment costs, the view that's starting to come out of the industry is that these things are very much a mixed blessing because the total lifecycle cost isn't necessarily cut. What you save on the initial cabling, you lose on configuration management, plus having to run around and change batteries and stuff. Also, where you allow people to deploy stuff in an ad hoc way, this may open up vulnerabilities, because if you connect industrial control systems that have got no internal authentication somehow to the internet, that's bad news, so perimeterisation is important, and lick-em/stick-em deployments are the enemy of managing perimeters. This is another data point which says that these sort of things are more complex than they look.

Anyway, to the beginnings of my conclusions. Trust, as Bob Morris taught us, is the ability to do harm. We may naively think that a trusted system is one that we feel all warm and gooey about, but you can't reason about that.

---

[4] The economics of resisting censorship, George Danezis and Ross Anderson, IEEE Security & Privacy 3(1), 2005, pp 45–50.

An equivalent formulation says that a trusted system or component is one that can break your security policy, and that we can reason about, so we prefer to use it. And if we're talking about brief encounters, then the big question is, why should you trust the principal with whom you have a brief encounter. It doesn't make sense does it? Now the ad hoc mechanisms that we've talked about have I think brought out the lesson that you're either dealing with trust that's been established exogenously, that is by some external mechanism, physical contact, or else trust that's established over time using tit-for-tat or social institutions, that's what happens when you've got a reputation system arising out of the operation of a peer-to-peer network. And if you don't have trust established in either way, will you hand over goods to a stranger? Well you can hand over goods in return for other goods, or goods in return for services. For example, Samuel Pepys saying to the lady of the night, well how's about it then dearie, and she says, that's half a crown squire. So transactions of a transient nature happen in real life, but there there is a good or a service on either side to actually be transacted. Now it is, as we know from the failure of DRM, it is somewhat difficult to have goods that can be transacted by purely digital devices. Services of course can be transacted, you could give a device some network connectivity perhaps in return for the use of some storage for a while, but then that brings us to the other problem with Mr Pepys encounter with the lady of the night, syphilis. Do you have some kind of social network transmittable ailment that you have to worry about in the digital domain? As you may recall, we had a paper come out at the weekend on social malware, so there are some issues there as well[5].

What's transient? As we try and deconstruct the thing further, we come to the conclusion that membership of a peer-to-peer system isn't properly a transient transaction, you join a network and you want to build up a reputation. Ducklings don't really give you a view into transience because a tachograph will be mated with the same gearbox sensor (you hope) for many years. Consumer electronics, the same story applies: if you go to the mall and come back with a pair of loudspeakers, you presumably hope that they will keep on working for five or ten years. Transferring a tune from A to B if DRM had worked, well maybe you could have a transaction whereby I give you this tune, and you in return give me back that tune, but as well all know now, that's not how the world has turned out to work. What about paying $1.50 for parking? Well here, in effect, the sensor, the payment card is acting as the source of trust, and of course people of a libertarian bent will greatly prefer the idea that trust in the future is largely mediated by payment rather than by identity. The culture of, that will be $1.50 mate, is an awful lot more easy on the British philosophy and way of life than the, Ausweis, bitte[6] culture that we have on the continent.

---

[5] The snooping dragon: social-malware surveillance of the Tibetan movement, Shishir Nagaraja and Ross Anderson, http://www.cl.cam.ac.uk/techreports/ UCAM-CL-TR-746.pdf, University of Cambridge Computer Laboratory TR-746, March 2009.

[6] Your papers, please.

But, as I think about these things, I'm afraid that I suspect that as society becomes fluid, and poses more transient associations, that's going to mean more protocol runs of one kind or another, whether identification protocols run with Google or Microsoft, or whoever, or payment protocols run with some kind of banking system, or shadow banking system, even if that is a reputation system on a peer-to-peer network. This has been flagged up for a long time. Lord Blackstone who wrote memorably about English law 200 odd years ago described the evolution of the law as a long march from status to contract. Perhaps we can see a more fluid and authenticated society as being merely the latest phase of this.

So how should we analyse this? I suppose the first thing to ask is, how long should security associations last? Don't be misled by the apparently transient nature of the establishment of some association. Ask who's guaranteeing what to whom. As Lenin said, when talking about power, the two questions you have to ask are, who and whom. And sometimes these things can be deceptive. Knowing someone's name, and thereby being able to tarnish their reputation, may be thought by the proponents of ID cards to be exactly what's needed. Well the people who gave their money to Mr Madoff knew his name, and they're now able to tarnish his reputation all they wish, but it doesn't give them their money back. So having pointed these things out, I would say that the big problem when talking about secure transient associations is to unpack that phrase and ask what in a particular application it really means.

Paul Syverson: There's lots of anonymous credential protocols, but as you were saying, there is something, it's not really exogenous, you set up an association in some way, but then you sort of guarantee some property is behind the whole thing. I did some stuff many years ago on linkable serial transactions in which you set up a subscription to something, but then any given transaction can't be linked to any other one, and so is in some sense transient, but you have some assurances specific behind it somehow.

Reply: Perhaps a good example of this is that in Britain once you are over 65, you can get a pass which entitles you to concessionary travel, free off-peak bus travel and stuff like that. In some parts of the UK this is truly anonymous in that you get a pass that simply has got your photograph and a number, and this enables the bus company to claim some government money. But there is perpetual pressure to associate this with names for marketing purposes, and to put more applications on the card, and what will probably happen in many parts of the country is that you will end up putting money on your bus pass and as soon as you refill it from your ATM card they'll know who you are.

Paul Syverson: There's also the issue of which identity you give up. I only make purchases online because my credit card company offers me single use credit card numbers. Now it's true that there's persistent vendors, but I go some place, I've never seen this guy before, and I'm not really worried much about the value of the transaction, I don't buy expensive things, and with a cheap thing, if I get ripped off, I don't know if I'll even pursue it, it's a risk I accept on the transaction. But what I'd really be worried about is if this complete stranger has my credit card number, and now I don't have to worry about that. So they know my name, but the credit card number would be the thing I really care about, and they don't have that.

Reply: I suppose this is contextual recourse. You go to the market stall and the chap there is selling bananas, right, and you take out your 50p piece and you pick up a banana, and you suddenly turn and run away. So the guy on the stall runs after you, and the policeman runs after you[7], and the probabilities of that are such that you only very rarely see people stealing food and running for it. I've seen it once in south London, I saw a couple of kids running off with fish and chips, but it's rare enough that the contextual guarantees kind of work. Now the problem is that in an online transaction you can't suddenly run after them.

Paul Syverson: Right, but I don't have to worry about actually protecting the transaction itself in the sense that I'm accepting that there's a moderate amount of risk that I will just lose on this transaction. It's not that I won't get the goods for what I paid, but that they will also have the credit card number, and that's what I'm trying to protect. I'm only willing to do the transaction because in fact it has been guaranteed in a sense to be transient.

Reply: I think you're actually willing to do the transaction because in America, thanks to Regulation E, your credit card company stands behind it.

Paul Syverson: No, because I'd never give them my persistent credit card number, I only give them a single use number. So it's because it's guaranteed to be transient that I'm willing to do it.

Ben Laurie: It's not really a two party thing then, I mean, you have a third party with whom you have a long-term relationship.

Paul Syverson: Absolutely, and I give them my name and those things, but I'm just saying that there is a guarantee of transience that's part of the transaction.

Ben Laurie: But it's relaying on a trusted third party.

Paul Syverson: Yes, absolutely.

Dusko Pavlovic: It seems to me that what you're saying is that what is transient is not only the content of the transaction but the notion of identity, and you don't care whether they have your name, your identity, and your transient identity in this case is your single use credit card number. So we're not just redefining associations, but actually the principals.

George Danezis: There is a lot of sociology that talks about the value of the weak tie, it started with the paper the kindness of strangers[8]. I think that our security world doesn't really support very well this idea that most people, if you

---

[7] And then your accomplices steal the remaining bananas ...

[8] The Kindness of Strangers: The Usefulness of Electronic Weak Ties for Technical Advice, David Constant, Lee Sproull and Sara Kiesler, doi: 10.1287/orsc.7.2.119 Organization Science vol. 7 no. 2 March/April 1996 pp 119–135.

actually sample them at random, are not going to try to attack you, and if you grab five of them and put them in a room then they won't all kill you together, and all that stuff. I think the fundamental question that poses is how well we can port that to assuring the quality of our interactions online, because if we cannot have these weak ties, it means that we cannot actually bootstrap strong ties unless we are doing it in very institutionalised ways, which is not very good, it creates social certification and all that stuff.

Reply: Well there's another aspect of that, which is I think almost never modelled in the protocols community, which is the means whereby principals are selected. We always take Alice, Bob and Charlie as a given, but how do you instruct your kids, or your grand kids, for example, how they should go about seeking help from a grownup if they get lost sometime. The obvious advice to give them is that if a grownup seeks you out and offers you help, scarper, but if you need help it's perfectly OK to approach a randomly selected grownup. Now we've got nothing in the digital world that comes close, as far as I am aware, to modelling that.

George Danezis: Right, Nikita Borisov actually has a very weird protocol that allows you to do secure random sampling in a peer-to-peer network in such a way that a Sybil attack, for example, cannot skew your probability of finding someone honest[9], even if they introduce a lot of bad nodes swapping at random and giving a higher probability of getting a bad node.

Reply: I presume for a protocol like that to work you have to have some pre-existing list of nodes that were thought to be honest at time t minus one, whereas one of the properties you have of the real world is that human beings can't do Sybil attacks. Therefore if the proportion of dangerous persons in society is 1 in 10,000, then a random selection of physically existing adults in a random street will with high probability give you a trustworthy one.

Paul Syverson: In the digital world it seems that it's also much easier, not just to multiply the identities, but also to choose. If there was a place where people tended to go and ask help from strangers, clever criminals would start to hang out there because it was statistically a useful thing to be solicited, maybe in a tourist location where people tend to ask strangers to take their photographs, could you take my picture in Trafalgar Square, or something, well maybe it's a good thing to stand around there waiting to acquire a camera. Although this doesn't happen so much in the physical world, I suspect online it's much more easy to figure out where people are going to gravitate, you know, probably

---

9 Prateek Mittal, Nikita Borisov: ShadowWalker: peer-to-peer anonymous communication using redundant structured topologies. ACM Conference on Computer and Communications Security 2009: 161-172; and in a classical time-travel paradox, Qiyan Wang, Prateek Mittal, Nikita Borisov: In search of an anonymous and secure lookup: attacks on structured peer-to-peer anonymous communication systems. ACM Conference on Computer and Communications Security 2010: 308-318.

something on Facebook, and then it's easier to figure out where to sit in this space to capitalise on the opportunity.

Reply: So what you're saying is that secure transient associations, whatever they mean or don't mean, are harder online than offline?

Paul Syverson: Because, for example, the thing you were saying about telling your child, I think that's also contextual with neighbourhood, in certain areas I don't want you going up to a random stranger because my guess is the average random stranger is not good, you want to get the heck out of that neighbourhood, and in other places it's fine, in most places hopefully. At least in the physical world you could look around and have a sense of the neighbourhood, but it's easy to set up a website that looks just like a bank, so how can you distinguish online neighbourhoods where trust is reasonable and where it isn't?

Reply: I suppose this is what Facebook is about, it's about forging the impression of a good neighbourhood.

Paul Syverson: Yes, exactly.

Jonathan Anderson: There are other contexts where you might find similar properties to the online world, there are occasionally these stories of a bunch of police all trying to arrest each other because they've all infiltrated the same child porn line or whatever, and presumably in certain criminal contexts, if you pick a random sample it could very well be that you're really nervous about whether or not this guy is going to be an informant or an undercover cop, so we might be able to learn simply by looking at those situations.

Joseph Bonneau: Paul's comment about being able to establish if you're in a good neighbourhood online, I mean, people actually do establish their trust based on how professional the website looks. But I think the assumption that it's easy to replicate a bank website, everybody throws that up, but they never do it, phishing websites are almost always terrible, and have typos, and they never look like the real thing.

Paul Syverson: Well this is something Bob Morris also has pointed out many times, that you don't realise how low the threshold is. It's easy to do, but they don't have to bother with even that level of effort because it works just fine without anything.

Sandy Clark: I think one of the important differences is that the digital world gives you the opportunity to set up your own neighbourhood, you don't have that in the physical world. So all you really have to do is watch trends, where people are looking, what they are interested in, how do I mimic that, there's just no easy way for me to go and buy up some real estate and creating this neighbourhood that people are going to go visit so I can take advantage of.

Bruce Christianson: That's called Second Life.

Reply: A lot of what we do with technology is simply enabling ordinary people to do what, in the 18th Century only the upper middle classes and above could do. Many of the things that we have perform the functions of servants, a car performs the function of a stagecoach, four horses, a coach, a groom, and so on, and it even does it better. Similarly, a word processor and email performs much the same function that a secretary used to do. Now you can use social networking software to do the functions that you would have done in the 18th Century by setting up a club, buying a nice house in St James', inviting a 100 of your friends to become members, and having some rules, and guys in uniform, and stuff. You can do that all in an afternoon online, isn't it great. How many of you have done it?

Paul Syverson: I also think there might be a point to be made here about how in different online scenarios, creating a new identity is much harder sometimes, and I think that makes a big difference. In the Facebook world the one thing that they do well is, when they do ban people they crack down hard on them: if they ban Ross Anderson from Cambridge, they will not let you rejoin with that same name and location, which makes the threat of being punished for something a lot higher, which is like it works in the real world.

Joseph Bonneau: Actually how do they do that, because I could imagine there's another Ross Anderson walking around Cambridge somewhere, and he just can't log in.

Reply: They don't care.

Joseph Bonneau: Yes, then they get complaints that they ignore, but ...

Sandy Clark: There's a recent example, because Kevin Mitnik could not get access to his own Facebook account because they wouldn't believe that he was Kevin Mitnik.

Reply: Well they're using unsocial embedding. It's less attractive for me, if I was banned from Facebook, to go back again as John Smith from Cambridge, because people would say, why are you John Smith, and I'd say, well because I'm a security guy, and they'd say, oh yes well.

Joseph Bonneau: I was talking to a Facebook security guy on Tuesday, he said their number one goal of their entire security team is to make sure that the mapping between the Facebook account and the person is one to one and it's your real name on Facebook representing you, because they bought into the notion that that's what they need to have Facebook be reasonably secure and support social protocols that exist in the real world.

Reply: So basically they're trying to achieve the same policy goals as the government's national identity register but using perhaps slightly better engineered software to do it.

Joseph Bonneau: No, it's not that well engineered.

Reply: I said slightly better engineering.

Luke Church: It's a pretty naïve view of social identity though. The whole of the faceted identity crowd would have us believe that if it's going to be a social platform as opposed to something that's to do with physical atoms that make up me, like the government care about, seemingly, then that's a pretty odd thing to attempt to achieve.

Joseph Bonneau: So you're saying it's desirable that people should be able to have different identities?

Luke Church: Sure, I mean, I have a different identity to you folks than I do to my family.

George Danezis: I think that it is not a different reality, in that you still have a unique identifier, namely your face, and when people from your different circles meet together probably they will start chatting about the different sides of your personality, which might be totally inappropriate for someone from your family and someone from your work

Luke Church: That meets more of the behaviour according to standard social norms.

George Danezis: Exactly, but this is not achieved by you wearing different masks physically when you meet different people so that they cannot physically link you, right?

Luke Church: No.

George Danezis: So Facebook can actually have a model like that. I don't advocate it, but it could have a model like that.

Luke Church: Sure, so I can present this aspect of myself to just these people.

George Danezis: And you just show different types of your profile but your name is the same.

Luke Church: In a fairly naïve way, yes.

Joseph Bonneau: Nobody does it but that they do have that functionality.

Matt Blaze: One thing that makes the online world more difficult here is that if we want to rely on social protocols to do this, there's not only the problem that you can create arbitrarily many identities, but that you can steal other people's identities. The equivalent of phishing and botnets doesn't exist in the real world in anywhere near the same way, nobody can actually take over my body and start behaving like me the way they can do it with my computers.

Reply: Don't go to Haiti then.

Matt Blaze: So we've got this problem from both ends, right, I can set up completely artificial, synthetic identities, and existing identities can be highjacked.

Reply: Well there's certainly a role for artificial identities, and many roles in fact, including professional roles. Perhaps our blog would be more successful if instead of calling it Light Blue Touchpaper we'd called it Giles Murchison's blog. Giles Murchison was a virtual person that various mathematicians and computer scientists used at various times over the last 30 years[10], perhaps the illusion of personality would be a good marketing thing. This laptop for example, is used 60% of the time by my wife, about 10% of the time by me, about 20% of the time by my daughter, and 10% of the time by my grandson, so Google may think it knows everything about everybody, but the body about which they know everything is not uniquely mapped to one particular individual. And I find it difficult to think that that is a bad thing.

George Danezis: There is a very nice argument against this, there is the physical identity which is your face, in the electronic world it's dubious whether that's the case. For instance there is an identity which is a complex combination of several different identities.

Paul Syverson: That's a composite person right there.

Reply: As security guys we've always known about compound roles and so on, maybe these roles may in time start to proliferate in the real world. They've existed in many fields, Her Majesty's Ambassador to France is a role that's inhabited by successive individuals, as is the Officer of the Watch on a warship. We've never had any difficulty socially with dealing with such roles.

Paul Syverson: Is this really the same thing? To the extent that this laptop is this composite thing, it's not so much a role, I mean, it actually is a reflection of you, and your wife, and your daughter, and your grandson.

Reply: In terms of syntax I am the Officer of the Watch of the kitchen laptop, but in terms of semantics, the social semantics, it's somewhat different.

---

[10] Probably best known for his classic "The Design and Implementation of an Operating System to Support Distributed Multimedia Applications". Contact: gsm10@cl.cam.ac.uk

Qualitative Analysis for Trust Management
Towards a Model of Photograph Sharing Indiscretion

Simon N. Foley[1] and Vivien M. Rooney[2]

[1] Department of Computer Science, University College Cork, Ireland
s.foley@cs.ucc.ie
[2] School of Applied Psychology, University College, Cork, Ireland
vivrooney@gmail.com

Abstract. Grounded Theory provides a useful approach for eliciting and justifying subjective characteristics of individuals. A Grounded Theory analysis is carried out on individuals who share pictures, with a view to developing a trust management policy model of indiscretion regarding the sharing of photographs.

1 Introduction

Psychologists, taking a social constructionist perspective, argue that *identity* is derived from recognizing, classifying, understanding, judging and otherwise conceiving and thinking about selfhood [25]. These are what characterize the individual and make them who they are.

From a Trust Management perspective [3], identity is regarded more in terms of determining some unique identifier for the individual than necessarily characterizing who they are. While schemes such as X509 [5] or SDSI [7] may provide identifier/naming frameworks for principals (including individuals), authorization attributes [3, 7] provide characteristics that further define the principal. Authorization attributes tend to be specified in terms of artifacts from the system with which the individual interacts. For example, their role, their clearance, their identification and the actions that they may engage, within an organization. They characterize the individual in terms of what they may do, and do not usually consider who they are, in the psychological sense.

We are interested in developing trust management schemes that better reflect the psychological identity of the individual. For the purposes of this paper, the problem is considered from the perspective of the electronic sharing of photographs. A conventional security/trust management approach might consider photograph sharing in terms of security artifacts such as access-control lists and group attributes (friends, acquaintances, etc.). However, in reality, decision making around picture sharing is based on a much richer set of characteristics which form part of the individual's identity. For example, in our study we found that some people can be quite indiscreet, arbitrarily disseminating personally meaningful photographs if they believed that they could not be identified as the originator. In addition to indiscretion, many other characteristics are possible

B. Christianson et al. (Eds.): Security Protocols 2009, LNCS 7028, pp. 298–307, 2013.

for an individual when it comes to sharing photographs. Identity tends to be subjective and the challenge is to devise a reliable method whereby relevant characteristics of the individual can be systematically elicited and justified for the problem domain.

Reputation schemes [15] could be thought of as providing a simple characteristics of the self. For example, Slashdot *Karma* gives an indicator of the individual's standing in that message board community. While apparently informative, it is unclear whether the subjective Karma attribute is actually a reliable indicator of how individuals see themselves within this community. Computing research on reputation metrics has tended to focus more on algorithmic and technical issues and not any systematic methodology for determining and justifying the attributes that make up the reputation.

While much has been published on the psychology of trust [22,26], this paper focusses on one basic form of trust, that is *well placed trust* [23], which regards trust in terms of relatively static attributes that are perceived by a trusting party. We argue that Trust Management is consistent with this view, whereby the static attributes of well placed trust coincide with the attributes and conditions that form the trust management policy.

The Trust Management literature provides plenty of examples that can be regarded as well placed trust policies, such as role-based policies [2, 17] and policies for specific applications, for example, using KeyNote in the Apache web server. However, a systematic methodology for eliciting trust policies has not been considered. Research on Trust Management and reputation metrics has tended to focus more on modeling, algorithmic and technical issues and not specifically on eliciting the attributes and conditions that form the policy.

We argue that Grounded Theory analysis [6] of semi-structured interviews can provide a methodological basis for eliciting attributes about identity when developing trust management policies. Grounded Theory is a qualitative research method commonly used in psychology for generating theory demonstrably grounded in data. A frequent application of Grounded Theory is in the area of health research. It has also been used to help elicit requirements in Software Engineering [24] and Compliance [4]. In the security domain, for example [1,9,11,20], Grounded Theory has been been used to help understand user behavior as part of better security (system) design, but not specifically for the derivation of trust management policies which is the subject of this paper.

The remainder of the paper is organized as follows. Section 2 provides an overview on the use of Grounded Theory for qualitative analysis. A Grounded Theory analysis was carried out on photograph sharing and some of its results are discussed in Section 3. This analysis was used to identify and justify attributes related to the issue of photograph sharing and Section 4 develops a trust model based on a number of these attributes.

2   Qualitative Analysis Using Grounded Theory

When experience with technology is confined to a particular perspective, for example, one restricted to a scientific mode of discourse, the result is partial, needing to be complemented by others [21]. Experiences with technology involve emotions, values and ideals, however, these aspects are neglected because they are considered too subjective [18]. Subjectivity, we are taught, is problematic because it undermines rationality. The Western tradition of scientific research values rationality, along with the comforting notion that a truth exists, one that is immune to interpretation, instead being detached, objective and unchanging [10]. Furthermore, from a rationalist point of view, users of technology are unlikely to experience resistance, doubt, ambiguity and suffering [18]. Among the aspects of user experience that need to be included when we consider experiences with technology are affective responses, concerning purpose, aspiration and relationships.

One difficulty in approaching the affective and subjective components of experiences is their complexity. Methodologically, the convenience of many methods lies in the results produced. Hence, the attraction of means of inquiry such as questionnaires, where results are obtained quickly and in a form readily adaptable to the requirements of designers. However, if we approach user experience in an holistic manner, the complexity and fluidity of our behaviour necessitates methods of inquiry that are correspondingly complex and fluid [13]. Qualitative methods of inquiry are ideal for such purposes, having the capacity to accommodate such requirements, as well as seeking to include the contextual and personal meaning of data.

The research method of Grounded Theory (GT) was first described by Glaser and Strauss in 1967 [12], since then it has evolved, and the constructivist approach to the method, as described by [6] was used for this paper. A feature of GT is the systematic procedures applied to the data, for example, those of constant comparison and coding. These ensure theoretical development that is both valid and reliable. Similarly, the use of written memos explicates the process of labelling and categorisation. Thus the emergent theory is demonstrably grounded in the data. Formulating a theory in advance of data analysis could lead to the imposition of a framework, thereby influencing both process and outcome. While the GT analytic process seeks to identify patterns in human experience, the subjective voices of participants - the meaning of experience for them - is retained. GT is particularly appropriate where participants are likely to produce a reflective account [19], and is therefore suitable to the study of photograph sharing, where personal significance is likely to be attached to the material. The theory that emerges does so as a result of a prolonged and intense engagement with the data, using the GT techniques.

3   Analysis of Photograph Sharing

This research began with a question concerning photograph sharing. The approach to addressing this question sought to understand how people made sense of sharing photographs. Thus semi-structured interviews were considered to be the most appropriate approach to gaining an insight into the individual's perspective. The semi-structured interview allows space for the exploration of participant experiences. Rather than a structured interview or questionnaire being used, the semi-structured interview facilitates a dialogue between the researcher and participant [16]. This approach seeks to lessen the weight of preconceived ideas concerning the content of the interview, instead allowing the dialogue to unfold, and as it does so, to take unexpected directions, thereby facilitating the exploration of individual experiences.

Seven interviews were audio recorded (duration: three hours and fifty minutes) and transcribed in their entirety (the text forming a document of just over thirty-six thousand words). The transcribed material was coded line by line. This analytic technique aimed at capturing the process taking place in the data, as described by the participant.

The initial coding sought to capture the meaning, or the phenomena, summarizing the actions therein, in light of the research question. This process accounted for each piece of data, with a view to the development of categories. Throughout this process the technique of constant comparison was used to compare segments of data and their assigned codes, with other data and codes. The purpose in doing so is to ensure that the labeling was proceeding in a valid manner. Initial coding is provisional, and subject to change as the process of constant comparison indicates nuanced relabeling of data, as the process develops iteratively.

The validity of the emergent theory relies on the painstaking nature of the coding as well as its transparency, for which memos provide an audit trail. Memo writing continued throughout the process of analysis, explicating, inter alia, initial ideas and possible categories. During the subsequent phase of focused coding, theoretical integration began: the initial codes were sorted and integrated, and from this synthesis of the codes, an abstract understanding of photograph sharing emerged. This process is iterative and carried out in tandem with memo writing as the conceptual framework is developed. Conceptual integration of the categories gave rise to theoretical development, suggesting relationships between the identified categories. For the purposes of illustration, the appendix provides short extracts from two interviews conducted as part of the study on photograph sharing.

In the attempt to understand experience from the perspective of the individual, then, there is a focus on their unique way of making sense of a phenomena. Using GT methods gives an opportunity to delve into this way of making sense. Rather than making a claim to be definitive in its scope, the validity of what emerges lies in the explication of the method used and the conclusions reached, ensuring transparency such that a reader can follow the steps taken, understanding them in the context of the research. Along with this committment to transparency and reflexivity, participants are the focus. In this research, their experience, imbued with values, ideals and aspirations, as played out against the background of photograph sharing, was elucidated.

4   A Qualitative Model of Sharing Indiscretion

In this section we explore the use of Grounded Theory analysis as the basis for an approach to eliciting a trust management policy for photograph sharing.

Our intention is not to provide an exhaustive model that considers all aspects of photograph sharing, rather it is to explore how grounded theory could be used to help elicit trust management policies. For the purposes of this paper, we consider just one aspect of picture sharing: a model of the potential for indiscretion when sharing photographs that might be considered sensitive and/or personally meaningful.

4.1   An Exploratory Approach

The Grounded Theory analysis (Section 3 and Appendix A) identified a range of categories that provide understanding for the meaning of photograph sharing for a selection of individuals from a user-population. These categories provide the attributes in terms of which a general trust management policy model for the broader user-population is constructed. These categories/attributes are treated as discrete probabilistic variables, representing the probability of their occurrence with respect to an entity of interest. For example, the probability that a particular photograph contains a child, the probability that a particular individual is deceitful, the probability that the holder is willing to share a photograph.

Interdependencies between categories/attributes can be identified as part of the Grounded Theory analysis. For example, an individual's willingness to share a photograph may be based on whether they own the photograph, how personally meaningful the photograph is to them and their own inclination for deceit, etc. This gives rise to a network of dependencies between attributes which, for ease of exposition in this paper we chose to encode in terms of a Bayesian Network. This provides a model of the knowledge about the domain elicited during the Grounded Theory analysis. Similar model building strategies have been used in the social and health sciences; for example, [8]

4.2   Deciding Whether to Share a Photograph

A person (the holder) in possession of a photograph makes a decision on whether and how to share a photograph. As the holder of the photograph, the individual has the ability to share the photograph regardless. The Trust Management question is one of how indiscreet would it be to share the photograph. This question is cast based on the attribute/category information available on the entities involved: the holder of the photograph, the recipient, the subject in the photograph and the photograph itself.

The Influence Diagram [14] in Figure 1 provides an abstract model for indiscretion over the sharing of photographs.

Probability variable personallyMeaningful represents the likelihood that the photograph has some personal meaning for the holder. For example, the more personally meaningful then the less likely that the holder will widely share the photograph. In practice, a holder also has her own personal value system regarding photograph sharing which can influence her sharing decisions. The variable jurisdiction provides the holder's belief on whether the photograph could be shared.

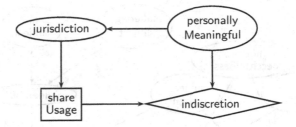

Fig. 1. Abstract model of photograph sharing indiscretion

Decision variable shareUsage represents the possible photograph sharing decisions that can be made by the holder. Note that if holder chooses, she can decide to share the photograph in a manner that is at variance to her own jurisdiction on the photograph. Utility function indiscretion indicates the extent to which the holder's usage of a photograph is careless. It is a function indiscretion : personallyMeaningful × shareUsage → $\Re$ for which we defined, in an ad-hoc manner, intuitive weights. For example, deciding to share a personally meaningful photograph with a wide audience indicates a high degree of indiscretion, while privately sharing a photograph that is not likely to be personally meaningful indicates a low level of indiscretion.

4.3   Indiscretion in Unconstrained Sharing

For the purpose of presentation, we consider unconstrained photograph sharing, that is, in deciding whether to share, the individual does not consider the identity of the recipient, other than whether the photograph is to be made public, shared privately, or not at all. Thus, the (shareUsage) decisions are none, private and public.

The Trust Management question is *how indiscreet is individual when deciding to share a photograph with some subject*, whereby,

- the photograph subject is characterized in terms of attributes: has given consent (to share), contains a suffering subject, contains a child subject, is contains candid subject and whether it is a public occasion;
- the photograph holder is characterized in terms of attributes: holder ownership and holder deceitfulness, and
- the holder decides to share according to shareUsage.

These are just some of the categories/attributes elicited during, and can be justified from, the Grounded Theory analysis. As probabilistic variables they may have observed values, for example, a photograph that is explicitly tagged as containing a child subject. Alternatively, the value might be determined from historical or user-profile information. For example, the health worker that tends to have photographs of suffering subjects, or a reputation metric that is used to score user deceit. In this paper we are not directly concerned with techniques for determining these values, rather, we are interested in how the attributes themselves are elicited and their use justified.

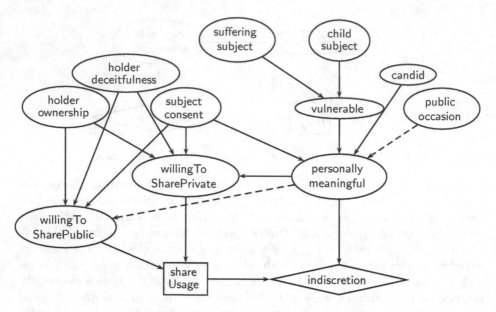

Fig. 2. Decisions about unconstrained sharing

Figure 2 provides an example of the sharing model constructed in terms of these attributes related to unconstrained sharing. Dependencies between attributes were identified qualitatively during the Grounded Theory analysis. Rather than requiring conditional probabilities to be (tediously) enumerated, dependencies were represented in terms of positive (solid line) or negative (dashed line) influences in the direction of the arc connecting attributes. These give rise to simple weightings that can be used to compute the conditional probabilities: a simple Qualitative Bayesian Network [27].

For example, the probability that a photograph is personally meaningful is directly proportional to the probability that its subject is candid, while it is indirectly proportional to the probability that it reflects a public occasion. While convenient for this paper, this approach can lead to a somewhat coarse-grained interpretation for the conditional probabilities, which could be manually adjusted by the analyst. In practice, it would be more effective to use all of the qualitative operators in [27] and/or to use machine learning over the attribute/category data sets in order to build a more precise model. This is a topic for future research.

5   Conclusion

In this paper we outlined how Grounded Theory can provide a useful approach for eliciting subjective attributes to be used in trust management policies. These are the attributes that contribute to characterizing the psychological identity of the individual.

One of the advantages of taking a Grounded Theory approach is that it is a transparent process and provides justification for the the theory developed. This theory forms the basis of a trust management policy which we encoded in terms of an Influence Diagram/Bayes Network. We do not consider this work to be limited to using only these model representations and in future research we plan to investigate their encoding into more conventional trust management credentials.

Acknowledgments. This research has been supported by Science Foundation Ireland grant 08/SRC/11403 and by the Irish Research Council for the Humanities and Social Sciences.

References

1. Adams, A., Sasse, M.A.: Users are not the enemy. Commun. ACM 42(12), 40–46 (1999)
2. Becker, M., Fournet, C., Gordon, A.: Design and semantics of a decentralized authorization language. In: 20th IEEE Computer Security Foundations Symposium (January 2007)
3. Blaze, M., Feigenbaum, J., Lacy, J.: Decentralized trust management. In: SP 1996: Symp. on Security and Privacy, p. 164. IEEE Computer Society (1996)
4. Breaux, T., Antón, A.: Analyzing regulatory rules for privacy and security requirements. IEEE Transactions on Software Engineering 34(1), 5–20 (2008)
5. CCITT Draft Recommendation. The Directory Authentication Framework, Version 7 (November 1987)
6. Charmaz, K.: Constructing Grounded Theory. Sage Publications, London (2006)
7. Clarke, D., Elien, J., Ellison, C., Fredette, M., Morcos, A., Rivest, R.L.: Certificate chain discovery in spki/sdsi. Journal of Computer Security 9(4), 285–322 (2001)
8. Daniel, B.K., Schwier, R.A.: A Bayesian belief network of a virtual learning community. International Journal of Web-Based Communities 3(2) (2007)
9. Dourish, P., Grinter, E., Delgado de la Flor, J., Joseph, M.: Security in the wild: user strategies for managing security as an everyday, practical problem. Personal Ubiquitous Comput. 8(6), 391–401 (2004)
10. Ellis, C., Bochner, A.P.: Composing ethnography, alternative forms of qualitative writing. Alta Mira Press, California (1996)
11. Flechais, I., Mascolo, C., Sasse, M.A.: Integrating security and usability into the requirements and design process. Int. J. Electron. Secur. Digit. Forensic 1(1), 12–26 (2007)
12. Glaser, B.G., Strauss, A.L.: The discovery of grounded theory. Aldine, Chicago (1967)
13. Hammersley, M.: The dilemma of qualitative method: Herbert Blumer and the Chicago tradition. Routledge (1989)
14. Howard, R.A., Matheson, J.E.: Influence diagrams. Decision Analysis 2(3) (September 2005)
15. Jøsang, A., Ismail, R., Boyd, C.: A survey of trust and reputation systems for online service provision. Decis. Support Syst. 43(2), 618–644 (2007)
16. Kvale, S.: InterViews: An Introduction to Qualitative Research Interviewing. Sage Publications, London (1996)

17. Li, J., Li, N., Winsborough, W.: Automated trust negotiation using cryptographic credentials. In: Proceedings of the 12th ACM Conference on Computer and Communications Security (January 2005)
18. McCarthy, J., Wright, P.: Technology as Experience. MIT Press (2004)
19. McQueen, R.A., Knussen, C.: Research Methods in Psychology. Prentice Hall Europe, London (1999)
20. Onabajo, A., Jahnke, J.H.: Properties of confidentiality requirements. In: 19th IEEE Symposium on Computer-Based Medical Systems (2006)
21. Pacey, A.: Meaning in Technology. MIT Press, London (1999)
22. Putnam, R.D., et al.: Making democracy work: Civic traditions in Modern Italy. Princeton University Press (1993)
23. Riegelsberger, J., Sasse, M.A., McCarthy, J.D.: The mechanics of trust: A framework for research and design. Int. J. Hum.-Comput. Stud. 62(3), 381–422 (2005)
24. Seaman, C.B.: Qualitative methods in empirical studies of software engineering. IEEE Trans. on Software Engineering 25(4), 557–572 (1999)
25. Stainton Rogers, R., et al.: Social Psychology: A Critical Agenda. Polity Press, Cambridge (1995)
26. Uslaner, E.M.: The Moral Foundations of Trust. Cambridge University Press, Cambridge (2002)
27. Wellman, M.P.: Fundamental concepts of qualitative probabilistic networks. Artificial Intelligence (44), 257–303 (1990)

A   Sample Coding of Interview Extract

In this extract from his interview, Conor volunteered to show the images on his camera phone. He is talking about a photograph of his friend John that he had taken recently. Names given are not those of the participants.

Interview	Focused Coding
Q: So, would you give that photograph to others, would you share that?	
A: No, I wouldn't send it to anyone, its just on my phone, its just a bit of fun, just kind of taking a photograph of him, it wasn't really a big deal.	reason for taking photos / significance of image
Q: Would you give it to John?	
A: I showed it to him but like you know, we're after a few jars so it didn't really matter like, he was like yeah, OK, whatever, it wasn't like an important photograph I suppose, but its kind of good, he's a good friend of mine.	photos of friends / significance of image / photos of friends

Interview	Focused Coding
Q: Would you give it to me, suppose I wanted to use it in a project or something like that, would you give me a copy of that?	
A: That's a good question, mmmm...	ambivalence
Q: You're thinking about it, what are you thinking about?	
A: I'm thinking, would he find out about it, like if you said it, I'd be like whatever, you know like, but if it was kind of printed on the front page of your project it would be a different story if someone in the class that knows him as well, or whatever, like, so he might be like 'that's a bit weird', so maybe not, no.	image traced to source ambivalence use of images image traced to source empathy
Q: Do you think you'd have to ask him first?	
A: Well, he's kind of an image conscious guy, so you know, he likes to look good and spend a lot of money on clothes, he might think its not the best photo, so I imagine he he might say no as well but having said that I don't think I, well, I know its a bit weird to say this, I wouldn't be in a situation where someone would ask me to do that, I suppose you're suggesting a hypothetical like, but I suppose, no.	empathy empathy social norms
Q: Is there someone else in that photograph behind him?	
A: It's in the bar, I've no idea	public venue
Q: There's another guy there	
A: A blurry guy, yeah, I think these people here behind us, see that guy there on the left, he's the ⟨official⟩, now that I look more closely.	images of bystanders
Q: If I wanted that photograph, but I wanted it because the ⟨official⟩ was in it, would you give it to me then?	
A: It depends for what reason, I suppose, I mean ...	uses of images
Q: Suppose you could get John out of it and it had someone you didn't know in it, would you give it to me then?	
A: Depends if it could be traced back to me, what you're going to do with it, I mean	image traced to source uses of images

Qualitative Analysis for Trust Management
(Transcript of Discussion)

Simon N. Foley

University College Cork

This is joint work between myself and my co-author Vivien Rooney, who's a PhD student in Applied Psychology in Cork. We were looking at the problem of how to come up with trust management polices that could be used to govern how photographs should be shared, not just applications like Facebook, but perhaps even photographs on telephones, whether or not it's OK to share a particular photograph with your friends. So I had this particular photograph here, which is just an example of a photograph from my iPhoto library, and I got to thinking, was it such a good idea to be showing people this particular photograph, I'm effectively sharing this photograph with the audience. Now I own this photograph but I don't know, is it good for me to be sharing it, you know, there's people in this photograph, it looks like it's a public place, but I haven't got anybody's consent for showing you this photograph.

Joseph Bonneau: Your security policy.

Reply: Yes, so when we share photographs between each other there's a whole bunch of different emotions that we consider, and it's not just a simple case of saying, oh I have my friends, and these photographs I'll share with my friends, and these other photographs I share with different people. And this is how we came to this particular problem of, well how do we come up with rules or policies that might govern how we could share our photographs.

Joseph Bonneau: When you say share, do you mean the act of making available, or somebody looking for it, or the act of actively saying, please look at this?

Reply: It could be either, in the particular study that Vivien looked at it was more the act of me saying, here's a photograph, please look at it.

Vivien Rooney: Or if somebody asks for it would you give it to them, would you be happy to do that.

Joseph Bonneau: Alright, but I think those are two different things.

Reply: So as computer security people, when we come to designing security policies, we're always thinking of the technical concerns. Very often our policies are based on artefacts from the computer system or from our business processes, transactions. They tend not to be based or rooted in the individual themselves in terms of how they may feel about allowing something to happen. From a traditional security perspective, we might think of our security policy for photographs

B. Christianson et al. (Eds.): Security Protocols 2009, LNCS 7028, pp. 308–320, 2013.
© Springer-Verlag Berlin Heidelberg 2013

to be something like this: users in category X are permitted access photographs in category Y. But we should really be thinking of the bigger picture where we think of the needs of the individuals and their relationships. One example is multi-lateral security with Kai Rannenberg's example, where somebody wants to make a telephone call to you, and you have your own requirement, which is you don't want to be bothered, but the person making the call has a requirement that they want to offer you some service. And so you have to somehow balance both people's requirements to meet a satisfactory outcome.

When we think of the needs of individuals and their relationships, we're not just talking anymore about tangible things, there's also all of these intangibles like people's reputation. And of course we need to consider things like human issues, so in this photograph here, it's not really just a question of saying, I have an access control list, and I'm going to put these people in the access control list to indicate that I'm willing to share this photograph with them. Really what goes through my mind is something like this: well it is a public setting, it is my own photograph that I took myself, but perhaps I shouldn't because some of them I think work for a government agency and I might be in trouble if I shared it. So there's all these things that I'm thinking about before I, as a person, consider sharing a photograph. But when it comes to writing or devising security policies, or trust management policies, to decide things like this, we often just sideline them, because it's extremely messy and complex to figure out, well how do I enforce this as a policy.

The work that we looked at was how do we start to address this type of issue, the more human side of trust management. And the particular strategy that we took was to interview a small number of people to try and understand their own feelings or perspectives on sharing photographs, and then we used some qualitative research techniques, in particular Grounded Theory Analysis to try and elicit from that the things that were considered important. Then we modelled the result in a Bayesian network. Now for this work it was convenient to model the policy in a Bayesian network, but we're not restricted or saying that it must be a Bayesian network, I'm sure there are many other models that could be used to capture the policy. The interesting thing really is how we do our elicitation of the policy, how do I figure out what's important for these users for this particular problem domain.

So the overview of the talk, I'm going to put things backwards. I'm first of all going to talk to you about the underlying policy model that we devised as a result of doing this qualitative analysis, just so you've got something concrete in your head to think about, and then Vivien will talk to you about the qualitative analysis, the Grounded Theory over semi structured interviews and what that gives us, and then we give an example of the derivation of the policy.

I view the problem as a trust management problem, where we have some principal who wants to know is it safe to do a particular action, we have a policy, there's presumably a PKI, but in this particular paper I ignored that aspect of it, all we really have is just a policy, so it's our standard reference monitor model, and somebody wants to know, I have a photograph, is it safe for me to share that photograph, so my question is this. From the principal's perspective, they're looking at a photograph, and there's a bunch of different characteristics that mean something to them, that they're going to use to decide whether or not they should share, or whether or not it's safe to share this photograph. And that's our policy. And here's a fragment of the policy that we devised, it's a Bayesian net, there's a bunch of attributes which characterise what we considered to be the important things, or at least what the results from the interviews decided were important, so things like whether or not there's a child in the photograph determines whether I'm going to share it, whether or not they're suffering, whether or not the people in the photograph have given me consent, whether or not I own the photograph. And these are effectively the probabilistic variables in the Bayesian net, and then there's the dependencies. And in this case, because I can just share this photograph anyhow because I have physical possession of it, what we're really looking for is some indication of how indiscreet I might be if I was to share this photograph, privately in this case.

In the paper we considered some other ways of sharing the photograph, but here we'll just take the very simple case of privately sharing this photograph. I'm not considering with whom I'm sharing it with, I'm just assuming, OK, so I trust this person in some way. And that's our policy, the basic policy model, the Bayesian net, and the answer from my trust management query is the likelihood that I'd be indiscreet when I share a particular photograph.

Now the individual's, or the principal's, photographs would have profiles which give us some values, or observed values if they're available for the probabilistic variables, so for example in this photograph presumably there wasn't any suffering so you could imagine there would be a tag for the photograph saying, there's no suffering in this photograph. Now of course we don't want to have to require a user to tag every photograph with an indicator as to whether or not there's suffering or a child in it, so perhaps the user, based on past photographs and past tagging, the likelihood that they'd have a photograph containing a child might be 0.4, so in this case why we have an observed value for suffering, in this case the likelihood of it having a child is 0.4, in this case I have no consent from these people to share this photograph, and I own the photograph.

This is the sort of the policy I guess maybe a computer scientist or a security person might devise and say, oh these seem like a reasonable bunch of attributes to build my Bayesian network, but how can I justify this, or where do they even come from in the first place. And that really is the interesting problem, how do we take a particular domain and from that synthesise or devise what's a reasonable and justifiable collection of attributes. And this is the work that Vivien then did when you were interviewing. Do you want to talk about this Vivien?

Vivien Rooney: I did semi structured interviews, the features of those would be that you would engage in a dialogue with the participants (who might be called subjects for some of you), and you would try to understand their perspective, and we tried to engage with them in a way that allowed space for them to explain their own perspective and bring their experiences to the fore in their own language so they can explain to you how their past has come into play and formulated how they see the world, and how they would do picture sharing. In a lot of psychological interviewing there's an emphasis on the psychologist as the expert, and the subject as somebody who's being examined and interrogated, but in semi structured interviewing and in qualitative analysis, you'd be emphasising that the participant is the expert and that you are joining in a dialogue with them to construct an understanding so that you can elicit what their world view is and develop that in their terms.

When you're interviewing in that way you don't have any set of questions, because to approach an interview in that way you might pre-determine what can be discussed or what can be talked about, and you might miss the individual's experience as they describe it in their own language. So then you transcribe the interviews and form a text which can be analysed, and for this particular project we used Grounded Theory analysis. I have an example of it in a minute so I can talk you through how it works. You take your data and summarise what's happening in the data, and try and capture the meaning of it with the research question in mind, and with the view to developing theoretical categories. So that's the first activity. The second activity is focus coding, which is taking you up a level so that you abstract the codes and develop categories from that. And as you're doing this, then you'd have your research question in mind, and you'd be also iteratively comparing your coding to what you've already done, and your previous interviews, and you'd be writing memos to justify that and explain it. The memos, they're like preliminary analytic notes so that somebody who's reading the Grounded Theory analysis afterwards can go back and see what you did and how you did it, and why you came to the conclusions that you did.

After that, based on the categories and your memos, and your synthesising of the categories and ordering them so that you can develop your theory, you develop your theory then based on that entire process. This is an example of one, she's talking, and this is the transcribed interview data here in the centre, and that's what it would look like when you start to code it. On the left here you can see the initial coding, this is the first step in the analysis, so you'd try to capture what's going on in the data here. The next step then is the focus coding, we'd be trying to synthesise and integrate it, so from your initial coding you'd be going to the focus coding here, which is a kind of a high level abstraction, and you'd do that, as I was saying, with the idea of developing your theory, and having the research question in your mind when you're doing that, and also iteratively thinking about what you have done and the process that you're trying to engage in, so as to develop it from the participant's point of view. Then you have theory development, and child, as a category, and then the vulnerability of a variable.

Reply: So the initial coding is getting a sense of what's happening in the text from the interview. And on the right hand side, the focus coding, I guess from a computer scientist's point of view, we think of this as identifying categories, or variables, attributes for our eventual policy. And then from that we're form-ing a theory about what people are thinking, or what they're saying, from the transcript of the semi structured interview. And so you can see that we have some categories here that are considered important, things that are considered important for this particular policy, the fact whether or not the photograph has a child in it, for example. Another issue that's a consideration is vulnerability. So we said, well we have category child and category vulnerability in general, these are our probabilistic variables, and there's a dependency from child to vul-nerability, the more likelihood that there's a child in the photograph, the more likelihood that we could have a vulnerability.

Now we systematically went through the focus coding and effectively drew a graph of generic variables plus the dependency errors between them, we have another example here, this is a more detailed example, and again you can see that we've got our vulnerability, this is an interview with a different subject, and again from the focus coding we identified more variables, in this case we identified a variable about suffering, in this case it was homeless people, but this is just a generic attribute called suffering. So in this case we've got a dependency from suffering to vulnerability, and from vulnerability there to somebody's willingness to share a photograph privately with somebody, and their willingness to share a photograph publicly. Now in this case we've got a dash line just indicating an indirect or opposite dependency, the more likely that the photograph is of somebody vulnerable the less likely you're going to be willing to share in public.

Now the actual construction of the Bayesian nets, if we sit back and look at the model for a second, you can see that in the Bayesian network, I just have these arrows, and so for the conditional probabilities here, I just filled those out in an ad hoc fashion. So I said, look, this is something like a qualitative Bayesian net, and where there's solid arrows it just means that it's a sort of an averaging,that the more likelihood that there's a child in it the more likely it's vulnerable. Wherever there were dashed arrows that means the more likelihood of one led to the less likelihood of the other. So it was quite an ad hoc approach to constructing the network.

In the end our hope is eventually to go from using this sort of ad hoc construc-tion of the Bayesian network to doing something like say a naïve Bayes classifier, which will just take large volumes of the data, and map it to something like this, which would compute the Bayesian network for us, it's the ultimate goal. We only did this on a very small experiment just to see what the process might be like. And again, remember the intention here is to be able to systematically identify the at-tributes for your trust management policy in a justifiable way, and having done the Grounded Theory, it means that every attribute could be justified back to the opinions on some of the actions, or what an individual is willing to do.

Matt Blaze: You looked at the standard trust management model which says, is it safe to do this, is this compliant with my policy if I do this? But in fact you're using it to answer a different question, which is, is it wise to do this, will I regret it later, in ways that are much harder to tell whether you've made a mistake.

Sören Preibusch: Simon talked about indiscretion, and that's far more complex than just considering the policy.

Matt Blaze: Right, so I can't tell if my system has made the right decision or not at the end, which seems to make this problem very hard. Also you're reducing this to objective properties of the photo, and when I think about my own photos, when I decide whether I'm sharing it, what I'm really asking is, taken as a whole, does this photo have some emotional property that makes me want to keep it private. And it's often not simply the sum of the parts. So those two things make this seem like an extremely challenging domain for a conventional trust management model.

Reply: Yes. In terms of the sum of the parts, in the Bayes net that we built, we just considered a small number of the attributes for the categories from the focus coding of the Grounded Theory, and as I just said, we treat this as a qualitative net, so these are just sort of averages across the dependencies. But presumably if we were to do a proper data mining across the data, where we could take all of our different participants, we'd build up a more accurate model about how people's views may influence whether or not a photograph is personally resonant.

Ben Laurie: I don't agree that this is different though. With all security policies, you're not sure what the outcome of applying them is. I mean, you know what the decision was, but you don't know whether it was a good decision, or whether actually it allowed an action you actually would have preferred to deny. I mean, when you get a virus, do you know you've got a virus.

Bruce Christianson: We've never seen an undetected security violation. [laughter]

Reply: The simply analogy with the conventional trust management system might be when you have compliance coming back from the trust management server, it's not just a yes or no, it's a compliance value saying, well, it's OK for you to authorise this transaction so long as you accept this risk, so it's not always this binary answer.

Sören Preibusch: I think we can also make an assessment in a longitudinal way, if we ask people again after half a year, one year, one year and a half, would you share this photo again, or would you make a different decision?

Ross Anderson: Also stuff like this is extraordinarily context sensitive. There have been a number of writings on this by Alessandro Acquisti and George Loewenstein, if you look for example at the blog of our Security Human Behaviour Workshop last year[1], there's some very interesting stuff reported. But whether these things are considered to be private, or are privacy violating, or whatever, will simply depend on the mindset of the person who approaches them. If privacy is to become salient to them, then surely these rights will become salient to them, and so that you can find that something that you believe is complete innocuous this year becomes terribly sensitive next year, because the

---

[1] http://www.lightbluetouchpaper.org/2008/06/30/security-psychology/

government has lost some more CDs, or because of a kid's picture that has been sold somewhere, or whatever. These are not, you know, static practices.

Reply: Yes, I agree. One could imagine that this might be your initial network, and then by doing it in a longitudinal fashion, where you're continually going back to participants doing follow-up interviews, their own views and feelings about how to share photographs could change, and then that would happen, and form the new policy.

Paul Syverson: You seem to be very much focused on the privacy aspects of this, but there's security things as well. For example, in your reference photo I would wonder how does a heavily armed libertarian feel about me sharing his photographs, as your reference photo was very popular.

Reply: Yes, that was one of my concerns showing the photograph.

Vivien Rooney: And the interviews themselves, like people admit to being liars, and they're quite happy to share things sometimes, if they think they won't be caught. So that kind of subtlety isn't really explained here but people very much worry about it.

Paul Syverson: That's a problem where the definition of privacy is the right to lie and get away with it.

Vivien Rooney: Yes.

Joseph Bonneau: When you define sharing, it seems like you've defined it as either you keep the thing private or you share it with the whole world, when in reality you can share with different groups of people, and then it's a very different decision.

Reply: In the interview data the subjects did make distinctions between how they'd like to share the photographs: how they'd not share, they'd share privately, sharing it openly and publicly, sharing it to be used for charitable purposes, sharing it to be used for commercial purposes. And so there's a whole bunch of different categories that were identified from the data, and as I said in this paper we only considered just a small number of categories to see, was it possible to think of how we share photographs in terms of some kind of policy.

Ben Laurie: I love this thing, but the difficulty is that it relies on the interviews and a kind of analysis, so I'm wondering if you think there's anyway you think you could do this stuff without the volunteers and analysis, and whether you can do it for yourself, for example?

Vivien Rooney: I don't know how you could do that actually. I suppose you could make up your own one.

Michael Roe: The interviews you'd only have to do once on a small sample, then you can generalise the network on a large population.

Ben Laurie: If you believe Ross' point (I do), then this change over time means that's not actually true.

Michael Roe: The change over time means, you have to think about what point in the time you generalise the population. Yes, I think I do agree with Ross that, for example, news stories will change things like whether it's OK to share photos of a airport. Something about terrorism, and suddenly pictures of government buildings and airports become much more of concern. There's probably all kinds of other things like that, so I've no idea what in two years time could be sensitive in a photograph.

Vivien Rooney: Yes, I know, not only do a lot of people change their mind over time, they change their mind within the space of the interview. They say, oh no, you asked me about that, maybe I shouldn't have done that, you know, I think I really would reflect on that, and maybe I'll think about it. So even in that short timeframe people will actually reflect on their own behaviour.

Ross Anderson: There's a very interesting experiment that Alessandro and George reported in that they manufactured a privacy meter[2], which is a series of questions of increasing intrusiveness: you know, have you ever had sex with a friend's partner, have you ever smoked drugs, have you ever cheated at exams, the usual sort of stuff, but arranged in escalating order, and the meter is to measure how many of the questions a student is asked before he baulks and stops answering questions. So three groups, a control group, and they measured how far people went. They then had a second group to whom they said, your stuff will be completely secure, we won't record your IP address, everything will be AES encrypted, blah, blah, blah, and do you think that people would be more privacy sensitive or less privacy sensitive? The strange answer is they're more privacy sensitive, as privacies become salient. And then in the third experiment they had a website that wasn't a respectable university website at all but, howbadareyou.com, with a little devil with red arms and a tail, go on, show us how bad you are, and the students went all the way. So these things can be appallingly counterproductive, and the context can depend entirely on what website it's being reproduced in.

Paul Syverson: Did they look at all at the extent to which there was a boiling frog issue? So that if you went straight toward the jugular, or just ask very gradually, and it's like, wow, I've already gotten there, what the hell? Was that part of how they did it?

Ross Anderson: That wasn't part of their research then.

Vivien Rooney: Grounded Theory is suitable for when people regard it as an important issue, so for a lot of people these kind of things are quite important, you know, their own photographs are something that they would have reflected on quite a lot. So it's not really suitable for what you were saying. For those kind of ones I think maybe they wouldn't work for a Grounded Theory like that, but

---

[2] John, Leslie K., Acquisti, Alessandro and Loewenstein, George F., The Best of Strangers: Context Dependent Willingness to Divulge Personal Information (July 6, 2009). Available at SSRN: http://ssrn.com/abstract=143048

if it's more important I think people might be more serious about their answers, or they might reflect more before they'd answer, positively or negatively.

Ross Anderson: Even important issues that people normally think they've got stable opinions on, can be enormously influenced by the order of questions. Tom Kuczinski, for example, has work on when you make a morality salient to someone, and then show them an anti-US essay written by a student. The probability that they are xenophobic against the student, depends almost entirely on whether you make the US constitution salient before you show them the essay, that reminds them of that they've got a constitutional duty.

Reply: Yes, I think that's the important feature of using the semi-structured interviews, you're not going through questionnaires or checkboxes with the subjects.

Jonathan Anderson: This self-imposed context doesn't work.

Joseph Bonneau: Are you thinking of someday turning this into an automatic system that will infer all these attributes in code, or is the user going to have to actually tag, I see a child, I think it's suffering, and all the other inputs that you put into your Bayesian networks.

Reply: The underlying Bayesian net is the policy, I guess. How we get the profiles and characteristics for individuals isn't our problem, because you don't want a situation where you say to somebody, well you have to tag every photograph, say that there's a child there or there's suffering. I guess for the individuals you can get a certain amount of information that's not observed attributes, so for example, one of the subjects uses camera a lot in a medical situation, and so say we highlight the photographs that he was taking were of people who were suffering, while in another situation, somebody who took a large number of photographs with children in it, and I guess maybe by building questionnaires at the beginning, so you get your Facebook account let's say, and then you go through a series of questionnaires, which you use to profile you according to attribute values for the Bayesian net, that might be a way to prime it. Then as time moves on the person can choose to tag the photographs as they see fit, and then that could then be used to feed back into the network.

Joseph Bonneau: It seems like, unless it's completely push button automatic, it's not usable because people can make the decision to share or not of themselves in two seconds. Maybe they aren't exactly right about it, but, if they have to spend 30 seconds tagging each photo I don't see what we've gained.

Ben Laurie: Yes, but maybe you get it so that, you start off with it untagged and it shows you which photos it's going to share, and you go, you shouldn't have shared that one, so I'll tag it so you don't, and that reduces the overall costs.

Joseph Bonneau: Yes, the goal should be making it easier to do the right thing, rather than going through and saying share, or don't share every photo.

Matt Blaze: Isn't tagging the photos more work?

Ben Laurie: Well the point is you only tag the ones that went wrong.

Matt Blaze: Oh so no image processing involved then?

Bruce Christianson: The question is, how is the user going to classify an untagged photo, what's the basis on which it's going to do that?

Joseph Bonneau: The thing is that people do go through and look at every photo, and then they're like: there's one of Mark, there's Mark, there's Mark, there's Jimmy.

Matt Blaze: Right, so there's some tagging going on anyway?

Jonathan Anderson: But not always. Part of the big appeal of using photo-sharing on social networks, is that you can just post the photos and then people who have more time on their hands deal with tagging all 20 people who were in it.

Matt Blaze: Right, but then I've already shared it.

Jonathan Anderson: And then you've already shared it, and it's too late.

Sandy Clark: I disagree with one of the things that you said. People *can* make the decision whether to share or not in a few seconds, but they may also regret that decision later, and frequently do. People now are finding that photos that they shared depicting themselves drunk turn up later, so these are things that they didn't think about.

Matt Blaze: Yes, actually, you want this system to be on the shutter button of the camera, not in the sharing.

Reply: You could use it in that case as a sort of early warning system, as a way to mediate the sharing of your photograph, because you're getting some feedback saying, maybe six months before it might have occurred to you that you're being indiscrete.

Luke Church: Another trap would be, next week you might take some embarrassing photos.

Joseph Bonneau: Sounds like the gmail feature, are you sending a drunk email.

Sandy Clark: Is a prospective employer going to Google for this or something?

Joseph Bonneau: What we really need is just to build the systems so that every photo you share gets automatically emailed to your mother. Once you know that, you start being careful.

Luke Church: I attempted to use Grounded Theory to elicit security policies previously, and ran into two problems. The first one, the generic one for Grounded Theory, is that it takes incredibly long periods of time to do. And the second one is, it keeps throwing up things which aren't computationally expressible anyway. Did you have either of these problems?

Vivien Rooney: What do you mean by computationally expressible?

Luke Church: Oh, a computer's view. The Bayesian network is one step towards progress but I could imagine things which would be very hard to express in a Bayesian network. So there is this general context which made me feel nervous about sharing this photo for no reason that I can particularly articulate.

Vivien Rooney: So that's kind of uncertainty and messiness?

Luke Church: Yes, and I found you ended up with a graph where everything pointed to everything to some degree that couldn't be quantified. None of this is particularly generative for building an access control list. Now I was working in a very different domain with a different audience who had less experience of western computer security models, so perhaps your users are already slightly embedded with the way with we think.

Reply: No, I don't think they were.

Vivien Rooney: Not the way you think, but probably the way I think.

Luke Church: So how long did it take you to do the analysis on how many?

Vivien Rooney: I don't know, because it's quite an intensive process, and it takes ages, and you really hate it, and you get sick of it, you kind of wonder why you started it, and yes, you can't think about anything else for quite a while[3]. I'd say it would take months to do it properly so that you can say, yes, I understand that data, I understand what's in it, and I am saying something that I'm willing to stand over as being an interpretation of it, a reading of it.

Luke Church: You were careful not to try and allow what technology can actually do to influence the decisions that were being made. So I kept finding people, for example, who wanted to retract things they'd published. It's not clear how to do that technologically.

Vivien Rooney: So you were doing interviews were you?

Luke Church: Yes.

Vivien Rooney: With the Grounded Theory, you end up with your focus code and categories, and then you use those to develop your theory. So in effect what we did was use the categories to develop and justify the theory, and the theory was this ad hoc transition going through the focus codes to the variables in the Bayesian network. It's not a mechanised step that's going from the focus codes to this. My hope would be that if we did look at something like machine learning that you might be able to automate more of that.

Luke Church: But machine learning brings a whole different set of hidden ontological commitments which mean that you're now biasing the kind of things your Grounded Theory is going to find.

---

[3] A bit like editing these transcripts really.

Vivien Rooney: Yes, it is difficult because you're trying to balance being able to do it at all with not imposing something positivistic on it, yes.

Luke Church: So I wasn't missing a step?

Vivien Rooney: No.

George Danezis: I'm mildly perplexed about what your goal is. I think that what you do has a lot of sociological value in terms of what people feel about photographs and sharing, but then you seem to want to automate it. Call me old-fashioned, but I don't like my computer being more illicit than me. There's some things that computers do very well, like maths and breaking keys, and some things that humans do better probably, which is having good taste, and now you're trying to make an expert system that will tell me what good taste is. You know, I have a feeling for what a good taste is when I share photos, and when I get it wrong, my mother will tell me, just as Joseph said.

George Danezis: So, as I get the feedback I want from the social mechanism we have, what then is the value for computers taking that decision.

Reply: Well the value would be that there are circumstances where you may not be present when the photograph is to be shared with somebody, so the deciding whether or not this photograph can be shared in certain ways might depend on a trust management system. So it's not that I'm always there as a user asking the question, oh I have a photograph and I'd like to share it with Bob. In this case if Bob maybe goes to my website and wants to look at my photographs, what I might have is a setting that says, the level of indiscretion that I have on my photograph website is 0.4, and so whenever somebody comes along to look at my website they will see photographs coming in at under that level of indiscretion.

Frank Stajano: Why would you even put photographs that had the value higher than that on the website in the first place?

Bruce Christianson: Because there might be other people sharing.

Reply: Yes, exactly, because there's different types of people visiting the website.

Paul Syverson: Yes, it's not a completely public website. Alice is presumably going to login, or identify herself. Bob might have his whole photo library there because he's not a security guy, he just thinks, why not, and then he has settings for who gets to see what, and this is a way that he doesn't have to be sitting there.

Reply: Yes, so it's instead of having the normal thing that we like to have, which are things like roles and access controls to groups. Instead of using that as the policy constraints, let's try to have a mechanism that matches more closely how the individual might be willing to share policies.

Frank Stajano: Aren't you reintroducing roles by the back door, when you are saying, well Bob is only going to have an indiscretion rating of 0.4 whereas Alice is going to have 0.6?

Reply: Yes, but the key thing is that by going through the process, you've got a justifiable link from your policy to the decision. So you can say, well, you know, I'm not just talking about say /.karma, which is, does it work or doesn't it work, I don't know. But in this case you can at least say that all the attributes in your policy are traceable back to the memos and the information from the Grounded Theory, which justify why, for this case, indiscretion is important. Because the whole model came from the Grounded Theory, so it's not that I started off at the beginning saying, right we're going to have a Bayesian network, and this is what we're going to do, it's only when we were looking at the data that the models emerged from that, and things like, you know, your willingness to share the photograph of this person, indiscretion, deceitfulness, etc, those are what came out of the data.

Establishing Distributed Hidden Friendship Relations

Sören Preibusch and Alastair R. Beresford

University of Cambridge, Computer Laboratory
William Gates Building, 15 JJ Thomson Avenue
Cambridge CB3 0FD, United Kingdom
{Soren.Preibusch,Alastair.Beresford}@cl.cam.ac.uk

Abstract. The social Web is going mobile and needs support for friend-ship management in a distributed manner, while privacy concerns mandate configuring the public visibility of one's friends. In this paper we leverage existing Web standards to describe a simple P2P protocol for establishing, enforcing, and revoking hidden friendship relations and report on an implementation for a mobile platform. We examine the suitability of hidden friendship links for bilateral and delegated access control and discuss how the social connotation of friendship can be preserved when concealing the friend's identity.

1 Online Friendship Relations and Privacy

The use of on-line and social networking websites is growing, and social inter-action through such systems is now part of the daily routine for many individu-als [4]. Whilst the development of social networking on the Internet originated from the desire to allow individuals to update their friends or colleagues with new personal or professional information, social networking techniques are now being used to enhance the performance of many other Internet services. For example, friendship links have improved Internet search content indexing and ranking by using HTTP requests made by friends [9]; Tribler [11] is an overlay on top of BitTorrent [10], allowing users to establish friendship links and form groups in order to increase download speed or improve content discovery.

Positive privacy of friendship relations. Once established, the friendship relation often confers additional rights or capabilities to friends, such as the ability to view personal photographs or send private messages (first use-case, UC1). In this context, friendship links on social networks are seen as privacy enhancing, since they restrict access to personal information. Unfortunately, the controls available to limit access to personal data or enhanced services are often quite primitive. Most sites allow users to restrict access to personal information to friends (of first or higher degree) and some sites permit permission to be configured at an individual level. There are only few sites which allow users to privately group individuals together and apply access control at the group level directly;

B. Christianson et al. (Eds.): Security Protocols 2009, LNCS 7028, pp. 321–334, 2013.
© Springer-Verlag Berlin Heidelberg 2013

such capabilities are required to provide more generic rôle-based access control facilities.

As online social networking sites increasingly become platforms on which relationships are setup rather than merely replicated from the offline world, networks provide trust metrics to guide the users in assessing other members' credibility. Despite its limitations, a user's friends count is used as a simple yet intuitive metric in contexts such as casual dating, business contacts, or electronic commerce (UC2).

Friendship links may also be used by the information consumer for incoming filtering rather than for outgoing filtering by the information producer. The access control function of friendship is replaced by an information overflow prevention function. For instance, user agents may only process broadcasted events such as status updates that originate from known friends; Sunday shoppers may only enjoy receiving promotional offers from stores that are on their favourites list (UC3).

The gate-keeping function of friendship relations is not restricted to pairwise encounters, but can be extended to multihop authorisation based on functional properties of the links, including but not limited to transitivity: friends of friends or, more generally, friends of nth degree may enjoy privileged access (UC4). Active consent of the original information holder or of the involved middlemen may be required for successful privilege propagation (UC5).

Negative privacy of friendship relations. The set of attributes and identities linked with a friend's online profile introduce a privacy-endangering facet into friendship relations. Having a friendship relation with somebody may be socially detrimental. For example, investigating journalists have a professional interest in keeping their sources secret (UC6). Executive professionals may wish to maintain secret ties with friends working at competitor companies (UC7). And teenagers may feel peer group pressure in choosing who they call friends (UC8). Pitfalls also arise within the online network itself when the number and kind of friends positively and negatively influence one's social status (UC9). There are also potential negative consequences outside the social realm. Companies rely on the formalised nature of friendship relations to mine connections between users along which personality traits and socio-economic characteristics are assumed to propagate. A potential employer may refuse a candidate because of her friendship with others; and users may receive targeted advertisements based on preferences and interests their friends publicised on the network site.

The nature of the friendship relation on social networking sites therefore requires the ability to hide friendship relations. Simply hiding all of one's friends does not solve the problem, because it denies the advantages of public friendship and ignores the symmetry of friendship relations, implying that either of the involved parties may reveal the existence of a link independently. In analysing an existing social network, the authors found that more than two thirds of users who chose to conceal friendships actually had exposed at least one of these supposedly hidden relationships [12].

Mobile networking. As the performance and capability of mobile phones increases, such devices increasingly host social networking applications. This movement provides richer (yet intermittent) connectivity, encourages greater levels of data entry, and allows the automated collection of sensor data, such as location information. Intermittent connectivity encourages more application state and functionality to reside on the device itself, rather than a remote server, and it is for this reason we believe that a move to decentralised social networks will occur. In the long term, mobile devices may function without any centralised facilities at all. Brief encounters amongst humans will trigger ad-hoc connectivity between devices. For instance, human mobility and opportunistic short-range networking may allow social networks to be built on top of delay-tolerant networks, for which, in turn, stable human connectivity traces suggest reliable routing paths [6, 16]. Also, a decentralised scheme potentially provides better privacy guarantees, since trusting social network operators is no longer a prerequisite—data are kept on the device under the control of the individual.

Our contribution. The contribution of this paper is twofold. Building on previous research into the architecture of hidden friendship relations [12], we propose a simple protocol for establishing, enforcing, and revoking selectively hidden friendship relations in a P2P scenario. In addition, we describe an implementation of this protocol for mobile devices, providing details of the user interface and on the integration with the phone's existing messaging and contact management facilities. We review our protocol with regard to security and functional requirements, to resource consumption, as well as to standard compliance. Based on nine use-cases, we examine the suitability of hidden friendship links to convey privileges and we discuss how the social connotation of friendship can be preserved when concealing the friend's identity.

2   Hidden Friendship Relations Protocol

Deployment scenario and protocol requirements. In a centralised scenario, hidden friendship links can easily be implemented by the central network server removing hidden friends from its response when serving a user's list of friends, based on the credentials the requesting client presents. In particular, the network operator is in a position to evaluate any credentials with regard to a strong identity since the user is typically session-authenticated. In an otherwise secure system, it is unlikely that user B could pose for A when presenting (replaying) one of A's credentials.

In a distributed scenario, however, checking the credentials of the requesting user represents a server-like task, implying that continuous connectivity must be maintained, which is incompatible with the assumption of intermittent connectivity and prohibitively resource-consuming for mobile devices.

One of the design challenges, which occurs when removing a central authority, becomes the lack of a strong yet simple proof of identity. A traditional decentralised public key infrastructure, such as GPG, or the web of trust imply a social graph in which identity can be mined to the detriment of *hidden* friendship.

Design goals and requirements. In order to support a distributed social network, it is desirable if a user's list of friends is immutable with respect to requests being made by different parties. A distributed hidden friendship protocol is further expected to fulfil the following design goals: (a) users should be able to selectively hide a self-chosen subset of their friends; (b) a friendship relation, whether hidden or public is symmetric; (c) users should be able to establish, to revoke, and to set the visibility of their outgoing friendship links uni-laterally, i.e. without coordination efforts; (d) a friendship is public iff both friends make it public and it is hidden iff both friends hide it; (e) a friend B of user A can check whether their friendship still holds by inspecting A's list of friends; (f) everybody should see public friendship links, and nobody except the involved parties should be able to infer a hidden friendship from either list of friends; (g) the establishment of a friendship relation requires the consent of both parties; (h) hidden and public friendship links are both made public, i.e. hiding a friendship link comes not from concealing its existence (no security through obscurity).

It is outside the scope of the protocol to specify what leads to establishing a friendship. This preceding interaction pertains to the social sphere.

Threat model. We outline the security goals and the threat model for a hidden friendship in general and its distributed deployment in particular. The fundamental notion is user A calling user B a hidden friend. This shall be manifested with an encrypted entry E_{AB} in A's public list of friends. The entry can be accessed by any other user since the list of friends is public. However, it shall not be possible for a non-related third-party $X \notin \{A,B\}$ to learn who B is from the entry in the list of friends. In particular, X is unable to locate the corresponding list of friends in which E_{BA} should be listed in case the hidden friendship actually exists through symmetrically calling one another a hidden friend.

The following assumptions are made with regard to a friend entry E_{AB}: (a) $E_{AB} \neq E_{BA}$ so that the symmetry of a hidden friendship is not obvious; (b) $E_{BA} \neq E_{CA}$ so that two users having a common friend is not visible in the friend list; (c) a friends list entry corresponding to a hidden friendship can be told apart from a non-hidden friendship link; (d) the validity of E_{AB} cannot be established by X, i.e. X cannot distinguish a real friends list entry from random data made up by A. It is assumed to be beyond the capabilities of an attacker to compute E_{BA} from E_{AB} and to infer B from E_{AB}.

Regarding the integrity of a list of friends, we assume that a user has sole control over her public list of friends and that requests to this list can be made in a secure manner. A potential attacker has the following capabilities: (a) monitoring traffic of users; (b) monitoring changes in the published lists of friends; (c) re-publishing hidden or public friendship entries found in other users' lists of friends.

Regarding the system environment, the following assumptions are made: (a) devices that offer tool support for distributed hidden friendship links have sufficiently synchronised clocks to assess lifetime expiry of documents such as friendship lists. Moreover, these devices experience periods of lost connectivity. We assume that (b) users checking for the existence of a device or a user do not immediately conclude the non-existence of a user from her non-reachability. As devices may cache friends lists, these cached versions may be outdated. No means for verifying cache expiry exists at periods of lacking connectivity, during which friendship revocation may occur. We, therefore, further assume that (c) users may rely on possibly outdated cache copies, (d) will implement safeguards such as short expiry times for critical applications, and (e) further delay the execution of critical friend lookups until connectivity is restored or cache validity has been established.

Further design goals specific to social networking applications. In addition to the design goals outlined above (p. 324), and for the purpose of sensible social networking applications, an additional property is desirable: any X can learn the number of hidden friends A claims to have by counting the entries for hidden friendship links. Such a requirement is in line with the use-cases UC2 and UC9. However, this further requirement conflicts with the design assumption (d) established above that validity of one's friends list entry is undecidable for an outsider. The remedy of counting one's inbound friendship links which should equal one's outgoing friendship links under the symmetry assumption is not possible for hidden friendship links. A well-formedness requirement may be another practicable approach to tell bogus entries and valid friendship entries apart. Still, the countability goal is not be achievable by withdrawing the assumption (d) only. Any user may have several identities that she could use for establishing friendship links between seemingly different users. There are therefore at least two techniques to boost one's hidden friends count, each of which cannot be precluded in a fully distributed scenario where identities can be created opaquely at low cost. We conclude that X can only learn a lower bound for A's number of hidden friends from latter list of friends. The satisfiability of weakened countability goals is discussed in Section 2, p. 329.

Social networks also rely on friendship as an access control criterion as described in use-cases UC1 and UC4. The existence of a friendship relation is enforced when accessing a secured resource. We distinguish between two cases: first, direct enforcement and, second, delegated enforcement. Bilateral enforcement relies on the design goals and is achieved since both parties involved in a hidden friendship can verify its continued existence in their own and the respectively other's records. A third party tests the existence of a friendship between two users by pairwise associating a friendship claim with a proof of identity.

Granting access to privileged resources may not be limited to one's direct friends but also friends of friends or, more generally, friends of nth degree. We discuss the compatibility of hidden friendship links with multihop friendship in Section 2, p. 330.

Leveraging existing technologies. The implementation of a hidden friendship protocol, discussed in the next Section on p. 326, can be built on top of existing Internet and security technologies, keeping the protocol itself concise while leveraging established and developing standards. In particular, the following infrastructure for publishing personal information in a semantic format and for transmitting information in a secure and concealed manner is used as a basis: (a) the vCard format extension to represent social network membership inform- ation for a single individual, in particular the publisher of the vCard file [5]; (b) the representation of latter in semantic HTML using hCard for direct em- bedding into personal or other Web pages, including distributed social network profile pages [1]; (c) the FOAF (friend-of-a-friend) standard to encode personal information and relationships in a machine-readable format; (d) FOAF+SSL, as an alternative to OpenId to allow for certificate-bound identities and distributed authentication across multiple social networks [15]; (e) a contact list private to the user's individual, such as a phone book, Outlook contacts or a private FOAF file; (f) means for encrypting messages and for concealing messaging interaction, using remailers such as Mixminion [3].

Implementation: establishing friendships. Public and hidden friendship links are both stored as outgoing friendship links, mutually pointing to the other party (Figure 1). For *public friendship links*, the link references the other user by her public identifier, K_A, such as a public key, a well-known personal Web page URI, an email address or the URI of her own list of friends. For *hidden friendship links*, the link references a public identifier specific to this relationship only and not otherwise used by either of the parties. Each party may freshly generate such an identifier as a (public key, private key) pair, unique to a directed friendship link. The referenced party maintains the private key K_i^{-1} associated with the public key K_i in the referencing party's public list of friends. Note that there is no need for sharing a secret. If secure channels are used for concealing the messages exchanged between two prospective friends, public/private keys used therein may be recycled.

Enforcing friendships. Friendship relations are enforced upon execution of a privileged action. A *public friendship relation* between A and B is enforced by A inspecting B's list of friends for the existence of K_A. B looks for K_B in A's public list of friends. In addition, any third party X may also check for the existence of a public friendship relation between A and B. A *hidden friendship relation* between A and B is enforced by A inspecting B's list of friends for the existence of the relationship-specific public key K_i that A once issued to B. Likewise, B looks for the relationship-key K_j she has issued to A. A third-party X is unable to check for the existence of a hidden friendship relation between A and B, since the relationship-specific keys do not contain a reference to the issuing party. This behaviour is intentional, as detailed in use-cases UC6 and UC7.

Revoking friendships. Friendship relations can be revoked unilaterally by either party removing the corresponding person- or relationship-specific public key from her public list of friends. Revocation can be detected through unsuccessful en- forcement. A unilaterally revoking party continues to have access to friendship- secures resources until the other party replicates the revocation.

Encoding in FOAF. FOAF is an established semantic Web format one can use to publish information about oneself and one's connections in standard and

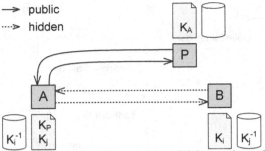

Public friendship relations are shown with solid lines, A ↔ P, and hidden friendship relations with dashed lines, A ↔ B. The list of friends (document) associated with a user is public, the individual contact list (database) is private. For a public friendship, the friends store the respectively other's public identifier in their own list of friends: A stores K_P and P stores K_A. For a hidden friendship, the friends store a public key issued by the respectively other for this friendship relation only. A generates a key-pair (K_i, K_i^{-1}): she keeps the private part and sends the public part to B who incorporates it into her public list of friends. B also generates a key-pair (K_j, K_j^{-1}) and performs the same exchange and integration tasks (Fig. 2).

Fig. 1. Encoding of public and hidden friendship relations with symmetric links

machine-readable manner. FOAF files are published by their author. In FOAF, foaf:knows-elements indicate relationships with other people. More specific variants, such as "closeFriendOf", "livesWith" or "parentOf" as exist as inheriting elements to further specify the quality of the relationship [2]. Such derived properties can be used to make the distinction between public and hidden friends explicit. However, this is not required because storing relationship-specific keys instead of person-specific identifiers is compatible with the syntax of FOAF. foaf:nickname or other RDF vocabulary may be used instead of foaf:name or rdf:resource may also be used to qualify the nature of the referencing identifier rather than of the reference itself.

For the friendship relations depicted in Fig. 1, the relevant fragment from A's FOAF file could be:

```
<foaf:Person rdf:ID="me">
  <foaf:name>A</foaf:name>
  <foaf:knows><foaf:Person>
    <foaf:name>P</foaf:name>
  </foaf:Person></foaf:knows>
  <foaf:knows><foaf:Person>
    <foaf:name>ae4f281df5a5d0ff3cad631f76d5c29b6d953ec</foaf:name>
  </foaf:Person></foaf:knows>
</foaf:Person>
```

The rôle of a central authority / delegated access control with distributed hidden friendships. As outlined in use-case UC1, friendship links form the basis for

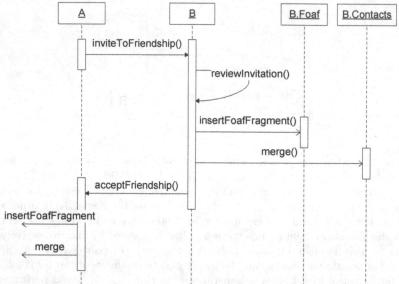

User A initiates the establishment by sending a friendship invitation to user B. A includes an identifying fragment, a public key specific to this friendship link for a hidden or her persistent public key (or other identifier such as a URI) for a non-hidden friendship. Her details such as email address or other communication details are included as sender information. User B reviews the friendship request and, upon approval, inserts A's identifying fragment into her own list of friends, such a B's public FOAF file (B.Foaf). B also updates her private contact database (B.contacts) with A's details and a pointer to A's public FOAF file for future friendship enforcement. B then replies to A with B's own identifying fragment (friendship link specific / general purpose public key). Finally, A performs the same integration tasks, by the end of which the friendship between A and B is established.

Fig. 2. Generic sequence diagram for a successful establishment of a friendship relation

social access control schemes. In particular, a user may publish a digital resource such as the photographs from the wedding or a video from the last rafting trip. Only friends shall have access to this resource. Typically, A does not want to host this material herself but relies on dedicated service providers to fulfil this server-like task since these offer continuous connectivity and have sufficient bandwidth and storage resources. Several social networks have grown around such media publishing. The idea of centralised content storage is compatible with and complementary to decentralised friendship control. Fig. 3 depicts a scenario where A publishes a restricted document using C's services and B, a hidden friend of A, wants to access the document. C shall be able to check whether B qualifies for access without having A to reveal her friends to C. Delegated access control is a major motivation for uniformly publishing hidden and non-hidden friends.

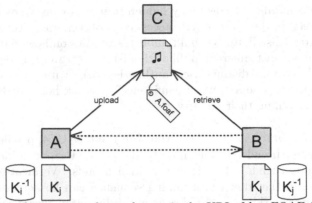

A uploads a document and attaches to it the URI of her FOAF file, which
shall determine who will have access to the resource. B, a hidden friend of A,
then wants to access the resource.

Fig. 3. A publishes a digital resource using C's facilities

Access to a secured resource will be determined based on a list of friends which
is referenced through a URI as part of the upload process. Linking to the friends
list instead of physically uploading it implies that changes in A's list of friends
will be reflected in C's decisions who shall have access with no need for A to alter
the uploaded content/ACL bundle. A may want to specify a resource-dependent
caching policy which allows C to base its decisions on local copies of A's list of
friends. Setting such caching policies is perfectly feasible when requests to the
URI of A's FOAF file are served over HTTP(S).

As soon as friendship enforcement relies on a cached list of friends relayed
by third parties, the authenticity of the caches needs to be sufficiently reliable.
Signing FOAF files guarantees their integrity and can be done using standard
XML Signature procedures. To ensure that the signer actually is the original
publisher (and not an attacker), the signature key needs to be linked sufficiently
strongly with the FOAF file author. Semi-centralised architectures such as institutional trust provide strong evidence as can a web of trust provided there
are enough public friendship links. Note that once established, the belief in a
signature key can be passed on over updates of the signed document.

A public friend is trivially granted access since anybody can enforce a public
friendship relationship. A hidden friend can prove her entitlement without revealing her identity: access shall be granted to a requestor who can prove to have
the private key associated with any public key located in the uploaders public
FOAF file. This challenge-response can be done using standard procedures. It is
not important under which hidden friends' public key a requestor authenticates
since all hidden friends have access anyway. A leaked private friendship key is
just the digital analogy to an unreliable friend.

Counting hidden friendships. As outlined in use-cases UC2 and UC9 counting
one's friends is another typical social networking application. Given a user's list

of friends, one can only tell how many hidden friends this user has at most (see p. 325). However, in the context of an access control scenario as the one outlined above, the content distributor C could publish statistics on how many successful authentications against different public friendship keys were made (still being unable to tell how many distinct users authenticated). A user may use a similar infrastructure to propose a "vote of confidence" and ask her friends to support her – without unveiling their identity.

Hidden friendship of nth degree. As outlined in use-case UC4, privilege propagation beyond direct friendship links may be desirable. Users can identify public friends (of public friends) of their own hidden friends. Verification of hidden friendship links further down in a linking sequence can be achieved on a per-case by applying the third-party enforcement / delegated access control model. As motivated in use-case UC5, successful enforcement of multihop friendship links requires cooperation from hidden friends along the friendship path. If, for instance, there was a path of friendship relations $A \leftrightarrow B \leftrightarrow C \leftrightarrow D$, all of them hidden, D would require (only) C's support for proving to A there is a friendship link of third degree. In general $n - 2$ cooperating intermediate friends are needed to to directly prove a hidden friendship of nth degree and $n - 1$ are required if A delegates the enforcement.

One-party deviation from the protocol. In a distributed friendship scenario, symmetry of friendship links is not enforced. As a result, each of two parties involved can change the friendship links in their FOAF files unilaterally. For a public friendship link, un-symmetric friendship links are obvious and may just be interpreted as unilateral appraisal ("fan") or as a transitory period during which one party has already established a link and is waiting for the other party to follow or one party has revoked the friendship.

The interpretation of unilateral hidden friendship relations is more subtle. A party deviating from the protocol may alter the visibility status of an outgoing friendship link or delete it. For all scenarios, it holds that the other party may detect such changes in the link structure to at least the same extent as a third party observer. Unilateral alteration of friendship visibility does not change the publicity of the relationship but breaks the relationship (as does revocation). The other party may respond by a corresponding action.

3 Tool Support for Mobile Devices

The feasibility and sustainability of the developed hidden friendship protocol is demonstrated by a mobile-device platform implementation of a "friend manager" application for which Figure 4 depicts the core functionality. The application builds on the Microsoft .Net Compact Framework, allowing deployment on devices running Windows [8], Symbian [14], or other various operating systems such as Linux on diverse architectures, Apple operating systems, SUN Solaris, and non-mainstream operating systems (for instance Nintendo Wii) via Mono.

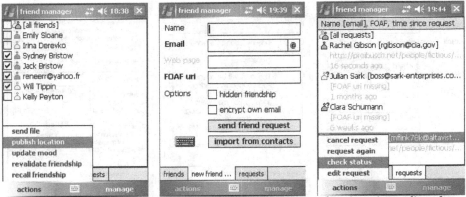

Using a tabbed user interface, the "friend manager" application gives a list of the existing friends, provides a form for generating new friendship requests, and allows a review of pending requests. **(left)** If a friend can be matched to the user's contacts, a real name is displayed instead of a communication identifier (e.g. reneerr@yahoo.fr). Shade and colour of the icons communicate the visibility of the friends (light: hidden; dark: publicly visible) and another property such as sex, which may be not available for some friends (grey icons). Multiple friends can be selected at once to perform a privileged operation such as informing them about one's current location. **(middle)** The form for creating new friendship invitations offers options for enhancing the privacy of the friendship. **(right)** Currently pending requests are summarised with the name of the potential friend, her contact details, and her FOAF URI if available. The visibility of the friendship is encoded in the icon. The time elapsed since the request was filed is displayed in a human-readable format. Requests with the FOAF URI missing are highlighted since their status cannot be checked. Filed requests can be edited to add such missing information at a later point in time.

Fig. 4. The "friend manager" user interface

The friend manager tightly integrates with the existing PIM infrastructure for messaging and contact management, Figure 5, hence improving usability and avoiding overlapping data silos. Close integration is of paramount importance for user acceptance as the contact book is the private manifestation of a person's social network and a source for finding opportunities for communication and interaction [13].

4 Discussion

The proposed protocol of encrypting identifiers for hidden friendship relationships presents several theoretical and technical advantages which are particularly valuable for deployment in distributed social networking. Public and hidden friendship relations can be encoded uniformly in a public FOAF file with no need to serve different friends lists based on the credentials a requesting client presents. Hidden friendship identifiers cannot be traced back to the actual

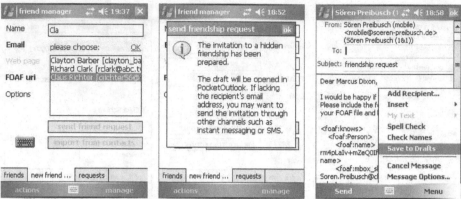

The "friend manager" application integrates with the existing messaging infrastructure on the device. (**left**) Upon creating a new friend request, user details can be imported from the contacts so that contacts matching in name will be displayed and updated as the user types. (**middle, right**) Friendship invitations are sent via PocketOutlook where a draft is generated for further edit prior to sending the message so the user can benefit from the entire existing messaging infrastructure. The application is prepared to handle alternative communication channels in addition to email.

Fig. 5. Integration with existing applications

users and several hidden friendship links of the same user cannot be merged. Semantics and syntax of FOAF are preserved as well as the various alternatives for publishing FOAF files – including third party repositories and distributed caching.

Hidden friendship relations are compatible with typical social networking applications such as direct or delegated access control schemes based on friendship. Friendship enforcement can be realised for multihop links. The number of one's outgoing hidden friendship links is an unreliable social metric since these links can be made up easily. Still, it is possible to anonymously count one's encrypted friend entries that are not bogus data.

The proposed protocol builds on top of encryption and the concealment of the friendship-establishing messaging. Nonetheless, should an encrypted identifier be intercepted, it cannot be used to establish a hidden friendship under a false name. However, challenges remain:

- Does the observable execution of a privileged action reveal enough information to detect the existence of a friendship link?
- Can users attach an individually negotiated privacy policy to a friendship link to govern the use of data received over this friendship channel?
- Is access control based on friendship relations of nth degree as sketched in this paper viable?
- To which extent can one leverage hidden friendship networks for anonymising the retrieval of Web resources?

- Can we build usable rôle-based access-control (RBAC) schemes for social networking?
- From an economic perspective what level of support for privacy settings does a social network operator optimally offers to its users? Do social network operators compete on privacy support anyway?
- How can metrics over hidden and public friendship relations still be computed in a useful manner?
- Is an escrow service (for instance dbpedia) required in order to ensure the same list of friends is presented to all users?
- Does the implicit understanding of what a friendship relation conveys differ across different networks to such an extent that joining friends throughout several networks would contravene the users' access control intentions?

References

1. Çelik, T., Suda, B.: hCard, http://microformats.org/wiki/hcard
2. Davis, I., Vitiello Jr., E.: RELATIONSHIP: A vocabulary for describing relationships between people, http://purl.org/vocab/relationship/
3. Danezis, G., Dingledine, R., Mathewson, N.: Mixminion: Design of a Type III Anonymous Remailer Protocol. In: IEEE Symposium on Security and Privacy (2003), http://doi.ieeecomputersociety.org/10.1109/SECPRI.2003.1199323, doi:10.1109/SECPRI.2003.1199323
4. Fisch, M., Gscheidle, C.: Mitmachnetz Web 2.0: Rege Beteiligung nur in Communitys. Media Perspektiven 7, 356–364 (2008)
5. George, R., Melnikov, A.: vCard Format Extension: To Represent the Social Network Information of an Individual. IETF, Internet-Draft (2009),
   http://www.ietf.org/internet-drafts/
   draft-george-vcarddav-vcard-extension-00.txt
6. Hui, P., Crowcroft, J., Yoneki, E.: BUBBLE Rap: Social-based Forwarding in Delay Tolerant Networks. In: 9th ACM International Symposium on Mobile Ad Hoc Networking and Computing, MobiHoc (2008),
   http://doi.acm.org/10.1145/1374618.1374652, doi:10.1145/1374618.1374652
7. Microsoft Corporation. Microsoft Launches MSN Messenger Service: Online Instant Messaging Service Enables Consumers to Communicate With More People Than Any Other (1999), http://www.microsoft.com/
   presspass/press/1999/jul99/messagingpr.mspx
8. Microsoft Corporation. Devices and Platforms Supported by the .NET Compact Framework (2009), http://msdn.microsoft.com/en-us/library/ms172550.aspx
9. Mislove, A., Gummadi, K.P., Druschel, P.: Exploiting Social Networks for Internet Search. In: 5th Workshop on Hot Topics in Networks, HotNets 2006 (2006),
   http://www.mpi-sws.org/~amislove/publications/PeerSpective-HotNets.pdf
10. Pouwelse, J., Garbacki, P., Epema, D., Sips, H.: The Bittorrent P2P File-Sharing System: Measurements and Analysis. In: van Renesse, R. (ed.) IPTPS 2005. LNCS, vol. 3640, pp. 205–216. Springer, Heidelberg (2005),
    http://dx.doi.org/10.1007/11558989_19
11. Pouwelse, J.A., Garbacki, P., Wang, J., Bakker, A., Yang, J., Iosup, A., Epema, D.H.J., Reinders, M., van Steen, M.R., Sips, H.J.: TRIBLER: a social-based peer-to-peer system. Concurrency and Computation: Practice and Experience 20(2), 127–138 (2008), http://dx.doi.org/10.1002/cpe.1189,
    doi:10.1002/cpe.1189

12. Preibusch, S., Beresford, A.R.: Privacy-Preserving Friendship Relations for Mobile Social Networking. In: W3C Workshop on the Future of Social Networking (2009), `http://www.w3.org/2008/09/msnws/papers/Preibusch-Beresford_Privacy-Preserving-Friendship-Relations.pdf`

13. Raento, M., Oulasvirta, A.: Designing for privacy and self-presentation in social awareness. Personal and Ubiquitous Computing 12(7), 527–542 (2008), `http://dx.doi.org/10.1007/s00779-008-0200-9`, doi:10.1007/s00779-008-0200-9

14. Red Five Labs. Net60 - Opening Symbian devices to .NET development (2009), `http://www.redfivelabs.com/content/datasheet.aspx`

15. Story, H.: FOAF & SSL: creating a global decentralised authentication protocol. In: W3C Workshop on the Future of Social Networking (2009), `http://www.w3.org/2008/09/msnws/papers/foaf+ssl.html`

16. Yoneki, E., Hui, P., Chan, S., Crowcroft, J.: A Socio-Aware Overlay for Publish/Subscribe Communication in Delay Tolerant Networks. In: 10th ACM Symposium on Modeling, Analysis, and Simulation of Wireless and Mobile Systems (2007), `http://doi.acm.org/10.1145/1298126.1298166`, doi:10.1145/1298126.1298166

Establishing Distributed Hidden Friendship Relations

(Transcript of Discussion)

Sören Preibusch

University of Cambridge

Welcome to the penultimate talk of the workshop. I will be talking today about hidden friendship relations, and I will introduce you to the concept of what hidden friendship relations are, say why we need them, and I will also explain how we can achieve them.

I will do so with the perspective on privacy, and focusing on distributed architectures. What has come up during the past few days is social networking in all of the scenarios that we have seen, and all the applications that can be run on these, and experiments we can do in social networks. Here you can see a screenshot of social network, it's a profile page for Friendster, and besides the fact that there's this nice guy, we have his friends over here, and friendship relations are the underlying relations that build a social network, so it can be used as a core to build higher level concepts. It's simple, but it's formalised, you can easily crawl it and so forth. There's also an interesting function property about friendship, that it's symmetric, so here we have Gwen, and if we browse to Gwen's profile page and look up her friends we see that Hennesey is again there. So we have the symmetry that is enforced across the network, that's an important property about friendship relations. Another thing is that they carry the property, to allow privileged actions, so if I have someone, you look over there to the left you can see that you can forward the profile page to one of your own friends but you can't forward their profile page to other friends. So this privileged action that is based on friendship can also have privileges that are with regard to resources such as hiding some things in the profile. This is what I will call the positive privacy of friendship relations.

Anyway we can see that friendship along with other relations between users is used to enforce some access control. And how this then results on the user requesting a profile page, you can see it on the right that this profile has been restricted, so it's private, and as long as you're not a friend to this user you can't see the details on what he's doing, his contact information, his activities, and so forth. So that's good.

However, there are what I will call the negative privacy of friendship relations, that there are friends you want to be friends with, but you don't want to be seen with these friends in public, that is because friendship relations carry also the understanding that social demographic information propagates along friendship links. There is a good analogy in the offline world that is the so-called red-lining, so if your neighbour doesn't pay his bills then you have a bad credit rating. We can think of this social networking also as red lining on a social graph, that

B. Christianson et al. (Eds.): Security Protocols 2009, LNCS 7028, pp. 335–342, 2013.

if your friends have properties that aren't socially acceptable, then this will have detrimental consequences for yourself. So if your friends are caught binge drinking then you might not get a job interview. An effect only last week was this, in the news, so that a prison guard was sacked because he was friends on Facebook with some of his inmates. So it would be good to be able to hide some friends, but still maintain the good things about friendship relations, that is, you want to have friends, and you want to show that you have friends, and you maybe want to show off with the number of friends you have. So that's why we need to be able to selectively hide friends, and purge people we don't want to be seen with in public from our list of friends.

We have a centralised architecture such as the Friendster network, or any other network, such as Facebook, MySpace and like in western Europe and the Americas, then we see that it's in principle very easy to hide friendship relations links selectively, because the network operator has strong credentials on who is requesting a list of friends, he has the login information this user is requesting to this provider with regard to the site. So if an unauthorised user is making a request then another list of friends will be served than if an authenticated user is requesting a list of another user's friends. Even so, implementation isn't always easy, security in theory doesn't mean it will work in practice. Because of this symmetry I've mentioned earlier there is a trap that unilateral disclosure friendship links may leak information, so if A is friends with B, and B wants to conceal this information but A makes it public, that means because of the symmetry we will know that B is also friends with A, so we would in fact need to hide both ends of the friendship relation. And some networks do not get it right, as we found out in a study on the existing medium size German social network, we've been seeing that we can infer lots of the friends.

To quantify this we had the exposure rate you're seeing: if we have all of the users who hide their friends, how many of these users have at least one friend exposed through incoming friendship links, that means that you have at least one privacy breach, and the answer is two-thirds. So there aren't many users who hide their friends. This network comprised 120,000 users, some of them more active than the other ones. Further pushing technology on this network, the feature to make a public list of friends was introduced as was an opt-out feature. The most active users opted out more often, but still they've been in a bad position because people who they've been friends with for a long time didn't change their settings and there are incoming links towards them. So two thirds of them did not succeed in enforcing their privacy well, and often it was not only one friend that was exposed, but nearly all of them. The in-friends ratio, the degree to which we can infer the complete list of friends, we can see it's almost all the friends that we can infer by inbound links only. So not paying attention to the symmetry of friendship links turns out to be quite bad if we really want to enforce privacy. Still, let's keep in mind it works in theory, which will not be the case if we move towards decentralised architectures.

The reason I want to consider decentralised architectures is because mobile is the future paradigm of social networking, and if we do mobile then doing decentralised is a good idea. So the drivers for having more mobile social networking are diverse. In the industrialised world it's mostly social economic drivers, so we see a blur between professional and private life, and the always on setting of mobile devices reflecting always on lifestyle. We're networking on the move, while on the plane you can now use your phone and do data service like social networking, and you want to keep in touch with your friends all the time because otherwise (having this always on mentality) they may think you're no longer there or have disconnected, so there is also some social pressure. And in emerging markets such as Africa or China, India, mobile platforms are much less expensive to deploy than centralised networks. Now these mobile devices then exhibit patterns of intermittent connectivity, they have power constraints and so forth, and even if you gain some flexibility in using a decentralised architecture with these mobile devices, it would be good that when you run out of battery, or if you don't want to connect to a central station, that you can make decisions on what information to share in a local way, that means making decentralised decisions. And coming back to the emerging markets, it may be much cheaper not to establish a link with the network operator, but networking with your friends in your community on a local basis.

So there are compelling reasons why we want to make social networking happen in a decentralised manner. And acknowledging we want to do so, then we must live with the constraints that come with it: the new architectures will impose new algorithms we need to deploy for having friendship relations selectively hidden in decentralised architectures. In principle, avoiding centralised authority is good because we no longer have one single point of trust failure, and because then we have our own list of friends that we self publish, and we link these lists of friends with other users, and we can change things on our lists unilaterally and deploy friendship links. So there are existing technologies that we can inherit from the semantic web stuff, there's the FOAF standard, friend-of-a-friend, we can use this to code these lists of friends in a decentralised manner and deploy them on our website. So the technology in terms of data format is there and we just need to deploy it.

But before I give the details on how this works for having a protocol for hidden friendship relations, let's be clear on the deployment scenario. We have mobile devices, and these have existing content management infrastructures, there's Outlook, your address book, and their embedding in the security infrastructure provides secure connections to retrieve information, exchange information, and also for concealing the act of messaging, so it's all there, it does not need to be reinvented. And the public list of friends we then had deployed on our own is immutable, with regard to requests: that is because making changes depending on who's requesting the list of friends would be a server like pass, and we don't want this, because it does not go well with the world of intermittent connectivity, and it's resource consuming deploying authentication schemes that are peer-to-peer in this world without having good credentials.

If we deploy friendship links distributedly we don't want somebody looking at my list of friends to see who I'm friends with. There's no epistemic inference if I have a friendship link that is hidden, that goes from A to B, I can't infer who is the target of the friendship link, just by seeing the hidden friendship link tell who's the other party who I'm friends with. And similarly if I have two links that are outgoing I can't tell if they're coming from the same person, and similarly I am not able to link common friends. And we also require that there is no symmetry, so if A is a hidden friend of B, and B is a hidden friend of A, they will have other things listed in their public list of friends. So we want to conceal that to users, our hidden friends, and ability to infer who are the individuals engaged in friendship relations. There is however the possibility that I can republish fragments that I find in the list of friends, because it's public by definition, and also I can change things unilaterally inside my public list of friends, because it's decentralised and there's no central authority that enforces symmetry, even though we still understand that symmetry is necessary to have successful friendship relations.

Also, even though we want to make decisions locally, it would be nice if we could delegate the task to a third party, so thinking of a content provider such as Flicker or YouTube, I can dump my data, my files, my music, my photos, and I can base access control on my list of friends that I tag along with the content I upload. So there would be something like Simon just mentioned, I have a photo and I want to attach some access control to it that is somehow made up in the first place. Also the existing social understanding of friendship links, such as counting friends for reputation, or building a WEP between users, should still be possible.

So how can we achieve this? We have a user who has attached a public list of friends, because it's public this list can be widely cached, but then we also have a private data store in which we can keep our contacts, and private information, especially private key information. And we have another user there, P, and A and P want to become public friends, let's just see how public friendship works. It's fairly simple, we need the symmetry, so A puts in his list of friends and identifies for P, this links towards P, then P does likewise and puts an identifier to his own list of friends, which then links again back to A. So we have a friendship relation that's public between A and P just by the fact that they put their respective other identifier in their own list of friends, so any third party can observe this and can say, OK, A and P are in fact public friends.

If we have another user, let's say B, and A and B want to become hidden friends, it's more complicated because the requirement is to embed the Groucho protocol, it can't infer that there is in fact a link, so nobody other than A and B should be able to observe this link. We start by A generating a public/private key pair, and keeping the private key for its own, and sending the public part to B who puts it in a file. This then establishes a link from B to A, and then B does the same, generates a public/private key pair, puts the private part into his own database, sends the public part A, and then we have the link between A and B. So these public/private key pairs are specific to the relation. It is not a user specific key, but a relationship specific key, and by definition nobody else is able to produce this key because it is a private key, so it has the properties that we want to achieve. We can then achieve enforcement of these hidden links just by inspecting the other user's lists of friends, seeing if the key is still there, and look if we don't have to leave our own key into the outgoing link, so this works pretty well. Revocation is of course unilateral, and just by deleting the entry inside the public file, so if B removes this entry then A can tell it's been removed, and A can tell, OK, B no longer wants to be hidden friends with me. So the properties of friendship that we want to convey are there.

Let's see how it works if we have delegated enforcement. So if as I said A dumps her photos or her music to Flicker, and only wants to have friends have access. Let's imagine A has been shooting some photos from the last holiday trip, uploads them all, and then only friends should have access to these holiday photos. So A tags along with these photos a list of friends, in particular we can imagine that it's not a public file that's attached but just a link, so a URL link to the original list of friends, so that we can inherit changes in the original file here. So the content that is now with C is linked with the list of friends from A. And if B is approaching C and tells C, OK, give me A's photos, then it should only work if B is in fact a friend, whether it's hidden or public friend, so C should be in a position to decide whether somebody who's approaching is authorised to access A's content based on A's list of friends. If the one who's requesting the photos is a public friend, it's not a problem because the symmetry is obvious and anybody can tell there is a friendship link. If B is a hidden friend it also works quite smoothly because then C knows this file by the link, and if B approaches, B just needs to prove that B is any friend of A, because all the friends have access anyway. So B chooses any of these entries in A's file, in particular the one that is with regard to their own friendship link, and proves to C that he knows the private key to the public key that is A's file using standard protocols. So C is in a position to verify hidden friendship without knowing the identity or learning any private keys of the involved parties. Even if we have repeated encounters C will be able to tell that they are different people requesting access because they authenticate under a different public key, but C will not be able to tell the identity of the people or link them if B is requesting, for example, for another user.

Joseph Bonneau: Why prove that you know the private key instead of just storing on C broadcast encryption to all of the public keys that are in A's friends lists. You mentioned that B will prove to C that it knows the private key that was then corresponding to some public key in A's friends lists, so why do that as some zero knowledge proof instead of just having a content be encrypted and then the proof is that, C will just transmit the encrypted content and it's useless if B's claim is false?

Reply: So then you would encrypt the content and pass on the key to B. Well for instance, you don't want to encrypt under the same key every time. If we assume that A encrypts under the same key every time and says, OK, you can always access my photo, and so new friends, if A updates her lists of friends this change is not reflected until A sends the link to B. So if A and B are unable to establish a connection because of intermittent connectivity ...

Joseph Bonneau: There's ways to deal with that I would think, but what you have works perfectly well. It just seems like zero-knowledge proof is more work than broadcast encryption, which would achieve the same property.

Reply Yes, well I don't claim it's a perfect protocol, of course. When we see that delegate enforcement works, it's also worthwhile examining whether we can use this to use multi-hop friendship links. Then we face a scenario where we have, for instance, friends of third degree, that means there are several hops between the original user A and then B who is a third degree friend, and if B now still wants to prove that he is friends with A of some degree then we need to leverage this delegated enforcement. The good news is that we only need the cooperation of one hop in the middle, that is H, because A knows that G is a hidden friend, and B can prove independently to A that he is a friend with H, so the only link that's missing is the one in the middle here, so that A can tell that H and C are hidden friends, to make it work so that B can prove to A that he is a hidden friend of third degree. So it's good news that only one person in the middle is required to prove a third degree hidden friendship link, that's not a lot of people, and subsuming that we know somehow who is in the middle, because otherwise B wouldn't be able to approach A in the first place, then may ask H to cooperate, which we can assume in a social context. If we have the scenario where A again delegates the enforcement, we need one more hop that is cooperating because of course C does not know that the link between A and G exists without having some information being passed on. But all this relies on the concept of having this delegated enforcement.

So far I've been examining hidden friendship relations for access control. If we briefly look at how we can use it for making aggregational friendship links as a social metric for trustworthiness, that is counting the number of friends to tell somebody else how reputable somebody is, then we have a problem because it works well for public friendship links because everybody can see if it is just a one-directional link or if it is indeed symmetry, so that we really have a friendship relation that is there, but we can no longer establish this symmetry for hidden friendship relations by definition because we don't want it, and for an outsider, encrypted friendship links, or hidden friendship links, looks just like random data. So the one who publishes the list of friends can make up these links and pretend there are lots of hidden friends, so the number of hidden friendship links inside a public list of friends, just gives an upper bound on the number of actual hidden friends, which is not a very strong property. So there are some downsides in having hidden friendship links, and especially that some web of trust cannot emerge.

Even so I think we have achieved some nice properties here. We can deploy hidden friendship links and public friendship links in an integrated manner, putting them in the same policy, the same public file, that enables distributed architectures, local decision making, there is no interactivity that is needed.

So A published the file, and then at any later point of time B can check if there is a friendship, or C can check on the behalf of A whether the user that is approaching C is entitled to have access to some photos or some videos. So A who published the list of friends and B who's requesting access do not need to be online at the same point in time, and there is no overhead as we see in other authentication protocols. It's quite simple, and we've been doing some tool support to see how users can be put in position to have mobile device software that helps them establishing and mounting their lists of friends.

We've come up with this protocol with a social context in mind but of course we can see this in the bigger picture. We have something that we publish, and it's public because everybody can see it, and can reproduce it, but still we keep it secret, and I think that this is a property that we can observe in other contexts as well, so that we have published information but have it encrypted so that only authorised users will be able to access it.

The remaining challenges, I've already briefly mentioned one, that is, counting. Counting is not obvious. Also the cooperation that's needed if we have multi-hop friendship links, maybe it's possible if we use privacy or morphisms for the encryption of friendship links that we can establish transitivity of friendship links. Without having cooperation another question maybe more challenging is, if we even want to have, or if it wouldn't leak too much information, or if it would make the assumption that somehow friendship is transitive, which we cannot assume every time. And of course the social dynamics are different for hidden friendship links because a web of trust cannot emerge, and network effects become not obvious, so the economics of hidden friendship links are quite diverse, and are not the same as we have for a public list of friends with only public links. And still we want all this keeping it simple so we can use it, and use it on devices that are limited in terms of user interface, methods of input, and storage, and so forth.

Joseph Bonneau: You said it's easy to verify public friends in a mobile scenario, but in the scheme you propose, that requires that if Alice claims she's friends with Bob, then you hear that from Alice but you have to go to Bob to verify?

Reply: Yes, if somebody else wants to enforce a public friendship link between two users, then this user just needs to inspect both lists of friends.

Joseph Bonneau: Right, but in the mobile scenario that might not be possible, if you're only able to communicate locally with Alice, and Bob is around the world, and you don't have network connectivity.

Reply: Yes, although the good news is you can widely cache these files, and if you deploy them on the web, embedded in HTML pages for example, can assume that they are delivered over HTTP, that means you inherit all the caching infrastructure, and can set cache policies on a lower level and say, OK, you can cache my friendship policies for one day, or for a week or so.

Joseph Bonneau: But what happens when you meet Alice in the middle of the Sahara Desert? I mean, you can only talk to Alice. I guess I wonder if you should supplement this with some sort of certificate from Bob saying, I am friends with Alice, until at least this date, and then Alice can carry that around as her proof that, yes, I'm friends with Bob.

Reply: Yes, of course. If we have caching that means that all individual users can cache, so A may want to cache B's list, and say, OK, this is an authentic list because it's signed by B. But then of course, how do you check that the certificate is authentic if you don't have connectivity? So maybe there is a third party you trust.

Joseph Bonneau: Well also maybe Charlie already has Bob's public key, because . . .

Reply: Maybe, we cannot live without assumptions there, and the validity of this assumption is very much dependent on the context we are examining.

Joseph Bonneau: I guess the scenario I'm thinking of is two people meet, and there's no outward connection, and so if Carol says, I'm friends with Bob, and Alice says, oh I'm friends with Bob too, and there's no way for them to prove that to each other, unless as you say they both cache Bob's friendship lists.

Reply: Yes, that works.

Joseph Bonneau: But that seems to go against your goal of not having a lot of storage to carry around, I mean, it's mobile phones.

Reply: Well having a text file doesn't really harm.

Joseph Bonneau: If for all your friends, you have to store their complete friendship lists to get this to work though, that starts to be pretty big if it's public keys for every one of those things.

Reply: The thing is, every user can decide on their own whether they want to cache it

Not That Kind of Friend

Misleading Divergences between Online Social Networks and Real-World Social Protocols

Jonathan Anderson and Frank Stajano

University of Cambridge
Computer Laboratory

Abstract. Current social networking technology provides users with little of the privacy that they expect and are promised. While some individuals may truly wish to be "open books," violating most users' privacy expectations leads to serious consequences for both the users and their network. We propose that, in order for users to truly be in control of their personal information, we need to respect and learn from the social protocols that have been built up over the millennia.

1 Introduction

Social networking technology is used by hundreds of millions worldwide to help them connect to and share information with others. Sometimes, however, the information they share reaches a wider audience than they intend [1, 2]. We believe that problem this stems from two primary sources: the implicit trust that must be placed in network operators and the exceptionally poor quality of users' access control.

In this paper, we propose a methodology which addresses these problems and seeks to truly put users in control of their personal information. We describe how a decentralized architecture, informed by the semantics of real-world social interaction, could provide the technical means for users to share information in a manner which they already understand how to manage. Rather than teaching users about the ins and outs of computer security, we should rely on implied social contracts; they are the foundation of social interaction and no technical details should obscure this. We will not make false promises about revocation to lure users into a false sense of security, nor will we use arbitrary constructs like friendship lists to provide incentives that do not exist in the real world.

2 What's Wrong with Social Networks?

Social network technology exists to assist people in connecting with others and managing their interpersonal relationships. The former, taken in isolation, is very easy. The latter, however, requires delicacy, confidence and privacy. Put another

B. Christianson et al. (Eds.): Security Protocols 2009, LNCS 7028, pp. 343–349, 2013.
© Springer-Verlag Berlin Heidelberg 2013

way[1], Facebook has the happy talent of helping you find friends; whether it is equally capable of helping you keep them is less certain.

Aside from obvious implementation details, we believe that there are two essential problems with today's social networking technologies:

1. network operators require implicit trust, and
2. users don't manage access control well.

2.1 Operator Trust

Most users don't think very hard about it, but using a social network ought to be a sobering activity. You tell a third party information that they can use to impersonate you [3], then tell them who all of your friends are – what keywords would be effective in a phishing attack against you [4], then post information which, should it reach an unintended audience, could get you blackmailed or fired [5–7].

Social network operators have databases of such information for millions of users. The value of this information is obvious, and the only thing keeping it from being stolen *en masse* by identity thieves is the competence and good will of the network operators and their employees.

The first of these qualities – competence – can be assumed to vary across the many social network operators in the market. The second quality – good will – is different, though. Many networks assert the right to share whatever information they like with whatever parties they deem trustworthy [8], and the only paying customers are their advertisers. In this light, consider a choice before a hypothetical social network:

1. spend time and money securing personal information against unauthorized access by corrupt insiders, or
2. spend time and money exposing personal information to advertisers to increase the value of their ads.

Which is more likely to be chosen?

I am not claiming that major social networks have been overrun by identity thieves or that they don't care about their reputation. I *do* assert, however, that the requirement for absolute trust in a large network operator is worrisome and there may be a chilling effect among some users: I'd share a lot less information with friends if I knew that strangers were recording a transcript of all my conversations.

2.2 Access Control

It is immediately apparent that a social network must allow information sharing in order to be useful. It is slightly less apparent that this sharing often depends on the *assumption* of effective access control – I share photos with my friends

---

[1] With apologies to Jane Austen.

and implicitly assume that my boss won't be looking at them. The system falls down when the assumption is not justified – as has been shown time after time on Facebook – but the system also fails to work effectively when its users allow the fear of poor access control to prevent them from sharing information.

Why isn't access control effective in social networking? A large part of the problem is that social networks are fun and easy to use, but their access control schemes are tedious and incomprehensible.

Tedious. People use social networking technology for the sake of their social relationships, not for the purpose of spending time in front of a computer. Faced with a choice between a) finding friends and chatting or b) entering meta-data and managing ACLs, most users choose option (a) [9].

Incomprehensible. Many of the implications of security policy decisions are not immediately apparent to users. These implications include problems with both fundamentals (e.g. a trust model with false in-/out-group distinctions or which assumes trust is transitive) and details (e.g. policy interactions that mystify PhD students in computer security).

3   What Can We Do about It?

How can we build a social network that doesn't succumb to these problems? Many data protection policies pay lip service to the concept of "putting people in charge of their own information," but we should actually *do it*: rather than "user control" consisting of a policy that users trust the system to follow, personal data ought to be protected such that if something isn't *authorized*, it isn't *possible*. Such a policy could be achieved by addressing the above problems of operator trust and poor access control, and we believe that privacy in online social networks could be greatly improved by observing real-world social protocols.

The human brain seems to be hard-wired to handle a fixed number of social relationships [10], and we have spend a very long time learning how to manage our social interactions with them. The great hubris of social network operators seems to be believing that they've fundamentally changed the way that humans beings interact, and we can see the results of this hubris played out all around – some people make bad access control decisions, but many people are afraid to use social networking sites and lose out on their potential benefit.

If we want to make a social network that behave as people expect, let's pay attention to the social understanding that people already have. Instead of trying (and failing) to teach users to think like a computer, let's train the system to figure out what the user wants to do [11] by following the semantics of real-world social relationships.

3.1   Centralization

One of the most obvious difference between online and offline social networking is the degree to which each is centralized. In the real world, no third party is required for you and I to be friends[2], but this model hasn't been picked up by social network operators. Instead, we have the all-trusted network operator. We can deal with the "trusted operator" problem in one of two ways:

1. stop trusting the operator or
2. stop using an operator.

The former solution has been proposed (e.g. "keep using Facebook, but encrypt everything in your profile"), but there is an economic problem with this model: you take away the central party's business model, namely the ability to serve highly targeted advertisements. This makes your system a *parasitoid*: a parasite which incubates within its host during its larval stage and eventually kills the host [12]. If your system is successful, it will kill the centralised network; if the network is smart, it will kill your system first.

This leaves us with the decentralized option, which brings us back to something which looks a lot like the offline protocol.

3.2 Social Contracts

Social networks need to make us feel safe enough to share our personal information (exactly *how* safe depends on the individual – some people will admit criminal guilt via public broadcast, but many would not). In order to accomplish this goal, network operators often provide "locks and bars" that make security feel like a technical problem, but security is fundamentally a *human* problem, and we would do well to consider the real underpinning of human relationships: social contracts.

In real-world social networks, there are no technical barriers to my close friends running around telling others my most personal secrets, so it shouldn't be surprising that the same behaviour is possible in an online setting. The only thing that really prevents this type of behaviour is an implied social contract: if I tell a close friend a secret, I expect them to keep it. If I tell a stranger the same secret, I have less expectation of them keeping it. If I allow a computer to share the secret with anybody in a group whose membership we don't really understand, however, then somehow we expect the secret to be kept.

We need to remove this layer of obscurity and clearly admit that social network security is based on an implied social contract, and that social contracts are not externally enforced [13]. Anything more is a promise we can't keep.

3.3 Revocation

One component of this obfuscation layer is the concept of permission revocation. If I tell you a personal secret, there is no way for me to make you forget (that doesn't involve a heavy stick). I can ask you to keep it secret, I can hope that you

---

[2] You could argue that a communications infrastructure is required in many cases, but it's not always true, and people can choose a wide range of communication options (phone, letter, "when you see Jon, tell him..." etc).

forget it and stop doing things that might remind you, but I cannot cut into your brain and remove the information. Current social networks, however, provide an interface which gives the appearance of perfect, retroactive revocation without actually backing it up.

This appearance of perfect revocation leads users to post things which they "can always delete later", but which in reality may never disappear entirely from the network. I can check a photo's ACL and see that only my University friends are allowed to view it, but if family members were ever allowed to see it, then who knows which browser cache or physical album the photo is tucked away in?

Better would be a system where the only revocation that is offered is *future* revocation. Such a system would serve the twin purposes of stripping the glossy veneer off of inherently risky activities and allowing users to view not just an optimistic guess at who we *hope* can view information, but an accurate picture of who *actually* can see it.

3.4 Friendship Lists

One of the main features of social networks – friend lists – may be their undoing in the long term. Such a concept simply does not exist in the real world, and there are several reasons why I think that pretending it does is a bad idea. These reasons include:

False Dichotomies. Social relationships are complicated affairs, but social networks would have us believe that they are binary in nature, and usually bidirectional. In real life, before sharing a secret with anyone, I think about my relationship with them, how reliable they are, etc. In a social network, however, the only easy-to-use access control is usually the question "is this person in my friend list or not?" Such a false dichotomy – either you're in my "inner sanctum" or the public at large – can lead to poor access control decisions.

Dilution. A friendship list can be viewed as a list of people with whom a greater degree of intimacy is warranted than with the general population. Often, "all friends" is the most restrictive access control that can be applied without significant effort (e.g. ACLs), yet a common complaint about social networks is that "your mother is on Facebook," so the friendship list doesn't mean what it once did. The larger and more inclusive a list gets, the less it differentiates people from the general population; conversely to how we usually think about network effects, increasing the size of a friendship list decreases its overall value.

Un-friending. In real life, "un-friending" somebody is easy: you stop inviting them to parties, revealing personal information, etc. until you've drifted apart. Such pruning should be easy, because it is necessary – the human mind can only accommodate so many close relationships. On a social networking site with hard binary relationships, however, letting a relationship go requires users to state, in effect, "I no longer value my relationship with Alice." Increasing the internal complexity of pruning friendships leads to a stale picture of current social relationships and access control decisions that no longer reflect the user's intentions[3].

Metric Gaming. If software engineering has taught us anything, we should know that introducing arbitrary success metrics (e.g. lines of code, bugs fixed) leads to actors maximizing their own "stats," often to the detriment of the larger group. Introducing the concept of a friend count incents users to make "friendship" links which they otherwise would not have made, as well as keeping links which they otherwise would not bother to keep. There are Facebook users with thousands of "friends" and MySpace users with millions; how many of these are actual friends, and how many of these "relationships" exist solely as a pair of mouse clicks between strangers? Keep in mind: this is a realm where "Only Friends" is as inclusive as many ACLs get.

3.5   Sharing Defaults

In the real world, ideas and secrets start out hidden away in one's grey matter, then are shared with friends via an act of will. Photographs follow a similar progression, with images being captured by a camera, developed (or downloaded) and then shared by the photographer's effort via paper and/or e-mail.

Since maintaining ACL metadata is tedious at best, current social networking technologies prefer to share everything by default. This can lead to unwanted information being shared, and is only mitigated by the [partial and ineffective] revocation promised by the network operators. We need not follow this poor practice, however, as long as we are not slaves to its precondition (poor access control). We can make a system whose default setting is "private" as long as sharing information is easy and understandable.

4   Conclusion

It we want to build a social network that people can use effectively while maintaining privacy, we should pay heed to the lessons learned over the last several thousand years of recorded civilization. Online social networking is not a fundamentally different thing from offline networking, so we should build virtual systems that work something like the real world.

An appropriate level of abstraction for social networks deals with concepts like friends, photos and events; we ought to hide details like transport protocols and encryption keys from users. It is *not*, however, appropriate to try to protect users from themselves by hiding social facts like "there is no such thing as true revocation." On the contrary, social networks should, to the user, look like the real world: decentralised and based on implied social contracts, with no concepts of perfect revocation, friendship lists or permissive defaults. If we make the computer network behave like real social networks, we just might provide a platform that people can safely use with confidence.

---

[3] In fact, such staleness is even bad for advertisers, who rely on the high accuracy of information in social networks in order to target their ads accurately!

References

1. Bennett, R.: Plea to ban employers trawling Facebook. The Times (2008),
   http://technology.timesonline.co.uk/tol/news/
   tech_and_web/article3613896.ece
2. Shepherd, J., Shariatmadari, D.: Would-be students checked on Facebook. The
   Guardian (2008), http://www.guardian.co.uk/uk/2008/jan/11/
   accesstouniversity.highereducation
3. Rabkin, A.: Personal knowledge questions for fallback authentication. In: Proceedings of the 4th Symposium on Usable Privacy and Security - SOUPS 2008, pp.
   13–23. ACM (2008)
4. Jagatic, T.N.: Social phishing. Communications of the ACM 50(10), 94 (2007)
5. Pilkington, E.: Blackmail claim stirs fears over Facebook. The Guardian (2007),
   http://www.guardian.co.uk/business/2007/jul/16/usnews.news
6. Randall, D., Richards, V.: Facebook can ruin your life. And so can MySpace,
   Bebo... The Independent (2008),
   http://www.independent.co.uk/life-style/gadgets-and-tech/news/
   facebook-can-ruin-your-life-and-so-can-myspace-bebo-780521.html
7. CBC News: Student recruits unfit for service, say former border guards. Canadian
   Broadcasting Corporation (2007),
   http://www.cbc.ca/canada/british-columbia/story/2007/10/01/
   bc-borderguards.html
8. Facebook Privacy Policy (2007), http://www.facebook.com/policy.php
9. Whitten, A.: Making Security Usable. PhD thesis. Carnegie Mellon University
   (2004)
10. Aiello, L.C., Dunbar, R.: Neocortex Size, Group Size, and the Evolution of Lan-
    guage. Current Anthropology 34(2), 184–193 (1993)
11. Yee, K.P.: Aligning security and usability. IEEE Security and Privacy Maga-
    zine 2(5), 48 (2004)
12. Godfray, H.C.J.: Parasitoids. Current Biology 14(12), R456 (2004)
13. Binmore, K.: Game Theory and the Social Contract. Just Playing, vol. 2. MIT
    Press (1998)

Not That Kind of Friend

(Transcript of Discussion)

Jonathan Anderson

University of Cambridge

It falls to me to deliver the last talk, so I'll try to keep you all awake.

We have this idea of social networks in the real world, and then there's this thing that we do on computers: they use some of the same language, syntactically they might be similar, but semantically they're completely different, and this leads to a lot of really appalling things.

Frank Stajano: Our group has been fairly active in exploring the security and privacy of social networks, and this is something where the old hands, like us, don't really understand what goes on. We were discussing yesterday with Matt, what is there in such a network that you can't do it just by having your own webpage? We don't get it, so we need some fresh blood, and this year we have had a good influx of smart people who are young enough to understand this stuff and have been using it since they were in college, and who, from the inside, can find so many holes. So this is an exciting time for this kind of exploration.

This is the last talk of a workshop where you are supposed to interact, so we do encourage you to interrupt as we go along. This is a topic that, as we have seen from the previous talks, resonates with many people; many of the issues that we want to bring up are things that people have been mentioning, so do chip in with your ideas. This is not about delivering received wisdom to you.

The problem that we are facing is that privacy issues in social networks, which stem from many things that are done in a appallingly poor way, not least of which is the choice of words even to describe what is being done, and what the social network people say they do has little match with the ordinary meaning of those words. So maybe what we seek to get out of this discussion in this last session is some clarity.

Reply: Everybody is aware of social networks at this point, no need to talk too much about them, they're popular with millions of people, and multiple social networks are ridiculously popular, and they're everywhere. They are becoming an essential part of the infrastructure of a lot of systems, so Facebook Connect is now the arbiter of identity on the Internet. Facebook says you are Bruce Christianson, therefore you are Bruce Christianson to the New York Times, and to whoever uses Facebook Connect, which is a lot of people. And of course there's been some pretty appalling privacy problems.

Bruce Christianson: What do you mean by privacy in this context, or are you just about to take a little bit of the wrapping paper off.

B. Christianson et al. (Eds.): Security Protocols 2009, LNCS 7028, pp. 350–364, 2013.

Reply: I'm talking about people's expectations. I'm going to define some terms a in a few minutes, but people's expectations aren't being met, basically. The first question is, who cares? People say, well you know, you're putting all this stuff on a webpage so you deserve whatever happens if anybody looks at it. Well, you might think that, but people really do have this expectation of privacy, and if that was all that there was to it, then you could chalk it up to people being silly. But in fact, social networks go out of their way to say, no, no, no, we give you control of your information, so if people are making promises like this then maybe we should build systems that can actually fulfil the promises. So people have this expectation of privacy, and we say, well are these things really important, I mean, who cares if anybody sees it.

Well there are real adversaries out there who are looking for lots of different kinds of personal information, and there are real threats, and we've seen things like people getting fired, and employers surveilling their employees, even if they're not necessarily firing them, they're still introducing weird things into the corporate culture. There's phishing that's going on, and there are blackmail things as well, at least one or two that we know about, but who knows how much blackmail is going on that we don't know about because that's kind of the point. And there's lots of frauds going on, the whole, help I'm lost in London with no money, please send me $900, thing.

We say that privacy is a problem, so what is the problem? These two categories divide into the two different definitions of privacy. On the top we're implicitly trusting the operator, this pertains to data protection stuff, my relationship with Facebook and all of the entities that are associated with Facebook. And the bottom is the access control side, which is more related to the personal privacy, my information getting out to friends, to people that I don't know, that sort of thing. So we contend that there are two big problems with the way that privacy is done in social networks. First you have to trust Facebook implicitly, and second, the access control mechanisms that are in place are quite silly.

So you're trusting the social network operator, you have to trust them completely, you give them all the information they could ever want to walk into Barclays Bank and say, hi, I'm Jonathan Anderson and I need to change my chequing account number, or whatever, and you give them all this information about personal relationships, which can be used to do really good phishing. If you can drop a few friends names into an email and make it look like it came from one of your friends, phishing rates go way up, so there's a lot of information here which is really sensitive. And the other thing is, you're not just trusting them completely with everything that you have, you're trusting them absolutely because there is nothing that you can do if some random Facebook application developer runs away with all of your data and sells it to somebody who wants to commit fraud, there's nothing you can do about it. But furthermore, there's no alternative, right, the only legitimate alternative to not trusting Facebook, MySpace, whoever the centralised provider is, is to just not use social networking. Some people say, OK, fine, I'll just not use social networking. But there are some legitimate benefits that you get out of social networks, in an online sense, and so it might be nice if people could participate in this.

The reason that we don't really like trusting these people falls down to competence, whether or not they're any good at what they do, and the answer in a lot of ways is kind of, no. They're good at some things, they're good at growing, whether or not they're equally good at retaining all of your personal information, well we've demonstrated in a lot of cases they're not. And the other thing is whether or not they really care about your personal information.

Ross Anderson: But what's different here? Lack of competence, lack of goodwill, no alternative, no redress, ... Doesn't this describe every information age monopoly from IBM onwards?

Reply: Right, and I'm saying this is a sphere in which we don't necessarily need to have an information monopoly, and if we could break this, then this would probably be a good thing for all the people who are being repressed by this monopoly.

Ross Anderson: But I think that everything bad that's ever been said about IBM, or Microsoft, or Google, or <put your favourite monopoly here>, can potentially be recycled for Facebook. The flipside of that is that anything we learn here about how to do things better will also apply for whoever comes along after Facebook.

Cathy Meadows: But there is some advantage to having like one single large supplier, in that we're all on the same network, and if you were going to have a bunch of tool suppliers, there's still going to be this problem of, how are you going to hook up from one network to another. So there is some economic reason to have one big network.

Bruce Christianson: At least if you buy IBM you know your software will be compatible.

Reply: Yes, absolutely. There are definitely lots of reasons why things have evolved in this way, and why you have big centralised providers, but there are some ways in which it's not necessarily required, and we could do things a little bit differently. Now, obviously if you have, some people are using Facebook, and some people are using Orkut, and some people are using MySpace, those people have no incentive to want to work together and make it easy for you to have a seamless social network experience. But we can go a little bit further than that, and still have one over-arching system, I'll get into that in a second.

Right, so the goodwill argument is, do the social networks really care about protecting your privacy, or are they too busy. If they're busy fighting phishing all day long, or whatever the scam of the day is, or stopping chain letters, which is apparently what they actually spend their time doing, putting out fires all day, then are they really sitting back and thinking about the insider threat, because so many people just have complete unmitigated access to your data. I have it from a good authority that Facebook no longer allows every employee to have unfettered access to your data, that's probably a good thing, but it's a little bit worrying that this was an ad hoc decision, and lots of people still do.

So to the access control side of things. Getting into the personal privacy side of things, the problem with the access control is not necessarily that they don't understand how to give you options, and give you pages and pages of options that will let you configure whatever role based access control scheme you want, there are some pretty sophisticated controls available in some networks, some not so much. But the problem with these is, one, they're tedious, so nobody wants to bother with them, you're on a social network to use the social network, not to go through pages and pages of configuration options. And some people are starting to do this more, but still the way it's done is really tedious, we could do a lot better. And the second thing, you can't understand it, the interactions between these things are such that a couple of reasonably intelligent PhD students looking at this say, no way, when you hit that tickbox all of a sudden it changes its behaviour in this other system, I had no idea you would have that interaction. So if you have all these hidden dependencies, how in the world are you expecting users to come up with an access control policy that suits their needs.

These are problems, what can we do about them? First, I think it's generally a good idea to minimise the number of people that you have to trust absolutely and implicitly, so if we can find a way to stop trusting the operator completely, that would probably be a good thing. Second, we need to start doing social networking. Say, wait a minute, isn't the problem that we're doing social networking? No, we're doing something that uses the same words, but isn't actually.

On the stop trusting the operator point, there are two things that you can do. One, you can just encrypt everything on the website, people have proposed this, so we'll use Facebook but we will encrypt our personal views and what I like to eat for breakfast. Well this makes you something called a parasitoid, which is a parasite that as part of its natural growth and development, kills the host. If you take away Facebook's targeting advertising revenue, by the time you're done, Facebook is dead, and then that really isn't good for anybody — it's like these little wasp larvae.

The other approach that you can take is to just stop being centralised. If we can build a decentralised network that would probably be a good thing to do, as an academic project certainly, but I also think that this has the potential to really help. And this has been toyed around with by lots of people, and if we could do it we could probably do something about the central trust problem.

OK, so we don't trust the operator anymore, that's great, fantastic. What about the second thing, let's start doing social networking. Now what do I mean by this? OK, we're not doing social networking currently. Currently we've approached the problem and said, alright, we are computer scientists, we know about passwords, we know about access control lists, we have lawyers who know how to write policies, OK, that's great, everything is going to be fine now. The great hubris of social networking operators is that they think they have fundamentally changed human interaction, it's like, we can do this on computers, therefore it is different from what we have been doing over the past thousands of years of recorded history. Well it's not. It's a new communication medium, but if we're going to build a system that people can actually use and that will actually work, I think we need to at least think about the way that things really work in the real world today, and see if we can maybe build a system that behaves in the way that people understand.

The bedrock of actual social interaction today is the social contract. In real time people want to negotiate their personal privacy needs with the environment around them, this is why sometimes you turn your phone off; if you're using an instant messenger you say, yes I'm here right now, or, I'm away right now; or you go to invisible; people want to pretend they're not home, they want to say, give out this much information right now, I don't want to give out so much. So in real time people want to negotiate this with their environment. A social contract isn't enforced externally, there is no government authority that will say, OK, well, you have told this person this, which they didn't want you to tell. Now in certain legal contexts you have something equivalent, but in a purely social setting, if I tell an embarrassing story to Ben and then he tells it to Ross, well I don't have a lot of redress from that.

Ben Laurie: A social contract says that you will never find me out if I tell it to Ross.

Reply: Right, that's the other thing, because it's not externally enforced, the social contract exists because all the players in this game believe that most people are going to abide by the social contract and therefore they can derive some benefit from playing by the rules and being a part of this system, and that's the only thing that keeps this going. Now this is a realistic promise to make, the moment we start promising that computers can do more than the social contract can do, and that introducing computers into the mix is going to make things better, this is the point where we start deceiving people, and they start doing really unsafe things.

So how about a few examples. Friends lists, this is my pet peeve as relates to social networks. We've introduced this concept of the friend list, and I believe it's caused all kinds of woe. The first problem with friends lists is you introduce false dichotomies into the system, you are my friend or you aren't, and that is the granularity of most access control decisions that are being made: either I once met you in a corridor at some point, or you could be my wife, somewhere in that spectrum; or else you're outside of that, and that is a completely mean-ingless distinction. Furthermore there's also false dichotomies between people who are on the network and people who aren't on the network, which again is meaningless. If there are 200 million people on Facebook then does it really matter whether you are in the network or whether you are not in the network, it's effectively the whole world. This idea of you're my friend or you're not, you get to see my stuff or you don't, this is a ridiculously simplistic view. Second, you have this metric gaming property, when you publish a list which says I have 700 friends, then people accept friendships just so they can have lots of friends, and there are lots of people who just want to look like they're really popular.

There's this long history of slapping metrics on things that are inappropriate, if you say, alright, we will pay you by how many lines of code you write, guess what, I'm writing more comments. People gain whatever metric you can slap on these things that isn't inherently appropriate to the situation, and this leads to loose and permissive access control policies just so that people can look like they're really popular. So you have dilution, there are all kinds of people on people's friends lists who aren't actually their friends, but you're treating them as if these are people who should have first rate access to your data, when they're just somebody you met once.

The final thing is this business of unfriending. In real life it is very easy to stop being somebody's friend: you just don't invite them to as many parties, or you don't tell them as many things as you used to, and sometimes you just move and then drift apart, or whatever; so a friendship changes. But here, because of this false dichotomy thing, you have the idea of, you are my friend, OK, and then I have to click the button, I have to pull the plug, you're no longer my friend, and there's this huge act of will that has to happen, which people almost never do, so these friend lists are incredibly stale.

Revocation is another example of how we're not conforming to the social contract. In real life this is what revocation looks like. If I tell you something, the only way I can make you forget is if I hit you over the head with a big stick or something, and then maybe you might forget it, but other than that there's no way to untell you something. I told you, oh I did such an embarrassing thing last night, I can't untell you that, you've been told. So when we have this idea of, OK, well if you just untick that box then revocation will be complete and no-one will ever see that photo, well no, because all kinds of people have already looked at it, they've printed it off and put it in albums, or they've got it in their browser cache, whatever; it's out there. And this is the barn door property, once it's out there, there's no putting it back in. And so if we let people think that there is such a thing as real true revocation, then they do unsafe things, they say, yes, I'll post this picture, and I can always take it away later, but no, no, no, you really can't take it away later, it's too late. If a politician said something really embarrassing when they were 21 and now they're 50 and they're running for office, well it was said, and if people remember it then it's done. So this leads to false assumptions like I said. The only thing that we really can provide, and we can make a good faith promise to is, alright, in the future we won't share this with anyone, in the future we won't tell anyone else, and maybe you can even ask your friends, hey please don't let that get out, but that's the only reasonable promise that we can give people.

Sharing defaults also don't look anything like they do in the real world. When you're on a social network the default settings are, if you post something, if you say something, everybody sees it, well just about everybody practically speaking, and then from there you can get more restrictive, if you want to put in the time and the effort then you can define an access control list. But this is not how it works in the real world.

Stefano Ortolani: Did you test this, like from its default settings on Facebook?

Reply: Yes, the default settings on Facebook are like MyFriends and Network, so anybody in Cambridge.

Stefano Ortolani: The network is added only for part of the network. By default it sets your information automatically as soon as you join a network.

Reply: Right, but then it's related to your network, which is still everybody in Cambridge, so the point is that you start with this ludicrously permissive policy, and if you want to bother then you can shrink it down, you can restrict it, and you hope that you do it before, so restrict the policy of your album before you add any photos to it, and things like this.

Joseph Bonneau: It's not just a Facebook thing either, we did an experiment, we signed up for forty-something social networks, and I think we found one or two that didn't have globally viewable as the default.

Ben Laurie: I predict that they were the least popular ones.

Joseph Bonneau: Yes.

Reply: So there are good economic reasons why you want to have these permissive defaults, people want to look at other people's stuff, right, people want to negotiate their own privacy, but they're also voyeuristic, so you say, look at all this stuff that you can see, join our network, and so there are reasons for this. But the way that things work in the real world is, if I have an idea it starts out in my head, and nobody knows it except me. Now it's very easy for me to promulgate this, right, it doesn't take a whole lot of effort to kick it out there to other people, but this is the way it works in the real world. It starts with private and then it goes out from there, as opposed to the default is, boom, it's everywhere and if you really want to put the work in you can restrict further.

Governance, this is an interesting issue actually. We recently wrote some comments on Facebook's proposed new governance idea, we called it democracy theatre. Facebook has 200 million active users, so this is larger than most countries, and they're learning the lesson that sometimes the peasants will all revolt, and get really angry about things, so in return you can either provide them with input into how things are run, or you can provide them with a semblance of input into how things are run. This is one area in which you could argue that Facebook might be learning some real world policies, having to move towards real world social systems.

And so these are examples of how the social contract ought to be guiding these things, rather than the concepts that we as computer science people have previously committed ourselves to. So social networks think that they've changed the way people interact, they've changed the *means* by which people interact, but human relationships have not changed in a fundamental way. What we ought to be doing is looking at the way people understand how their social network works, the way people relate to their actual social networks, and look at the structures that are implicit in real social networks. If we can have the humility to learn from these historical lessons, then maybe we could build something that actually works a little bit more like people understand it: so that if we use the same words it has the same effect, or else at least we don't use the same words; and therefore people might be able to manage it a little bit better and get the system to actually meet their expectations.

Ben Laurie: And they'll be less popular right?

Reply: That's quite possible, it might be less popular.

Ben Laurie: So what, what's the actual point, I mean, OK, you can do this in theory, but in practice the one that will get used is the one that doesn't do it, the one that is insecure.

Reply: The one that will get used by a lot of people, yes, but there are a lot of people who are not doing social networking at all because they're afraid of it for reasons that they don't fully understand, they're like, I hear there's bad privacy stuff.

Joseph Bonneau: Yes, because that's what we tell journalists.

Reply: Yes, that's because that's what we tell journalists, right.

Joseph Bonneau: I have a couple of complaints here actually. One, I think that you're saying both that we should be more like real social networks, and that we shouldn't. Because democracy is very rare in the real world, but we're saying in Facebook we think it shouldn't be like the real world, it should have this perfect democracy instead of this sort of ruling class.

Reply: I'm not claiming that for Facebook at all, all we said in the Facebook thing was that Facebook shouldn't go around making promises they don't intend to keep.

Joseph Bonneau: That's what happens in real governments. I mean, the Facebook governance thing is exactly how most pseudo-democracies work in the real world, so there is a case where it's doing exactly the real social protocol, and that's bad. And then the other case is where we think it's different, we think, oh it should be doing the in the real world social things.

Dusko Pavlovic: But this isn't the government in the real world?

Joseph Bonneau: Yes, but once again we're saying, let's do it better than real people do it, but then for other stuff, let's do it like real people do it instead of trying to do it better.

Frank Stajano: Somehow that makes sense, I mean, copy the good things that real people do, when it's good things, people also do lots of bad things, why should we copy that?

Joseph Bonneau: Yes, that's my second point. I think the argument that we should just try and make a carbon copy of real social protocols falls down for two reasons. One, there's no such thing as the real world social protocol, it's very different across time and culture. I mean, in the West now we have more of a notion of privacy, but 300 years ago when people lived in villages that didn't exist, and it's a standard that everybody in the village knew everything about everybody else in the village, and there's certainly a culture where that's still the case. But I also don't think it's the case that people want to recreate.

Reply: It's not actually true that just because people live in these isolated communities that there is no sense of wanting privacy.

Joseph Bonneau: But it is very different.

Reply: Oh it's very different, sure, but the point is that this ought to be driven by user choices, not by policies that we lay down.

Joseph Bonneau: Well that's my other point, I think you're assuming that what we want is to just recreate the real thing, but the main appeal of social networks is that they let you do all these things that weren't possible 20 years ago: you can keep in touch with 50 friends from High School, because it takes only five seconds to get caught up on what's going on in their life, whereas previously that would have been really hard.

Reply: But that's not actually any different than what people used to have, it's just faster in a lot of ways.

Joseph Bonneau: Faster is different though.

Reply: You could have said, here is a telegraph that I'm going to send to 50 people, Western Union go and take care of it. So they have changed the game in that they have made communication quicker and easier, but they haven't changed the game in that it wasn't impossible to do these things before.

James Malcolm: The change of scale is so dramatic that ...

Bruce Christianson: ... there's qualitative changes as well.

George Danezis: The key difference is that we saw that as a person-to-person communication channel. I think that these social networks changed the game in that they have created a social space, so it's more like suddenly all my mates from school are all the time in the same room. That creates a proximity and a visibility that totally changed the game, it's not just that I talk to them faster or in a more automated way, it's like we are together all the time.

Cathy Meadows: And instead of sending your telegrams to 50 different people, you're posting it in the town square.

George Danezis: It gives that piazza or town square kind of feeling, where everybody is there all the time and we can basically grow old together.

Reply: So it's like something that used to be there hundreds of years ago.

Sandy Clark: But your model assumes choice.

Bruce Christianson: Perhaps we ought to be making social networking more like reality TV.

Ross Anderson: But that's how it's becoming! If you go to the sort of villages where there is still a deep local social structure, the feel of the place is different, you walk along the street and people say hello to you. Now that is something that Facebook and its ilk have not been able to recreate, and given that the theme of the workshop is transient encounters, in a traditional society transient encounters would very quickly develop into at least passing friendships, are you from out of town, come and have a cup of tea, tell me what the outside world is like.

Joseph Bonneau: Ross that's not true. Even on Facebook you play scrabble, you play with a stranger, you chat with him, and any friend, it happens all the time. A lot of people use Facebook only to keep in touch with their real world friends, but there's a huge class of people who do interact with strangers and meet them playing games, and doing other applications.

Dusko Pavlovic: Yes, and now the bandwidth is much smaller, they invite you to real tea, they send a bunch of letters, and that's the big difference.

Sandy Clark: Yes, if you want that sort of thing you get it on Second Life.

Joseph Bonneau: Yes, Second Life and World of Warcraft are a lot stronger for that, but it happens on Facebook too.

Dusko Pavlovic: It's ridiculous really, because it's trying to compensate for this bandwidth, and instead of having a bunch of words you get this something trying to be a person.

Paul Syverson: There's large groups of people who primarily have online friends, and they spend a lot of their time, and they've never met these people except there. So it's not capturing something from real life, it *is* their real life as far as they're concerned.

Matt Blaze: You mentioned earlier in your talk the possibility of a decentralised version of this. Many of the worst privacy problems that you have identified, seem that they would be addressed straightforwardly by a distributed social networking system, in which my Facebook page is simply a webpage I maintain on the server of my choice with some tools that let me link in to other people's pages. It seems like nothing that the current web does is fundamentally incompatible with this, or requires a centralised service. Facebook and all these other social networking sites got there early and made it more convenient for people, but they don't seem to have any absolute fundamental advantages here.

Joseph Bonneau: It is because of the latency, if you want an 18 year old to use Facebook, and you increase the latency by one second per page they would freak out.

Matt Blaze: But caching fixes a lot of those problems, it's an engineering problem that it seems the direction technology is going in is likely to advantage us in solving.

Reply: That's the thing, the combination of broadcast and unicast communications channels that people had before were starting to look a bit like that. When people used to model social networks before Facebook they would look at large datasets of who's been sending email to whom, for example within a company, and it was effectively the same thing. Now they have made this, more streamlined process, and there's less latency and of all these kinds of things, but they're not actually bringing anything to the table that didn't exist before, they're just doing it better.

Matt Blaze: So my question is, if you had a lot more time than you probably do, or a lot more help than you probably have, could you just develop a set of tools that would put all these centralised social networking sites, for all their ills, out of business.

Joseph Bonneau: I think there are other issues, more fundamental scalability problems that you can't do in a distributed thing, basically it gives you a stream of 200 friends with real time updates, which is pieced together from your friends because they all go into the centre, and then Facebook sends them out to the right people.

Reply: But Facebook also has a lot silly latency things that you wouldn't see in a distributed network. When you're talking to Facebook servers, most of the time you're spending on that interaction is not those three or four lines of, this is what happened in this person's life, it's fetching all this information that you've already seen before, information that is three days old. Pictures that were posted last week, I just haven't looked at them yet.

Joseph Bonneau: The browser caches some of that. If you try and do basically this stream aggregation in a decentralised way, I'm not sure that you can do it in any reasonably efficient way.

Matt Blaze: But you know, I'd make the same argument about a centralised server, 200 million people on a single server, under a single administrator control, well obviously that can't possibly work.

George Danezis: I'm not really sure why you make that argument, Joseph, I mean, RSS feeds exist, and people do aggregate RSS feeds.

Matt Blaze: So is what you're describing simply an artefact of the way the market in social networking has happened, some accident in the way that market has evolved, or is there actually some fundamental reason for these potentially evil centralised servers?

Reply: Well my whole point is that I don't think there is a fundamental reason for social networks to have their current form. There are good reasons why they are there, and why they became really popular, and why things are done in a centralised way, and some of those reasons are quite compelling, but they're not fundamental. Reasons that rest in human dynamics obviously show that we don't have to go this way.

George Danezis: But it is a bit of an accident. I feel that if the web was invented today it would be centralised because we have datacentres, but the web was invented in the 1990s, when you couldn't have datacentres, we just didn't know how to build this stuff. Social networks are invented today whereas the web was invented in the context of a centralised phone system that was extremely centralised and tightly controlled, and people said, maybe we want to do something a little decentralised for robustness properties.

Dusko Pavlovic: I think the issue is a little bit economic. I think the web remains decentralised because people who could have grabbed it didn't realise that it was important. Last year there were three groups of people who were looking for funding for social network aggregators, and they had convincing technology and they didn't get the funding because no-one believes that they could pull it off, and that social networks would allow themselves to get aggregated.

Joseph Bonneau: But haven't they sued to shut down people who were doing that?

Dusko Pavlovic: Yes, so the issue is not the technology, whether it's nice or whether it is good, but the issue is that there is this growing world government and they're in it for money.

Luke Church: There's another interesting point that relates back to your decisions as to how much should we just replicate things that exist. One of the reasons I suspect social networking became popular is because it existed as a concept, so one can go to Facebook, and this provides people who would never have thought of the idea of behaving in this way with a set of protocols that they can engage with. So its centralist nature may have been central in suggesting an affordance with nervousness about the term. That plays into your questions as to, how much do we want to model the natural world, and how much do we want to co-evolve the technology with the natural world. So don't think of it only as a technical thing, it's also a very human thing.

Reply: Right, that's very true, that people look at things differently, and think about things that they maybe didn't think about before when there wasn't something in front of them for them to think about, which I contend, it's not that it wasn't there before, it's just that people didn't see things that way, or they didn't think about it.

Luke Church: So putting it all in one place makes them think about it?

Reply: Right, and so it changes. I also contend that we could do an architecture which doesn't involve trusting a central repository of data, and still do it in a way that's very familiar. I've built a little prototype that you go to a webpage and then it downloads a little Java application in the background, and it looks like a webpage, but meanwhile all this information is being stored on your computer with appropriate sandboxing mechanisms, blah, blah, so that your data isn't all stored in the clear on somebody else's server where they can sift through it and take it out and sell it at will.

Luke Church: Yes, this is precisely the point, that now we've used the central system to teach them the behaviours, to teach them what they can do, you can now replace the technology underneath it at will.

Ross Anderson: The other way of looking at this is economics. The economic analysis, it's firstly that there are very strong network effects in this, because once most of your friends are in Facebook, there's no point in being in MySpace, so that the markets are tipped naturally, and that makes it more difficult to deploy any competing network including a decentralised one. And second, there's this enormous conflict of interest between Facebook, which wants to sell all your information to advertisers, and users who want the appearance of privacy, which is why you've got these very unusable, very obfuscated access control mechanisms with very bad defaults, that is exactly what you expect given the incentives facing both the network operator and the users. Now one has to face up to economic reality, how are you going to shield the world from that?

Reply: So the first point says why it will be hard, and the second point says, well I think it's essential.

Ben Laurie: Facebook doesn't let you choose what you show to advertisers, it only let's you choose what you show to other users.

Ross Anderson: It's like an NHS system, you can choose what you show your doctor, but you can't choose what you show the civil servants, and Whitehall see everything.

Dusko Pavlovic: Don't you think that this imbalance is a chance for a breach of the first on the market principle? In all other areas there is this gravity who gets there first, you know, who gets there first gets the monopoly, but here, who gets there first, their interest is directly and necessarily not the interest of their customers. So you know, there will be the game all the time, customers will revolt, it's already started, so depending on how skilful they are in this balancing act, they may fall off the road, and the second on the market may take over.

Joseph Bonneau: There's actually a strong history that people forget about, which is that six degrees was social networking in the late 90s, and then that became less popular and Friendster was really popular, and then Friendster died, and MySpace took over, and then MySpace has died and Facebook is taking over. So it hasn't been static. If you could provide something that people actually wanted more than Facebook, they would switch eventually. But the vast majority of people want Facebook, and the people who don't want Facebook end up going on Facebook anyway because they're friends with a lot of people who want Facebook.

Ben Laurie: Facebook is not the only winner though, I mean, it depends where you live.

Bruce Christianson: If Facebook did effectively become a monopoly then we could start using some kind of trust laws to make them accept third party plugins I guess.

Reply: The solution is not to put another plug in interface into Facebook, but your point as I take it is that, it's not so much our game to win, it's Facebook's game to lose. If an academic research project develops something that would be a viable alternative, if only Facebook didn't have this extraordinary position that it has, then when they do fall ...

Dusko Pavlovic: The question which the academic or non academic project needs to address is finding the alternative business model where your model will not be adversarial to the interest of your customers. If you achieve that, then the monopoly is yours.

Joseph Bonneau: I think what we're all assuming again is that the only thing Facebook has is it's users, which is the main thing it has, but also it has a pretty good website that works, and compared to the other social networks it's actually a lot better, it's cleaner, and things are faster, and it's easier to do what you want. So there's a lot of engineering effort that they have invested there that shouldn't be discounted.

Reply: Yes, but a lot of that engineering effort only came after they became really popular and all of a sudden had the money and the access to venture capital to do that level of engineering. I mean, how it started looks nothing like how it is today, it started as the most naïve implementation one would do.

Joseph Bonneau: Going back to your original question though, how do we make social networking more like real world social networking. I still don't think this is the right question. I think Frank's thing of what do we want and what do not want, is the right question, because it's naïve to think that you can do anything that would be exactly like the previous thing.

Reply: OK, yes, we can't be exactly like the real world because there are subtle differences. But if we're going to go around using some of the language of the real world, let's see whether or not we're able to make it actually behave like the real world when we're using the same kind of language. And if it's not the same thing as the real world, well that could be fun, that might be a choice that people want to take, but provide people with the ability to make that choice, don't call it the same thing, because I think that level of misunderstanding is what causes a lot of these personal privacy problems.

Joseph Bonneau: I think it's like email came out 25 years ago, and they thought it would just be a simpler way of sending a letter to somebody.

Bruce Christianson: It came out of the typical science nerd community.

Joseph Bonneau: It got popular though and became something that non-technical people started using, and now there's a completely different social protocol around email, and it mostly works, and it's fine. Social networking will probably go the same way, that for the first few years people exist by weak analogy to the real world, and then eventually we will embrace it as a separate thing, like Luke was talking about, and then we'll be OK. The question is just, when it is this separate thing, what do we want that separate thing to be.

Reply: Right, and what we want that thing to be, we want it in some way to do some of the things that we already do in the real world. Some of these things I'm just saying have been done really poorly because we've said, OK, so we know about access control lists, and we know about set theory, let's go. Whereas if we say, what is it that we actually want to do, and how is it actually done, then maybe we could have built something, or maybe we still can build something, that looks a little bit more like something people actually understand how to use.

The Final Word

The only way to retrieve a secret, once it is known, is to replace it with a lie; then the knowledge of the truth is once again your secret.

Orson Scott Card, Xenocide

B. Christianson et al. (Eds.): Security Protocols 2009, LNCS 7028, p. 365, 2013.
© Springer-Verlag Berlin Heidelberg 2013

Author Index

Anderson, Jonathan   343, 350
Anderson, Ross   282, 285
Arsac, Wihem   41

Backes, Michael   143, 149
Bangerter, Endre   51
Barzan, Stefania   51
Bella, Giampaolo   41
Beresford, Alastair R.   321
Blaze, Matt   24, 28, 34
Bonneau, Joseph   189, 199

Card, Orson Scott   365
Chantry, Xavier   41, 48
Christianson, Bruce   1, 171, 179
Clarke, Stephen   171
Compagna, Luca   41

Danezis, George   87, 93

Foley, Simon N.   298, 308

Gligor, Virgil D.   157, 162
Gordon, Andrew D.   69

Krenn, Stephan   51, 63
Kůr, Jiří   3

Maffei, Matteo   143
Matyáš, Václav   3
McDaniel, Patrick   24
Meadows, Catherine   240, 262
Mitchell, Chris J.   269, 275
Mukhamedov, Aybek   69, 82

Pavlovic, Dusko   240
Perrig, Adrian   157
Preibusch, Sören   321, 335

Rooney, Vivien M.   298
Ryan, Mark   69
Ryan, Peter Y.A.   111, 131

Sadeghi, Ahmad-Reza   51
Schneider, Thomas   51
Stajano, Frank   343
Švenda, Petr   3, 18
Syverson, Paul   213, 231

Teague, Vanessa   111
Tsay, Joe-Kai   51

Xiao, Hannan   171

Zhao, Jun   157